On the Outside

On the Outside

Prisoner Reentry and Reintegration

DAVID J. HARDING,
JEFFREY D. MORENOFF,
AND JESSICA J. B. WYSE

THE UNIVERSITY OF CHICAGO PRESS   CHICAGO AND LONDON

The University of Chicago Press, Chicago 60637
The University of Chicago Press, Ltd., London
© 2019 by The University of Chicago
All rights reserved. No part of this book may be used or reproduced in any manner
whatsoever without written permission, except in the case of brief quotations in critical
articles and reviews. For more information, contact the University of Chicago Press,
1427 E. 60th St., Chicago, IL 60637.
Published 2019
Printed and bound by CPI Group (UK) Ltd, Croydon, CR0 4YY

28 27 26 25 24 23 22 21 20 19   1 2 3 4 5

ISBN-13: 978-0-226-60750-4 (cloth)
ISBN-13: 978-0-226-60764-1 (paper)
ISBN-13: 978-0-226-60778-8 (e-book)
DOI: https://doi.org/10.7208/chicago/9780226607788.001.0001

Library of Congress Cataloging-in-Publication Data

Names: Harding, David J., 1976– author. I Morenoff, Jeffrey D., author. I Wyse, Jessica J. B.,
   author.
Title: On the outside : prisoner reentry and reintegration / David J. Harding, Jeffrey D.
   Morenoff, and Jessica J. B. Wyse.
Description: Chicago ; London : The University of Chicago Press, 2019. I Includes
   bibliographical references and index.
Identifiers: LCCN 2018037843 I ISBN 9780226607504 (cloth : alk. paper) I ISBN 9780226607641
   (pbk. : alk. paper) I ISBN 9780226607788 (e-book)
Subjects: LCSH: Prisoners—Deinstitutionalization—United States. I Employment re-entry—
   United States.
Classification: LCC HV9304 .H265 2019 I DDC 365/.647—dc23
LC record available at https://lccn.loc.gov/2018037843

♾ This paper meets the requirements of ANSI/NISO Z39.48-1992 (Permanence of Paper).

FOR OUR RESEARCH PARTICIPANTS AND THEIR FAMILIES

Contents

Acknowledgments   ix

Introduction   1

CHAPTER 1.   Trajectories   19

CHAPTER 2.   Transitions   48

CHAPTER 3.   A Place to Call Home?   76

CHAPTER 4.   Families and Reintegration   107

CHAPTER 5.   Navigating Neighborhoods   139

CHAPTER 6.   Finding and Maintaining Employment   175

Conclusion   215

Appendix: Data and Methodology   243

Notes   257

References   269

Index   293

Acknowledgments

We are indebted to the twenty-two individuals who shared their experiences of imprisonment, reentry, and reintegration with us as research participants in what came to be known as the Michigan Study of Life after Prison. For up to three years they participated in regular interviews, opening their lives to us and trusting us with sensitive information about their past and present experiences and hopes and fears for the future. While it would be impossible to capture the nuances of all their lived experiences in a book such as this, we hope we have lived up to the trust they placed in us by faithfully representing the common experiences they shared as they left prison and began the process of reintegration.

This project would not have been possible without the cooperation, support, and advice of the Michigan Department of Corrections (MDOC), especially its research and evaluation unit and senior management. MDOC staff should be acknowledged for seeing the value of collaboration with academic researchers despite the potential risks of sharing their administrative data and granting us access to prisoners for interviews. They aided us in the process of securing access to administrative data, explained the workings of Michigan's prisons and parole systems, and advised on the interpretation of our data. Although the conclusions we have drawn from the data they helped us collect and analyze are our own and they are unlikely to agree with everything we have written in this book, we hope we have been faithful to the lessons they have imparted to us based on their years of experience in corrections and public service. We thank in particular Doug Kosinski, Steve DeBor, Jeff Anderson, Ken Dimoff, Dennis Schrantz, and former director Patricia Caruso.

We are especially grateful to Paulette Hatchett and Charley Chilcote. Paulette was a partner in this project from the very beginning, managing the process of securing our access to research participants in MDOC prisons, providing us with administrative data, and supervising research assistants who worked on the project in the MDOC headquarters in Lansing. As the project progressed and Paulette eventually retired from MDOC, she continued to advise us on a weekly basis for many years regarding MDOC practices and data systems and to track down answers to our many queries. Charley joined the project at a crucial time, developing and managing the process of coding the parole agent case notes that became the backbone of the administrative data on families and communities. His commitment to producing data of the highest quality was integral to the success of the project. This project would not have been possible without Paulette's and Charley's dedication and generosity.

Many research assistants labored tirelessly to code, clean, and analyze both qualitative and statistical data for the Michigan Study of Life after Prison. We thank Brenda Hurless, Bianca Espinoza, Andrea Garber, Jonah Siegel, Jay Borchert, Amy Cooter, Jane Rochmes, Claire Herbert, Jon Tshiamala, Katie Harwood, Elizabeth Sinclair, Carmen Gutierrez, Joanna Wu, Clara Rucker, Michelle Hartzog, Tyrell Connor, Madie Lupei, Elena Kaltsas, Brandon Cory, Elizabeth Johnston, Ed-Dee Williams, Cheyney C. Dobson, Erin Lane, Kendra Opatovsky, Adam Laretz, Emma Tolman, Josh Seim, Keunbok Lee, Zawadi Rucks-Ahidiana, Carla Ibarra, Steve Anderson, Megan Thornhill, Tyler Sawher, and Phoebe Rosenfeld.

We are also grateful to colleagues whose advice and feedback were critical to the design and execution of the project. We thank Silvia Pedraza, Al Young, Sarah Burgard, Elizabeth Bruch, Bill Axinn, Yu Xie, Jennifer Barber, Sandra Smith, Loïc Wacquant, Michele Lamont, Black Hawk Hancock, Bruce Western, Chris Winship, Rob Sampson, Heather Harris, Dave Kirk, Chris Wildeman, Kristin Turney, Sara Wakefield, Chris Uggen, Megan Comfort, Andrea Leverentz, Issa Kohler-Hausman, Shawn Bushway, John Laub, Mario Small, Scott Allard, Kurt Metzger, David Martin, Steve Heeringa, and Zeina Mneimneh.

Finally, we are grateful to the entities that have funded our research. This project was supported by the Office of the Vice President for Research, Rackham Graduate School, Department of Sociology, Joint PhD Program in Sociology and Public Policy, National Poverty Center, and the Center for Local, State, and Urban Policy at the University of Michigan, as well as the Russell Sage Foundation, the National Institute of Justice (2008-IJ-CX-0018), the National Science Foundation (SES-1061018, SES-1060708), and the Eunice Kennedy Shriver National Institute of Child

Health and Human Development (1R21HD060160 01A1); by center grants
from the Eunice Kennedy Shriver National Institute of Child Health and
Human Development to the Population Studies Centers at the University
of Michigan (R24 HD041028) and the University of California, Berkeley
(R24 HD073964); and by the National Institute on Aging to the Population
Studies Center at the University of Michigan (T32 AG000221).

Introduction

The Mackinac Bridge, one of the world's largest steel suspension bridges, connects Michigan's Lower and Upper Peninsulas. DeAngelo Cummings, then twenty-seven years old, crossed that bridge for the first time around noon on a blustery winter day in 2007, in route from the "Reception and Guidance Center" prison in Jackson to the Hiawatha Prison in the Upper Peninsula, where he would live for the next six months. He peered through the grated windows of the prison bus at the icy gray waters connecting Lake Michigan and Lake Huron hundreds of feet below. It was during this crossing, over two miles in length, that he realized the full weight of this separation, both geographic and symbolic. Though he had been to prison once before, it was in the Lower Peninsula. He was now over three hundred miles from the streets of Detroit where he grew up, from the restaurant where he worked as a waiter, and from his four-year-old son. The only bridges back to his former life would be few and far between; the long trip up north to "the UP" would mean no visitors, and phone calls, at a cost of $8 for twelve minutes, would be brief. "That's when I realized I was really in a different world, just how far away from home I was," DeAngelo explained almost a year later as he awaited his parole date in the Cooper Street Prison back in Jackson, wondering with some anxiety how he would find work, reconnect with his family, and avoid the depression and drinking that contributed to his incarceration. The challenges of reentry and reintegration lay before him again, and his anxiety was palpable, as his prior reentry failure was constantly in the back of his mind. In the months and years ahead, he would succeed at finding a job, establishing his own household, gaining custody of his son, and forming new relationships, but he would also struggle with depression and anxiety, alcohol, and unemployment and eventually find himself back in prison, only to start over again.

DeAngelo's experience of reintegration is far from unique. Over 700,000 individuals leave American prisons each year and reenter society, a "reentry boom" that is the inevitable result of four decades of rapidly rising incarceration rates in the United States, a change that has been likened to an epidemic of "mass incarceration" (Chesney-Lind and Mauer 2002; Garland 2001). Our nation now imprisons more people and has a higher incarceration rate than any other country on earth. On any given day, one in one hundred Americans is in prison or jail, and one in thirty-three is under the supervision of the criminal justice system, that is, in prison or jail, on probation, or, like DeAngelo, on parole supervision after release from prison (Pew Center on the States 2008). As a result, our nation is now grappling like never before with the social and economic reintegration of formerly incarcerated individuals.

Prior research shows that the steady flow of people into and out of prisons has played an important role in increasing inequality in recent decades, primarily by reducing opportunities for employment and lowering wages among those already most disadvantaged, the stigma of a felony conviction hampering one's ability to find a job (Pager 2003; Western 2006). More broadly, incarceration represents an important change in the life course and affects individuals' well-being, that of their families, and that of their communities in many domains, from the economic to the social to the political (Braman 2004; Clear 2007a; Comfort 2007; Manza and Uggen 2008; Wakefield and Wildeman 2013). Moreover, incarceration is disproportionately experienced by young, low-skill, African American men. More than half of all African American men with less than a high school education go to prison at some point in their lives. These patterns mean that the criminal justice system is as important an institution for understanding contemporary urban inequality and poverty as is the education system or the labor market (Western 2006).

Yet, despite the growing size and scope of the criminal justice system as an influence in the lives of many Americans, social scientists are only beginning to understand the challenges men and women face when returning from prison and attempting to reintegrate into society. Criminological researchers tend to view prisoner reintegration through a narrow lens, focusing on recidivism as the primary issue, and seeking to identify the key risk factors accumulated *before* or *during* prison that predict recidivism, such as criminal history, education, and family background. In *On the Outside*, we examine the lives of formerly incarcerated individuals as they pass out of the prison gates and return to society (and sometimes back to prison) and situate their experiences within the broader framework of poverty and inequality in the United States. We consider the challenges they face in securing stable employment, housing, and transportation and often struggling with drug and alcohol problems. Our overarching argument is that successful reintegration depends not only, or even primarily, on the traits and proclivities of individuals when they entered prison but also on the family, community, and institutional contexts they encounter after prison and on the social roles and identities they construct for themselves after release. In other words, we move beyond a narrow focus on recidivism by examining the process of *reintegration* more broadly.

The Prison Boom, Mass Incarceration, and Prisoner Reentry

Since the mid-1970s, the United States has experienced an enormous rise in incarceration. Whereas in 1975 the population in jails and prisons on any given day was roughly 400,000 people, by 2003 this number had increased more than fivefold to 2.1 million people (Western 2006). Although the upward trend in incarceration has begun to level off in the last few years, the number of individuals in state and federal prisons was over 1.5 million at the end of 2011 (Carson and Golinelli 2013). Compared to other nations, and compared to earlier periods in US history, current incarceration rates are unprecedented (Raphael and Stoll 2009), leading to what some have termed *the era of mass incarceration* (Chesney-Lind and Mauer 2002; Garland 2001).[1] Because almost all prisoners are eventually released, mass incarceration has in turn produced a steep rise in the number of individuals reentering society and undergoing the process of social and economic reintegration (Travis 2005). Over 700,000 individuals are now released from state and federal prisons each year (West, Sabol, and Greenman 2010).

How did the United States end up incarcerating so many of its citizens? Prior to the 1980s, the incarceration rate in the United States was similar to those in other high-income countries and Western democracies, but a series of policy changes both at the federal level and in statehouses across the country led to more people being sentenced to prison and to more time served in prison (Raphael and Stoll 2013). Drug offenses, other public order crimes, and violent offenses in particular are now subject to harsher sentencing. Specific policies enacted into law across the country are responsible for these changes. Determinate sentencing laws took discretion away from judges and required more prison sentences and longer

sentences. Truth-in-sentencing laws require inmates to serve some fraction of their sentence before they can be let out for good behavior or
on the basis of other evidence of rehabilitation while in prison. Repeat
offender laws such as California's three-strikes law require long prison
terms for repeat offenders, even when the second or third felony is nonviolent. Raphael and Stoll show that other explanations for the prison
boom—such as changes in crime rates, the deinstitutionalization of the
mentally ill, demographic changes, or joblessness among minority men—
are at best only a minor part of the story. In short, individuals who would
have been sentenced to probation or jail four decades ago are now being
sentenced to prison, and individuals who would have been sentenced to
a short prison term four decades ago are now being sentenced to longer
terms. As Raphael and Stoll put it: "Many Americans are in prison because
we are choosing through our public policies to put them there" (2013, 27).
The costs of this expansion of prison systems across the country are stag-
gering. For example, in 2007, the federal government and state and local
governments spent over $74 billion on corrections—which includes jails,
prisons, and community supervision—representing a tripling of per capita
expenditures since 1980 (Raphael and Stoll 2013).

These policy changes are only the proximate causes of the prison boom.
Most analysts trace the origins of these policy decisions to a Republican
response to the changes brought about by the civil rights movement (Beckett 1999; Jacobs and Helms 2001; Tonry 1996; Weaver 2007; Western 2006).
Tough-on-crime rhetoric recast urban problems as the result of lawlessness
and criminality rather than poverty and racial oppression, capitalized on
racial stereotypes about crime, and appealed to white voters threatened
by new rights and freedoms for African Americans. Unable to mount an
effective rhetorical counterattack, and suffering at the ballot box, Demo-
crats also shifted focus to crime control, and the above-mentioned policy
changes were made under the leadership of both parties, including most
notably harsh federal sentencing laws during the administration of President Bill Clinton. Though the prison boom has these racial origins, poor
whites were also affected by these policy changes.

The prison boom and accompanying expansions in jails and community
supervision (see below) must be understood as part of a broader cultural,
political, and institutional shift toward order, control, and the use of punishment to solve social problems, particularly those associated with poverty or ethnoracial minorities. In *The Culture of Control*, Garland (2001)
argues that this cultural shift in the United States and Britain extended

not just throughout the state but also to civil society as well, leading to the legitimization of criminal justice and crime prevention logics in many fields, and remaking many of our society's fundamental institutions in the image of "intense regimes of regulation." In *Governing through Crime*, Simon (2007) shows that practices related to crime prevention or the regulation of disorder, such as surveillance, punishment, and risk assessment, have become increasingly necessary for legitimacy in other institutions. In other words, the logic of regulating disorder has seeped into many other institutions as well.

Criminal justice system practices have become templates for problem solving in diverse institutional sectors, such as schools, the family, and the workplace. One example is school discipline, where police tactics and security technologies have become commonplace. These cultural and institutional changes are particularly evident (and particularly relevant to reintegration) when it comes to social welfare policy. As Wacquant (2009) argues, the rise of state logics of punishment has coincided with the shrinkage of the welfare state and a move toward more punitive practices toward the poor. Examples include the shift from Aid to Families with Dependent Children to Temporary Assistance for Needy Families and the use of the criminal justice system to exclude the homeless and other destitute individuals from public spaces in American cities (Beckett and Herbert 2010). Similarly, mass incarceration can be understood as a newly legitimized way to manage poverty, economic and social dislocations, and mental illness and addiction.

Understanding prisoner reintegration requires an appreciation of four key features of the prison boom. First, the rise in incarceration has been disproportionately experienced by minorities, particularly young African American men, and those with low levels of education. One in nine African American men age twenty to thirty-four is in prison on any given day (Pew Center on the States 2008), and, among those with less than a high school degree, the number is approximately one in three (Western 2006). Over half of African American men with less than a high school degree go to prison at some time in their lives (Pettit and Western 2004). Some scholars argue that the prison system now plays the same role in racial domination and exclusion as slavery, Jim Crow, and the ghetto did in previous historical periods, separating African Americans from whites, and tainting African Americans with a mark of inferiority (Alexander 2010; Wacquant 2001).

Second, although almost all communities are touched to some degree by prisoner reentry, poor urban communities bear a disproportionate share of the burden, in terms of both prison admissions (Clear 2007a; Sampson and Loeffler 2010) and releases (Morenoff, Harding, and Cooter 2009). As a result, the criminal justice system now touches nearly as many people in poor communities as the education system or the labor market. Many formerly incarcerated individuals return to communities to live alongside other formerly incarcerated individuals, a situation that carries implications for competition for scarce resources, criminal opportunities, and the effectiveness of formal and informal social control. As Clear forcefully argues: "Concentrated incarceration in those impoverished communities has broken families, weakened the social-control capacity of parents, eroded economic strength, soured attitudes toward society, and distorted politics; even, after reaching a certain level, it has increased rather than decreased crime" (Clear 2007a, 5).

A growing body of scholarship with important implications for prisoner reintegration has documented the impact of mass incarceration on the communities and families on which formerly incarcerated individuals rely (Chesney-Lind and Mauer 2002; Johnson and Waldfogel 2004; Travis and Waul 2003). This literature shows that the incarceration of a family member increases household material stress, increases the risk of foster-care placement, leads to behavioral and schooling problems in children, and affects both mental and physical health (Braman 2004; Comfort 2008; Johnson and Waldfogel 2004; Lee et al. 2014; Wildeman and Muller 2012). Reincorporating a formerly incarcerated family member into the household may exacerbate some of these problems, especially in the short term (Braman 2004). These findings suggest that formerly incarcerated individuals may have difficulties securing social support on release, particularly those from already-disadvantaged families and communities.

Third, incarceration appears to exacerbate already-existing racial and socioeconomic inequalities by making those who are already disadvantaged even more so (Wakefield and Uggen 2010). Released prisoners typically reenter the community with very low levels of education, spotty work histories, and frayed social networks as well as high rates of histories of substance abuse and other forms of mental illness (Visher and Travis 2003). The flow of people into and out of prisons has contributed to increasing inequality in recent decades, primarily by reducing opportunities for employment and lowering wages among formerly incarcerated individuals, but also by decreasing the prevalence of two-parent families (Western 2006). One factor driving these effects is the stigma of having a felony record and serving time in prison (Holzer, Raphael, and Stoll 2007; Pager 2007b). Others include the so-called collateral consequences of felony convictions and imprisonment, *collateral consequences* referring to statutes and administrative rules that bar those with a criminal record from means of social, economic, and political reintegration, including laws and rules disqualifying some from receiving public benefits, holding certain jobs, voting or holding political office, and monetary penalties and fees levied on individuals under community supervision (Alexander 2010; Chesney-Lind and Mauer 2002; Harris, Evans, and Beckett 2010). As a result, the communities that are most affected by incarceration are faced with reintegrating individuals who often have poor prospects for employment and struggle to make ends meet (Harding, Wyse, et al. 2014).

Finally, the prison boom was accompanied by an even larger boom in community corrections. The number of individuals on parole and probation also increased dramatically, to a point where one in thirty-one American adults is either on probation, on parole, or incarcerated on any given day. Moreover, racial and class disparities similar to those for incarceration are also evident for community corrections supervision (Pew Center on the States 2009). As Wacquant (2001) notes, the carceral state now extends further into the community via probation and parole supervision than it did a few decades ago.

Conceptualizing Reintegration

Most scholarship on formerly incarcerated individuals focuses on recidivism and desistance from crime, much of it guided by theories of social control, particularly how social control changes over a person's life course (Laub and Sampson 2003; Sampson and Laub 1992; Shover 1996). This framework emphasizes the importance of social bonds—particularly those resulting from marriage, employment, and military service—in deterring criminality and encouraging desistance (Laub, Nagin, and Sampson 1998; Laub and Sampson 2003; Sampson, Laub, and Wimer 2006). These bonds can be strengthened by key life events, so-called turning points that potentially increase social control by altering daily routines and stabilizing prosocial roles. Those who are most motivated to desist may actively seek out social control and prosocial roles. Moreover, formerly incarcerated individuals who experience such changes in their social roles and relationships may also adopt new identities or self-concepts (Laub and Sampson

2003; Maruna 2001; Paternoster and Bushway 2009; Sampson and Laub 2016). Thus, owing to the role played in it by employment and social relationships, desistance from crime is intimately tied to social and economic reintegration. In much of the past scholarship, social and economic reintegration has been viewed as a means of explaining recidivism. In this book, we focus on reintegration as an outcome and a process worthy of its own study as we attempt to understand how and why some formerly incarcerated individuals fare better than others on its various dimensions. In other words, desisting from crime is just one component of successful reintegration. Indeed, as chapter 6 will show, employment stability is not as tightly linked to desistance as we might expect.

More generally, we see a profound disjuncture between the pathways to desistance emphasized in the predominant theories of desistance from crime and the social circumstances our participants confront in the era of mass incarceration. While prior scholarship emphasizes the importance of engaging in prosocial activities that knife off one's past from one's present, such as finding steady work, serving in the military, entering into marriage, and becoming involved in one's community, such pathways to desistance and reintegration are no longer viable options for many returning prisoners—even those motivated to desist—in contemporary American society. Job opportunities are scarce for formerly incarcerated individuals (especially those that pay a living wage), military service is closed to most convicted felons, marriage is rare in this subpopulation, and many deliberately withdraw from community life to avoid the temptation of drugs, crime, and other sources of trouble. And opportunities for civic involvement, such as voting or serving on a jury, are often closed to those with a criminal record (Lerman and Weaver 2014; Manza and Uggen 2008). Thus, renewed study of the postprison experiences and interactions with a wider set of social relationships, social contexts, and institutions of formerly incarcerated individuals is required to understand the contemporary experience of reentry and reintegration. Here, we take a step back to describe the conceptual framework with which we approach our study of prisoner reintegration.

Like the scholarship on desistance (Bushway 2003; Bushway, Piquero, et al. 2001; Laub and Sampson 2003; Sampson and Laub 1995), we view reintegration as a process that unfolds over time, although not all dimensions necessarily advance in concert. The formerly incarcerated individual rebuilds old relationships and forms new ones, develops new social networks and reactivates old ones, becomes incorporated into key social institutions such as the labor market or the health care system, and engages in various forms of community such as religious and community organizations or political activism (Fox 2015). Ideally, economic and social stability increases over time and involvement in the criminal justice system declines as involvement in other institutions intensifies. The process of reintegration need not be unidirectional. As will be clear in the chapters that follow, even our participants who fared relatively well along these dimensions experienced many setbacks and diversions. The term *reintegration* might be read as indicating that formerly incarcerated individuals are integrating back into the social, economic, and institutional positions in which they were embedded before prison, but that is not what we mean to convey. We view the question of who finds new settings in which to integrate after prison as a critical one.

In order to develop a conceptual framework for understanding variation across individuals in terms of reintegration, we draw on insights from the literature on immigrant incorporation, which addresses broadly parallel questions of social, economic, and cultural integration (Kaufman 2015). The manner and degree to which immigrant groups or individual immigrants become incorporated (or integrated) into the new society can be thought of as a function of both the resources they bring with them and the context of reception (Pedraza and Rumbaut 1996; Portes and Rumbaut 2006). The immigrant's resources may be economic, social, or cultural, and the context of reception can be the economy (e.g., agriculture, industry, information technology), culture (e.g., attitudes toward different ethnoracial groups), community (e.g., religious organizations, neighborhoods, presence of fellow immigrants), or institutions (e.g., laws governing access to the education system or the labor market). The state plays a critical role in the political incorporation of immigrants, enabling or blocking their civic and political participation and their ability and opportunity to exercise political and human rights (Bloemraad 2006; Soysal 1995).

The immigration literature shows us that the fit between resources and the context of reception is central. For example, low-skill immigrants arriving in a tight labor market for manual labor will likely fare better than low-skill immigrants arriving in an information technology economy. Because there have been multiple waves of immigration characterized by different immigrant groups and different contexts of reception, immigration scholarship also highlights the way in which the particular historical moment conditions resources, the context of reception, and the fit between them (Portes and Borocz 2007). Comparative research on immigrant incorporation shows us that the specific programs, policies, and resources that the state devotes to political and civic incorporation of new arrivals determine their involvement in political and civic institutions—and whether they eventually achieve full citizenship—to a greater degree than their premigration experiences or the specific routes they have taken to their new home country (Bloemraad 2006; Soysal 1995). Applied to prisoner reintegration, these ideas suggest that the experience and extent of reintegration will be a product of (1) the social, economic, and cultural resources with which the individual leaves prison, (2) the social, economic, and institutional context to which he or she returns, and (3) the fit between the two.

Former prisoners' limited economic resources—whether human capital, such as education and work experience, or economic capital, such as minimal savings or assets from before incarceration—and dearth of resources in the receiving context all make attaining economic stability and security a significant challenge. As we describe in chapter 1, low levels of human capital, poor health, and lack of work experience also pose barriers to formerly incarcerated individuals' economic stability and mobility. At the same time, however, because formerly incarcerated individuals leave prison with almost universally low levels of education and work experience, human capital itself does not go as far as we might expect in helping us explain why some are more successful than others in eventually achieving some degree of social and economic integration. As we detail in chapters 5 and 6, the economic context to which former prisoners return includes both legal and policy restrictions on employment and social benefits for those with criminal records and labor market discrimination against those with a felony record.

The literature thus far has taught us much about the importance of economic resources but has said less about the importance of the social and cultural resources to which an individual has access (Leverentz 2014; Maruna 2001), so we focus much of our empirical analysis in the chapters ahead on these two factors. Social resources include social support from family or friends, job networks, or other forms of social capital. Cultural resources include cultural capital that allows for the navigation of complex social institutions and knowledge of particular class-based conventions or dress, speech, or cultural knowledge that might facilitate access to employment, schooling, or other opportunities.

Yet the social contexts that shape reintegration are even more important than these individual characteristics. The ones on which we focus include families, neighborhoods, living arrangements, and other aspects of community such as religious organizations. We show in the chapters ahead that these contexts can be supportive, for example, when a family member takes in a formerly incarcerated individual and provides material and emotional support, a neighborhood is near jobs available to those with a criminal record, or a homeless shelter prevents the formerly incarcerated individual from experiencing hunger and exposure to the elements. Social contexts can, however, also be challenging, for example, when a neighborhood provides easy access to drugs or a family member is emotionally abusive. Economic context includes the nature of the economy and the current state of the labor market, particularly as it relates to jobs available to those with a criminal record or the skills typical of those coming out of prison. Cultural context includes attitudes toward formerly incarcerated individuals and the identities they hold, particularly race, gender, and disability status.

Our core economic, political, and civic institutions are also important contexts for reintegration. The contemporary labor market for individuals with low levels of human capital is particularly challenging owing to low wages, poor job security and high turnover, unstable work schedules, and the prevalence of part-time work. Gone are the days when someone without a high school degree can find meaningful, if physically taxing and repetitive, work with a steady paycheck that supports a family. Even for those without a criminal record, gaining and keeping a foothold in the low-skill labor market is a constant challenge (Kalleberg 2011). In chapter 6, we explore how our formerly incarcerated subjects navigate the low-skill labor market and why many struggle not just to find a job but also to hold on to one for any meaningful period of time.

State institutions—both their presence and their absence—also determine the context of reception. As Wacquant argues (2009), mass incarceration is part of a larger shift toward neoliberalism that has increased punishment, reduced the welfare state, and all but criminalized poverty. Institutional contexts include the scope, power, and resources of the criminal justice system, government programs to provide services and supports to formerly incarcerated individuals or the poor more generally, and institutional practices such as criminal background checks for employment and housing, which the state leaves largely unregulated. In sum, formerly incarcerated individuals are returning to a society and economy in which many others like them are competing for scarce government and economic resources and in which they face intense and heightened institutional scrutiny.

A critical aspect of the context of reception for formerly incarcerated individuals in the United States is the current era of mass incarceration. Studying reintegration from the perspective of those experiencing it suggests a more multifaceted and nuanced view of incarceration and reintegration than is currently present in the mass incarceration literature, which tends to view prison either through the lens of deterrence or as a uniformly negative influence that reinforces criminal trajectories by stigmatizing and negatively socializing inmates. Our participants' experiences tell a more complex story about the effects of incarceration and how they work. To be sure, our participants were highly critical of the prison system, but many of them also acknowledged that prison had given them the opportunity to cool down, sober up, reflect, and mature. In fact, when we first interviewed them in prison, most were surprisingly optimistic about their chances of staying clean and working hard to make a living on the outside, a finding documented by other scholars as well (e.g., Comfort 2012; Seim 2016). In this sense, imprisonment has the potential to be a positive turning point for some people, providing a window of opportunity to desist from crime and substance use and rethink goals and identity. The key is to understand for whom prison is a turning point and for whom it is a source of continuing disadvantage.

Whereas many scholars have called attention to the disproportionate impact of mass incarceration on poor and minority communities, few have considered the role of criminal justice institutions in structuring the lives of the poor even outside the prison walls. Of particular importance for this study, the era of mass incarceration coincides with a shift in the institution of parole toward a greater emphasis on punishment, deterrence, and surveillance (Burke and Tonry 2006; Simon 1993). An outgrowth of the juvenile justice system, parole was originally intended both to rehabilitate and to control former prisoners and also later served to help relieve prison overcrowding (Simon 1993; Stemen, Rengifo, and Wilson 2005). In the late 1970s, the rehabilitative goals of parole came under question in the influential "Martinson Report," which argued that nothing works in offender rehabilitation (Lipton, Martinson, and Wilks 1975) and helped usher in an era of more punitive criminal justice policies in which parole came to be seen as a soft approach to crime (Burke and Tonry 2006).

The shift toward punishment and surveillance in parole was institutionalized in the late 1980s and early 1990s as part of a broader set of institutional changes in the criminal justice system that Feeley and Simon (1992) have called *the new penology* and that involved more efficient management of growing caseloads, actuarial methods of risk assessment, and a focus on preventing offending rather than rehabilitation or reintegration. This era also brought about changes in the role of parole officers, whose primary responsibilities were reframed as managing risks to public safety rather than providing treatment or services to parolees (Simon 1993). The benchmarks by which parole officers' work is evaluated shifted toward parole violations and revocations resulting from detection of prohibited behavior (Feeley and Simon 1992; Seiter and West 2003; Simon 1993; West and Seiter 2004). The use of violations and sanctions concomitantly expanded (Burke and Tonry 2006). Lynch (2000) has argued that, although the current discourse on parole pays lip service to rehabilitation, resources are primarily focused on punishment and surveillance. We show—from the perspectives of our participants—how parole supervision can dominate day-to-day life by dictating how and where one spends one's time and by imposing so-called intermediate sanctions that generate residential instability, hamper efforts to find and maintain a job, and disrupt ties to loved ones.

The social control and punishment experienced by formerly incarcerated individuals after their release is not limited to the state itself, however. Nongovernment organizations that provide housing, job training, substance abuse and other mental health treatment, and myriad other services to those who have recently left prison often serve as agents of the state, or what Haney (2010) has called *hybrid state institutions*, which represent privatized state functions (Kaufman 2015). Such organizations provide much-needed services but also monitor drug and alcohol use or curfews, report suspected deviance to parole authorities, inculcate and reinforce particular belief systems stressed in prison about the importance of personal rather than societal failings, and regulate emotions and presentations of self (Haney 2010). As we will see in the chapters that follow, our participants were often both beholden to these organizations, their staff, and their cultural logics to meet their basic material needs and frustrated by their inability to provide viable pathways toward economic and social independence, given the meager resources they made available. Few such organizations are able to move beyond control and surveillance to providing real prosocial opportunities (Kaufman 2015).

Race, gender, and health are central to our theoretical framework for understanding reintegration as they play important roles in determining both the individual resources to which formerly incarcerated individuals have access and the social and institutional contexts in which they are embedded. In other words, the resources with which the formerly incarcerated leave prison and the opportunities they have to use them productively in their reintegration are strongly conditioned by race, gender, and health status. Moreover, race and gender, separately and in concert, play critical roles in determining exposure to the past traumas that are so often a source of addiction and other mental health problems facing individuals leaving prison (Burton and Lynn 2017; Richie 2012). We will see the effects of race, gender, and health throughout this book, but here we provide a few examples. Formerly incarcerated African Americans return to poorer neighborhoods with fewer institutional and social resources, face heightened stigma in the labor market, integrate into families with fewer material and social resources than those of their white counterparts, and face greater challenges securing effective mental health care and social benefits.[2] Women face risks of physical, sexual, and emotional abuse in their homes, neighborhoods, and workplaces, while men must contend with narrow definitions of working-class masculinity that define worth through physical work and masculine family roles. Those with known histories of addiction or other mental health conditions face heightened scrutiny and formal social control from the criminal justice system and its hybrid state agents who provide treatment and care.

The Study

On the Outside is a study of prisoner reintegration based on the experiences and perspectives of formerly incarcerated individuals as told to us in over 150 interviews with fifteen men and seven women. We randomly selected these participants from a list of prisoners with impending release dates in late 2007 and early 2008. When we first met them in prison, these men and women were serving time for a diverse set of crimes, including violent offenses (e.g., manslaughter, armed robbery), property offenses (e.g., burglary, retail fraud), and drug- or alcohol-related offenses (e.g., selling drugs or repeated drunk driving). After their release from prison, we conducted regular follow-up interviews with our participants over a period of time that lasted up to three years. Our conversations, in coffee shops, diners, and participants' homes, covered a wide range of topics, including community context, family roles and relationships, child support and contact with children, criminal activities and experiences, experiences in prison, services sought and received, employment and other sources of income, and general health and well-being, both mental and physical, including drug and alcohol abuse. We followed our participants through marriages and breakups, drug relapses and sobriety anniversaries, births and deaths, employment and joblessness, and completions of parole and returns to prison. The appendix explains our methodology in detail and discusses the challenges we faced in conducting this research.

In presenting the results of our research in book form, we highlight the experiences of six individuals who participated in our study whom we term *focal participants* and introduce to the reader in chapter 1. We selected this group for its variation in race and gender and for its variation in experiences. Our aim in focusing on these six participants is to provide the opportunity for the reader to gain deeper insight into the lives of these individuals. We will revisit their experiences repeatedly throughout the book as a device for conveying our findings in a way that will allow the reader to follow a small set of individual stories. We emphasize, however, that, while we prioritize these individuals when we provide examples of our findings, our findings are based on systematic analysis of all our participants (and the reader will find the experiences of many other participants discussed throughout the book as well).

Although the book will focus on the firsthand accounts we obtained through these in-depth qualitative interviews, it will also draw from time to time on another original data source: a quantitative longitudinal study in which for seven years we prospectively followed every state prisoner in Michigan released on parole during 2003 ($N = 11,064$). The administrative data we compiled provide a comprehensive view of not only their criminal history and sociodemographic background but also their postprison experiences with the criminal justice system (e.g., conditions of supervision, substance use tests, absconding warrants, parole violations, arrests, and new convictions and sentences), employment, and earnings. Our research team also read and coded parole agents' narrative case notes on a one-third random sample of this cohort to collect data on their living situations, residential mobility, and neighborhood context and more detailed information about their employment, education, and contact with the criminal justice system. We will draw on this quantitative study to contextualize the accounts from our qualitative interviews. Although our use of the administrative data will differ somewhat from chapter to chapter, we will typically use it to establish key descriptive patterns. The qualitative data will then be used to understand the sources or consequences of those patterns.

Both sources of data are unique and were possible to collect only after establishing a collaborative partnership with the Michigan Department of

Corrections. These data will allow us to understand participants' prison experiences and postrelease expectations as well as examine how their struggles with employment, housing, substance use, health, family reintegration, and parole supervision are interconnected and unfold over time, from the uncertainty and anxiety of the first days of freedom to the long-term challenges of building a stable and productive crime-free life.

As we report our results in this book, we endeavor to avoid terminology that subtly engages in othering and essentializing formerly incarcerated individuals—words such as *former prisoner*, *ex-offender*, or *parolee*. Such language risks viewing our research participants as a separate and dangerous class, implicitly reinforcing and legitimizing the cultural mentalities that have led to mass incarceration in the first place. Instead, we prefer terminology such as *formerly incarcerated individual* and *returning citizen* that has been adopted by those who work directly with individuals who have been recently released from prison and by those individuals themselves. Such language indicates that, while committing crimes and experiencing imprisonment are key life experiences for our research participants, we must understand those experiences within the broader context of their lives as individuals embedded in families and communities with multiple identities and possible life paths ahead.

Plan of the Book

Chapter 1 serves as an introduction to our focal participants. It will introduce in detail six participants whom readers will come to know throughout the book, including their biographies, personalities, challenges, and experiences after release from prison. This chapter highlights the social and individual characteristics of formerly incarcerated individuals that have largely been ignored in public discourse, including addiction and mental health, community context, and family roles and identities.

Chapter 2 describes the transition home from prison as experienced by our participants. It shows through their eyes the prison experiences as both punitive and rehabilitative. Though prison is cold, isolating, and dehumanizing, it can serve as a time-out from drug and alcohol use and a time for reflection. This chapter documents the overwhelmingly positive hopes and expectations at the point of release and the challenges of adjustment to a new social environment and the new pressures that come with freedom, including reconnecting with family, avoiding old places and old faces, finding stable housing and employment, and conforming to onerous supervision conditions.

Chapter 3 explores the challenges formerly incarcerated individuals experience in securing a stable home, the foundation on which successful social and economic reintegration will be built. This chapter examines why returning to preprison homes is relatively rare, and then documents and explains the reasons for high rates of residential mobility after release from prison. A result of such residential instability is that many formerly incarcerated individuals struggle to meet basic needs for food and shelter. Rebuilding family relationships proves to be critical to achieving any measure of stability and economic security.

Chapter 4 examines the role of families in the reintegration of formerly incarcerated individuals beyond the role of material support examined in chapter 3. The effects of family relationships are complex and countervailing. Romantic partners, children, siblings, parents, and other family members are important sources of material support, informal social control, and emotional support. They also provide salient sources of positive social identities to individuals denied access to prosocial roles in almost every other context. However, these same relationships often also ease the path back toward substance abuse or crime, through opportunities for criminal behavior and substance abuse, emotional stress, and role strain.

Chapter 5 examines the role of neighborhood context in reentry and reintegration. It addresses how formerly incarcerated individuals resist the opportunities for crime and drug use and avoid police supervision, both of which are more common in poor neighborhoods, as well as how one's geographic location affects the reintegration process through influences as diverse as access to transportation, social services, and job opportunities and the availability of drugs and opportunities for returning to crime. We describe the strategies that our participants use to avoid their neighborhood's crime and violence as well as the unintended consequences of those strategies.

Chapter 6 explores the experiences of our participants as they embark on the daunting task of searching for work, exploring how and where they find work, and the stigma management strategies they use, both successful and unsuccessful, in an era of instant background checks and intense parole supervision. It analyzes which participants overcome other barriers to employment, including weak job skills, low levels of education, and transportation difficulties, and how the expansive net of the criminal justice system has resulted in particular niches in the labor market where formerly incarcerated individuals often find more receptive employers. Moreover, maintaining employment often proves as difficult as finding a job, so this chapter examines who is able to keep a job in the longer term and rise into the working or middle class.

The conclusion summarizes the key points of the book and discusses the lessons that our participants' experiences and perspectives hold for policies designed to reduce recidivism and promote the social and economic reintegration of formerly incarcerated individuals.

CHAPTER ONE

Trajectories

I'm trying to strive every day to be a better mother than I've been.... It's like learning how to be a new person all over. I'm learning myself more and more every day, my likes and dislikes ... how to identify with my feelings, my thoughts.... I didn't know how to do that because I stayed so intoxicated.... I didn't give myself a chance to feel or to even think without being intoxicated. It was from the time I woke up until days and days and days until I would absolutely pass out.... It was, I think, the only times in the last four and a half years I have clean time is if I was locked up in rehab or asleep. And that's the truth, and that's just something I have to remind myself.... I cannot forget where I came from. I cannot forget... them old patterns, ... and it's difficult, but it'll work out because that's what I want to do. I want to stay clean, and in the past I would get clean for ninety days or whatever, and I'd go right back out and use because I wasn't ready to stop it.... And I can see clearly now. I can see that all the damage I've done to myself, my children, my loved ones, and I just don't want to do it anymore. I was killing myself slowly. I have a heart problem. I have liver damage now, kidney damage now. And I'm ready to move on and live now because before that wasn't living. I was killing myself. So I'm just really, really ready for change in my life, and it's well past due.

Jennifer

Jennifer is a thirty-eight-year-old white woman with a soft, round face, honey-blond hair, and a warm, open demeanor. Around her neck she wears a gold chain proclaiming "100% drug free," while her nervous smoking hints at the struggle she faces maintaining that sobriety. The youngest of six, Jennifer was born into a working-class family in Ypsilanti. Her mother worked at an auto plant, and her father was a truck driver. There were many good times in her childhood: "My parents were good to us.... We lived like middle class. Always had food. Always had a roof over our head, clothes on our back. Other than the drinking, I'd say it was good.... My brothers were in football, went to a lot of football games. Really, I had a real family-oriented life when I was younger, much younger. And

then alcohol started . . . progressing in my parents' life, and fights started."
What was once weekend drinking increasingly spilled into the week, the
fighting and violence escalated, and Jennifer began missing school. Her
grandparents intervened and brought her into their home when she was
in the fourth grade, initiating a calm period of regular school, church, and
family life.

Yet, outside her grandparents' home, Jennifer continued to hang out
with her siblings and other older kids from the neighborhood. She began
experimenting with marijuana, alcohol, and powder cocaine, and eventually her sister introduced her to crack. Not long after moving back to
her parents' house, Jennifer's yearlong, casual sexual relationship with an
older boy resulted in pregnancy. She bore her first child, Jason, at thirteen.
Jennifer never returned to school. She explains how early parenthood and
other stressful life events were linked with her deepening addiction: "It
had a lot to do with having kids and stuff at a young age, and then I lost
Dawn's dad, and . . . I kept spiraling down. Then I lost my grandmother
and my baby's dad, then my mom, and then it just, from there. . . . It was
one thing after another, and it just kept going deeper and deeper and
deeper into it . . . for like to comfort me. And then, before I knew it, I was
so addicted that it was the only thing I knew and the only thing I wanted."

By sixteen, Jennifer had borne another child, and the three were living in "a dope house." While her daughter was raised by her father, her
oldest son, Jason, remained with her and became deeply involved in her
criminal offending. At eleven years old, he was helping her deal drugs and
guns. Just a few years later he shot and killed a man in a confrontation that
escalated. She explains how her behavior was implicated in this tragedy:
"He was taught—literally taught—and my sick thinking taught him that,
that you sell drugs, you carry guns, you wear bulletproof vests. This is what
life's about because I was so messed up. . . . The kid was eleven years old,
walked in and caught me with a needle out of my arm, and I'm slumped
over the toilet. He thought I was dead. . . . What type of mother does that?"

Yet, even after her son was arrested for manslaughter and his prison
sentence began, the drug use continued through her third pregnancy, and
her son Lucas was born addicted to crack. Jennifer lived with him just two
years before sending him to live with other relatives. She moved in with
her fiancé, Stan, thirty years her senior, and spent years largely confined to
their home, using drugs and watching television: "I stayed in Stan's house
just smoking my brains out, with blankets and stuff over the blinds so it'd
be dark in there. And the dope man would bring the dope right to the

door. Stan would go get my cigarettes and alcohol, I'd smoke five packs of cigarettes a day . . . just in a corner in the living room on the couch doing my drugs and drinking my alcohol with the TV on mute, burning up, just running the TV . . . the lamp on constantly day or night right next to me, just sitting there."

When Jennifer did leave, it was often either to buy or use drugs. Although she had "probably broken every rule there is" when it came to her addiction, her incarceration history consisted only of two short bits in jail for driving under the influence (DUI). It was her third DUI that landed her in prison this time. When she was stopped by the police driving the wrong way down a one-way street, she knew she was going to prison.

Jennifer was scared initially entering prison and remained withdrawn and on edge throughout her sentence: "You have to mind your p's and q's . . . weave your way through." Nonetheless, she came to see prison as a blessing: "[Otherwise] I would've never got sober." She explains: "It helped me to find out who I am and gave me a foundation of clean time." Prior to prison she had not spent more than a few months sober in twenty-three years. In prison, with little to occupy her time during the eight months she served aside from "walking the track," she was able to reflect on what she had done with her life and where she wanted to go in the future. She recognized that her addiction had caused great suffering for her children, from Jason's imprisonment to Dawn's adoption and Lucas's learning disabilities. She made a decision to turn her life around, to become a good mother for her children.

In her first interview following release, Jennifer explained how her commitment to motherhood shaped her choices: "My kids make me very strong. . . . Having to take care of them and doing the mommy thing and just being with them reminds me every day that somebody needs me. . . . And I'm needed, and I can't do both. I can't use and be a productive mother; I can't use and take care of my children. I can't have them two both worlds, so I choose not the drugs, I choose my kids." This narrative sets up a fundamental opposition between her past self, the selfish addict who would do anything for drugs, and her current self, the person who lives her life for her children. Her sense of herself as beginning anew, having experienced a complete personal transformation for her children, allowed her to begin to forgive herself and move forward. This narrative would sustain her in the hard months to come as she experienced the challenges of independent living, motherhood, and sobriety.

With a great deal of material and emotional support from her family as well as a personal commitment to God, Jennifer began to establish a life for herself and her youngest son. The two moved into a trailer a few weeks after her release, and Jennifer began seeking out public assistance. Over the months that followed, she shared her excitement at being able to live independently for the first time in her life, learning to pay her bills, manage a household, and mother her son. She secured welfare assistance, food stamps, and supplemental security income, learned to read with the help of a tutor through a free adult education program, and strengthened her relationship with her children and her girlfriend, Rachel, whom she had met in prison. It was not just personal responsibility that was new to her; it was also having a mind unmuddled by drugs and alcohol. She explained that every day, when she woke up and her head was clear and not in a fog, it amazed her.

Despite these positive developments, Jennifer also experienced significant challenges throughout her reentry period, many of which were linked with the social world in which she was embedded. Several of her neighbors were former drug buddies or people she had either bought drugs from or sold them to, and drinking and drug use were common in the trailer park. Many of her family members had substance abuse problems, including two brothers who had been incarcerated for drunk driving and continued to struggle with addictions. Even Rachel, who was a crucial emotional support for Jennifer, continued to struggle with alcoholism, and the two fought frequently over this. In an early interview, Jennifer explained: "Everybody else that I absolutely know in my life [aside from Luke's father and some men helping repair her trailer] is in some shape or form involved with the drug atmosphere." Yet, because she valued her sobriety so highly, she pursued strategies to keep substance abuse at bay: she remained in her trailer rather than hanging out outside, banned Rachel from her home when she was drinking, and kicked her brother out once she learned he was using again. Ensuring that she was not directly exposed to drug or alcohol use helped her maintain her sobriety.

A second set of challenges revolved around physical and mental health problems. Though only thirty-eight years old, Jennifer had already had two crack-induced heart attacks. She suffered from anemia, hypothyroidism—for which she inconsistently took medication—and had the early symptoms of emphysema. She also struggled with depression and anxiety. She dealt with her physical problems largely by ignoring them—worrying that, were she to spend time thinking about and treating them, she would become overwhelmed and perhaps return to drug use. Her commitment to the maternal role also helped keep her on track. For instance, she forced herself to get out of bed to get Lucas to school in the morning, even when she was dragging.

In this chapter, we introduce our six focal participants, whose experiences and perspectives we will return to again and again. Although the analyses offered throughout the book are based on our entire sample and we will draw examples and illustrations from everyone in the sample, our focal participants provide narrative continuity, linking our arguments together across life domains through their lives before, during, and after prison. An intimate understanding of these six individuals and their successes and failures at reintegration will ground this book in the experiences of specific individuals. The theoretical framework sketched in the prior chapter emphasizes the fit between individual resources and contexts of reintegration. This chapter presents a portrait of the resources with which formerly incarcerated individuals, individually and collectively, begin the reentry process.

Difficult Pasts, Uncertain Futures

Is Jennifer an outlier in terms of her traumatic past, serious addiction, low education level, and health problems? As we present the descriptions of our focal participants and their trajectories, from their young lives through the close of the study, it will become clear that disadvantage, often from childhood, was the norm. Just like Jennifer, many experienced high rates of abuse as children and had parents who abused drugs and alcohol and were criminally involved. Nearly all grew up either poor or working-class, and addiction was rampant in adulthood. But does this portrait square with that of imprisoned individuals nationally? Before returning to our five remaining focal participants, we briefly address what is known about the characteristics and experiences of prisoners and formerly incarcerated individuals across the United States.

The disadvantages that incarcerated individuals experienced during childhood have been well established. Nearly 13 percent of state and federal inmates report residing in a foster home or correctional facility in their youth, almost one-third report that their parents abused drugs or alcohol, and 18 percent report that a parent spent time in prison or jail. Poverty in the family of origin is also common, with 45 percent of African American, 22 percent of white, and 33 percent of Hispanic inmates reporting parental receipt of public assistance. While white inmates are more likely to have spent time in foster care and have parents with substance abuse problems, African American inmates are more likely to report experiencing economic hardship (Uggen, Wakefield, and Western 2005).

Abuse is also common. Among state prison inmates, one in four women and one in twenty men report being the victim of sexual abuse prior to age eighteen, while one in ten men and one in four women report childhood physical abuse (Harlow 1999).[1] These numbers represent self-reports, leave the definition of abuse up to the respondent, and were collected in a single interview with each respondent, so they are likely to underestimate the prevalence of abuse. For instance, a small survey of New York State prison inmates utilizing a tool that imposed a precise definition of abuse found that 68 percent of the sample of incarcerated adult male felons reported some form of childhood victimization. Nearly 35 percent of the sample experienced physical abuse, nearly 16 percent neglect, and more than 14 percent sexual abuse (Weeks and Widom 1998).[2] Victimization into adulthood is also common, with over one-third of women experiencing abuse at the hands of an intimate partner (Greenfeld and Snell 1999). Men experience high rates of violence and exposure to trauma in adulthood as well (Carlson and Shafer 2010).

Disadvantage also marks prisoners' education and their work lives. Dropping out of high school is common; 40 percent of state prison inmates have not completed high school (Harlow 2003). Among young men, 90 percent of those twenty-five to thirty-four in the general population hold a high school diploma, while only one-third of young incarcerated do (Uggen, Wakefield, and Western 2005). Unsurprisingly, low education levels tend to translate into low-wage, low-quality jobs. Individuals entering prison are also much more likely to be unemployed or out of the labor force at the point of prison entry than is the general population (Wakefield and Uggen 2010). Of male inmates aged twenty-five to thirty-four, only 55 percent were employed full-time prior to entering prison (Uggen, Wakefield, and Western 2005).

Disadvantages uncovered in family of origin, education, and employment history are mirrored in physical and mental health status. A study by the Urban Institute found that eight in ten men and nine in ten women leaving prison had a chronic health condition that required treatment or management (Mallik-Kane and Visher 2008). One-half of men and two-thirds of women had a chronic physical health condition such as asthma, diabetes or HIV/AIDS (Hammett, Roberts, and Kennedy 2001). In 1997, nearly one-quarter of those living with HIV/AIDS, nearly one-third of those bearing a hepatitis C infection, and more than one-third of those with a tuberculosis infection were released from a prison or jail (Hammett, Harmon, and Rhodes 2002). Fifty-six percent of state prison inmates have a mental health problem, with female inmates evidencing a significantly higher burden: 73 percent versus 55 percent among men (James and Glaze 2006). The high burden of mental health disorders was documented by another study looking broadly at those ever incarcerated, whether in prison, jail, or another correctional institution. Schnittker (2014) estimates psychiatric symptoms at a level twice that of the never-incarcerated population, impulse control disorders 2.4 times as common, and comorbidity (the prevalence of two or more disorders simultaneously) 2.7 times higher.

Drug and alcohol abuse is also prevalent. An estimated 80 percent of incarcerated individuals have some kind of alcohol or drug problem, and 20 percent have a history of injection drug use (Hammett, Roberts, and Kennedy 2001). The 1997 Survey of Inmates in State and Federal Correctional Facilities reveals very high rates of drug and alcohol abuse among inmates. Eighty-three percent of state prison inmates reported past drug use, 57 percent reported using drugs in the month prior to their offense, 51 percent reported that they were under the influence of drugs or alcohol when they committed their offense, and 19 percent of state and 16 percent of federal inmates reported committing their offense in order to obtain money for drugs. Nearly a quarter of state prison inmates are classified as alcohol dependent (Mumola 1999).

As will become evident in the stories that follow, the men and women in our sample have experienced many of these same challenges, and these characteristics shape not only their criminal involvement but also their ability to reintegrate into society successfully.

DeAngelo

DeAngelo is a handsome twenty-seven-year-old African American man whose brow often creases with worry; he speaks slowly and methodically, pausing often to choose his words carefully. Sometimes his voice lowers to barely a whisper as he reflects on his life experiences and his future prospects. Other times, he laughs nervously when describing his most traumatic experiences, as if to comfort the listener and dispel the tension.

De Angelo locates the beginning of his troubles in childhood, growing up as one of six children in a chaotic, impoverished family. When he was just four years old, his mother left his father, a violent man who beat her and the children. Their troubles did not end there, however; as money was scarce, the family moved frequently within Detroit and subsisted largely on welfare. When DeAngelo was thirteen, his mother remarried. His step-father was also abusive, locking the children in the house and padlocking the refrigerator to keep them from the food. Throughout his childhood, DeAngelo was exposed to violence:

> All day, every day. I seen people getting shot, people getting jumped and beat up every day. Just everything. Seen my mama getting beat up every day. We got beat up every day. Just you name it, we seen it. I seen my daddy kill somebody. The second time I seen somebody get killed I was like nine years old. They killed this dude right in front of our house 'cause he had broken into the dope house right across the street. When they caught him in there he came running out, they shot him up right in front of our house.

He links this exposure to violence with his lifelong mental health problems, afflictions that would have important implications for his later involvement in criminal offending and substance abuse:

> I believe that's where my anxiety comes from. 'Cause I never felt protected. I never felt like anybody ... would love me or like me. . . . I'm always thinking about what they think about me, what they think about me, what they think about me? They probably don't like me. . . . My mama used to . . . she had her fair share of beating me, too. So I never felt that comfort. The people that's supposed to like me, I didn't get that from the people that's supposed to, so how can I think anybody else could?

This anxiety led DeAngelo to withdraw; he described himself as a loner who struggled in school: "Back when I was a teenager I was extremely shy, low self-esteem, insecure. So ain't had no friends, I didn't talk, I was always nervous. And, if they could let me sleep through a whole class, I'd be asleep through a whole class." He began drinking to ease his anxiety and soon found his niche socially as a gang member. Around this time, his mother put him out of the house: "My mom would put me out on the streets when I was fifteen, still in high school . . . in January [*laughs*]. So I'm walking up the street with two garbage bags, you know, with nowhere to go and snow all on the ground." He was angry and resentful: "I mean, I didn't have no reason to be happy. . . . I didn't even think happy existed. I would see somebody smiling, and . . . I would . . . resent them . . . because . . . they . . . obviously . . . got it better than me. . . . I used to . . . want to go beat them up [*laughs*]." Once he was immersed in the gang, his criminal activity quickly escalated: "I joined a gang, and things really got bad then. Started robbing people, got shot, got stabbed, riding around just . . . finding rival gang members . . . breaking in houses, stealing cars . . . robbing bars. . . . The more . . . bad things I do, the next time it'll be something worse than the last thing I did." By the time we first met with him, he had accumulated three probation, eight jail, and two prison sentences.[3]

Yet this description tells only a partial story. Despite his gang affiliation, DeAngelo successfully completed high school and moved on to community college, completing two semesters of a custom collision and paint certificate before dropping out. At twenty-three, he married and had a son whom he cared for full-time while his wife attended college, until he and his wife separated when his son was fourteen months old. He also held a variety of jobs, including janitorial, factory, and construction work, retail sales, and restaurant work. Prior to his most recent incarceration, he had been employed as a waiter and was doing construction on the side.

Despite these markers of successful adulthood, alcoholism also cast a long shadow. DeAngelo initially began drinking to cope with his social anxiety, as we have seen, but, as his drinking escalated, he found that it caused him to lose friends: "When I was drinking a lot, I talked stupid, I acted stupid." It also had important health consequences, DeAngelo had been hospitalized three times for alcohol poisoning. Further, when he was drinking, which was frequently, he did not worry about college or the fact that he had been out of a job for six months; he was "living in the moment." It was his third DUI conviction that landed him in prison most recently. This period of imprisonment proved critical for DeAngelo, providing ten months of structured sobriety and a chance for the fog of alcoholism to lift:

> By my drinking, it kind of clouded my . . . vision . . . the things that I really wanted to do. Once I . . . got locked up this third time . . . I noticed the difference. I noticed how much more I can see where my life was heading and where I wanted it to go. . . . And I don't want that cloud back in front of my face . . . blurring my vision, you know, turning . . . turning back to the bottle. . . . So, you know, that just gives me that much more drive to do what I want to do, knowing that I've got the willpower and the strength to say no to that.

In prison, without the crutch of alcohol to turn to when anxieties arose, DeAngelo had to learn to deal with uncomfortable feelings in other ways.

He found that, the more he did sober, the more comfortable he became living his life without drinking: "It became easy, well, normal." He also credits his positive attitude with his ability to change: "You gotta psyche yourself up sometimes. You gotta make yourself believe something. You know, the impossible, if you feel it's impossible, make yourself believe it." Within a few months, he found that his depression and anxiety had lessened.

Leaving prison, DeAngelo was lucky to have a great deal of support from his girlfriend, Laura, and her mother. The fact that these two believed in him was vitally important—he knew that returning to crime and heavy drinking would let them down. This support contrasted dramatically with that from his family of origin. They were not surprised when they found out he had been to prison. Rather: "It's almost expected." DeAngelo described his mother's interaction with him as superficial and "fake," while his relationship with the brother he was closest to was built on a history of shared drinking and drugging. In contrast, his new family provided a safe and secure landing. Not only did the two provide housing, food, and transportation to his many weekly appointments; they also monitored his comings and goings, thereby providing informal social control.

This social context allowed DeAngelo to aspire to a new social role, that of a mature family man. He hoped to secure a job quickly to be able to give back: "Working, you know, providing . . . what a man's supposed to do." He also hoped to reconnect with his now four-year-old son and eventually gain custody. He feared the boy was being neglected or even abused by his wife and her boyfriend, who both smoked pot "from sunup to sundown." In contrast, he hoped to be a positive role model: "I don't want him to be a street dude or a hood dude. I want him to be respect-able. . . . And I want him just to come up right. . . . I gotta be right for him to be right." He knew that, if he did not want his son to take the path that he had, he would have to change. His interests had also changed since he was younger: "I think your mind just changes as you get older." Whereas in the past he had sought excitement and drama, now he appreciated stability and responsibility. He described how he felt caring for his son: "I like the sense of responsibility. . . . It motivates me. It keeps me going. It makes me feel good on the inside."

Just months after leaving prison, DeAngelo was pleasantly surprised at how smoothly the transition was going. He had secured a job as a waiter, was attending AA and therapy, saw his son regularly, and had been pre-scribed medication to treat his anxiety and depression that seemed to be really working: "It's almost like I'm just, like, right back in the groove . . . in less than two months."

Yet, only months later, troubles began to arise. First DeAngelo lost his job when his manager was unwilling to be flexible with his work schedule to accommodate his schooling. Then his girlfriend began to exhibit signs of mental illness. Her increasing jealousy and violence drove him out of the house. Over the next two years, DeAngelo became involved with five new girlfriends (many of whom he lived with), was kicked out of a subsidized apartment provided by a reentry program after neighbors complained of too much noise from his unit, and supplemented his sporadic employment with plasma donation, collecting cans, and cutting hair. He was also briefly returned to prison on an open-container and driving-with-a-suspended-license charge. He explains how this occurred: "I think I had too much freedom at that point. Because, when I said I'd never drink again, I had support, people around me. Like, Laura and her mama. And my [parole officer] was kind of on me." Also contributing was a reconnection with friends from the past who partied and encouraged him to drink. His drive to attend treatment, AA, and therapy would fade the longer he remained out of prison, as did his dedication to work, particularly when a girlfriend could support him. Still, over the three years, his basic commitment to sobriety and his son remained intact.

Three years after we first met, DeAngelo was sharing an apartment with his son, attending a program in culinary arts full-time, selling Avon products, and cutting hair on the side. If he had not fully succeeded, he seemed to be on his way. He described his vision for his life five years down the road: "Working some six days a week, making some nice money. I want to be married sooner or later, have a real family. . . . Just live a normal life. I ain't never really lived a normal life. So I kind of just want that. Be a productive citizen in society. A law-abiding [one], of course. But I just want—I just want to live the dream."

Lenora

Lenora is a tall fifty-one-year-old African American woman. She speaks with composure and deliberateness. She views herself as different, a step above the women who have all too frequently surrounded her during her adult life: in prison, homeless shelters, and substance abuse treatment facilities. Unlike these other women, she had "a beautiful childhood," graduated from high school, completed a number of college courses, and prioritized work and family over sex, drugs, and street life. She remembered: "Some of the [prison] officers used to tell me that, 'Dag, Lenora, you don't act like the rest of them!' Because I didn't pick up the prison mentality.... I have my own mind, and I make up my own mind, and I don't be in no crowd or no clique or 'So-and-so doing this; I'm going to do it.' I think for myself." And after eight prison bits she had made up her mind that enough was enough.

Lenora grew up with five siblings and married parents in Southwest Detroit. They were working-class, with her mother employed as a maid and cook for various white families, while her father was a supervisor in an auto parts company. The family went on summer vacations and away to summer camp. The only trouble she could recall was her mother's drinking: "My mother drank; my dad drank sociable. But my mother is the one that started having problems with the alcohol. And that's what killed her, too. Her whole liver was gone.... My mother, when she would get drunk or whatever, my father would just take up the slack. She worked every day, so she was a functioning alcoholic. She worked till the day she died." Despite her mother's serious alcoholism, work remained a defining feature of her life—a quality that was mirrored in Lenora's own.

Lenora locates the beginning of her trouble at her father's death when she was just fourteen. She made this connection recently in a prison-based residential substance abuse treatment program, a class that helped her understand why she kept returning to prison, why she was "getting high and all that mess." She noted: "[At first] I wasn't doing nothing but drinking a little Hennessey and maybe taking some uppers." But soon she met a drug dealer who introduced her to heroin and cocaine. She explained: "I used him to fill the void.... I was the baby girl.... He liked me and used to give me all this money all the time ... so I got overwhelmed.... I was [planning to go] to modeling school, and I got toot powder in my nose, and OK, forget that, I'm gonna do this fast money." She was subsequently kicked out of high school. She stayed with this boyfriend, a "kilo dealer," until his violence toward her escalated. After suffering two black eyes and a pistol-whipping, she left him.

But the stage had been set, and the addiction and criminal involvement were only beginning. Over the next thirty-five years, Lenora was constantly cycling in and out of prison and jail. In the early 1980s, she bore two sons, both while she was incarcerated. Her family cared for the babies until she was released from prison, a year and a half and one month later, respectively. Her mother was initially the children's primary caretaker and later her sister. When she was not incarcerated, she would see her sons every day, but she was frequently incarcerated. Each time she was released she would move back in to her mother's old house, the home she had lived in since she was fifteen. Although the neighborhood had deteriorated in the 1990s, with middle-class families moving out and drugs and crime taking over, her family remained.

When not incarcerated, Lenora was committed to work and school. She was tremendously proud of her education and work history. She had completed her GED while in jail and gone on to get an associate's degree at a community college after her release. She hoped to complete her bachelor's degree in the next few years. She was also proud of her job skills: "Factory on the line, line leaders, I worked at three different factories, nursing orderly. Computers, the presser at the dry cleaner, I did all that. As manager, I cleaned by myself. I've did a lot of jobs. I've worked at the Marriott. Emptying the trays that come in from the rooms and setting them up so the dishwasher can wash them, I've worked there. Let's see, restaurants. I've worked at White Castles." Yet interspersed with these legitimate jobs were stints selling drugs. She would make between $5,000 and $8,000 per week as the middleman, selling crack and heroin to other dealers. Problems would arise when she began dipping into the product: "When I'm selling, I'm using. Eventually you'll become your own best customer." Indebted to the buyer, she would be forced to steal to make the payment. Still, she saw herself as different than other drug dealers. She might sell a package or two, "make a couple of grand," but she would never stay inside getting high all day. Rather, she spent time with family out in the community. She also attended church: "I went and got saved, but I had a half-pint in my purse." Throughout her adult life her conventional activities were woven into the unconventional.

Lenora's most recent eighteen-month period of incarceration resulted from absconding while on probation and parole. The original crime had been retail fraud—the same crime Lenora had been sentenced to many times in the past. She describes how that crime unfolded: "I was at Marshall Field's in the Donna Karan area, and I think it was six sweaters and six pair of jeans I took. And, when I got ready to leave, this man grabbed my arm before I was leaving out the door. And I just went on with him. I knew I was caught."

Eighteen months in prison were nothing new for Lenora, but they nonetheless made her tired and firmed her resolve to stay out for good:

"I'm tired of disappointing my kids and my family.... I'll be fifty-two next month. I'm not getting younger, I'm getting older, and I'm tired of leaving, I'm tired of being in a prison cell. I told my son, I'm tired of being locked up. I want to enjoy my kids and my grandkids and do something with my life because ... I'm thankful all that crime and drug life I didn't get shot, stabbed, cribbed. I'm healthy, so I'm blessed I can still work and I can still think properly." She also recognized that she had gone astray in the past because she continued to drink. She knew now that she would not be able to drink at all.

Discussing her upcoming release from prison, Lenora expressed high hopes. While typically she would return to her family home, this time her sister had denied the placement. Lenora did not acknowledge this, suggesting instead that she had chosen to live in commercial placement because it would help her work harder to meet her goals. She explained that her family had enabled her substance abuse in the past and let her "get slack," staying home and watching movies rather than focusing on school and job search. Her sister, with whom she was very close, was herself an addict and alcoholic, and the two would often use together. This time, with the support of a prisoner reentry program, her rent would be paid at a substance abuse treatment facility for four months. She planned to enroll in school at Wayne State University, using the financial aid money to buy one or more houses to fix up. She would cast a wide net in her job search, looking online, in the newspaper, and at the employment center Michigan Works! for any opportunities: "Coming out of prison you'd accept anything. You have to crawl before you can walk." She was confident that her hard work would help her advance: "I'll work up the ladder to be manager."

Yet several months in the community proved that her reentry would not go as smoothly as Lenora had hoped. First, her living situation was more challenging than she had anticipated. The facility required that each resident engage in job search from 7:30 to 3:00 each day, with a break for lunch. So, regardless of weather, the residents would walk the streets, submitting applications and talking to shop owners about jobs. The young women also grated on her; they were messy and negative and did not treat the facility like a home, which she felt signaled that "they're still in their addiction because they still have their dope fiend behavior." After 120 days, she had to move out and began paying $300 in rent to her nephew, money that she could not afford.

Securing even a minimum wage job also proved difficult. On the recommendation of a family friend, she was hired within two months of her release for a busser job at a local entertainment venue, and the work paid $55 per event, but she worked only once or twice weekly. Still, she gave it her all: "I did excellent my first day. Usually I do good work, anything I do I do to the best of my ability; that's how I was raised." She later enrolled in a training program that combined job skills training in the morning with afternoons working on the factory line. The job paid minimum wage but was only short-term. Following this program, she secured another transitional job through the reentry program. For ninety days it paid participants to work twenty hours per week in community placements in the hope that these positions would lead to permanent jobs. In Lenora's case it did not, and she later confided that this disappointment led her back to drinking, and with the drinking came the stealing.

Lenora described the negative cycle that ultimately led her back to custody. First, she absconded from parole and began spending a lot of money on others, particularly when she was drinking. She described the fall: "When I absconded, and when I quit reporting, that's when the red flag go up and they would send me a letter: 'You either violating your probation or parole.' So I wasn't getting no food stamps. So that's why I had to buy my food. So it really was going fast then, so I started ... I want to say in September. I started going to Macy's and pfftt. I went about four times." She estimated making about $1,500 each time. She also credited school—"school was no joke"—and a negative relationship with overwhelming her and leading her back to drinking and drug use. Finally, while her family provided a great deal of support, she had also returned to using drugs with her sister.

Released again from a different substance abuse treatment facility nearly two years after her prison release, Lenora remained optimistic despite the substantial challenges she faced. In the short term, she returned to living with her nephew and saved any money she could from the odd jobs that came her way. Yet this residence would be only temporary as her nephew's house was about to be foreclosed on. She planned to move into a shelter and had high hopes that a counselor could help her find more permanent housing. And she hardened her resolve to find a job, regardless of how difficult that might be:

> I've got to get me a job. Really serious because I've got like two months. I'm giving myself that much time.... I'm fixing to start tomorrow. Going to the temp place ... I have to be out there at 4:00 [a.m.] ... I would have to get up at 3:00.... Probably fix my breakfast the night before, boil some eggs.... OK,

catch the Livernois bus all the way to Vernor, catch the Vernor bus to Erl-
wal.... And then Wednesday I'm going to go [to] Labor Ready ... I have to be
down there between 10:00 and 12:00 and fill out the application. I went down
there twice and at 5:00 in the morning, and then I still be sitting there at 1:00,
[but] I have to try.... If I go out tomorrow, I know they'll call me back because
I do a good job.

Confident in her abilities as a worker, she would push forward with her
job search. After all, she had no other options, "You just don't know how
it feel when you don't have nothing, just nothing." She had no more at
her final interview, nearly two years later, than she had at prison release.
Though she knew the challenges of the job market and what disappoint-
ment could lead to, she planned to stay out of prison by sheer force of will:
"I know if I catch another case it's not going to be no misdemeanor and
they're going to send me right back. And I got off parole, and I'm happy.
And I'm going to stay. I'm not going back. I know that. I'm never going
back to prison. They had a good time with my life.... I'm never going
back. I'm never even going in the jail cell, in the county or no. I'm not
going to do anything wrong, I'm going to just not."

Leon

Leon is a thirty-seven-year-old African American man with short dread-
locks and a wide, infectious smile. He grew up in a middle-class Detroit
family in the Rosedale neighborhood. His parents sacrificed to send the
children to private Catholic school, and going to college was expected.
And his parents' hard work paid off: all three of his siblings were college
graduates. In contrast, Leon began dabbling in crime in elementary school:
"I'm not sure, I was like maybe eight or nine ... and stole bubblegum
from the store. And ... I guess I liked what I got for free and just kept
stealing. Then I would just steal from stores and just shoplift. And then I
just stopped shoplifting one day, I don't know why." By high school, surrounded by people for whom stealing was not a norm, he no longer saw
it as an option and stopped completely. Although he did poorly in high
school, he did graduate and enrolled in a small college in the South. He
soon realized that the ultraconservative Christian school was not for him.
"They wouldn't even play Bobby Brown's 'My Prerogative' at the dance,"
he explained. He dropped out and soon after enlisted in the army. He de-

scribes his six years of service as "the best experience" of his life: "I liked my job; I did well. I traveled." In interviews, he frequently mentioned this European travel as well as his college education as experiences that set him apart from others.

Although things were going well in his career, Leon stumbled back into crime when home on leave:

> I had B&E [breaking and entering] when I came home on leave. That's how it started because I wanted some nice stuff and I didn't have a lot of money. And I broke into a store out in Birmingham, got caught.... And then I went over to ... back to Germany ... but I had stole [somebody's personal] checks and went back to cash them in Germany. I just went and got a forged ID, a military ID that was fake, and just was cashing them, about maybe, thirty thousand dollars worth of checks.... I went crazy.... And Germany's like about the size of Michigan, so it's smaller. So bases are maybe an hour away, and that's not really far on the autobahn. So I would just open another base and cash the checks. That's how I'd do ... and I got arrested by the military ... and sent to Leavenworth for like two years, eight months.... Then I came back home, and I decided, "Well, hell," you know, "can't cash ... checks. I don't like messing with drugs.... I don't know nothing about it." So I said: "I know I can arm rob some places." So that's what I did, just because I was giving ... I was a poor manager, man. I just thought about spending for me.

Leon further explained that the thought of turning to robbery first occurred to him when he owed $600 on a car debt. He had worked at an Arby's in high school and knew that each location typically took in $1,200 on a weekend, which would easily pay off his debt. He secured a gun through a friend and robbed the restaurant with an unloaded gun. He waited about six months, then struck again: "Once you've done it once, it makes it easier to do it the next time."

Alongside these criminal actions, Leon began to put down more conventional roots. He first worked for a community newspaper, making "great money," but ultimately left following a strike. From there he worked in the auto industry for a few years. During this time he met and married his wife, Stella. Stella was three months pregnant when he was arrested on five counts of armed robbery and two counts of firearm possession. Pulled over by the police just blocks from the site of his most recent robbery, he was terrified but also "glad it was over, in a way."

Over the ten years of his incarceration, Leon began to transform. He began working as a tutor in the GED program early in his prison bit and found that he really enjoyed the work. His relationships with most family members improved as he became more mature. Following the birth of his son, he looked forward to visits with him three to four times a year. And, perhaps most importantly, his perspective on criminal offending changed dramatically. About seven years into his prison term, he realized that he would never return to prison again. "It was an epiphany," he explained. He realized how precious freedom was and knew that he would never sacrifice something so valuable again. "To jeopardize that, I could never do anything like that again. I mean, it's so embedded in me. That's all I thought about when I was locked up." Although he did not pinpoint the exact cause of this change, he was engaged in a rehabilitative prison program, Assaultive Offenders, at the time and in regular contact with his wife and son, which may have been contributing factors.

At release, Leon planned to move in with his father and stepmother and begin to search for a job. He knew that the process would be slow and that he would have to be patient. But he also knew that he would have a lot of support. His father and stepmother were well-off financially, living in a gated community on the Detroit waterfront, and they would be able to help with transportation, food, and other material needs. In the longer term, and once he was off electronic tether, he planned to look for a place of his own, preferably outside the city or in a nice neighborhood inside the city. He hoped to find a good school district where his now ten-year-old son could enroll. His relationship with his wife had deteriorated, and, with concerns about her parenting, he hoped to gain joint custody.

Although reentry proceeded relatively smoothly for Leon, it was by no means easy. He began applying for jobs right away. It was not long before he had applied for forty to fifty jobs and received only one callback. Yet his rich social network soon bore fruit. His uncle knew someone in a social service agency that was hiring and asked that the manager give his nephew a chance. Leon got the job, and two months after his release he was working forty hours per week as a relief worker, making $9.20 per hour. He worked at night and had to travel two hours each way by bus to reach his job site. Still, he felt that the position was worth it, both for the money as well as for the sense of self-worth that working in a helping profession provided: "I wouldn't be the same person today if I didn't have that job, actually. 'Cause I love the work. I don't mind working at all. And that's like, defines me a little bit as far as just being useful to society in some type of way." After securing this position, he began looking for his own apartment. This, too, proved a challenge as each rental application required a criminal background check as well as a fee, effectively barring him from residence. After a brief stint living in a subsidized shared-housing situation, he moved in with his sister in the posh suburb of West Bloomfield.

Throughout this difficult transition period, Leon relied on conversations with a therapist to keep him emotionally stable and on track. Soon after his release, his father had put him in touch with a psychiatrist living in the building who agreed to see him for free. He found these sessions invaluable:

> See, I talk to Dr. Weber, and she's a psychiatrist. And ... she actually tells me how it is about me. . . . She spotting my problems immediately. . . . I wish more men could have something like that, some one-on-one counseling where somebody tells you, look, this is what you're doing, and, if you continue to do this, you aren't going to grow at all, you're going to go back to whatever you used to do. . . . Because it's easy to get frustrated out here, and it's easy to make excuses for ourselves. . . . And this right here I swear has helped me a lot. Because there have been times where ... just the frustration builds up and then you just try and block it out and not deal with it instead of learning how to deal with it at the time. . . . And that's what she's teaching me, is how to deal with me, get myself together. . . . I swear, if everyone would come out and get that type of counseling once or twice a week, no one would go back to prison.

He relied on these sessions and the strategies the therapist suggested to get him through periods of self-doubt and longing for the easy money of his past.

On the one-year anniversary of his prison release, Leon reflected on the year that had passed: "When ... the new year came, I was like OK it was a tough year, walking a lot, struggling to stay up with my job, try to move ahead and get a better position, but that's how life is. You've got to work hard to get something, and everything's not easy. But you know I'm getting more comfortable with living my life, let's say that." He recognized that accepting the challenges of his job (a four-hour commute, night work, low wages, and no benefits) was necessary for him to advance, and his perseverance soon began to pay off.

Within two years of his release from prison, Leon had secured a raise, benefits, and full, daytime work at the agency. He had moved in with a supportive woman he had met at work who inspired him to continue to better himself, and his relationship with his son continued to blossom in a way that astounded him: "He just loves being around me. He could have went roller skating with his friends; instead he wants to come over and be with me. I'm like, 'Wow.' I mean, this boy loves me to death, and it scares me. . . . I mean, I don't want him to get older and think: 'Oh, my dad really wasn't this or he really wasn't that.'" His investment in these relationships strengthened his resolve to grow both personally and professionally.

With substantial social support from family, self-knowledge, coping strategies learned in therapy, and a renewed commitment to work and fatherhood to motivate him, Leon kept to a reentry trajectory that was slow but steady, straight, and true.

Randall

Randall's soft brown eyes tug slightly downward, as does his mouth, ringed by a scraggly beard. Randall is a thirty-two-year-old African American man whose hard life is written plainly on his face and tall, lean frame: bad luck and bad decisions have taken their toll. Fully immersed in a world where criminal or antisocial options are plentiful and conventional people and opportunities rare, he describes a life pushed and pulled by forces he feels are largely outside his control.

Although Randall described very little of his childhood, it is clear that it was marked by sadness. He was the victim of sexual abuse when still very young. His mother disappeared when he was just eleven, and he knows nothing of her whereabouts. His father left Michigan for California when Randall was very young, and Randall has not seen him since. He and his two brothers were taken in by a woman he refers to as his grandmother, busy with fourteen children of her own. Randall dropped out of high school in the ninth grade, at which point "everything just collapsed." It was then that he began doing "dumb stuff."

It was a cousin who first introduced Randall to crime. At the time a family friend who was a chef had connected him to a job in a restaurant:

> And she had a connect on getting me a job, like, "You want a dishwasher job?" "Yeah. I want a dishwasher job." You get paid, you get everything. I was making almost $13.00 a hour just to wash dishes. So I ran into one of my cousins, he's like, "Do you want a ride out here with me?" That's when he was staying in Inkster. I was like, "Yeah, I'll ride out there with you." Two or three weeks went by, and the next thing I know he come and pick me up. I'm out there sit-

ting in the dog house. The ... next thing I know I'm selling at that point. And I done quit the job. ... Everybody cussed me out for that too.

Interviewer: Why did you decide to go with him and do that rather than stay with the dishwashing job?

Because ... that money was coming fast. It was coming too fast. And me, I'm the type ... I'm addicted to going shopping. I'm addicted to shopping, trying to ... impress people.

Falling into crime, he abandoned his job in favor of the easy money of drug selling.

Over the next few years, Randall worked sporadically in fast food, temporary labor, and, with a cousin, repairing cars. Throughout this time he also continued to engage in criminal behavior, selling drugs and stealing cars. For about five years he caught "random cases" before entering a brief period of calm: "I settled down for a minute." He was living with his grandmother, was working as a manager at Arby's, and had met and had a child with his girlfriend. He identifies their breakup as a turning point: "I think basically what really got my mind off, though, was when my baby mama bust up with me and my daughter. Everything went downhill then. I just had no care in the world." When his ex-girlfriend asked him to babysit for their daughter, he dropped the girl off in Ypsilanti with her grandmother and never came back. Another factor that influenced his criminal descent was linked with the childhood sexual abuse he had experienced. As an adult he shared this history with family, and they chose not to believe him. This rocked Randall and deeply affected his stress level and mental state.

Randall had racked up an extensive criminal history over his criminal career. Of his nine felony convictions, "four [were] for dope, one for weed, two for car theft, and two for firearms." He had been sentenced to probation four times, jailed three times, and imprisoned twice. His recent imprisonment resulted from a parole violation. Thirteen months after his initial release and absconding from parole, his girlfriend at the time had called his parole officer and told her where to find him. He was arrested coming home from the store.

In prison, Randall began to understand the roots of his problems as stemming from the negative influence of others. In response, he employed a strategy of isolation while incarcerated, believing that avoiding problematic individuals—those ensnared in prison gangs and those with long sentences who had nothing to lose from provoking fights—would be the key to his success. He had vowed to reform. Yet in prison he began breaking rules right away. Because he had no one contributing money to his account, he held contraband for other prisoners in order to earn money for toiletries, purchased in the prison store. He was also drawn into fights with other prisoners because of the neighborhood he was from. Yet, for the most part, he kept to himself and spent his time working on improving his GED scores.

Randall knew that he faced an uphill battle following release. His family was fed up with him, and he expected little in the way of support from them. He could not return to the home he had been staying in prior to his imprisonment; his cousin had been kicked out along with her three children. He would be paroled first to a substance abuse treatment center and then to a homeless shelter. Ultimately, he hoped to return to Detroit and begin working, possibly with the help of his cousin Xavier, his closest friend and the lone remaining source of family support. In the longer term, he planned to complete his GED and return to school to study culinary arts. Though he did voice some goals, he was far from confident about his future. At his first interview after his release he stated: "I couldn't even predict ... the future right now because I can be here today, dead tomorrow."

Although he had hoped to avoid troublesome influences, particularly his brothers, he quickly found that this would not be possible. Following his stint at the treatment center, he spent a few weeks at a homeless shelter before being kicked out for drinking and transferred to another shelter. He then moved into his brother's basement for about two months. He cleaned the house, watched the kids, and donated his Bridge card (food stamps) to pay his way. The arrangement was largely successful except for when his brother was drunk and would taunt and shame him in front of his friends. When drunk one night, his brother threw him out of the house, initiating a period of homelessness in the Detroit winter.

The job search was similarly beset by problems. Initially, Randall had hoped that Xavier could help him find a job, but he soon discovered that this was not to be: "He got his [job] through a temp service, and ... they really do background checks. He ... said it's a waste of time." He did help his cousin occasionally with odd jobs, but Xavier tended to pay him with marijuana, which he encouraged Randall to sell for a profit. The only flaw in this plan was that Randall's brother would demand the drug in exchange for housing. Over the months and years that followed, Randall estimated that he applied for fifty jobs without receiving a single callback. He subsisted on his Bridge card and the money he earned by doing yard work and odd jobs and through donating plasma, which earned him $35 a session.

After his bout of homelessness, Randall began to stabilize somewhat. First, he found a more permanent, less turbulent residence with his half sister and her father, staying with them for roughly six months. Although generous with transportation, food, and shelter, the two were under their own material stress, and the home lacked food and electricity at various times. Randall began an employment-training program at a social service agency, where he pursued his long-term goal of becoming a cook. He was thrilled by the promise of a guaranteed job following the program. His daily drinking began to taper off, until he was drinking just beer on the weekends, although he admitted this was partially due to a lack of income. About a year after his initial release he began to get serious with a new girlfriend, Janelle, who worked for a security company and had been clean and sober for one year. The two attended NA together, and he identified her as a good influence. He began to talk more seriously with us about searching out the young daughter he had not seen in three years.

Yet, not long after Randall and Janelle had moved in together, he committed a crime that sent him to jail. Still unable to find employment, and increasingly desperate for money, he returned to the plasma center. After a long wait, he was informed that it was not his scheduled donation day and that he would be unable to donate. Frustrated, he saw a Blackberry lying in the lobby and snatched it on his way out the door. The phone belonged to a security guard, and he quickly found himself in jail. Over twelve days he was unable to leave the small cell he shared with seven other men, "the four-man cells they turned to seven-man cells, that's how tiny it was." Officers would come by to check on the men once an hour, and food was delivered through the bars. Ultimately, he was convicted of a felony for larceny and received a parole violation but was not returned to prison.

Moving in with Janelle proved a mixed blessing. He described both positive attributes, such as her encouragement to avoid alcohol, and negative attributes, such as her controlling impulses and their frequent conflict. Stressors arose from her desire for marriage and a baby, which Randall felt unready for and resisted. Still, the two kept each other "from doing something stupid." Soon Janelle became pregnant. Randall described his excitement at two milestones coinciding: "And, as far as getting off parole, I was happy. 'Cause I was figuring like, Damn, I'm getting off parole, and I'm about to have a baby. Get off parole, then had the baby the next day.

I was happy. 'Cause I saw them when they cut the umbilical cord." The baby, born prematurely, died shortly after birth. Randall stayed at home a lot following the death, helping Janelle with her recovery: "All I do is I go to school, play with my dog. Straight, I don't mess with the neighborhood. I don't mess with nobody in the neighborhood. I just stay in the house." Yet his old strategy of isolation could not protect him from problems at home, the conflicts and jealousies. The two began fighting, and Randall decided to move back in with his half sister and her father for a time. Aware of his money trouble, a cousin gave him some crack to sell. He made $450 selling the drugs before deciding that kind of life was not for him and moving back in with his girlfriend. Soon after they married.

Nearly three years after his initial release, Randall explains how his wife helped him finally secure a job. She had been driving a bus but was forced to stop because of carpal tunnel syndrome. He tells the story:

> And then she was getting that workers comp. But they weren't giving her nothing but like $300. And she felt that wasn't enough. Then she started going off on me and all that. She went in the Yellow Pages one day while I was sleeping, wrote down every restaurant in the Yellow Pages. Called them. She was trippin'. . . . She was telling me to call them. But she woke me up with attitude; we were arguing every day. But one day, I got up on a Monday, I went and put the application in on a Saturday. And I just woke up out the blue on a Monday and, while she was gone, called them. And then I come in for the interview. The next thing I know, I'm working that following Monday.

With a lot of pushing from his wife, he landed a full-time job as a cook, making $7.50 an hour. He describes his daily routine: "Thousands of burgers a day [*sighs*]. Flip burgers, and eat fries. Gotta wash dishes piled this high." When asked where he saw things five years into the future, he responded: "Hopefully better. Better than it is."

Christopher

Christopher is a thirty-eight-year-old white man whose easy, lighthearted manner seems out of sync with the troubles he has faced in his life. "It's always something," he's fond of saying. With a shaved head, a scraggly goatee, and multiple tattoos, he can present himself as tough and menacing when he wants to by giving you a hard stare, but such a mug quickly breaks into a sly smile, as if to let you in on the joke that he is really a teddy bear on the inside. He grew up in a middle-class family on twenty-seven acres in rural Michigan. The second of three children, he was adopted at five months old. He describes a childhood free of the violence and substance abuse common among our other participants: "Early 1970s. Everything was cool, neighbors on both sides, across the street, the whole street, we all knew each other. . . . Dad never hit me, ma didn't hit me, no sexual abuse." Although his mother was an alcoholic, she had been sober for the majority of Christopher's life, and he had no memory of her drinking. His father was an accountant, and the family moved five times across his youth around the eastern half of the United States.

Although loath to discuss it, Christopher identifies sexual abuse at the hands of a neighbor as the incident initiating the onset of his addiction, around age twelve: "There was a little sexual abuse in '82 maybe from an individual in my neighborhood. That was really about it. And then from that point on, from when that happened, then I started using." He began hanging out with other kids who drank and used drugs, accessing drugs easily available in his neighborhood. Although his addiction to both alcohol and crack cocaine quickly accelerated, he managed to graduate from high school on time. Thereafter, his addiction soon became the dominant force in his life, determining and limiting his relationships, jobs, and freedom.

When we first spoke with him in prison, Christopher stated that he had been free "on the street" and out of prison only eight months since 1990; the rest of his adult life he had spent incarcerated. His criminal history is composed of a variety of ill-fated crimes, mostly conducted while drunk and high and searching for money for even more drugs and alcohol. He describes his recent charge for attempted kidnapping: "I'm broke, high, out here at Five Mile and Middlebelt in Livonia. I see this lady come out of this restaurant, she goes to get in her van. I run up, grab her, 'Get out of that van.' She turns around and starts scratching me with her keys. So I looked, there's two kids in the car. I took off, 'See ya,' I don't want nothing to do with these kids. That was where the attempt to kidnap came in. But that was another one of these spur-of-the-moment things. 'I'll just run over and take this shit.'" For this and other crimes, he had been imprisoned four times and jailed four times in Michigan alone.

Christopher had been imprisoned for sixteen months on his most recent charge. To manage through his incarceration he kept his distance from others and maintained a positive attitude. He explains that, unlike most guys in prison, he acts "a clown," not letting the institution or guards get him down. His positive attitude was facilitated by a lot of coffee and exercise; he estimated walking twenty-five miles each day around the yard. He also worked both in the kitchen and on the yard crew, which he believed taught him responsibility. He spent his remaining time sleeping, watching television, and staying informed by listening to the BBC or CBS news on the radio. The only thing that set this period of incarceration apart from past bids was the loss of his father's support. Early in his bid, Christopher's father informed him that he would not contact him until Christopher had been out in the community and sober for a full year, and the two had not communicated in a year and a half. This loss was a blow, one that would make his reentry even more challenging.

Christopher voiced few goals for his release, and those he had were simple: "I'm just trying to stay free from prison for a year. That would be unbelievable." Just the thought of it was exciting: "It's like another world." He also hoped to get back in touch with his father, get a job, and go back to school. Initially, he would move into a homeless shelter in Ann Arbor, where he knew he would have to sleep in a chair for several weeks until a bed opened up. From there he hoped to move into a residential treatment program for about a year; he knew that living independently would be too much. Eventually, he hoped to get his own apartment close to a job. Establishing a relationship or a family was not on his agenda. As he said: "Even the thought of it is too much." He expressed high hopes for his release: "I would say I have about a 97 percent chance of staying out, for good. . . . And that's because I'm not out here on some bullshit like I normally am." Things would not go as planned.

Christopher initially moved into the homeless shelter and spent his days attending AA, riding the bus, going to the library, and getting free meals offered around Ann Arbor. He signed up for and received financial aid for an auto body and auto restoration course at a community college but never attended. He had little luck on the job search, applying for more than seventy jobs and ultimately securing only a part-time position at the Salvation Army that provided housing and a small stipend. He quickly lost this job and, with it, his housing. Most importantly, he began drinking heavily almost immediately after release. He justified his drinking by claiming: "It's not really the alcohol as much as it is that cocaine. . . . Telling you what, man, that cocaine is a monster." Homeless, and beset by suicidal thoughts, he went on a drinking binge that ended in five days in a detox facility. Only two months after release, and already longing for an external restraint, he bemoaned: "I don't want to go back to prison, but lock me back up because … I'm a mess out here. I've turned into a complete wreck." Following his detox, he secured housing at a transitional facility but was soon kicked out for spending several nights away with his new girlfriend, Janice. The two then moved in together.

Christopher had met Janice at an AA meeting soon after his release. In addition to a struggle with alcoholism, the two shared a history of criminal offending, and Janice was also on parole. Janice had five children ranging in age from sixteen months to thirteen years, all of whom had been removed from her care. They were now cared for by her parents, her ex-boyfriend, and foster parents. Janice was an important emotional support for Christopher, one of the only such supports he had given his disconnection from family. Yet, despite her sobriety, this relationship was not enough to keep him sober. He continued to drink heavily once the two moved in together and through a ninety-day temporary job he had secured through a prisoner reentry program, although he had earlier claimed both isolation and joblessness as triggers for drinking. Another trigger arose when he received his financial aid money: "I saw that lady counting out all them hundred dollar bills, I was sick to my stomach. I couldn't think of her [Janice]. All I could think about was getting high, and I did. I went right down to Detroit." He went on a week-long crack binge. Finally, he called Janice, and she came to pick him up: "I was sick. I told her, Get me out of here right now." Subsequently ordered to a treatment facility by his parole officer, he continued drinking on release, even after he found out that Janice was pregnant with what would be his first child. He was subsequently arrested and sent back to prison for a parole violation linked with drinking when he "blew a .29 [blood alcohol level]" in a visit to the parole office. Before he was sent away, he and Janice married. Released just four months later, he vowed that this time would be different. As he said: "I know when the baby comes it's no drinking. There will be no drinking."

On release, he was fortunate to be returning to a job as an auto detailer, plus he had support from Janice and a motivation to reform—his unborn son. One year after this second release, things seemed to be on track. He had successfully remained sober for almost a year, he was rebuilding his relationship with his father and learning to parent both his infant son and Janice's thirteen-year-old, and he had opened an auto-detailing business with Janice. But, under the surface, things were beginning to unravel. Christopher stopped going to AA and began smoking pot. Then, while in the liquor store buying beer for Janice's cousin, who was staying with the family temporarily, he began envisioning buying "some tiny bottles of vodka" that had been stocked near the register. Looking at them, he thought to himself: "The bills are paid, everything's OK, I got it together now." He began drinking again and soon became desperate for alcohol.

One day, while driving to work, he realized that he was too drunk to go. He decided to stay in his truck and drink more vodka. He fell asleep and was woken by the police placing him in handcuffs. He later found out that, while blacked out, he had gone in to his own bank and slipped the teller a note demanding $500, although he had more than that amount in his own checking account. Following the robbery, he had driven across town and fallen asleep in a parking lot. As Janice explained: "When the police got there, he had the $500 in his hand, and the truck was running, and he was passed out drunk. And they couldn't even wake him up. They had to physically carry him into a police car and handcuff him." He was ultimately convicted of bank robbery and sentenced to a term of two to nine years in prison.

Christopher's addiction coursed through and directed his life, seemingly without rhyme or reason. When unemployed, he blamed excessive free time for his drinking, yet, when employed, he drank as well. At times he recognized that as an alcoholic he could not drink at all and could manage his drinking only with the support of AA, yet at other times he believed that he could return to drinking and abandoned the support of AA. Although he faced a variety of stressors and temptations that might have contributed, he did not attribute his return to drinking to any of these factors. Reflecting on the relapse from his prison cell, he stated: "I hate to say it was inevitable for me to relapse but . . ." For Christopher, nothing could match the power of his addiction. Facing another long prison term, he had no other explanation to offer for his predicament.

Conclusion

How can we understand the reentry and reintegration experiences of Jennifer, DeAngelo, Lenora, Leon, Randall, and Christopher and the hundreds of thousands of other individuals who leave prison ever year in the United States? How and why do some, like Jennifer, DeAngelo, and Leon, manage to stave off their addictions, construct postprison lives for themselves, and emerge from the shadow of the criminal justice system, while others, like Randall and Lenora, struggle simply to feed and house themselves and still others, like Christopher, remain caught in prison's revolving door? In the next chapter, we begin to answer these questions, beginning our analysis at the point when we first met these six individuals and the rest of our participants, readying to leave prison and adjusting to life in the community in the first days, weeks, and months after release.

CHAPTER TWO

Transitions

S everal times a day a prisoner transport van manned by county sheriff's deputies drives through the outer fence of the Charles Egeler Reception and Guidance Center (RGC) in Jackson. Each van stops at another gate at the entrance to a tunnel made of chain-link fence that leads to the prison's intake areas. Men in jail jumpsuits, shackled in cuffs and chains, exit the van one by one and shuffle to the sounds of rattling chains through the chain-link tunnel into the custody of the Michigan Department of Corrections (MDOC). Some have come from jails in the northern parts of the state hundreds of miles away, while most are from the more populous parts of the southeastern parts of the state, including Detroit. Whether this is their first time or their tenth, all male prisoners start their custody at the RGC, where they are processed in quarantine before transfer to one of the general population prisons scattered throughout the state. Most will spend thirty to forty-five days in what inmates call *the bubble*, a prison block seemingly straight out of Hollywood with inmates two to a room barely high enough to stand up in and barely wider than two beds, stacked several stories high and behind steel bars, all enclosed under a glass and steel outer structure that tries in vain to keep out the cold of Michigan's winters and the heat of its summers. These days pass slowly with little to do as inmates are confined to their cells except for meals, a brief time in the yard each day, and appearances for various tests and assessments that will determine the course of their experiences while serving time. Most spend this time reading or sleeping, exhausted from the chaos of the local county jail, or enduring the drug- or alcohol-withdrawal symptoms that only slowly subside. Women prisoners go through a similar process, starting their MDOC custody at the only women's prison in the state, the Huron Valley Correctional Facility in Ypsilanti, a few miles away from the University of Michigan's flagship campus in Ann Arbor, but a world apart.

Almost sixty years ago the sociologist Erving Goffman described prisons and mental institutions as "total institutions," "a place of work and residence where a great number of similarly situated people, cut off from the wider community for a considerable time, together lead an enclosed, formally administered round of life" (Goffman 1961, xiii). Goffman would not be surprised at the institutional practices on display at the RGC and Huron Valley. Each new inmate is stripped of many of the last vestiges of individuality and oriented to the rules and regulations of the prison environment. Any personal possessions other than photographs, paperwork, reading material, and medically necessary items are forfeited. Uniforms from the county jail are removed, the inmate is searched and showered, and prison blues are issued, complete with one's MDOC identification number stamped on the back. Fingerprints and photos are taken, and the photos are used for a prison ID card, law enforcement databases, and a public database of prisoners, probationers, and parolees available on the Internet. Orientations explain how to behave in prison and services that are available. Each inmate is tested for communicable diseases such as tuberculosis, hepatitis C, and HIV, assessed on mental and physical health, addictions, personality disorders, disabilities, education and literacy skills, and security threats. Staff members make decisions regarding services, programming, and counseling to be provided, and the inmate is classified along multiple dimensions. During this time, there is little contact with the outside world as no visitors other than lawyers or clergy are allowed, although short phone calls are permitted.

These procedures and practices can be understood as the first steps in what Goffman termed *institutionalization*, the socialization of inmates into their new social role and position within the prison. The process of institutionalization (or perhaps reinstitutionalization for those who are returning to prison) continues as the inmates move on to other Michigan prisons and have more occasions to interact with other inmates, guards, and staff and to be exposed to prison programming and culture. Goffman was also concerned with the consequences of institutionalization for the reintegration of the inmate after release. In his ethnography of another type of total institution, the mental hospital, he argued that inmates were likely ill served by institutionalization, as the behavior patterns, identities, and roles adopted in the institution leave them less capable of functioning in free society (at least temporarily), a problem he called *disculturation*. In particular, the highly structured life of the total institution stands in stark contrast to life in free society. Goffman's framework suggests a number of factors that will be important for understanding the reintegration of formerly incarcerated individuals: the experience of incarceration itself, the social separation and isolation of prisoners, how prisoners think about their social identities and roles, and the period of adjustment immediately after release.

With these themes in mind, this chapter begins our investigation of the process of prisoner reentry where this transition starts, in prison and in the days and weeks after release. We first analyze our participants' accounts of their experiences in prison and the impact of their incarceration on their family ties and other important relationships. We then describe their transition experiences immediately after release as their institutional identities and roles are shed and the process of social and economic reintegration starts in earnest. We pay particular attention to our participants' experiences of parole and the legal and financial obligations that accompany parole supervision.

From a theoretical perspective, the experiences our participants recount in this chapter reveal the importance of two contexts that will be critical to their reentry and reintegration and that we will revisit in future chapters. One is the families, loved ones, or other informal social networks from which they have been separated by imprisonment and to which they hope to return after their release. For some, social ties are severed by imprisonment, but, for many others, imprisonment serves to strengthen one's closest ties, particularly to family. One's ability to rely on such ties for food and shelter as well as emotional and social support will prove critical to the reintegration experience. Parole supervision is a second key context. The rules and requirements of parole will structure much of the parolee's time and actions in the days and weeks after release. Access to services and supports from nonprofit organizations will also come at the cost of surveillance and control. Far from being an escape from the state's grasp, release to parole—and the state's contracted surrogates—imposes a new form of scrutiny that is, in many ways, even harder to live up to.

Prison Life and Social Isolation

"You're doing everyone else's time too"

We sat down with Leon at the Cooper Street Prison in Jackson three weeks before his parole date to discuss his past, present, and plans for the future. When our conversation turned to what he was most looking forward to on the day of his release, his response was simple but vague: "freedom of choice." What did he mean by this? "Getting up at night and using the bathroom without having to get someone's permission." Leon is referring here to the regimentation of life in prison, the almost complete lack of personal control over even the most basic of human activities. Also implicated in his response is the lack of privacy that life in prison entails. Except in the most high-security prison cells, inmates eat, sleep, bathe, and use the restroom in crowded conditions. Prisoners in Cooper Street, a minimum security prison, sleep eight to a room in a "cube" originally designed for four. Leon's account also hints at a third key aspect of prison life, the deference that must be paid to guards, whose own safety depends on their ability to control the behavior of inmates by tactics other than physical force, and who therefore insist on complete obedience. Inmates who refuse to follow a direct order, talk back to a guard, or even let their pants sag below the belt line risk a misconduct "ticket," which can result in loss of privileges, and which the parole board takes into consideration when assessing readiness for parole.

Moreover, crowding, regimentation, and deference are not the only unpleasant aspects of prison life. Prisoners endure extreme temperatures— the heat of Michigan's summers and the cold of Michigan's winters— with the state providing only the most rudimentary of clothing and shoes and the thinnest of winter coats. Our participants described the food as nutritious but bland and inadequate in quantity. An inmate without money in his or her commissary account to purchase extra food at the prison store would either go hungry or resort to stealing from other inmates.

Another challenging aspect of prison life, primarily for men, is its brutality and the risk of physical assault. As Paul, a veteran and former substance abuse counselor whose own addictions led him to rob a video store and a pharmacy, explained, in prison you are not just doing your own time: "You're doing everyone else's time too." In the closed world of the prison, status among prisoners is largely but not entirely negotiated physically, as it is on the streets of the poor and working-class neighborhoods from which many prisoners hail. This is especially the case at the medium- and high-security men's prisons housing the most violent criminals and less so at women's prisons and lower-security prisons where many inmates have a parole review coming or a parole date scheduled. Our participants described multiple strategies for negotiating position in the dominance hierarchies and avoiding victimization, strategies that parallel those used in other settings such as the streets of violent neighborhoods (e.g., Anderson 1999; Dance 2002; Harding 2010).

One strategy is to join a group for mutual protection. Another is to establish a reputation for toughness, as someone not to be messed with, by fighting when necessary. Leon described these strategies at his interview at Cooper Street. He says that some people join groups for protection. A lot of guys are "so used to being on the block and being part of something." The only thing different about experiencing prison firsthand is that "you don't see the true brutality on TV as you do in live action." This brutality took a strong mental toll on him: "It makes you more cynical, nontrusting." He thinks it necessary to defend oneself in prison and that guys constantly have to do it: "Let's say you're playing cards with a group of people and one of the guys is like, 'You're an asshole for winning,' and he calls you a derogatory name, and you say, 'You're an asshole.' . . . You have people up here who are truly malicious. . . . Guys can come in and just take stuff from you. . . . What are you gonna do?" He mentioned that you can go someplace else, you can "go tell," or you can fight back. Fighting back is the "wiser choice": "Even if you get beat up, hopefully the police will get there fast enough." He added: "The hardest thing is going to be leaving here and leaving that kind of thinking behind."

A third strategy is to isolate oneself as much as possible and make friends very carefully. DeAngelo followed this strategy, as he explained in his first postrelease interview, exactly one month after his release:

> It's the certain way you got to carry yourself while you're in there. The less you talk, the less a guy know about you, and the more reluctant they are to try to because they don't know what you about. They don't want to find out the hard way. . . . I'm pretty much the laid-back, keep-to-myself quiet guy. . . . It was my system for avoiding problems. And I would . . . I leave there so quiet I can just scope everybody's demeanor, you know what I mean? I can't be cool with them because I see he a troublemaker. That dude over there I see him steal. He gonna get his head cracked, and, if I'm with him when he get his head cracked, I might get mine cracked too. So I can't be around him. So, if he comes in and tries to be friendly one day, I cut that short.
>
> But if you . . . if you one of these old uppity friendly guys that want to [know] everybody as soon as you get there and all, you don't know what type of people you bringing in around you. So they might have to get into something just by being around the wrong people. So I just kind of like had a few guys who I kick it with. I surround myself with people just trying to go home. That's what kept me from getting tickets and helped me from staying out of trouble.

Staying safe within prison required a constant vigilance and attention to one's own demeanor.

The prison conditions that our male participants describe—overcrowding, isolation from the outside world, threats to physical safety, seemingly arbitrary systems of punishment and control, and minimal supportive programming—are consistent with the scholarship on the psychological effects of prison life or what psychologists call *prisonization* (Haney 2003). Over time, prisoners may become reliant on institutional structure and regimentation, losing the capacity for self-direction and internal control. Constant threats to physical safety may lead to hypervigilance, distrust, and feelings of suspicion. Strategies to manage such threats, such as high levels of emotional regulation, may lead to emotional overcontrol and psychological distancing, social withdrawal, and isolation (on the *carceral habitus*, see Caputo-Levine [2013]). Prison culture is often characterized as including *norms of exploitation* that may be internalized over time. Lack of privacy, security, and control over one's own body can lead to diminished self-worth. Finally, the chronic stress of the prison environment can lead to posttraumatic stress disorder and related symptoms (Haney 2003). Empirical research on the health consequences of incarceration in prison shows that it leads to elevated levels of mood disorders, including major depressive disorder, bipolar disorder, and dysthymia, although many of the psychological disorders observed among prisoners (anxiety disorders, impulse control disorders, and substance abuse) develop earlier in life and likely contributed to incarceration rather than resulting from it (Schnittker, Massoglia, and Uggen 2012).[1]

While much of the experience of imprisonment was similar for men and women—the cold and loneliness, boredom and power negotiations between guards and inmates—women described a different social context within the prison. Specifically, fear and threat of violence from other prisoners seemed less pervasive than they were among the men involved in our study. Rather, our female participants most often described other prisoners as immature and irritating, as did Jada, a thirty-one-year-old black woman imprisoned for trying to smuggle drugs to a boyfriend in prison. "Women all the time, yech! Women is treacherous. They're irritating, they talk all the time, they're in each other's business." For those new to prison, the social dynamics came as a surprise, as is evident in field notes transcribed from an in-prison interview, again with Jada: "At first [Jada] thought it would be like it was on TV: with bars, people getting raped. She had all kinds of thoughts about prison. She was scared when she came.

She's found being in prison that the only hard thing is not being with her kids or her family, not being able to come and go when you please. She gets homesick. Also having to wait to use the toilet, etc. She says, 'Really it's like a college campus.'" Others described prison as "kiddie camp" or "junior high."

Indeed, age and maturity seemed to be important organizing categories within women's prisons. Asked about prison gangs, Jennifer responded: "The only thing there really is are age-group cliques in prison." Participants highlighted their own age and/or maturity relative to other inmates and described forming friendships largely with "older" or "mature" women. Kristine is a forty-year-old white woman with a history of shoplifting, drug selling, and prostitution to support her longtime addictions to crack and heroin. Her relative maturity was highlighted in her relationships with younger women, to whom she served as an adviser and maternal figure. She recounted counseling them: "Please, make this [incarceration] your learning experience." One young woman—"twenty-five and she was doing twenty-five years"—even called Kristine "Ma."

Further, all our female participants had formed relationships with other inmates, and most characterized these relationships as important to them. For instance, Jennifer met her girlfriend in prison and remained with her throughout the study period. Others formed friendships or pseudofamily relationships, as was the case with Kristine. Yet, for most, these relationships would fade in importance once they left prison. The rules of parole expressly forbid associating with other parolees or even responding to letters from prisoners. Participants also worried that friends might change once they returned to the community. Lenora recounted learning through prior imprisonment that people tended to change for the worse once they left prison, often becoming involved once more with drugs.

While much of what has been described about the prison experience was similar for both men and women, in terms of their relationships with other prisoners women's experiences differed. While the threat of violence was not absent, particularly in higher-security women's prisons, our female participants did not feel it so keenly and were able to avoid threatening or violent encounters. Perhaps for this reason, transition from prison to the community seemed to require less recalibration of affect and demeanor than was the case for men. As Jocelyn—a thirty-seven-year-old black woman with convictions related to drug dealing and weapons possession— described: "I'm me. I don't change. I treat you the same way you treat me. That's all that is. You know, I treat you with respect, you treat me with respect, and everything's all right."

Staying in Touch with Those on the Outside

Many of the aspects of prison life described above will probably not be unfamiliar to consumers of popular media presentations of life behind bars on television and in the movies. While most of our participants found ways to adjust and adapt to crowding, regimentation, temperature extremes, poor food, and even threats to physical safety, one of the most difficult aspects of life in prison was social isolation—separation from loved ones and removal of social roles that provided meaningful forms of social identity (parent, brother, daughter, friend, worker) on the outside. This separation is the result of both practical challenges and the often-strained nature of such relationships before prison, though, as we describe below, imprisonment can often be an occasion for rebuilding family relationships that became frayed in the period before incarceration.

The practical challenges that prison poses for maintaining contact with those on the outside include distance, the rules regarding prison visitation, the cost of phone calls in prison, and the difficulties of letter writing. Michigan is a large state, with most of its population concentrated in the southeast part of the state and some in the southwest, but its state prisons are located throughout the state. DeAngelo received only a few visits from his girlfriend while he was "up north," but in the months before his release, when he was moved to the Cooper Street Prison in Jackson, she visited him regularly, as it was less than an hour's drive from Ypsilanti. A visit to a prison up north could mean a two-day round-trip drive plus the cost of lodging, food, and gas while on the road, expenses many prisoners' families could ill afford. Some avoided visits because prison is an unpleasant place. Inmates and their families have no privacy, they face strict rules about physical contact, even with children, and visitors must adhere to dress codes and strict visiting hours and undergo security screening before entering the prison and at times unpleasant treatment from guards on the lookout for people smuggling contraband into the prison. Some of our participants did not want to subject their loved ones to these experiences. This is an example of what Comfort (2003, 2008) calls the *secondary prisonization* of inmates' families, who are subject to long and unpredictable waits, searches of person and property, and frequently changing and seemingly arbitrarily applied rules governing attire and personal possessions when visiting loved ones in prison. Greater family contact during incarceration is related to greater family support after release (Mowen and Visher 2016).

Other participants, however, approached visitation with considerable ambivalence. Sometimes they did not want their loved ones to see them in the prison environment. Prison blues, lack of privacy vis-à-vis other inmates, surveillance and control by guards, and the crowding of the prison visiting room all challenge the inmates' identities on the outside in the eyes of family and friends. For example, although Paul, whose addictions lead to a fall from his comfortable middle-class status, described his social circle as "rallying around" him and he received many requests for visitors, he limited visitations to only his wife. He did not want others to see him as a prisoner.

For participants who had been to prison multiple times, family members' patience with the challenges of staying in touch in prison had already worn thin. This was Lenora's experience. Family members did not want to visit as they were fed up with her drug abuse and repeated bouts of incarceration. Lenora preferred to write letters, thus avoiding directly experiencing her family's frustration: "They're tired. This is my eighth time [in prison]." Her sister had told her that she did not feel that she was taking her life seriously. Lenora had not bothered to fill out a visiting form for any family members. She describes why: "Shame. I just wanted to deal with myself, find myself. And I really did."

For others, brevity and infrequency of visitations are stressful. The pain of separation is felt acutely every time a visit ends, and it is simply easier to get used to having no in-person contact with loved ones while in prison. For example, Lamar—a forty-three-year-old black man imprisoned for armed robbery and parole violations—explained why he avoided visits: "Once it is over, I feel like something is breaking." It is too stressful being able to see people only briefly. He described it as a "spiritual strain." His niece wanted to visit, but he told her not to come. Another challenge to maintaining relationships with family is the expense of phone calls. A fifteen-minute phone call cost $8 at the time our participants were in prison, a high price considering that their prison work assignments often paid less than a dollar a day. The cost of phone calls can quickly add up for families on the outside, who are often struggling to make ends meet and help their incarcerated loved one with money for commissary (Grinstead et al. 2001).

Instead of visitors and phone calls, Lamar tried—largely in vain—to encourage his friends and family to write to him. At first, they would write only half a page and not say much. In his own letters he would coach them to write more and to be more descriptive and expressive: "So it's like they are writing a novel describing their lives." Most did not have the time to write. In an age of text messages, email, and social media, long discursive letters are increasingly rare. But Lamar found that his relationships with those whom he was able to develop an extended written correspondence grew and that he felt closer to them as they began to reflect more deeply and to express themselves more vividly than they might in person or over the phone.

Letters are also different from phone calls and visits because they are tangible possessions, permanent links to the outside world. The memory and feeling of a visit will fade, but a letter can be read and reread. Along with the photos that often come with them, letters become some of an inmate's most important possessions. In an environment in which few material possessions are allowed, interaction with the outside world is limited, and there is much time that needs to be filled, letters and photos take on incredible symbolic value. They are a source of validation and a link to positive roles and identities that are largely unavailable in prison. DeAngelo wrote to everyone he could think of in the hopes of getting a letter in return, asking his mother or girlfriend to look up addresses for him. He explained the importance of letters. "These people you ain't talked to in ten years [you contact just so] you have somebody. . . . So, can you drive past this house and get this address for me? 'How come I haven't heard from you in a while? I just wanted to say, "What up?"' You know, and hopefully . . . they write you back. Just for you to get mail. Mail is everything when you're in the joint, when the officer passed me my mail. There ain't no worse feeling than when he just walk right past your bunk."

Separation from loved ones can also be experienced as a feeling of helplessness and lack of control. While in prison inmates can do little or nothing to help a family member having problems. They miss important milestones like children's birthdays, school graduations, or weddings, and, although furlough is sometimes allowed to attend a funeral, they miss the chance to see aging and sick parents or grandparents before their death. At his first interview after release, DeAngelo reflected on why he felt so much stress in prison. He described his frequent anxiety over not knowing whether his girlfriend might be cheating on him while he was in prison and the impact this had on their relationship after release:

A lot of people have wives or girlfriends and stuff like that when they locked up, and while you're in there you're always thinking, "What is my girlfriend out there doing?" It's almost like you don't believe nothing they say. You're always thinking in the back of your mind that . . . that they probably been messing around behind your back and all that, so that creates like a wedge in between the connection. It's just kind of like your whole brain is just totally different when you come out because of the simple fact that you've just been gone for so long. It's like they could be there for you spiritually, and they can be there for you, but you almost have to doubt that they can be there for you a hundred percent.

These challenges of maintaining relationships with people on the outside while in prison that our participants faced had important consequences for their social networks. Without exception, they reported that their social networks shrunk, as many social ties withered without frequent contact. In particular, ties with friends, coworkers, and more peripheral family members were lost. However, some participants experienced a strengthening of relationships within what sociologists call their *primary affiliations* or *primary groups*, social groups with close, personal, enduring relationships that are independent of formal institutions such as workplaces or churches. Like most Americans, our participants' primary groups consisted mostly of family members and romantic partners.

The strengthening of family ties during the time our participants were in prison was due both to changes experienced by the inmate and to changes in the family. For the inmate, prison can be a time for reflection, leading to greater focus on relationships of particular importance (Comfort 2008, 2012). This reflection can help the inmates see their own actions through the eyes of their family members and the impact of their own behaviors on their family. The inmate also has time and energy to devote to rebuilding relationships through writing, phone calls, and visits and becomes more emotionally involved in relationships (Comfort 2008). Particularly for those with severe drug addictions, the sobriety that prison forces on them provides an opportunity for a new clarity of mind. Finally, the experience of separation also highlights the importance of those relationships, as does the need for emotional and material support while in prison.

Jennifer described her family relationships as growing closer while in prison. With both of her parents deceased and the fathers of her children long since estranged, she focused on rebuilding her relationships with her two sisters. In her prerelease interview, she described how much she planned to depend on her sisters after her release. With little formal education and no job skills or work experience, as we will see in future chapters, she in fact did rely on them considerably after release for help with housing and other material needs.

We know from research on the family members of prisoners that prison also has a big impact on those "doing time on the outside" (Braman 2004) or "doing time together" (Comfort 2008).[2] These effects are material (loss of income to the family, the cost of commissary, phone calls, and visits), emotional (the strain of separation from loved ones, the insults and injuries of secondary prisonization), and social (residential instability, disruption of social networks, the stigma by association of a family member's incarceration). These consequences accrue in many domains, including health, economic opportunities, and child development (Comfort 2007). Despite these effects, family members often rally around an incarcerated loved one, providing emotional and material support. Going to prison serves as an indication of deep personal crisis, and family members and romantic partners have a huge stake in helping sons, wives, sisters, or coparents turn their lives around. Efforts by the incarcerated loved one to rebuild relationships can send a strong signal to those on the outside that a change is possible.

Yet not all our participants were able to rebuild primary relationships while in prison. Sometimes this was because individuals they did want to reconnect with had too many of their own problems. For example, Leon was never able to reconnect with his mother, who was struggling with her own mental health problems and was unable to face the reality of her son's imprisonment. He had no contact with her for three years. In other cases, our participants had simply "burned too many bridges" after years of criminal behavior and/or drug addiction and many periods of incarceration followed by a return to old behaviors. For example, Christopher never connected with his father during his latest period of incarceration, which he attributed to his father's lack of confidence that he would change.

Randall also had trouble reconnecting with most of his family while in prison. He received just one letter from his grandmother during his latest period of incarceration, and a cousin sent him photos and money for commissary. He felt that the rest of his family expected him to return to prison after release because that is what they told him the last time he was paroled, that he would be back in prison in a matter of weeks. During this period of incarceration his brothers did not write him or send him any money. He interpreted this as abandonment when he was most in need. Although his brothers have their own problems, including addiction and involvement in the same sorts of criminal activity that landed Randall in prison, we will see in future chapters that Randall had no other options than turning to them for help after his release. When that help was short-lived, Randall was left homeless and hungry.

Coming Home from Prison

"In prison I can't disappoint anyone; out there I can"

As difficult as the prison environment is, and no matter how detailed the plans made in anticipation of freedom, the days and weeks following release can be especially challenging. Formerly incarcerated individuals must quickly shed the vestiges of their prison disculturation, juggle the demands of parole supervision and required treatment programs, and begin to put their lives back together after a long time away. Our participants found this to be a period of highs and lows. The joys of reuniting with family and other loved ones, eating one's favorite foods again, and simply being able to do what one wants without asking permission were contrasted with long waits at the parole office to report to one's parole agent, long rides on the bus to attend various programs, navigating the dangers of the streets of new neighborhoods or of old beefs, struggling to find stable housing or to get along with staff and fellow residents in residential postrelease programs, and—perhaps most importantly—expectations regarding work and sobriety. Some described it as feeling like they needed to make up for lost time despite not knowing how to do so. Or as Randall explained as he anticipated his parole date just days away: "In prison I can't disappoint anyone. Out there I can."

The days and weeks after release from prison are full of risks. The risk of reoffending is high during this period. As a result, parole agents keep their charges on a tight leash, insisting on regular drug tests, weekly check-ins, and in some cases alcohol, curfew, or GPS tethers, electronic ankle bracelets that monitor location or alcohol use. One out of every twenty parolees in the 2003 Michigan cohort failed a substance use test in the first thirty days after release. Thirteen percent failed a substance use test within ninety days of release. Cumulatively, 22 percent failed a substance abuse test within the first six months of release, while 55 percent failed sometime while on parole supervision. These numbers likely underreport the prevalence of substance use as parolees often fail to report for their tests when they have been using drugs or drinking heavily. One out of ten is arrested in the first four months after release, and one-quarter are arrested in the first year. One out of twenty absconds from parole in the first four months after release, and almost one-fifth abscond within the first year. Almost 10 percent of parolees are cited for a parole violation in the first month after prison release. At three months, one-third of parolees have received a parole violation, and, by six months, half have. Ten percent of parolees are returned to prison for a technical violation or a new crime within nine months of release.

The risk of death is also very high during this period. Binswanger et al. (2007) report that, among formerly incarcerated individuals in Washington State, the risk of death in the two weeks following release was almost thirteen times that among the general population. These statistics have been attributed to increased risk of drug overdose, homicide, and suicide. Tolerance for hard drugs falls while in prison, reentry leads to new stressors, and old conflicts reemerge after release. We see similarly high rates of death in the 2003 Michigan parole cohort.[3]

The First Days

DeAngelo's girlfriend picked him up at the prison in Jackson on the day he was paroled in fall 2007. They drove for a little over an hour, heading east on I-94 to the home where she lived with her mother in Ypsilanti and where DeAngelo would also live for the next few months. The day he had been awaiting for over ten months had arrived, yet, before he even arrived home, the joy of freedom was quickly replaced with anxiety about what the future would hold. The challenges that lay ahead—finding a job, getting along with his parole officer, and even basic social interactions in free society with different implicit rules than the prison—were front and center in his mind:

> My first day was the worst ever. I didn't have an actual anxiety attack, but my anxiety was just so bad. Because, when we were in there, it's like you don't have to do anything on your own. Your dinner's prepared for you. Everything's just kind of laid out for you. And once they let you out it's like you, you're on your own now. Fend for yourself. Basically, that was the hardest, and the most intensive challenge for me when I first got out was the anxiety. . . . It's not just a jittery nervousness. It's like . . . you're just scared shitless . . . overwhelmed with just life. As soon as you get in that car and you drive off, it's like everything hits you like, all the responsibilities you've got to take care of and just getting everything back on track.
>
> It was crazy. The anxiety didn't hit me until [his girlfriend] pulled onto the freeway. . . . I see all these free people in their cars driving, just going along. "Wow. I'm out here. I'm free now!" You know, I was really nervous, and it was hard for me to talk to people. . . . I had to get over that before I could even think about going to get a job. . . . It's a lot of mental humps you got to get over.

So, if you can get over that, that's the first step to get back into the regular groove of society.

I had to go see my PO [parole officer]. Then I had ... to make a whole bunch of rounds like to see the insurance agency. I just handled a whole lot of business my first three days. ... Soon as you get out, you got to do all of this stuff. ... You be so overwhelmed as to where you just scared. You don't know where to start. And, if you don't get one of those things done in that first day, you feel like you messed up already, and you almost panic.

Although DeAngelo is somewhat unique in the level of anxiety and "nervousness" this moment provoked, our other participants also described the first days out as a mix of exhilaration and anxiety as the reality of reconstructing one's life on the outside set in. Most prisoners leave prison with almost nothing, perhaps just a change of clothes and less than $100 in "gate money." As DeAngelo described, the first responsibility on the day of parole is to visit your new parole officer. But many other tasks must be accomplished, usually without the use of a car. A new state ID must be procured, social benefits such as DeAngelo's county health insurance for the indigent must be applied for, and various postrelease programs related to drug and alcohol abuse must be attended. For some, it was actually enough to produce some nostalgia for the simplicity of life in prison, as DeAngelo described:

I miss having time to myself where I can just write all of my thoughts on paper because I write raps and I write a little poetry and stuff. I can just sit on my bunk and just write for two hours. It was just so calming and soothing, and I would just feel so refreshed after sitting down by myself. ... [At home] you ... got all this stuff to deal with. ... You got to go look for jobs, you got to worry about whether your PO like you. ... In there you ain't got no responsibilities. ... [In prison] you can just block everything out and just have your time. You're not worrying about your bill got to be due next week.

Jane, a forty-eight-year-old white woman who served one year for heroin possession after being arrested for driving erratically, expressed the same mix of happiness and fear. Like DeAngelo, she felt overwhelmed by the transition home and all the challenges that went with it:

I think it's a different overwhelming feeling. Like it's a happiness, but it's a big fear, too. And it's a fear of just not for yourself but failing your family. Fear for my kids. Fear for my life. Wow, I'm out here, I have to make it, I have to do this. And if I don't everything it's gonna crumble. And at the same time, being that I been in and out, in and out, in and out, each time I try to pick up something that I could do different. That's why I really don't have a job now. Not that I probably couldn't get one. Yes, if I went out and pursued it. . . . I wanted to get comfortable just being in my own skin at home. And that was a big thing for me, just being comfortable, just doing nothing and not feeling like this over-whelming desire that I have to be something. . . . It was probably like maybe a week or a few days after when I started to get edgy. I don't have no money, I don't have a car. My husband was borrowing my vehicle, and then I was tak-ing him to work on some days, like I had to go report and different things. But for the most part, no, I don't have a car. And that got on my nerves.

For Jane—a self-described heroin addict who started using drugs at age nine after being sexually abused by an uncle and was addicted by age twelve—a primary challenge was staying away from drugs and alcohol. Her thoughts turned to drugs almost immediately. She was fortunate to return home to a husband who could support her, but he was himself an alcoholic and part-time drug dealer. It quickly became clear that he did not trust her to stay clean and sober, which itself stirred thoughts of using again:

My husband had, got some new watches while I was gone [in prison], and I happened to go in the drawer to get something while he was at work, and I found this nicer watch. And I was like, you know, Rolex. . . . And I tried it on and went back to go put something back in there after he had come home the next day. I went to go in there to try and see, and it wasn't in there. And I thought, Did my husband think I was gonna steal it? That was my first thought, and then with that on my mind, and I'm sitting here broke. But I went to an [AA] meeting.

The pressures are not just internally generated. Formerly incarcerated individuals fortunate enough to have a family to come home to often find that family members were struggling in their absence and that there is new pressure to get a job and contribute to the household. James is a twenty-seven-year-old African American man from Detroit who served two and half years after driving while intoxicated and causing an accident that killed his passenger. James explained that the "honeymoon" period following prison release ends quickly:

I was so used to being confined. Like I find myself now, in my room. But I'm so used to being by myself, so it just . . . felt kind of funny, the first day. Then, about three or four days later, I started feeling a little more comfortable. . . . You know how people bless you when you get out, they give you money and stuff? So I didn't need no money at the time. But when reality hit, that everybody's used to me being at home, it's time for me to make my own money, it's like, "Oh, man." Like, before I went to prison I was used to making money. But now when I get out it's like, aw, I'm thinking like I'm like I was before I went. But it's hard out here now, it's even harder. I put my life on hold, and I got to pick up the pieces. And it feels like sometimes I be kind of mixed up, like confused.

James's account also highlights the additional challenges of moving from the highly structured environment of prison to the unstructured environment of life on the outside, a theme that we can see as well in the excerpts from DeAngelo's and Jane's first postrelease interviews offered above. While James talked about feeling uncomfortable around other people, other participants focused on the difficulties of shedding interactional styles developed in prison to deal with the threat of violence. Leon explained how he continued to approach social interactions, especially those with men, with an interactional style characterized by aggression. In Goffman's terms, it took him some time to shed the disculturation that comes from living in a total institution like a prison:

It's hard really integrating back. When you socially try to interact with people with so many roadblocks, it's frustrating, but I can't worry about that because this is what I have to deal with.

Interviewer: When you try to sit back and assess for yourself objectively, do you still have any of that prison attitude in you?

Yeah . . . some of it's always going to always be there. Like dealing with my wife's boyfriend. I lay down the law there. . . . It shouldn't be like that, but that's how it is. Dealing with other men is where it's at. Women naturally, it's a whole different setup because you just weren't around women so much, but . . . as far as like men that are in your path in any type of way, is where you show your aggression at.

David, a twenty-eight-year-old white man from the working-class suburbs west of Detroit with a long-term heroin addiction, explained a similar experience. He had to get used to interacting with people on the outside in a different way than he had in prison, where any sign of weakness might be taken advantage of:

> I've been to some high [security] prisons, and that's where your skin becomes callused. You put on an alligator skin and it's hard to penetrate. And then when you get out here, you expect the same respect from everybody else that you would get in there. But this is society and people don't know where you've been.... In prison you can't expose any weaknesses ... I'm suspiciously alert at all times, and I have to live like that ... It's hard for me sometimes to understand that people don't know, it's not the same out here that it is in there ... I'm still adjusting. To this day, I get panicky at times.

For David, navigating such social situations in the days after release proved to be too difficult. He was initially released to a residential reentry program for those convicted of a drug offense run by an established nonprofit organization. After a tearful phone conversation with his mother, he got into a fight with another resident of the program who insulted his masculinity after seeing him crying. He left the program, thereby absconding from parole. He managed to avoid capture by living with a former girlfriend whom parole authorities did not know about, but a few months later he was returned to prison for committing a burglary and then fleeing the state.

However, most of our participants eventually adjusted to life on the outside over the course of the first few weeks after release. They shed their prison demeanors, adjusted to social interactional styles in free society, and learned to navigate the web of parole requirements, service providers, and programs that would structure their lives while under state supervision, a topic we return to below. Many of our participants adopted a strategy of isolation to deal with the stresses of social interaction. For Randall, these stresses came from conflict with his brother, whom he lived with for lack of any other option. Although Randall got along well with his sister-in-law and two nephews, his brother was an alcoholic who treated him poorly, telling him he was just going to end up back in prison. Randall developed a habit of going on long walks through the deserted streets of Detroit while listening to music to "clear [his] mind," occupy his time, and stay away from interactions with "negative people" like his brother. He pursued a similar isolation strategy in prison to avoid entanglements:

> I like to walk ... I just get a clear sense of mind. I don't want to be out there looking for trouble or nothing like that; I just walk. It's just the thing, like what

I'm going to do now, what I'm going to do later, what I'm going to do tomorrow, that's how I be thinking while I be walking, thinking about my brother and
all this negative stuff he said about me, that's one thing I wrote down before
I got out of prison that I'm going to stay away from negative people. People
who don't want to see me succeed, stay away from them. . . . I ain't never did
nothing to my brother. Nothing. And still he want to pick. I don't like that. He
don't know what's on my mind. He don't know what I'm going through, this
parole and all this stuff. I might just snap out of this, just trying to throw me off
my square, and I told my PO these words, she's like, "You better calm down,
I don't want to send you back." So I've been straight up.

Jennifer uses the social isolation strategy as a way to avoid people and
places that have served as triggers for the drug and alcohol abuse that
have led to crime in the past. She is focused on her addiction recovery,
and she must be constantly vigilant for old patterns of behavior and associations that might lead back to drug use. From there it is a short path
back to prison:

I don't want to get too relaxed because, if I get too comfortable in what I'm
doing now, I could slip off, so I just got to always keep myself and remind myself that wherever I go or whatever I do or whoever I see, just remember that
it's very easy to fall back into my old patterns and it wouldn't take nothing to
end up in a dope house. And the first time I do that I'll be right back in prison.
    That's just something I have to remind myself that it's just a struggle. I can-
not forget where I came from. I cannot forget them old patterns. And if I see
myself thinking a certain way or thinking there's a friend of mine that I haven't
seen in a couple years and he's a user and we used to use together and he's a
really nice person but I know that he's probably still in his addiction, so therefore I can't even go by and say hi to him because all it will take is him pull it
out in front of me. . . . It's just so, so many different things in life that I've got
to learn to build my life around, and it's difficult, but it'll work out because
that's what I want to do. I want to stay clean, and in the past I would get clean
for ninety days or whatever, and I'd go right back out and use because I wasn't
ready to stop it.

Lenora went so far as to avoid her old neighborhood altogether as
much as possible, lest she come into contact with people she used to drink
and get high with what, mimicking treatment programs, she refers to as
"wet places and wet faces." She came to the conclusion that such people
care little about her and are mostly interested in feeding their addictions:

If I was in the old neighborhood I would see people I know, which I've went over there 'cause I had to go get my purse and I seen a few people and just, hi, I'm OK, give them a hug, and I'm gone. I don't care. I don't even care what they doing. But I don't stop to see them.... That's when I messed up before, going to wet places and wet faces. Soon as you go around there and they drinking, they smoking crack, and they using heroin, and they ask you for some money.... Then, if they don't know where I'm staying, that's how it's gonna be. I'm not letting nobody know where I [live] but my kids and my family.

The Experience of Parole

As his first days after release stretched into weeks, DeAngelo gradually adjusted to the routines and interactional styles of life in free society. Indeed, he had little choice but to do so. The requirements of parole and the time it took to get to and from various meetings and appointments on the bus quickly filled his days. There was little time to dwell on the transition home. When asked what he had been doing since his release, he listed a busy schedule of treatment programs, reporting at the parole office, and mandatory meetings with service providers. His drunk-driving conviction meant that he also had to wear an ankle bracelet, or electronic tether, that continuously monitored him for alcohol use through contact with his skin. Indeed, it can seem like being on parole is itself a full-time job (see also Halushka 2016), particularly in the first few weeks after release when programming, reporting, and job search are most intense:

Five AA meetings a week, two groups a week, reporting, I report twice a month, I report every other Tuesday. MPRI [Michigan Prisoner Re-entry Initiative], I've got to go down to Power once a week. I got to do Work First every day. I had to do that meet and greet thing.... Meet and greet is at this Catholic Social Services. Basically, when you first get out, they have like a whole bunch of different agencies come do presentations and things like that to let you know what's out there that'll benefit a person just getting out of prison.

The challenges of meeting all these requirements are compounded by lack of transportation. Public transportation infrastructure is limited in many parts of Michigan, and few parolees are allowed to drive when they are released. Even fewer have their own vehicles. This often means that parolees must rely on friends and family to drive them around. Jennifer described the difficulties this posed when such transportation was unreliable:

My sisters take me or my brother drives me in his van. His [her former fiancé's] van's there, he left the van for me to have somebody drive me around because I was having a hard time because when he got sick he got to the point where he couldn't drive me to report. Then my little niece that was staying here with me, she wasn't showing up to take me to my appointments. I missed a dental appointment for [my son] because of her. So I was like I can't rely on her, I'm going to have to find another way. So I started telling my sister that she's not showing up to help me and I can't do that for my parole. There's no way I can just tell my parole agent, "Oh well, my ride didn't come, and I'm not on the bus route." He would have said, "Well you should have walked here." You don't play around like that. You get there because that can send you back [to prison].

Although our participants usually managed to beg rides and cope with riding the bus for the intense but relatively short period of time after release when requirements were at their peak, we'll see in chapter 6 that reliable transportation often proved to be an even more difficult problem if and when a steady job was landed.

Many of our participants lived in institutional settings such as treatment programs or other residential programs for formerly incarcerated individuals, either as a requirement of parole or because they had nowhere else to live after prison. Fewer than three-quarters of Michigan parolees live in a private residence immediately after release, and over half reside in some sort of intermediate sanction program at some point while on parole (Harding, Morenoff, and Herbert 2013). Although these programs can reduce the burden of meeting parole requirements, they can feel like prison all over again. Christopher explained his frustration with a job-readiness program for formerly incarcerated individuals run by the Salvation Army to which he turned to avoid having to live in the local homeless shelter:

When you go in there, requirement, your Bridge card [food stamps]. If you ain't got one, we're taking you down to the [welfare office], and you're going to apply for it, and we're taking it when you get it. So I have to pay $155 to Jesus' organization, and I don't mean to say it like that, . . . but this is a Christian fellowship, Salvation Army. OK, so why do I have to give you my Bridge card? Why do I have to give you my food shit? They drain the 155 out. Take it out every month. There's 222 guys there. Do 222 times 150, OK. That's actual monetary. But figure, what's minimum wage, $7.15? Times 60, times 202. That's the weight, the work that you got out of us. No wonder they don't hire people. . . . I'll tell you, the food there, it's exceptional, perfect, but, if I'm paying you 155 dollars a month and I'm giving you 60 hours to 70 hours a week for a dollar, I want porterhouse every night. Spaghetti, spaghetti, spaghetti, spaghetti, that's all it ever is, spaghetti, tacos, institutional food. It's prison. Know what it is? You know what I started calling it as a joke? That's the Fort Street Correctional Facility.

The group living quarters, institutional food, regimentation of daily life, lack of privacy, and disrespect from authority figures are more than reminiscent of life in prison.

The institution of parole has shifted from treating parole agents as providers of services to emphasizing surveillance, and the kind of training parole officers receive is more akin to that of law enforcement than social workers, stressing, for example, monitoring and arrest rather than service referrals (Blumstein and Beck 2005; Lynch 2000; Petersilia 2003; Simon 1993). Because parolees are still in the legal custody of the criminal justice system, their constitutional rights are severely limited (Petersilia 1999). Parolees must, among other requirements, report to parole officers when directed and answer all reasonable questions, notify the parole agent of changes in residence, submit to mandatory drug tests, and not leave the jurisdiction without permission (Travis 2005). If the conditions of parole are violated, the parolee is subject to sanctions, one of which may be a change of residence (Travis 2005). Parolees may be returned to prison or temporarily moved to a variety of institutional settings other than prison. Drug treatment facilities, for example, may be rehabilitative settings, but they can be used as punitive measures of control (Gowan and Whetstone 2012; Lynch 1998). Parole violations are a product of the behavior of the parolee, the intensity of supervision, and the "official markers of dangerousness" contained in criminal justice records (Ryken and Lin 2016).

Parole supervision requirements vary from person to person but generally involve regular reporting to the parole office, getting approval for any change in residence, regular drug and alcohol tests, attending treatment programs, curfew, not associating with other felons, not living in a residence where there are weapons, and working, looking for work, or attending school. Parole agents in Michigan check and approve before release the residence that the parolee will live in after release and then make periodic home checks to make sure the parolee is still living there. The frequency of reporting to the parole office varies by the parolee's risk level as determined by a risk-assessment instrument, which is updated over time. In particular, those who are employed often have to report less frequently, and reporting requirements become less onerous with good behavior over time, with the lowest-risk, long-term parolees reporting only by telephone or, in rare cases, mail. A high-risk individual may have to report multiple times a week when first released. Some parole restrictions are also specific to the parolee and his or her past crimes. Former drug dealers may be restricted from owning a cell phone or pager (one-quarter of parolees in the 2003 Michigan parole cohort experienced this restriction). Car thieves or drunk drivers are restricted from having a driver's license or driving a vehicle (one-quarter of parolees). Those convicted of fraud are restricted from having bank accounts or credit cards (about 10 percent of parolees). Those convicted of a sex offense probably face the most stringent requirements, including restrictions on where they can live, whom they can live with, and whether they can access a computer (about 9 percent of parolees).

Parolees are also required to pay supervision fees and usually have also been ordered by the court to pay fines, court fees, and restitution to victims.[4] Supervision fees are higher for those required to wear ankle bracelets. Such fees, imposed on an already economically marginalized and often destitute population, represent a form of secondary punishment, one that is largely invisible to the general public. However, the collection of fees is uneven across individuals and counties. Our participants reported being asked to pay the fees, and many tried to contribute something, even if only a token amount, each time they reported to their parole officer. While failure to pay fees could not result in an extension of one's parole beyond the statutory maximum sentence, it could prevent a parolee who was otherwise compliant from being discharged from parole early. We discuss the consequences of supervision fees for material well-being below.

Constant, electronic monitoring by means of a GPS ankle bracelet may also be required by the parole board for parolees deemed to be at highest risk. Leon was required to wear such a bracelet for the first ninety days after he was released to enforce the restriction that he leave the house only to look for work during a set period of time each day. His movements were so closely monitored that he was once verbally reprimanded for going to the store to buy something to eat after the tether revealed his movements to his parole officer:

> You can't leave.... You can only be gone from eight to one. And you can only go to places that are assigned. So she gives me a sheet of paper like a week later and tells me to have people sign this wherever you go.... She just asked where

I was because they showed something on her computer. I went to store, and she'll be like, "You know you can't go to the store, being out from eight to one. You know, you're only supposed to look for a job." You can't go get anything to eat or nothing like that. You're only supposed to be gone from eight to one, just to job hunt. And then she knows I catch the bus, and it takes me a hour to get downtown.

The community supervision system is large, highly bureaucratized, yet loosely coupled. Each year in Michigan, there are over seventeen thousand parolees and over fifty-seven thousand probationers being supervised by over twelve hundred field agents at over 120 local offices throughout the state at a cost of over $170 million dollars a year ("Michigan Department of Corrections Annual Report" 2008). Although there are procedures that parole agents must follow, there is also considerable room in many situations for discretion. For example, agents have a strong incentive to request an absconding warrant when a parolee fails to report because the issuance of such a warrant frees them from any responsibility for the parolee's actions. Yet some agents issue a warrant more quickly than others. Some will do so the day after a parolee fails to report, while others will wait a few weeks to see whether the parolee will reappear. The decision of course also depends on the risk posed by the parolee and his or her history and patterns of criminal behavior. This individual discretion and complexity of decision making means that, from the perspective of the parolee, a working relationship with one's parole officer is critical, and the experience of parole can vary considerably both among parole agents and among county parole offices. As a result, from the perspective of the parolee, each weekly, biweekly, or monthly report to the parole office carries with it the fear of being returned to prison for a parole violation.[5]

Parolees' anxiety about violation stems, in part, from the fact that violation and reincarceration can result from behaviors that would rarely, if ever, result in imprisonment for the average citizen—fighting, drunkenness, petty theft, or possession of small amounts of drugs, for example, can quickly mean a return to prison for someone on parole. This is because parole is understood by agents as a privilege, not a right, and a replacement for serving time in prison. Parole violations do require a hearing, but that hearing happens in prison after the parolee has already been reincarcerated. DeAngelo explained how careful one must be while on parole: "It's overwhelming how you just got to keep yourself composed. Regardless of what the situation might be, because of the situation that you're in. I can have an argument with somebody and maybe just push him and walk away. It would make you go back to the joint. But, if I had never been to the joint, it would have been nothing. It's like now that I'm on parole and I'm out it's like I got to be a thousand times more careful than anybody else who had never been to the joint."

This intense scrutiny also means that others can manipulate the system to their advantage over a parolee. The parolee is rarely given the benefit of the doubt. Information about possible parole violations or criminal behavior reported to a parole agent is taken seriously no matter the source or extenuating circumstances. Police contact is also taken seriously by parole officers, making many parolees hesitant to call law enforcement even for their own protection. Jennifer explained how her son's father was trying to use the parole system to exact revenge on her. To protect herself, she informs her parole agent of her side of the story before he can tell his: "I'm always letting [my agent] know—whenever he threatens me, I'll call my agent and tell them he verbally threatened me or he left another message or he brought the cops over. And he said just keep them informed and don't use, don't violate, and whatever he says is just, he say, so there's really nothing, he can't stop them. He doesn't even know what agent it is, he's just leaving messages up there about me. And saying this, that, and the other, [my son's] dad, trying to get them to violate me."

The extra scrutiny, numerous programs and reporting, and various requirements of parole are designed to provide structure and control for individuals who have had trouble exercising self-control in the past, as many of our participants readily acknowledged. Just keeping busy meeting requirements can prevent problems. As Jennifer explained, parole requirements kept her from enrolling in school, but they also kept her from having the free time even to think about the drugs and alcohol that were the source of so many of her past problems:

> I'm not doing nothing about school, but I want to do it as soon as I get through with my rehab because with the trailer [see above] going on and then my community service going on and then reporting once a week and rehab it's just way too much. And then trying to be with my son too and help him with his homework on a daily basis and just be in his life every day because I'm not living with him yet. That's a ways to travel. It doesn't sound like I do much in a day, but to travel.... I'm afraid for my daily schedule to die down because that leaves room for thought, and that thinking can get me in a dope house or something which I can't afford.

Legal Financial Obligations and Monetary Sanctions

Another aspect of being on parole is legal financial obligations or monetary sanctions, a complex and confusing web of accumulated fees, fines, restitution orders, and payments associated with criminal justice processing and time served. Such fees are numerous and may range from restitution for crimes committed, such as an obligation to repay a victim for the value of items stolen, a daily fee assessed for being supervised on tether or housed in a county jail, a monthly fee for being supervised on probation or parole, or lawyer fees assessed by a court-appointed attorney assigned to indigent defendants. Many participants were saddled with "driver's responsibility" fines—specific to Michigan—which we discuss further in chapter 5. These monetary sanctions affect a substantial majority of those criminally convicted in the United States and have important consequences for those on whom they are levied (Harris 2016; Harris, Evans, and Beckett 2010). First, payments represent a substantial financial obligation relative to annual income, typically in the range of 30–60 percent. Second, debt contributes to the erosion of credit scores, which limits access to key reintegrative resources, such as housing and education. And, third, failure to pay debts can result in criminal justice sanctions, including the potential for warrants and reincarceration.

Among our participants, only three of twenty-two had no legal debt. The average legal debt (including restitution, court and supervision fees, and driver's responsibility charges) was $3,585 and the median $2,345. With virtually none of our participants in a financial position to pay debt down, the dominant debt-management strategies were to have family members pay fines or simply not to pay and hope for the best. In addition to these strategies, two participants were using college financial aid to cover monthly payments, and one took out a loan that enabled him to pay his debt in full as well as get off parole. Among all our participants, only one, Paul, was able to pay off a substantial portion of his fees with his own earnings, but Paul's middle-class background made him more advantaged than our other participants.

His debt profile and the challenges James faced paying it were fairly typical. He owed $2,500 in restitution charges linked with the deaths he had caused while driving under the influence as well as $1,200 in supervision fees that he had accumulated while on tether, which charged a daily fee for use. The debt had recently gone to a collection agency, with which James had negotiated a $200 monthly payment despite the fact that he earned no more than $800 a month during the entire study period. Several months following the renegotiation he had yet to begin paying, which had resulted in additional fees charged atop the original fee each month. Prioritizing his expenses, he explained: "Fees ... the parole ... my license, then school." In other words, he would be able to direct money toward his education only once his legal debts were dealt with.

For others, payment of legal debt was even further out of reach. This was the case for Henry, a fifty-two-year-old African American man who was incarcerated for auto theft and owed $1,000 in supervision fees and $457 in restitution. He believed that he would be unable to get off parole unless he paid his restitution: "If I get some money ... you know some money in there I can spare, I'll start paying. Because I've seen guys be on parole seven, eight years because they don't pay the money." Yet, because he was unemployed throughout the study period, surviving together with his fiancée and two stepchildren on one child's supplemental security income payments, even the $10 per month payment he believed would prove his commitment to his parole officer was impossible.

We found that these legal financial obligations were significant not just because of the substantial economic burden they represented for our participants (and, more often, their families) but also because of the implications of payment for supervision. Parole officers seemed to view payment toward fees as an indication of a client's seriousness about completing parole. Those who were not able to make payments were thus understood to be not simply poorer or lacking family resources but less invested in their own reform. Some participants also believed that they could not be free of parole supervision until these fees were paid, heightening anxiety about inability to pay.[6]

Conclusion

Understanding where formerly incarcerated individuals start the process of reintegration is critical to understanding the challenges they face and how it unfolds over time. In the introduction, we conceptualized prisoner reintegration as determined by the resources with which the individual leaves prison, the social, economic, cultural, and institutional contexts he or she enters, and the match between the two. This chapter has described the experiences of our participants in prison and the first days and weeks after release as they began the process of reintegration. These days and weeks are a period of adjustment to the routines and norms of life in free society, but, more importantly, they are the formerly incarcerated individual's first exposure to the contexts that will affect his or her reintegration process. Relationships with loved ones, stable housing, and the institutional practices surrounding parole supervision are three salient contexts during this initial period after release. Perhaps paradoxically, the power of the state and its surrogates to surveil, control, and punish is felt most strongly in the period after release from prison—power that is often felt particularly strongly by women and people of color. We now turn to in-depth analyses of the social contexts in which formerly incarcerated individuals are embedded—families, romantic relationships, and neighborhoods—in order to understand their role in prisoner reintegration. Chapter 3 focuses on the challenges of rebuilding family relationships and our participants' efforts to create stable home lives for themselves and their families.

CHAPTER THREE

A Place to Call Home?

When we first met Leon in Jackson Cooper Street Prison three weeks before his parole date, he was eager to talk about the challenges he would soon face on his release. He worried about how he would find work and spend time with his son, who had been born just after Leon was imprisoned, while conforming to the curfew that his electronic tether would enforce for his first ninety days. He worried about how he would get along with his now-estranged wife and whether she would be patient with his inability to help out financially. He worried about whether he would build a relationship with his son—whom he had seen three or four times a year while incarcerated—and whether he would be able to get joint custody of him given his criminal record. His goal was to be a father and provider for his son, but it was not entirely clear to him how he was going to do that after a decade spent in prison.

Yet Leon also knew he would leave prison with a relatively high level of social support, primarily from his father, with whom he would live in a middle-class neighborhood near Detroit's riverfront. He would leave prison with some advantages relative to other returning citizens, including time in the military, an extensive work history before his incarceration, and a year of college. He also hoped his extended middle-class family would prove helpful in finding a job, yet this was less certain. Although he had a brother and two sisters, he had had little contact with them during his incarceration. His mother—long since divorced from his father—had not talked to him in three years and had never visited him in prison. Leon attributed her distance to her mental health problems, including bipolar disorder, and her inability to come to terms with the course his life had taken. In short, the joy of his upcoming release was tempered by questions about how he would meet his family responsibilities and rebuild family relationships.

Family relationships were a critical part of other participants' postrelease plans as well. Jennifer, for example, virtually glowed with excitement as she told us about her plans the day before her parole from the Women's Huron Valley prison. Excited to have a visitor to talk to, and optimistic about starting a new life, she looked forward to seeing her youngest child, eleven-year-old Lucas, and her sisters, who would pick her up at her release. She planned to live with her fiancé, Stan, for a few weeks until her sisters could help her get set up in a place of her own, a trailer once owned by an elderly aunt where she and Luke could live together. The sobriety and time for reflection that prison offered had "made [her] see where [she was] in life," including the effects of her long-term addiction on her children. Her eldest son, now nineteen, had been heavily involved in her own criminal lifestyle from an early age and was now incarcerated for manslaughter. Her middle child, seventeen-year-old Dawn, had lived with her father her entire life and did not even know Jennifer was in prison. Jennifer's sisters and his father cared for Luke while Jennifer was in prison, and her release represented the possibility of a new start at motherhood, a chance to hit reset and rebuild her relationship with her youngest son.

Jennifer's sisters sent money for her commissary account, wrote to her regularly, and facilitated weekly phone calls with Luke. (Stan, now sixty-eight, was too saddled by his own intense drug addiction and age-related health problems to be of much support.) With only a seventh-grade education, almost no work history, no experience living sober outside prison, and her own serious health problems, Jennifer would need the continued financial and emotional support of her sisters to land on her feet and achieve her goal of maintaining a stable home for herself and Luke. They had arranged for the trailer and were working on finding a trailer park with a lot rent that Jennifer could afford. The only option would turn out to be more drug infested than the quiet neighborhood where she lived before prison smoking away her days in a drug-induced fog. Given his poor health, Jennifer wished she could care for Stan as well, but his continued drug addiction presented too much of a threat to her own sobriety for continued involvement with him (he would die not long after her release). In short, she focused intensely on motherhood as a bulwark against relapse. She envisioned it as her primary role and identity as she tried to start a new life for herself after prison.

The hopes and fears regarding family relationships that Leon and Jennifer articulated are typical of those expressed by our other participants as they anticipated their upcoming releases. On the one hand, the release from prison eases the pain of separation and is a chance to start fresh and make up for past mistakes and lost time. As we documented in the previous chapter, many family relationships strengthened during prison as relationships with friends dropped off. Although prison increases physical distance and puts up procedural and economic barriers to family contact and interaction, it also focuses inmates' attention on their loved ones and spurs reflection about the importance of family. Romantic partners, parents, siblings, and other family members often rally around their incarcerated loved one by providing emotional and material support.

On the other hand, the moment of release can be a test of these seemingly strengthened relationships, which are suddenly thrust into daily interaction and are tried by the challenges of reentry and reintegration. What will happen when these relationships must be negotiated and developed in the outside world, which is full of pressures to contribute care and financial resources and successfully navigate connections to a wider social network? We find that some family members are sources of critical material and emotional support while others turn out to be potential burdens whose needs compete with those of the formerly incarcerated individual to find work, meet parole requirements, and stay sober and away from crime. Family members with whom relationships were difficult before prison can be sources of stress, while others present opportunities for criminal activity or substance use. Still others have their own mental and physical health problems, for which the returning citizen needs to provide care. Frayed relationships with former spouses or romantic partners can make reuniting with children more challenging. Past problems with parenting or providing financially serve as a reminder of past failures rather than an uplifting motivation to persevere despite the challenges of reentry and reintegration. Finally, as we documented in the previous chapter, many formerly incarcerated individuals do not have family they can return to and end up living in shelters, treatment programs, or other types of institutional housing as they struggle to get their economic footing without the support of one or more family members.

Whether participants reconnect with family and establish a stable home will prove to be critical for their social and economic reintegration after prison and their ability to stay away from drugs and crime. The theoretical framework we introduced in the introduction emphasizes the importance of social contexts and institutions and the ways in which individual characteristics and resources articulate with the opportunities and constraints imposed by these contexts and institutions. Families, households, and institutional living situations will prove to be central contexts for social and economic integration among formerly incarcerated individuals. This chapter also discusses our participants' experiences with institutions of parole supervision and public benefits programs as they relate to residential stability and the broader question of economic security.

In this chapter, we begin our analysis of the role of families in reentry and reintegration. Because of the importance of coresidence to family relationships, and because of the high rates of residential instability among formerly incarcerated individuals, we consider residential stability and security key concrete markers of family relationship stability among these individuals. We use them as a window into the process of rebuilding family relationships throughout much of this chapter while also playing close attention to nonresidential family relationships and supports. We examine three core questions regarding finding and maintaining a stable home and family life after release. First, why do few formerly incarcerated individuals return to their preprison homes? Second, why do they experience high rates of residential instability and insecurity? Third, how are some able to achieve stability while others are not?

In this chapter, we also detail the role of families and other sources of material support in helping meet day-to-day needs for food and shelter, not just in the period immediately after prison, but also—for many—in the longer term as well.[1] The importance of family to our participants' reintegration process will be examined in future chapters as well. Chapter 4 describes the role of family—both positive and negative and including both desistance from crime and continued sobriety—in the social reintegration of formerly incarcerated individuals. Material needs and the assistance family members provide can override other, more negative aspects of family relationships. In examining the role of neighborhood context in prisoner reintegration, chapter 5 shows how our interview participants tended to avoid neighbors, further underlining the importance of family relationships. Chapter 6 shows the importance of families for employment, particularly the role of working- and middle-class families, in setting their returning loved one on an upward economic trajectory in the labor market.

As we consider the role of families in prisoner reintegration, we define *family* broadly, to include not just parents, siblings, and romantic partners but also more distant relatives and nonblood relations that nonetheless serve the same social and economic functions as family members. This reflects the reality of the diversity of meanings of family and home among formerly incarcerated individuals. This diversity is evident in the first residences where Michigan parolees lived after prison (according to our

administrative data). These include living with parents (33.6 percent), living with spouses or partners (11.4 percent), living with siblings or cousins
(11.2 percent), living with other family members from a generation older
than that of the parolee (6.3 percent), living alone (6.0 percent), living with
an acquaintance or a friend (2.9 percent), and living with an adult child
or younger relative (1.3 percent). This private, noninstitutional housing
accounts for only about three-quarters of first residences. The remainder of parolees move into institutional housing when they leave prison,
either because they cannot find anyone willing to take them in or because
such residences are required by the parole board. These residences include
criminal justice institutions similar to halfway houses (13.1 percent), hotels (5.2 percent), homeless shelters (3.3 percent), and substance abuse
or mental health treatment programs (3.6 percent). Even these numbers
understate the diversity and fluidity of family life after prison. Qualitative
work by Donald Braman (2004) and Andrea Leverentz (2014), for example, shows that extended and nonnuclear families are common among
formerly incarcerated individuals and that there is a great deal of flux in
household composition.

Coming Home after Prison?

We begin our discussion of rebuilding family relationships after prison with
a startling fact that motivates our interest in residential stability and family
integration: few formerly incarcerated individuals return to the homes or
neighborhoods where they lived before prison. Less than one-third of parolees in our administrative data returned to an address within a half mile
of their preprison residence on their release from prison, and only 41 percent ever returned to their preprison neighborhood in the first two years
after release (Harding, Morenoff, and Herbert 2013). This means that most
formerly incarcerated individuals are starting over when it comes to finding a home, both physical and social, for themselves after prison. Although
in some cases their families have moved while they were in prison, formerly incarcerated individuals are often negotiating new places in households rather than returning to familiar households.

Why do few formerly incarcerated individuals return to their preprison residences or neighborhoods? First, the families and communities
from which they come themselves have higher-than-average rates of residential mobility, the poor having high rates of residential mobility (Gram-

lich, Laren, and Sealand 1992). During the time a family member is in prison, the household may have moved. For example, Leon lived with his wife before he was incarcerated, but she moved not long after he entered prison, and returning to live with her was not an option owing to their estrangement during his time in prison. A move is particularly likely when the prisoner provided the main source of household income or was the homeowner or renter.

Second, family members may be unwilling to continue to support a formerly incarcerated individual, particularly when he or she has been in and out of prison multiple times or brings substance abuse or other criminal behavior into the household. As discussed in the previous chapter, family relationships may fray with frequent contact with the criminal justice system and frequent and prolonged separation owing to incarceration, particularly when it comes to extended kin. In such cases, treatment programs, corrections centers, hotels, or homeless shelters may be the only postrelease housing options. Even at two years after release, at least 13 percent of those who are still on parole and still in the community (i.e., have not been returned to prison) are living in some form of institutional housing (Harding, Morenoff, and Herbert 2013). At that point in time, the most common is jail (4.1 percent), followed by treatment programs and custodial programs for technical violators (2.7 percent each).

The role of institutional housing becomes even clearer when we look at the entire span of the first two years after release (see table 3.1). Over half of parolees experienced an intermediate sanction such as a jail, technical rule violator center, treatment program, or correctional center, accounting for almost 8 percent of nights (we address the role of the intermediate sanctions and the criminal justice system more generally in generating residential instability below). Many formerly incarcerated individuals spend at least some time in institutional housing. Nine percent ever spent a night in a hospital, 9 percent ever stayed in a homeless shelter, and 9 percent ever lived in a hotel. Twenty-eight percent ever lived in a residential treatment program for substance abuse or other mental health problems, but such programs are generally short, accounting for only 3 percent of nights. Finally, about half ever spent time in a county or city jail, accounting for about 5 percent of nights.

Third, formerly incarcerated individuals preparing for release may not be well served by returning to preprison social environments. Sometimes, the formerly incarcerated individuals recognize this for themselves and intentionally stay away from potentially risky environments, particularly

TABLE 3.1 **Residence types during first two years after release**

Residence type	Ever resided (%)	Mean nights (%)
Intermediate sanctions		
Jail	49.1	4.6
Treatment program	28.3	3.0
Correctional center	25.2	1.9
Probation detention, technical rule violator or reentry programming center	23.4	2.8
Any intermediate sanction	64.9	12.3
Any sanction other than jail	52.5	7.7
Other residence types		
Private residence	96.2	74.4
Transitional housing	6.2	1.3
Hospital	9.0	0.4
Hotel	8.5	1.6
Shelter	8.9	1.3
Homeless	1.2	0.1
Unknown residence	32.9	8.6

Source: Harding, Morenoff, and Herbert (2013).

residences in hotels or homes where there are fellow drug users. In other cases, parole boards or parole agents may make this determination and require or encourage a new start in a new environment. For example, Randall intentionally avoided requesting to live with his brother, sister-in-law, and two teenage nephews in Detroit because of his brother's past involvement in crime, their contentious relationship, and his brother's continued use of alcohol and drugs. Instead, he paroled to a drug treatment program, although he would later move in with his brother when he had nowhere else to go. David provides an example of institutional housing mandated as a condition of parole. Although he would have preferred to live with his mother, brother, and sister-in-law in the working-class suburbs west of Detroit, he was required to participate in a residential drug treatment and work program in the city owing to his history of drug abuse. His criminal history included multiple crimes committed while under the influence of drugs, so the parole board mandated that he enter drug treatment as a condition of his release.

Low rates of return to preprison homes also mean that most formerly incarcerated individuals are starting their postprison lives without strong prospects for housing security and stability, a key foundation for economic and social reintegration after prison. Some researchers have argued that secure housing is the most pressing, immediate short-term need for returning prisoners (Lutze, Rosky, and Hamilton 2014; Metraux and Culhane

2004; Roman and Travis 2006), and parole officials cite housing as the biggest need for parolees (Petersilia 2003). Moreover, stable housing may be the foundation on which other aspects of successful reentry rely (Bradley et al. 2001): it can be difficult for returning prisoners to find and maintain stable employment, maintain family connections, receive consistent and timely physical and mental health care, and avoid substance use without stable housing (Lutze, Rosky, and Hamilton 2014).

Prior research suggests that homelessness and incarceration are closely intertwined as homelessness increases the risk of incarceration and incarceration increases the risk of homelessness. Homelessness can affect incarceration because the lives of homeless persons are increasingly controlled by laws and ordinances that criminalize their daily activities and the homeless experience frequent law enforcement surveillance and contact. Lacking private, personal space, the homeless must use public spaces to engage in private activities such as sleeping, urinating, drinking, or using drugs, and many cities have enacted antihomeless campaigns that criminalize performing these private activities in public spaces (Donley and Wright 2008).[2] For example, in Seattle and several other West Coast cities, simply sitting or lying on the sidewalk is illegal (Beckett and Herbert 2010). Homeless persons are also more likely to engage in behaviors like heavy drinking, stealing money, or stealing food that make them more likely to enter the criminal justice system (Gowan 2002; Greenberg and Rosenheck 2008). Individuals with long criminal records who experience homelessness may be particularly at risk of further punishment because of the frequent police contact and criminal justice system involvement that homelessness entails.

Residential Instability

Looking beyond the first residence after release from prison shows that housing stability and security are key challenges for formerly incarcerated individuals. By any standard, formerly incarcerated individuals experience a remarkable level of residential instability. According to Harding, Morenoff, and Herbert (2013), the typical formerly incarcerated individual in our administrative data changes residence two and half times per year in the first two years after release, and other researchers find similar levels of housing instability and insecurity (Ditton 1999; Geller and Curtis 2011; La Vigne and Parthasarathy 2005; Metraux and Culhane 2004).[3] Some of this residential mobility is surely positive—moves from institutional or group housing to live with family or moves to more desirable housing or neighborhoods once work is found. Yet this number also suggests the fragility of living arrangements. It also suggests that integration into a household takes considerable time for many formerly incarcerated individuals. A home is both a shelter and a place of social belonging, emotional support and security, and social exchange. Evidence from our administrative data supports the close link between family support and residential stability (Harding, Morenoff, et al. 2016). Family living arrangements played a critical role in providing residential stability after prison. Living with a parent or romantic partner greatly reduced the probability of moving relative to other private living arrangements, and living at one's preprison address reduces the probability of a residential move. Residential stability, in turn, was negatively associated with arrests and substance abuse, although it was not associated with finding employment.

High rates of residential instability are also clearly evident among our qualitative interview participants. The number of residences ranged from 1 to 20, with a mean of 5.7 and a median of 4. Figure 3.1 illustrates this graphically by showing moves over time since release for all twenty-two of our participants. This figure also illustrates the importance of institutional housing among our participants as institutional residences are clearly quite frequent. Finally, it shows that there is considerable variation across participants in experiences of residential instability and institutional housing. In this section, we explore the primary causes of this residential stability for our participants.

Randall is one participant who struggled with housing insecurity and homelessness. As he considered his housing options during his prerelease interview, his eyes fell to the ground. He knew that he would not be able to go back to the apartment he had shared with his cousin and her three children prior to his imprisonment; the family had been evicted. Other family members were fed up with his criminal behavior and promised little in the way of support. The Michigan Prisoner Re-entry Initiative would pay for his residence at a drug treatment center for two weeks (though he was not an addict), but he had no plans thereafter. He also worried about finding a job. While he had worked at Arby's and Burger King in the past and had some experience as a construction day laborer, he feared that his criminal record would stand in the way of securing even these minimum wage jobs. Further, while he had been eking out steady improvements in his GED scores while in prison, he had not yet managed to pass. With

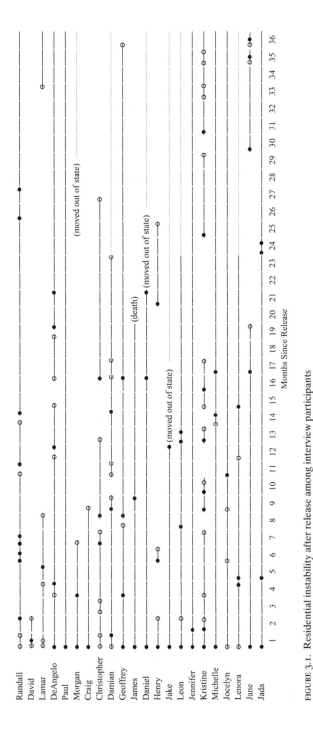

FIGURE 3.1. Residential instability after release among interview participants

Note: The black line denotes time not incarcerated in prison or jail and under study; the gray line denotes time not incarcerated in prison or jail but not under study; the open circles are moves into institutions or institutional housing; and solid circles are moves into private residences.

little family support, little human capital, and no possibility for securing substantial government benefits, he seemed beyond worry, almost resigned to the future.

This resignation proved prescient. Over the three-year period following release, Randall applied for more than fifty minimum wage jobs, from Taco Bell to White Castle, from which he heard not one response. His monthly resources consisted of $200 in food stamps and the sporadic money he earned doing yard work, selling marijuana, or blood plasma. He bounced between problematic family residences, homeless shelters, and even homelessness—living for a few days in an abandoned building in the middle of a bitter cold Michigan winter. Six months after release, he described his desperate economic circumstances:

> It's hard as hell out here. But [if] I didn't have [my friend] A.B. and my sister, my PO [parole officer], I don't know where I'd be. Like I said I was going up in that vacant house. Man it's cold, windows broke out, I mean it's just freezing, dog barking all night next door, basement flooded, so you know the walls sweating and it's cold.... I used to wake up like at 4:00–5:00 in the morning, feet be so cold they'd be burning.... Try to go in there and try to get me something to drink and knock me out. I can't even do that. I wake up, and I'm still freezing. I ain't like that and then ... I got to walk around and debate if I'm going to knock [and anyone would] ... let me in.... [*Pause.*] That's how hard it is. That's exactly how hard it is.

Soon thereafter, Randall began drenching his sheets in sweat at night and passing blood through his urine. Because he had no health insurance, he simply ignored these symptoms, hoping they would pass. When he finally secured insurance through Medicaid, he was in the hospital for days: one of his kidneys had swollen to a dangerous level and was pressing against his spine. Although he could have qualified for insurance earlier, he had put off filing because he had no permanent residence to which the card could be mailed. Once he finally did get the card, he explained: "I carry this around with me all the time ... because I might get sick or something ... people might want to know who I am. I ain't no John Doe." Living so completely at the margins, he saw death as a real possibility. Life on the outside was for him even harder than life incarcerated. And, though he wanted to stay out, his nearly desperate situation made this goal very difficult to achieve.

Given the difficulty of landing a job, Randall and others returning home from prison simply cannot survive on a daily basis without significant family or government support. Cobbling together short-term residence with family and stays in homeless shelters and treatment facilities kept a roof over Randall's head for the most part but gave him neither a reprieve from financial stress nor a foundation on which to build.

While Randall's economic situation was dire, it was by no means exceptional. Results from our administrative data show relatively low rates of outright rooflessness or shelter use among formerly incarcerated individuals but very high rates of residential instability. We also find that the probability of a residential move decreases dramatically after the early weeks at a particular residence; 50 percent of the moves occurred within the first eight weeks. In other words, there is an inverse relation between housing tenure and the probability of a move; the longer a parolee lives in a residence, the less likely he or she will be to move from it. This means that instability begets instability. When a formerly incarcerated individual moves, he or she is put at heightened risk for another move (Herbert, Morenoff, and Harding 2015).

Why do formerly incarcerated individuals experience so much residential instability? Previous research shows that, in part, the challenge returning prisoners face in finding a place to live is a reflection of their personal economic circumstances, including poor work histories and poor credit histories. Many of the obstacles to successful prisoner reentry overlap with the obstacles facing the insecurely housed and homeless populations. Both populations are at risk for mental health problems (Beck and Maruschak 2001; Burgard, Seefeldt, and Zelner 2012; Lee, Tyler, and Wright 2010; Shaw 2004; Travis 2003) and substance abuse (Mumola 1999; Shlay and Rossi 1992; Visher and Travis 2003). Family support is associated with lower risks of housing insecurity (Burgard, Seefeldt, and Zelner 2012), homelessness (Bassuk et al. 1997), and recidivism (Nelson, Deess, and Allen 1999; Visher and Travis 2003). Formerly incarcerated individuals face great difficulty finding and maintaining employment (Bushway, Stoll, and Weiman 2007; Travis, Solomon, and Waul 2001; Uggen and Massoglia 2003; Visher and Travis 2003; Western, Kling, and Weiman 2001), and experiencing unemployment can be a precursor to housing insecurity (Burgard, Seefeldt, and Zelner 2012) and homelessness (Shlay and Rossi 1992).

Above and beyond these personal circumstances, however, returning prisoners face an additional set of institutional obstacles that make their housing security especially precarious (Geller and Curtis 2011; Metraux, Roman, and Cho 2008; Roman and Travis 2006). First, many private

landlords require applicants to disclose their criminal history and are reluctant to accept applications from those with felony convictions (Helfgott 1997; Holzer 1996; Thacher 2008). Aggravating an already difficult
economic situation, many parolees also face mounting fees for supervision, restitution, and child support (Alexander 2010), and their criminal
records preclude them from obtaining many types of public assistance,
public housing, and housing subsidies in most states (Geller and Curtis
2011; Petersilia 2003). Returning prisoners even face obstacles in seeking temporary shelter with friends or family members who live in public
housing. Under the US Department of Housing and Urban Development's
one-strike-and-you're-out policy (Donovan 2011), public housing tenants
can be evicted if any other household members or guests are involved in
drugs or other criminal activity on or off the premises, even without the
tenant's knowledge, which may make them reluctant to offer assistance to
someone with a criminal record.

   In order to understand the key sources of residential instability among
our qualitative participants, we analyzed participants' reasons for residential moves. Our data are consistent with the focus in the literature on
lack of economic resources as a key driver of residential instability,[4] but
they also revealed three other key sources of such instability: (1) conflicts
that prompted our participants to move out of a family member's home,
(2) substance abuse relapses that prompted moves out into housing more
conducive to regular drug use or into residential treatment, and (3) moves
and challenges finding housing related to community supervision. However, not all moves were precipitated by negative events. Some moves followed advances in economic independence that allowed participants to
establish their own households, often by coupling their own income with
that of a romantic partner.[5]

Family Conflict

Seven of our twenty-two participants experienced at least one residential
move that was the result of conflict with the family or friends with whom
they had been living. As we will see below, for those with few economic
resources to fall back on, maintaining connections to family and friends
can be an important buffer against hunger, homelessness, and housing
instability. Yet, when those relationships sour, residential instability can
result. Geoffrey, a forty-five-year-old white man with a long history of
cocaine use and drug-related crimes, provides an example of the role of
family conflict in generating residential mobility. When he entered our

study, he was being released from prison for the fourth time. In his case, his relationship with his longtime on-again, off-again girlfriend improved during his prison term, but relationships with his own family had long since frayed. Although he listed their home as his intended residence while on parole, his relationship with his parents was poor, owing to conflicts over his past drug use and involvement in the criminal justice system. He ended up moving in with his girlfriend, who owned a house in the suburbs of Detroit. Although he set to work making long-neglected repairs to the house, drawing on his skills as a carpenter and home remodeler, he was never able to find formal work. He lived with this girlfriend and her pregnant adult daughter for three months, until he was kicked out for hitting on the daughter.

This conflict put Geoffrey onto a trajectory of residential insecurity for about six months, ending with a bout of homelessness. After leaving his girlfriend's house, he had few other options. Because he had not told his parole officer he was living with the girlfriend, he could not move in with his parents without risking being put in custody for absconding and a parole violation. He managed to parlay his carpentry skills into some remodeling work in exchange for staying in the house he was remodeling. That provided him a residence for five months, but, when the work was done, he had nowhere else to go. A similar deal fell through after friends canceled their remodeling plans partway through. He turned to his siblings, from whom he had been long estranged, but got no support. Unable to access any formal services because he was still absconding, he was considering sleeping in a park: "You know that park down the street? That's what I was thinking about. It's warm . . . I could always pull up a blanket. Might get eaten up by bugs, I don't know. But there's a bathroom down there. I mean, I've never had to live this way in my life. Never, I swear to God I haven't. I've always made good money. I've always been able to take care of myself. I been taking care of myself since I was fourteen years old."

After he spent a week in the park, the girlfriend took Geoffrey back in, but her house was undergoing foreclosure, and they moved again, this time to an apartment. He then experienced a period of relative stability, living there for over a year and half.

Substance Abuse Relapse

Substance abuse was also a common cause of residential mobility. For those participants with serious substance abuse problems, relapse could prompt a period of living rough on the streets, in abandoned houses, or in cheap motels where they could engage in drug or alcohol use away from friends or family and easily purchase drugs nearby. Relapse could also trigger moves in and out of jail or treatment programs. Such residential mobility tended to be concentrated among fewer of our participants (about a quarter) but caused repeated disruptions in their housing stability and security. As we will see below, substance abuse also played a key role in preventing them from taking full advantage of the social support offered or available from family members. Stable housing and other material assistance such as food, clothes, and transportation provided by family members were not always enough to ensure social reintegration and avoidance of drugs and crime.

Kristine credited prison with providing her new clarity regarding the direction she wanted her life to take, including helping care for her now elderly and partially disabled mother and rebuilding her relationship with her adult daughter. Yet she also faced severe obstacles. Aside from the time she was pregnant, she spent her entire adult life fully consumed by meeting the demands of her addictions and moving in and out of jail and various drug rehabilitation programs. She has only a ninth-grade education, only a small amount of work experience as a waitress, and serious health problems, including severe back pain from a car accident and hepatitis C, which saps her energy. She believes she has an undiagnosed learning disability as she can barely read and forgets things easily. She also believes she may suffer from bipolar disorder and often finds herself feeling depressed. She wonders whether this is linked to the sexual abuse she experienced as a child, for which she never received treatment or therapy. She cannot legally drive again until she pays thousands of dollars in driver responsibility fees and her license is reinstated. Aside from her mother and daughter, all her adult relationships have been with other drug addicts and revolved around securing and using drugs.

Kristine moved in with her mother and daughter after release. This situation had the potential to provide her with a strong foundation on which to rebuild her life. Her mother had lived in the house for thirty-five years, and the house was located in a safe, working-class neighborhood in the suburbs. Kristine contributed her food stamps to the household, and that combined with her mother's income from social security and some light housekeeping work in the neighborhood was sufficient to keep the family afloat. Although her own medical problems prevented her from finding a job, Kristine did assist her mother with the informal housekeeping work. Unfortunately, her substance abuse proved to be the source of considerable residential instability. She moved at least twenty times during the period she participated in our study, rotating between her mother's house, jail or rehab mandated by her parole officer, and periods of intense drug use during which she lived on the streets, in drug houses, or in motels with fellow drug users. Two months after her release from prison, she described being depressed by her inability to get a job, her discomfort from her back pain, and missing her ex-boyfriend, who was still involved in drugs. She also experienced drug cravings. Her first relapse came about a month later and was spurred by a conflict with her daughter over the daughter's boyfriend. She returned to theft and prostitution from time to time to support her habit, which led to the periods of time in jail, and she failed multiple drug tests administered by her parole officer. When our study ended, she had just moved out of her mother's house again to enter a month of residential drug treatment mandated by her parole officer.

Community Correctional Supervision

The criminal justice system is also intimately connected to residential instability among formerly incarcerated individuals. In Kristine's case, arrests and brief periods in jail or mandated drug treatment led to residential instability that was a direct consequence of the criminal justice system's response to her continued involvement in drug use and petty crime. Yet the criminal justice system and parole supervision play a role in residential instability in other ways as well. Much of formerly incarcerated individuals' housing insecurity is linked to features of community supervision, including increased risk of arrests, intermediate sanctions, returns to prison, and absconding (Herbert, Morenoff, and Harding 2015).

First, the conditions of parole impose restrictions on where returning prisoners can live. For example, those convicted of a sex offense are usually restricted from moving near schools or day-care centers. Some parolees are also subject to electronic monitoring and thus must wear an ankle bracelet and live in a house with a working phone that can transmit data (via modem) to their parole officer (our administrative data indicate that about 8 percent of parolees are on electronic monitoring at release [Siegel 2014]). In some states (including Michigan), parole agents closely supervise parolees' living arrangements—often through home visits—and restrict them from living with others who have felony records and in any place where there are firearms or drugs on the premises. Restricted housing options can make finding stable permanent housing more difficult.

Second, prior research documents the way the intense surveillance of formerly incarcerated and wanted men leads to residential mobility in order to evade surveillance or arrest (Brayne 2014; Goffman 2014). Goffman illustrates the intense presence of law enforcement in the lives of wanted men in Philadelphia, where searches and seizures are commonplace. She shows how contact with family can put men on the run at risk of arrest and reincarceration as parole officers keep track of family members' residences and search there for individuals who have absconded. Recall how Geoffrey could not return to live with his parents once he absconded and also felt that he could not seek out homelessness services or health care owing to his absconding status. David had a similar experience. After he absconded from a drug treatment program at a halfway house, he could not live with his mother or siblings because his parole officer knew where they lived, so he moved in with his child's mother at an address unknown to law enforcement. Indeed, parole officers raided the home where his mother, brother, and sister-in-law lived in search of him.

Third, being on community supervision such as parole or probation subjects an individual to surveillance and monitoring of compliance with the conditions of parole; failure to follow these conditions may constitute a parole violation. Sometimes these behaviors are illegal, such as drug use or petty theft, and sometimes they are violations of the rules of parole, such as alcohol consumption, curfew violations, failure to report to one's parole officer, association with other parolees, or contact with crime victims. Often, a formal parole violation involves multiple infractions; the typical first violation in our Michigan administrative data is for two to three rule violations. The most common infractions involve failing to report to parole officers (73 percent), failing to attend or complete programming (61 percent), substance use (51 percent), living at unapproved residences (50 percent), violating curfew or other movement restrictions (49 percent), associating with other felons (29 percent), possessing weapons other than firearms (29 percent), and driving without permission or without a license (22 percent) (Siegel 2014). About 40 percent of parolees abscond at some point in the six years following their release from prison (Morenoff and Harding 2011).[6]

While parole violations can sometimes prompt a return to prison, less serious violations can result in brief spells in custody in so-called intermediate sanction facilities such as jails, residential treatment centers, and programs for technical rule violators (Harding, Morenoff, and Herbert 2013). Intermediate sanctions are often intended to stop such behavior from escalating to more serious offenses. For example, a parolee who fails to report to his parole officer and is suspected of using drugs may be sent to a residential drug treatment program or a technical rule violation center for a week or two in order to detox. Typically, a parolee will not receive such a sanction for a rule violation until he or she has either accumulated multiple infractions or displays behaviors consistent with prior crimes. Another common intermediate sanction is spending time in jail. This occurs when a parolee is arrested by the police for a minor crime and either serves a short jail sentence (e.g., ninety days) or has the charges dropped before prosecution. Parolees may also spend a few days in jail as an intermediate sanction at the behest of parole agents. Treatment programs can also be used as an intermediate sanction by parole officers. Seeking to evade such intermediate sanctions, parolees may move out of their registered residence and/or avoid locations where a parole officer might look for them.

Our estimates from our administrative data indicate that about a quarter of residential moves are generated by the criminal justice system in the form of entries to and exits from short-term custody for parole violations (Harding, Morenoff, and Herbert 2013). In addition, in almost a quarter of residential moves to intermediate sanctions or drug treatment facilities, we find that the individual does not move back to the home where he or she was living before the sanction or treatment. Thus, these moves (and/ or the behaviors that precipitated them) appear to affect important family relationships and social support. Apel (2016) shows that short jail stays interrupt residential romantic partnerships and, in the longer term, reduce the probability of future marriage (but not future cohabitation).

The case of Christopher—whose residential trajectory was heavily influenced by his involvement in the criminal justice system, in ways both good and bad—shows the interconnections between community supervision and residential instability. Including moves in and out of correctional housing, treatment programs, jails, and prison, he moved thirteen times during the three years we followed his experiences. On the positive side, a state program for reentering prisoners provided him with housing at times. For example, when he had nowhere else to parole to, the program put him in a hotel in downtown Ann Arbor for two weeks until he could secure a bed at the local homeless shelter. After he spent three weeks at the shelter and had no luck finding a job, his parole officer moved him to a Salvation Army employment program that provided food and housing in exchange for working part-time sorting donations and preparing them for sale. On the negative side, the state's responses to his addiction relapses and rule violations also played a role in his residential instability. After he was accused of stealing from the Salvation Army and forced to leave the program, which led to a three-week period of homelessness, the state program again put him up in a halfway house and quickly thereafter moved him to a residential substance abuse program. Yet, when he broke curfew rules there and was expelled from the program, he became an absconder and moved in with his girlfriend, Janice. Soon thereafter he relapsed. Again, the official response to his parole violations was swift. He was arrested for absconding, spending five weeks in jail and then sixty days in a custodial treatment program run by the Michigan Department of Corrections. After he was released, he returned to living with Janice in a house in Ann Arbor that they were renting from his father. Four weeks later he was imprisoned on a parole violation after a positive drug test was detected by his parole officer. He spent four months in prison before returning to live with Janice. His experiences illustrate how criminal justice system involvement can be both a product and a cause of residential instability, both of which are also linked to substance use and criminal activity.

Achieving Stability

Thus far we have documented the main causes of residential instability among formerly incarcerated individuals, including economic circumstances, family conflict, substance abuse, and the criminal justice system. Yet not all our participants experienced high levels of residential instability, and even those who did often had intermittent periods of stability as well. This raises the question of how formerly incarcerated individuals overcome the challenges to residential stability?

Not surprisingly, our analyses of the administrative data confirm that employment is a robust predictor of residential stability, but we also found family support to be critical. Those who are living with parents or romantic partners are less likely to move than average, and those who are living in their preprison residence are also less likely to move, an effect we interpret as stemming from living with otherwise stable family or friends. We approached the question of how returning citizens achieve residential stability by first analyzing our participants' trajectories of material hardship, categorizing them into four trajectories (continual hardship, survival and marginal stability, long-term stability, and upward mobility). We then compared those participants who achieved long-term stability to those

Trajectory	Name	Race	Gender	Age*	Months from Time of Release											
					3	6	9	12	15	18	21	24	27	30	33	36
Hardship	David	W	M	28												
	Henry	B	M	52												
	Christopher	W	M	38												
	Kristine	W	F	40												
	Lenora	B	F	51												
	Jada	B	F	31												
Survival	Craig	W	M	37												
	Morgan	W	M	33							Moved out of state					
	Lamar	B	M	43												
	Randall	B	M	32												
	Geoffrey	W	M	45												
	DeAngelo	B	M	27												
	Damian	B	M	71												
	Jane	W	F	47												
Stability	James	B	M	26												
	Jake	W	M	27					Moved out of state							
	Jocelyn	B	F	37												
	Jennifer	W	F	36												
Mobility	Leon	B	M	37												
	Daniel	W	M	32							Moved out of state					
	Paul	W	M	48												
	Michelle	W	F	22												

*Age at release

FIGURE 3.2. Postrelease trajectories of economic stability and security

Source: Harding, Wyse, et al. 2014.

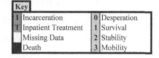

Key

I	Incarceration	0	Desperation
T	Inpatient Treatment	1	Survival
	Missing Data	2	Stability
	Death	3	Mobility

who struggled with continual and marginal stability to understand what set them apart (Harding, Wyse, et al. 2014). Figure 3.2 graphically illustrates these four trajectories and how they varied across participants.

This analysis revealed that family support was critical to long-term residential stability. Employment alone was insufficient, largely because wages were low and job insecurity was high. While this is consistent with the results from our administrative data, the qualitative data also showed the importance of public benefits for long-term residential stability. In short, only those participants who were able to couple family support with either sporadic employment or long-term public benefits were able to create a stable household for themselves in the long term.

Family Support

Family and romantic partners were the primary providers of housing and other forms of material support for our participants. This direct provision of material resources, or what might be termed *instrumental support*, has been defined as "the use of the relationship as a means to a goal" (Lin 1986, 20). Most commonly this came in the form of providing food and shelter, both immediately after release and in the longer term as well. All but four of the fifteen male participants lived with family or romantic partners immediately after their release, including romantic partners (four); parents (six); and siblings (one). Only one male participant (Lamar) remained independent throughout the study period (living with a brother only during the first week after his release). All but two of the seven female participants lived with family or romantic partners immediately after their release, including romantic partners (two) and parents (three). The remaining two female participants lived initially in institutional arrangements (a treatment program and an adult foster-care facility) and were later housed by family and a romantic partner. Family members also provided many other forms of material assistance, including transportation to look for work, parole meetings, treatment programs, and school, gifts of clothing, contributions to savings toward independent housing, assistance with completing job applications, and paying off legal fees and other debts.

Often such instrumental support came in exchange for caregiving of some sort, particularly in the early period after release. In some cases, caregiving was directly compensated care work for family members, who offered financial support in exchange for services such as cleaning and other household chores, babysitting, or caring for adults with serious health problems. Our participants engaged in various caretaking roles and responsibilities, ranging from routine household chores such as cooking and cleaning to acting as a full-time caretaker for a disabled adult and child. Indeed, caregiving and care work often proved to be the most straightforward way for our participants to find meaningful roles and responsibilities in their new households, given their difficulties in the labor market. Eight of the twenty-two participants assumed some sort of primary caretaker role, either for an adult (three) or for a child (five). An additional five engaged in some other sort of care work that provided monetary or in-kind compensation during their time in the study. Most study participants— even those not engaged directly in caregiving or care work—had personal health challenges (e.g., disability, illness, addiction) or lived with other family members who did.[7] As we will see below and in the next chapter, these caretaking responsibilities proved to be meaningful and fulfilling for most of our participants, but many also found themselves juggling their own needs along with those of household members, leading to a great deal of stress. We saw no clear racial or gender distinctions in care work, caregiving, or the experience of living with a family member with health-related challenges (but our small nonrandom sample precludes any sort of statistical analysis or strong conclusions in this regard). Yet, as we will see in the next chapter, care work and caregiving often had different implications for men and women. These roles seemed to be a source of stress and frustration for the men, who felt that they were taking on these roles largely because they did not have full-time employment.

In some cases, care work became a form of informal employment. For example, Henry moved in with his fiancée (who was unable to work owing to a disability), her eleven-year-old daughter, and her eighteen-year-old son (who suffered from cerebral palsy). Although he found a few days of informal work as a handyman, he struggled to contribute to the household and hoped to become certified by the state to provide state-paid care for his fiancée's son. In the meantime, he provided care for free, saving his fiancée $150 a week. Another example comes from Kristine. Her mother was able to cover household expenses with social security, food stamps, and some informal cleaning work. When Kristine was unable to find work of her own after release, in part due to her own health problems (back pain from a car accident, hepatitis C, and depression), she took over her mother's work, cleaning the homes of a neighbor and her sister for pay.

Whether in exchange for care work or not, family support is central to the material well-being of formerly incarcerated individuals. Its role is illustrated by comparing the experiences of Lamar and DeAngelo. Lamar is a single African American man in his forties with no children who served two prison terms for armed robbery. A high school graduate raised in a foster family, he got involved in the party scene in his late teens and early twenties and eventually committed multiple armed robberies. At our first interview, he was being paroled for the third time. On release, he lived for a week with his foster brother before moving to the city's homeless shelter. Though his foster family was emotionally supportive, this short period of housing assistance was the primary material resource they offered during his transition. Absent additional resources, Lamar relied heavily on a soup kitchen and food stamps for food and a homeless shelter for housing while he pursued a dogged strategy of job application. He estimates that he applied for over two hundred jobs in the months after release. His persistence paid off with two part-time jobs, one stocking shelves and another in a fast-food restaurant. With these new sources of income and help from the state's prisoner reentry program, he secured a subsidized room in a boarding house. Meanwhile, he also continued to party and use cocaine on the weekends, carefully timing his use to avoid detection by his parole officer. Soon thereafter he landed a full-time job as a line cook but then

lost it after a conflict with the manager. Not long before his room subsidy
was set to run out, he got a job as a taxi driver, and, with this new income,
meager savings, and some help from the reentry program, he secured his
own apartment.

At this point, Lamar had, by his own admission, become a little too
comfortable with his new economic stability and success on parole and
began to make mistakes. He skipped appointments with his parole officer
when they coincided with the most lucrative taxi shifts, bought some stolen
money orders from a neighbor for a fraction of their face value, and was
accused by his sister-in-law of stealing and pawning jewelry (though this
later turned out to be a misunderstanding). This was enough to result in
another parole violation, and he was returned to prison for almost a year.
All the progress he had made toward economic stability and all the possessions he had accumulated were lost when he was arrested and returned
to prison. Almost two years after his last parole, he was paroled again,
returning to a rooming house for parolees, but this time entering a reces-
sionary economy. Once more deploying his strategy of applying for every
job he could, he eventually secured a food service job through a temp service and rented a small apartment of his own but lost the apartment when
the job failed to become permanent. Over three years after we first met
him, Lamar moved back to the homeless shelter. He had little to fall back
on besides his own tenacity in searching out employment and social services. Because these were often short-term, he was frequently left at risk
of homelessness.

In contrast, DeAngelo was able to rely heavily on the support of romantic partners, who provided housing, food, and other forms of assistance.
Living with his girlfriend, he felt the security of a roof over his head and
food to eat, at least for the time being. This home permitted him a period
of readjustment to life outside prison and gave him the time needed to
secure health insurance through a county program, begin treatment for
his mental health problems and addiction, and look for a job that paid a
living wage. His girlfriend also shuttled him to appointments and job interviews because he had lost his license following his drunk-driving conviction. About three months after his release, he revealed that the negative characteristics of his girlfriend and the relationship were beginning to
outweigh the benefits, which eventually led him to leave the house and the
relationship, at least for a time. The relationship had frayed; his girlfriend
had her own mental health problems, and the two of them were constantly
fighting. Although the breakup occurred relatively quickly, the relation-

ship nonetheless had important material consequences for him; because he had been able to save money during his stay, he was able to get first a subsidized room in a boardinghouse and then his own apartment.

Soon thereafter, DeAngelo began taking courses in auto body repair, and a new romantic partner moved in to his apartment. She had her own public benefits and cared both for her own child and for DeAngelo's son. His employment did not last long after he realized that the household could get by on his girlfriend's benefits and his financial aid. About nine months after his release from prison, he was arrested again, this time for driving without a license, and was returned to prison for a technical violation.

DeAngelo served another six months in prison and, like Lamar, lost everything he owned when the landlord emptied his apartment for non-payment of rent. When he was paroled, he went immediately to another subsidized apartment provided by the state reentry program. He quickly reconnected with the first girlfriend, who in the meantime had begun dancing at a club and had established her own household. She drove him to appointments and interviews on her days off and helped him with groceries. When his time in the subsidized apartment was up, he moved in with this girlfriend and his son. The girlfriend quit her job, applied for and received supplemental security income (SSI), and helped care for DeAngelo's son. The couple made ends meet with her SSI benefits and help from her family, supplemented by some income DeAngelo made by cutting hair and doing odd jobs. Four months later he found another restaurant job, this time as a line cook at a restaurant two bus rides from home. Then he broke up with his girlfriend again. Without her support, he lost his access to reliable transportation and a babysitter, and a few months later he lost his job after his schedule changed and he could not get to work on Sundays on the bus or work in the evenings, as his job demanded, because he needed to care for his son. He has since enrolled in a culinary class while his son is in school and makes ends meet by selling beauty products, cutting hair, and doing odd jobs. He is behind on bills but managing to make rent every month, at least for now.

While the comparison between the experiences of Lamar and DeAngelo demonstrates the importance of social support, social support was not always sufficient for participants to achieve economic stability in the long term. Whether it could be leveraged into a long-term trajectory of economic stability was dependent on the quality of resources the family could offer as well as the characteristics of the family. While some families offered access to extensive job networks and material resources, for instance, other families had members who were themselves out of work and struggling financially. Further, some family members' own emotional disorders or addictions meant that the support they offered could pose a danger to our participants' own sobriety or emotional stability.

A small number of participants had families able to provide instrumental support that went beyond helping meet basic needs such as food, housing, and transportation to include assistance with finding more stable jobs and building careers. Only more advantaged families were able to provide such assistance, which included loaning or gifting significant amounts of money to help cover the costs of schooling or job training and leveraging their own social networks to help their loved one secure a job that could provide stable employment with a living wage and prospects for upward mobility. One example is James, who relied heavily on social support, primarily from his mother, but also from siblings and extended family. A chief source of support was the housing and transportation provided by his mother, who was on disability, and eventually a romantic partner with whom he later lived and split rent. Moreover, unlike many of our participants, he received support in establishing a career as a barber. Prior to release, he stated that he had tentative plans to go to barber school. Multiple family members served as role models for this career path, including a brother, a stepbrother, and cousins who were all barbers (including one cousin who owned a barbershop). Further, James reported that his brother provided advice on this career and that his sister paid for his barber apprentice permit and financial aid application fees to help him attend barber school.

While James struggled to find any work during the study period outside barbering (receiving no guidance in this job seeking), he started informally engaging in barbering at his mother's house and then transitioned to working at a barbershop two months after his release. Not long after, he began barber school, but he quickly dropped out to work more hours to earn more money, saying he intended to continue his formal training in the future. He returned to work at the barbershop where he had originally started and built up a clientele. Not long after, he moved in with his girlfriend. Through the instrumental support he received from family, he was able to gain and maintain stable employment that then helped him become economically independent. Sadly, James was killed in a home invasion only nine months later.

Public Benefits

For formerly incarcerated individuals released into the community with no job, no savings, and few resources, public benefits would seem to be an important way for them to meet their material needs. Yet substantial barriers exist to their access to these benefits. First, cash assistance to the poor is increasingly tied to participation in the labor market. Following the 1996 reform, welfare became subject to work requirements and time limits (Danziger 2010). Currently, the largest federal cash-assistance program targeting the poor is the earned income tax credit, a program that supplements the income of *working* poor families through the tax system (Grieger and Wyse 2013). The Supplemental Nutrition Assistance Program (SNAP), that is, food stamps, remains an important exception, providing benefits to over 45 million people regardless of labor force participation (US Department of Agriculture 2018). Second, those with a felony conviction also face restrictions on their access to some benefits, such as housing, food stamps and financial aid (Demleitner 2002; Freudenberg et al. 2005; Godsoe 1998; Pinard 2010; Rubinstein and Mukamal 2002; Travis 2005). The situation in Michigan specifically is somewhat better, with no limitations placed on the receipt of welfare or food stamps, although access to public housing may be restricted.

Reflecting the limited pool of benefits available, particularly for men, of the fifteen male participants, only one was supported primarily by public benefits (Damian, who was elderly and received SSI). Eight of the male participants were supported in part by public benefits received by romantic partners and family, and at least nine received some food assistance via SNAP or housing and transportation resources, which were provided to some participants through the state prisoner reentry program. All seven female participants received some resources through public assistance. Two gained support in part through family members' public benefits; three relied predominantly on their own public assistance—SSI and Temporary Assistance for Needy Families (TANF)—and six received food assistance or housing and transportation resources. The two receiving TANF and housing assistance both lived with their young children.

The significant role that public benefits can play in residential stability can be seen in the comparison between Jennifer and Lenora. Jennifer initially relied heavily on her sisters for material support, but later public benefits came to play a crucial role as well. Established in her own home, she regained custody of her young son, who brought in $125 in food stamps

monthly, not to mention the SSI payments he received on behalf of his
father, who suffered from rheumatoid arthritis. These benefits provided
a source of economic stability while Jennifer sought out her own government benefits: applying for Medicaid, SSI, food stamps and TANF. Her
TANF and food stamp award granted her an additional $600 per month.
Soon after, she was approved for SSI, both for illiteracy and for the chronic
injuries she had sustained as a result of a car accident. She and her son
together received roughly $1,100 monthly in government benefits that her
sisters and her girlfriend supplemented occasionally with money or food
stamps as needed. With the help of a great deal of family support, substantial government benefits, and a strong commitment to sobriety, Jennifer
made it, attaining economic stability (albeit at a level below the poverty
line), and never relapsing or committing another crime.[8]

In contrast to Jennifer, Lenora was unable to establish substantial long-
term benefits and, thus, never stabilized, despite the fact that she had an
extensive employment history and was resourceful, motivated, and en-
ergetic. On release, she brought this energy and enthusiasm to her job
search as well as to her search for charitable and government benefits. She
first landed in a halfway house in Detroit, and for four months the state's
prisoner reentry initiative covered food and rent. At the halfway house,
she and the other residents were required to be out of the house for the
entire day, searching for jobs. She stopped by a university in Detroit and
discovered that she qualified for financial aid. She signed up, believing that
financial aid could be her ticket out, as discussed previously.

Over the following months Lenora took advantage of job skills training
at Goodwill Industries, free clothing at a local charity, a short-term position subsidized by the reentry initiative, and supports and services offered
by a number of other Detroit-area charities. Yet her frustration at not
being able to get a full-time, permanent job led to a several-month bout
of relapse and retail fraud that ended when she was assigned to inpatient
drug treatment. Both the relapse and the inpatient residence disrupted her
education plans, compromising her chance for additional loans and grants.
Following her completion of the inpatient treatment program, she stayed
on as a resident trainee for four months, earning $75 a week plus room
and board. She hoped to be hired on to a permanent position. She was
not and thereafter moved in with her nephew, paying $300 in rent a month,
and subsisting on food stamps and sporadic temporary employment. The
last we saw of Lenora, her nephew's house was being foreclosed on, and
she was planning to move, possibly into a homeless shelter. She admitted

that her stress at having no income aside from food stamps and the threat of losing her housing had led her back to drinking and that drinking triggered thoughts of stealing. Despite her resourcefulness—accessing a half dozen charitable organizations, employment support, transitional housing services, and financial aid for education—the short-term nature of each of these supports never provided her with economic security. Each employment or housing opportunity came with a time limit, after which she had to struggle again to meet her basic needs. Though she sought out public benefits, she was, unlike Jennifer, never eligible for those that provided longer-term stability.

The comparison between Jennifer and Lenora reveals the importance of substantial public benefits for residential stability among formerly incarcerated individuals who struggle with employment. While many of our participants pursued long-term benefits such as SSI, only a few were able to secure them. Nominal or short-term benefits never served as a stepping-stone to residential stability through sustained economic security. And, while substantial benefits provided an economic foundation on which to stand, they were not sufficient to bring participants above the poverty line.

The New Welfare?

When family support was absent or insufficient and public benefits unavailable, our participants also turned to other programs to help them make ends meet and maintain a stable household or living arrangement. Given the severely restricted benefit pool to which many of our participants had access, many turned to government aid programs not traditionally considered income-support programs for the poor. In particular, SSI—an income-support program intended for those with limited financial resources whose physical or mental disability prevents them from working—and financial aid for education were pursued as a way to meet basic material needs (on the use education loans as a survival strategy among the poor more generally, see Seefeldt [2015]). Such was the case for DeAngelo, who decided to apply for SSI after splitting up with his girlfriend and finding himself struggling to make ends meet; he hoped SSI could support him until he was able to find a job: "I'm in therapy now and they got me on medicines again. . . . And my work history gap is a lot longer. . . . Hopefully that'll hold me over till I can find something. I don't know how long it's gonna be till I can find a job, so. . . ." Although DeAngelo did have mental health problems, he was dealing with them effectively with medication. And at the point that he had applied for SSI, nearly three years after his initial release from prison, he had already worked in three different restaurants full-time.

Although six of our participants applied for SSI (and even more talked about the possibility of applying without following through), only three ended up receiving it. Of these, Jocelyn had serious health problems that precluded employment, and Jennifer was barely literate—although she did want to work and had pursued employment at release, she was never successful. Finally, seventy-one-year-old Damian was eligible owing to his age. Currently averaging $1,166 per month for a single person, SSI disability benefits provide a low level of material subsistence but nonetheless something of an economic foundation (Social Security Administration 2016).

Similarly, although clearly not designed as an antipoverty program, financial aid for education was also turned to by participants unable to secure employment as a way to make ends meet. Eleven of our participants applied for Pell Grants and Stafford Loans, and, though many were enthusiastic about returning to school, a primary motivation was often the up-front monetary award. Such was the case for Damian, enrolled in an introductory sociology course, and Jocelyn, taking an online business administration course. Both received SSI and talked of using their educations to enhance their career prospects. Paid in a lump sum, financial aid represented a windfall for our participants, who felt lucky to secure even part-time work at the minimum wage.

Such was the case with Lenora, who was determined to utilize all available resources to put herself on a more positive trajectory. Despite the fact that she was just beginning her reentry process and actively struggling to maintain sobriety and secure stable housing and employment, she prioritized enrolling in a course (ironically, Introductory Criminal Justice) for the rewards school attendance offered. At an interview just one month following her release from prison, she explained why she was eager to get back to school: "I'm gonna try to see if I can start now, Jessica, 'cause you know they give you money when you go to school. And then that's my ticket outta here. [Buy] a house, furnish it. And, you know, get me a little vehicle or whatever." For Lenora, financial aid was a pathway out of the grinding poverty and homelessness she could not seem to escape.

While Lenora was ultimately able to complete her course, she also absconded, returned to stealing at Macy's, relapsed, and was sent back to detox and drug treatment. Far from the ticket out she had hoped for, school was, she later realized, simply one more factor that had contributed to the feeling of being overwhelmed to which she attributed her relapse. Further, because she was no longer enrolled in school, she would soon have to begin paying back her loan, with interest.

Indeed, the long-term implications of student loan debt were already being felt by Leon, whose cash flow was substantially squeezed by a $4,000 student loan in default. Each month he faced a $395 payment ($180 toward his loan and an accompanying $215 fee) that represented about a third of his monthly take-home pay. Given the impossibility of meeting these obligations, he did his best to be "proactive": "I play the lottery once a week, the Megamillion. I put two dollars on it every week. . . . For me, everything's in God's hands. . . . If you aren't proactive, . . . it's not gonna fall in your lap. It is in God's hands, but you have to do something yourself." Since he clearly had no way to make the monthly payments required to clear up his lingering debt, playing the lottery each week gave him hope that he might eventually get out from under the burden.

In the end, education loans turned out to be more of temporary income support than a pathway to long-term upward mobility in the labor market. They were a way to supplement income when family support, earnings, or income from other programs was irregular or insufficient. Whether participants returned to school intending to enhance their employment prospects, for short-term financial gain, or for some combination of the two, most faced numerous barriers to completing their courses. From ongoing criminal offending and return to prison or jail, relapse, or a disrupted schedule brought on by a new job or parole condition, their lives were in substantial flux, and courses could easily fall by the wayside. Poorly suited as an income-support program, financial aid received by our participants rarely seemed to translate into education or career advancement.

Conclusion

Finding a place to call home proved to be an elusive goal for many of our participants, even as they endeavored to realize their plans to rebuild family relationships and care for loved ones, both children and adults. Many returning citizens struggle mightily with meeting their most basic material needs for food and shelter and with achieving the residential stability that can serve as a stable foundation on which to build a postprison life. Typically unable to return to preprison households, and with bleak prospects in the labor market, their ability to build this foundation is challenged by family conflict, substance use relapse, meager or unavailable public benefits, and the restrictions and surveillance of community supervision. As a result, social and material support from family and romantic partners is critical to establishing economic stability and a place to call home. In the next chapter, we continue our examination of family life after prison by addressing the complex and often-countervailing roles of families in social reintegration more broadly defined, turning to their effects on social and emotional well-being as well as substance abuse and involvement in criminal activity.

CHAPTER FOUR

Families and Reintegration

Jane sat at a table amid a group of other inmates, laughing away. She seemed to be quite comfortable in the prison setting, and in some ways she was, having been imprisoned four times and jailed sixteen. Yet she felt certain that this time was going to be different. As she explained: "This time, I have something to go back to." Prior to her most recent incarceration she had married Sid, a widower with two teenage children. She felt that having a family and a home to return to would make all the difference, for, were she to slide back into drug use and the crime that so often followed, she was certain to lose it all. It would also ease the reentry transition—with her husband's financial support and a home to return to, she would not need to begin her job search right away. Rather, she planned to make her home her "oasis," slowly adjusting to life on the outside and "that wife role" that she had never filled before. Her husband would thus play a key role in her transition, supporting her both emotionally and financially until she felt ready to reemerge into the world of work (and possible temptations stemming from associations, money, and place). At our first postprison interview, she explained that her relationship with her husband kept her clean and sober: "It's very good [the marriage] because I'm doing the right things, and it makes him happy. And, when he's happy, I'm happy."

Yet, as was so often the case with the hopes voiced by our participants within prison walls before their release, this vision proved to be overly optimistic. While Sid had recently secured a job as a welder working on the factory line, he had also sold drugs on the side for years—including the crack and heroin Jane was viciously addicted to—as a financial supplement. Indeed, Jane later revealed that the two had first met when he ventured into the suburbs to sell drugs to her. And, though he had managed to kick his own crack addiction years previously, he continued to abuse alcohol. Further, the teenage children who completed the family unit had serious troubles of their own. Sid's son was currently incarcerated in a juvenile facility, and his daughter would attempt suicide during the course of the study.

Jane would soon find that, although her new family role would provide a motivation to stay clean, it would also present both opportunities and triggers for a return to drug use and crime. At first, her husband strongly encouraged her sobriety, but he continued to drink sporadically. Over the months that followed, Sid's hours at work were cut back again and again, and to replace this lost income he increased his drug selling and spent more and more time away from home. He also began drinking more and more. Seven months after her release from prison Jane revealed that she had relapsed just days previously, using the drugs that her husband kept easily accessible in a bedroom closet. He kept them there believing that, because he had been able to kick his drug habit with relatively little effort in the past, she should similarly be able to master her cravings. Following this relapse, he stopped allowing her to use the family car, gave her less spending money, and threatened to cut off her cell phone. He also monitored her daily activities by calling to check on her multiple times each day.

Over the months that followed, Jane's and Sid's addictions began to feed off one another, spiraling out of control. A little over a year after she was released, whispering and crying quietly, Jane revealed that the night previously Sid had suggested that she take part in a threesome with two of his customers for just $40. She was humiliated that her husband would suggest such a thing and for such a small sum. Later, backtracking, he claimed that he was just trying to "geek them up." Jane responded: "Well, you could have geeked 'em up about another girl . . . not your wife, not the love of your life!" The man who had once represented the chance for family and the conventional identity that she longed for had turned the relationship into just another trick.

Jane recognized that her relationship had the potential to both help and hurt her: "My husband, it's kind of like [*pauses*] we hold each other up or we pull each other down together. And we're in that pull-down phase." She elaborated: "He'll start drinking, and then that makes me want to smoke crack, and then if he's not drinking and then I want to smoke crack, you know, and he's trying to get his brain on the right track, and here I come. And, 'Oh, well, fuck it.' And so we both end up doing it, you know, bouncing off each other in our addictions and stuff." Despite the ups and downs the relationship would suffer over the months that followed, in our final interview more than three years after her initial release from prison, the two had been clean and sober for two months and were holding fast, trying to support each other in sobriety.

On the other end of the spectrum was Henry. Not only did he not have the family financial support to return to that Jane did; the demands of providing for his family financially had motivated his crimes in the past. As he explained: "Work got kind of slow, and I needed more money close to the holiday." However, he also admitted that "drugs had something to do with it." Partnering with a friend who ran a regular car theft racket, he decided to "move some cars" and was arrested driving a stolen car worth about $200.

At release he worried about how he would be able support his family without relying on the criminal means he had in the past. His fiancée, Tammy, was suffering from serious health problems and required surgery; he feared she would never work again. The two also provided for two teenagers, including Tammy's son, whose cerebral palsy required extensive care. They also resided in a dangerous neighborhood with few employment prospects and where drugs were commonly sold and used. The asphalt plants where Henry had worked in the past had closed, relocating to suburbs that were difficult to access without a car, which he did not have. He knew that it would take time to secure a job, but he also feared that food stamps and the social security income on which the family would be subsisting entirely would prove insufficient to cover basic needs. As a result, while he believed that he would "be crazy" to go back to stealing cars, he also did not rule out crime as an option of last resort. On the other hand, Tammy provided him with a place to live and a welcoming household, one where he was both needed and supported.

In short, although both Jane and Henry cited their relationships as a primary motivation for criminal abstention in early interviews, characteristics of their partners and the realities of their relationship dynamics tempered these relationships' capacity to play that role. For Jane and Henry, as for most of our participants, family relationships were linked with material, social, and emotional well-being, reintegration, and desistance from crime in ways both complex and countervailing. While our participants recognized that family relationships could encourage as well as discourage their criminal behaviors, for returning citizens who were flat broke and otherwise socially isolated, staying out of relationships and away from family was often not a real option. Since, as we saw in the previous chapter, they had severed ties with criminally involved friends or associates, romantic partners and other family members were often our participants' only source of material and emotional support. Family relationships also proved to be key sources of identity construction.

In this chapter, we explore the role of family relationships in the reintegration of returning citizens. Romantic partners, children, siblings, parents, and other family members are important sources of material support, informal social control, and emotional support. They provide food, clothing, housing, and transportation. They monitor potentially risky behavior like staying out late at night or spending too much time with peers, provide routines that encourage good behaviors like spending time with children and family, and motivate efforts to stay sober and find employment. Especially for our male participants, family members provide a sympathetic ear when stressful events arise and emotional support that can help participants weather daily frustrations. However, these same relationships often also ease the path back toward substance abuse or crime. They create role strain and motivation for crime when formerly incarcerated people struggle to fulfill family role obligations, particularly the obligation to play the provider role and bring money into the household. They provide opportunities to use drugs or reengage in criminal behavior and in some rare cases actually actively coerced participants into new criminal activity. They serve as sources of conflict and emotional stress that can lead to a return to the poor coping strategies of the past, particularly substance abuse. Thus, relationships with family members are critical social contexts that affect the process of reintegration after release from prison.

Romantic Relationships after Prison

Those looking forward to returning to stable family relationships on prison release recognized how fortunate they were in this respect. For the material support that partners and families provided allowed these participants crucial breathing room to find the right job, rather than simply settling for the first possible opportunity, and the freedom to adjust slowly to life on the outside. Further, families provided emotional support that took the edge off this stressful transition. As Paul, married twenty-seven years, explained, not only had his wife supported him "emotionally, financially, spiritually, and every other way that's possible . . . every step of the way," but, after his release, her lucrative job in the auto industry also freed him to return to school full-time. He recognized how different his situation was than that of most formerly incarcerated individuals: "I'm a very fortunate guy, and I . . . it's not lost on me that I am." His wife had no criminal or addiction history, was fully employed in a lucrative position, and had no significant personal challenges. In these respects, both she and the relationship were exceptional among those to which our participants returned.

However, prosocial relationships with family members were not universal as family had previously played roles in introducing our participants to drug use, as Jennifer's example illustrates. For those leaving prison without such strong, prosocial family attachments, the story was quite different. In these cases, participants were quick to recognize the substantial role that romantic partnerships and other family relationships had played in their past offending, often through pathways linked with substance abuse. Some, like Jennifer, felt that former partners had enabled their drug use in the past. She explained that her former fiancé "fully supported" her in her drug addiction. For others, past partners had essentially been partners in crime. This had been the case for Christopher, who explained that past relationships "always turn out to be a bit partying, you know, turns into a big drug fest." For him, relationships and the criminal lifestyle "go hand in hand."

For others, not just drug use but criminal offending had been both mirrored and validated by their romantic partners or family members. As Lamar told us: "There was times when I was in relationships with people who liked ripping and running the streets and was very street oriented, so they didn't care about me doing crime, so that made it a lot easier because it wasn't like I had to hide anything. Then I can just come home, and she'll know already that I ain't got no job, so she'll be like, 'Well, where you get all this money from?' And I can just be like, 'Well, I went and robbed.'" He recognized that relationships formed with such street-oriented partners had encouraged his criminal actions in the past. While such pairings were more common among our female participants, they also characterized some relationships formed by our male participants. Recall that Randall described being drawn into drug selling by a cousin who lured him away from a low-wage but steady job with the lure of fast money, teaching him the basics, and helping him get started.

Others worried about the emotional effects relationships could have. Consider the recently divorced twenty-seven-year-old Jake, who was released from his second term in prison after serving three years for drunk driving. He explained: "The biggest trigger for relapse would be her [his ex-wife]. . . . She has a good way of fucking up my feelings." Our participants expressed the fear that forming new relationships or becoming entangled in old ones would present stress and emotional challenges they were ill prepared to weather. Damian explained: "[Women] are a hindrance. . . . I don't need extra problems." Faced as he was with tremendous challenges on release, searching out a relationship was the last thing on his mind. As we will see below, he also worried about reconnecting with his adult children, who had problems of their own, including drug addictions, that might entangle him or distract him from his own goals.

Overall, however, participants were most wary of romantic relationships, preferring to rely on parents, siblings, children, or other family members first if at all possible. While many of the reasons men and women voiced for remaining single were shared, some were gender specific. For instance, some men planned to avoid relationships because their dire financial state meant that they would be unable to be the kind of partner they envisioned and were comfortable being. Lamar, explained why he has no interest in a serious relationship: "Have you ever been in a relationship and been the broke party? It doesn't make a good relationship where it's difficult for one to reciprocate. So let's say if I'm unemployed, I'm broke, and you have someone who has finances, and it's like they're giving, and I'll just say for me, I don't feel comfortable not being able to reciprocate." While he describes this concern as emanating out of his own role expectations, he added that some partners could also pressure men to fulfill the provider role, reinforcing the stress of relationship involvement. Or as Craig, a thirty-seven-year-old white man imprisoned for drunk driving and fleeing police after an accident involving injury, described: "What the hell kind of boyfriend could I be anyways right now? . . . Without . . . money and a car and, I mean, I don't have a job." The notion that one must first achieve a particular financial status prior to entering a relationship is reminiscent of Liebow's account of why so many of the men he encountered on a Washington, DC, street corner opted out of marriage more than fifty years ago. As he described: "Marriage is an occasion of failure. To stay married is to live with your failure, to be confronted by it day in and day out. It is to live in a world whose standards of manliness are forever beyond one's reach" (Liebow 1967, 87). Men felt that avoiding relationships would protect them from the feelings of failure that would arise were they unable to fulfill their own role expectations. As we will describe later in the chapter, such feelings did arise for some men once involved in relationships and could initiate a cascade of risky decisions.

Women, too, voiced a unique motivation to remain single, a belief that seemed to stem directly from lessons learned either within drug treatment programs or criminal justice supervision (Wyse 2013). These participants described a sense of self or identity that was simply too weak to be successful in a relationship. Often employing identical language lifted directly from treatment programs to describe this motivation, they explained that they needed to focus on themselves at release, taking the time needed to learn who they were clean and sober before diving into a relationship, which had the potential to rob them of their budding sense of self. As Kristine explained: "Right now it's just about me getting myself together, getting back to know me and getting with my family. I'm in no hurry for no relationship." After all, she continued: "I don't even have a relationship with myself!"

For these reasons, most of our participants were wary of forming new romantic attachments soon after release, instead planning to go it alone or rely on parents, children, or siblings. Rather than jumping into relationships, most hoped to establish themselves before starting a new relationship, whether that meant a substantial period of clean time, securing a new job, or simply waiting patiently until the right partner came along. Lamar eloquently voiced the rationale behind this strategy: "I'm just going to be cautious and take my time and, you know, let the right apple fall into my basket. I'll walk around this apple tree and just walk around with an empty basket. And when that ... when that apple falls, that right apple falls, it'll ... it won't be bitter and I won't have ... I won't catch a worm when I bite it." Rather than jumping into a relationship with the first woman who came along, he would have patience and wait for a "good woman," one who was supportive of his desistance goals.

Yet many participants became involved again with former partners they vowed to stay away from, broke up with partners they expected to remain involved with, and started relationships with new partners after detailing the threat such an action might pose for their reentry. Such was the case for Christopher, who, when asked whether he hoped to have a family in the future, professed in his first in-prison interview: "Even the thought of it is too much." However, only three months later he had initiated a serious relationship with a woman who was the mother of five children. While it is difficult to pinpoint why so many participants changed course, both emotional and material motivations seemed to underlie the decision. The most significant reason was simple: the universal human desire for companionship overcame any worries about relationships' potential negative effects. The need for material support and housing played a role as well.

Partners, Families, and Informal Social Control

The caution with which many of our participants approached romantic relationships—and in some cases family relationships—reflected the complex and diverse experiences those relationships had posed in the past. While in some cases, like Paul's, family relationships represented a material and emotional safety net, in others past relationships had initiated a cycle of addiction and crime that participants hoped desperately to avoid in the future. This complexity has received surprisingly little attention in the larger literature on relationships and criminal offending and desistance, which has focused rather narrowly on the power of a strong bond to a conventional romantic partner, particularly the power of a marriage to a law-abiding wife, to promote the desistance of a man with a criminal history.

An impressive body of research has emerged to support the finding that men who enter into marriages characterized by high levels of attachment are more likely to cease or reduce their participation in criminal activity (Laub and Sampson 2003; Sampson and Laub 1995; Sampson, Laub, and Wimer 2006). Much of this research was sparked by Sampson and Laub's analysis of a cohort of men who were first selected for study by the Gluecks in 1940 when they were adolescents living in Boston (Glueck and Glueck 1950). The desistance implications of marriage are understood to occur via processes of informal social control through four primary pathways (Sampson, Laub, and Wimer 2006). First, marriage increases the potential cost of crime because criminal activity may threaten the bond of attachment and lead to its dissolution (Hirschi 1969; Sampson and Laub 1995). Second, it may keep people away from situations and social relationships that present criminal opportunities and influence, the so-called routine activities explanation (Cohen and Felson 1979; Osgood et al. 1996; Warr 1998). Third, it provides structure and supervision, particularly when the partner expects the individual to have a legitimate job, contribute income, support the household, and avoid activities that might threaten the family's economic stability. Fourth, it can provide both partners with identities that are inconsistent with criminal behavior. Marriage may change the way people see themselves, their responsibilities, and their relationships with others, strengthening the ability of conventional norms to govern behavior, lest criminal activity conflict with role expectations, such as that of the provider.

Despite the crucial importance of this finding, the prevalence of marriage itself continues to decline, especially among people who have committed criminal offenses or been incarcerated. For example, the rate of marriage among incarcerated men is only half that of nonincarcerated men (Western 2007), and nearly half of incarcerated women have never married (Greenfeld and Snell 1999). Moreover, studies of formerly incarcerated individuals have found high rates of involvement in cohabitation or other nonmarital romantic relationships (Giordano, Cernkovich, and Rudolph 2002; Leverentz 2006). Nonmarital childbearing has also risen to 40 percent of all births among the population at large ("Unmarried Childbearing" 2016) and is likely to be higher among the formerly incarcerated. In stark contrast, more than three-quarters of the men in the sample selected by the Gluecks in 1948 and later followed up by Sampson and Laub were married by age thirty-one (Glueck and Glueck 1968).

Reflecting these larger trends in marriage and cohabitation, only two of our twenty-two participants were married at our first, in-prison interview. In spite of the marriage rate in our sample, many of our participants became quickly, and sometimes seriously, involved in relationships over the course of the study, and we found that these relationships, too, could play a crucial role in returning citizens' reintegration processes (Wyse, Harding, and Morenoff 2014). Such a finding is in line with recent ethnographic work on the importance of intense but fleeting disposable ties in the survival strategies of the urban poor (Desmond 2012). It seems that, given the dearth of resources, attachments, and identities to which many formerly incarcerated individuals have access, romantic and family relationships of even the most tenuous sort may prove deeply influential.

We draw on the theoretical concepts outlined above, augmented with other criminological theories, to describe the processes and mechanisms through which not only romantic partners but families more generally may affect reintegration outcomes. Table 4.1 lists the family processes that are, we argue, most critical to prisoner reintegration and categorizes them on the basis of the theoretical pathways through which they are connected to reintegration outcomes: by affecting material circumstances, informal social control, or emotional support or stress.

It is important to note that most, if not all, family relationships generate a mix of both positive and negative influences on reintegration. For example, even the most emotionally supportive relationship can at times create emotional stress, and provision of material support for an extended period of time can be critical to material survival as well as generating

TABLE 4.1 **Theoretical mechanisms through which family relationships may affect prisoner reintegration**

Mechanisms	Theoretical traditions
	Material circumstances
Instrumental support	Control theory, strain theory
Role strain	Strain theory
	Informal social control
Monitoring/supervision	Control theory, differential association, routine activities
Coercion/negative social control	Strain theory, differential social support, coercion
	Emotional supports and stressors
Expressive support	Control theory, strain theory, social support theory
Relationship stress	Control theory, strain

Source: Wyse, Harding, and Morenoff (2014).

role strain, especially for men whose conventional role within the family has been that of economic provider. In other words, this is a typology of processes, not a typology of relationships. As our larger theoretical framework would suggest, how a relationship with a family member or a role in a household influences reintegration will ultimately depend on the characteristics of the family member, the nature of the relationship, and the characteristics of the formerly incarcerated individual. As men and women often enter into relationships with different role expectations, gender will also be influential.

The Provider Role and the Dark Side of Material Support

In chapter 3, we argued that family is a crucial source of material support for formerly incarcerated individuals, who enter the community often with little more than the clothes on their backs. In particular, family members proved to be a key source of residential stability, the foundation on which successful social and economic reintegration is often built. Yet, for both men and women, material support could pose risks as well, particularly when, lacking their own resources, participants felt dependent on their partners. For women, the possibility of domestic violence was ever present, as nearly all had experienced serious abuse in past relationships and financial dependency would make leaving the relationship far more challenging.[1]

For men, the risks, though less severe, were nonetheless consequential as dependency challenged an important identity and self-concept: that of provider. In other words, reliance on others for material support could also have negative consequences, especially among men, because these situations could lead to role strain. Role strain occurs when an individual is unable to fulfill the expectations of a given role (Agnew 1992; Ganem and Agnew 2007). Failure to fulfill the provider role through conventional means may then lead to criminal activity as an alternative. Role strain is made more likely given the difficulties our participants faced finding employment and contributing to the household over the long term. Moreover, the stress of role strain may lead to substance abuse, which can in turn lead to reoffending. One way to cope with role strain is simply to exit the role, which in this case would mean leaving the household or breaking off the family relationships that lead to role strain, yet this outcome would create residential instability, which brings its own challenges.

When Henry left prison, his commitment to his fiancée and her children was a primary motivation for staying away from crime: "I'm blessed because she waited on me. . . . So I don't plan on going nowhere. . . . See, I can't just think about me, me, me all the time. So first thing come is the family and the people who love me and put up with me." Yet, when he encountered the familiar stresses posed by poverty, addiction, and criminal opportunity, this motivation was simply not enough to keep him away from crime. In fact, his commitment to his family and his identity as a provider became prominent reasons that he offended again.

Leaving prison, Henry knew that he had to find a job quickly. Yet he had few job options available to him. Recall that the asphalt company he had worked for in the past had moved to the suburbs. Without either a license or a car, he was not able to make it to the new job site. Over the months following his release, he was able to pick up work for only a few days at a time, either as a handyman or at the asphalt plant when friends could give him a ride. He never attained steady employment at any point across the three-year study period. As a result, the family subsisted entirely on the teenage son's SSI benefits and food stamps, which jointly netted less than a thousand dollars a month. At less than half the federal poverty level for a family of four, the benefits were nowhere near enough to meet even basic needs. Henry hated being broke and, even more, hated not being able to provide the children with necessities like clothes for school and food.

The financial stress and personal frustration came to a head following a four-month period during which Henry was jailed for a crime he did not commit. On release, he was angry and desperate for money. He returned to one of his criminal haunts and stole a car "with rims" that he thought would be worth a substantial sum (it turned out to be worth only about $200). He later admitted that he had also been high on crack at the time of the robbery. In a drug-induced haze, he hit a parked car and wound up sentenced to a year in jail. Although for Henry his family was a major reason to stay straight, his identity as a provider also made his poverty even harder to bear.

For men wedded to an identity as a provider for family, relationships could pose something of a catch-22: while providing crucial resources on release, because they provided resources they could also inspire an identity crisis that could encourage a return to offending. Henry was not the only one for whom this was the case. A few days after David was paroled, he left his drug treatment program early and failed to contact his parole officer—an act of absconding. Unable to stay with his mother or other family members for fear that the authorities would find him, he was taken in by his former girlfriend, Loretta, the mother of his child, and they soon resumed a relationship, living together in a low-income housing complex with their daughter and Loretta's two other children. To get by, they relied entirely on Loretta's public benefits, including rent vouchers and food stamps. Over time, David became increasingly stressed about not bringing any income into the household. Four weeks after release, he explained that he even considered limiting his own eating because he was not contributing income: "I wasn't eating for a minute ... I felt like I was taking out of the children's mouth; that's not my food." Still, he continued living with his girlfriend, who bought him not only food but also cigarettes and beer. After he was returned to prison, he explained that the strain of living off his girlfriend's largesse was one of the main factors that led him to resume criminal activity. He had noticed that one of his girlfriend's neighbors often left her apartment for weeks at a time. Just weeks after our interview, he burglarized the apartment after a night of drinking. He explained that the main reason he committed the crime was that he could not continue living in the household without contributing financially. He had planned to pawn the stolen goods to help with household expenses, but the police arrived the next morning.

For David, his role as a father and a romantic partner in the household initiated a particular role expectation that served more as a motivation for criminal involvement than a protective factor. Such role strain can be understood as closely linked to traditional gender norms dictating that men should provide material resources for their family—the breadwinner role. Such role strain often manifested itself in unpredictable ways. As we discussed above, some single men in our sample cited their inability to fulfill the role of breadwinner as a reason for avoiding romantic relationships, while others appeared to limit their contact with children when they were unable to help provide for them (see also Edin and Nelson 2013). Instances of role strain were most common among men living with romantic partners and children. We did not observe the same degree of role strain among participants living with their parents, nor did we see it among our female participants, who seemed more comfortable adopting a caregiving role as a way to contribute to family.

In some instances, the men in our study were also able to resolve potential role strain by substituting the caregiving role for the breadwinning role when they struggled to find employment. Although caregiving was common among women and conformed to gender norms and conventional household roles, comfort in such roles came less easily to men. Men who engaged in caregiving still viewed their household roles as far from ideal, but caregiving helped them reconcile their identities as a family member with their challenges in securing stable employment. Several of the men described their completion of household chores, such as repairs and yard work, as an economic contribution to the household, thus viewing the household as a place where they engaged in work despite being unemployed.

This was the case for Randall, who did not obtain stable employment until nearly three years after his release from prison. During this time, he pieced together informal jobs and engaged in various forms of caretaking in the different households where he lived. For example, not long after his release, he moved in with his brother, sister-in-law, and their two teenage sons. Unable to find a job, he contributed his food stamp benefits to the household, did odd jobs for other family members, and briefly sold marijuana to generate a small income. Despite these contributions, he felt badly about his unemployment and being unable to contribute more to his family financially: "It feels like I'm taking food out they [the kids'] mouth when I'm eating in the house, and I ain't working. But all she [sister-in-law] wants me to do, basically, is keep the house clean." Randall thus helped around the house and contributed his food stamp benefits, biding his time with an expectation that his brother would eventually connect him with a job through his employer. That job prospect fell through, however, leading to a rift in the relationship that was also related to the brother's drinking and accompanying verbal aggression. Two months later, Randall was kicked out, feeling used by his family, who had spent his monthly food stamp allotment. He then faced a prolonged period of unstable housing until eventually landing in a more permanent living arrangement with his chronically unemployed stepsister and her father, a retired blue-collar worker whom Randall referred to as an "uncle."

Despite finding a place to live, Randall was still unable to find work, and he never quite felt secure with his place in the household, especially after his stepsister's brother retuned from prison to live in the household as well. On multiple occasions, Randall packed his bags to leave, only to have his uncle insist that he was welcome to stay. He repeatedly expressed his anxiety over not having a job and being so dependent on his uncle:

> One night about two weeks ago I told [my stepsister] I didn't feel comfortable being here, I keep throwing that in their face because I feel I ain't doing nothing. And I told her I ain't feel that [her father] wanted me there. Then she takes me back like, "He ain't mad at you. He said he like that you ain't out there just running the streets and that you take care of your business." I fixed the room up, and it's been good ever since. Then I don't ask her for nothing because I feel I don't have to ask for nothing, he's already doing the best he can for me.

Randall eventually came to accept his contribution to the household in terms of his household labor:

> [My stepsister's brother] had a talk with me one day, and I told him flat out, "I don't feel comfortable being here, that's why I always leave because I feel like I can't help around this house as far as contributing food or money or anything." And he like, "My dad ain't asking for much, he just wants you to do something around here. You can keep the house clean, anything, he'll appreciate that." And I be having the house clean, every morning, I get up. He's like, "Treat this like you treated your own cell when you was locked up." I keep the whole house smelling fresh.

These arrangements required constant negotiation and encouragement. Despite reassurances from his uncle that he was fulfilling his household role, Randall continued to feel conflicted about his dependency and hesitant to ask for further support. At the same time, his ability to engage in care work helped assuage these insecurities, and he lived with his uncle and stepsister for over a year, leaving only when he formed a new household with his fiancée and her son in the suburbs.

Another form of role strain can occur when caregiving and care work interfere with meeting one's own needs. In these situations, our participants were torn between the roles they developed for themselves in the family after release (and the desire to assist family members in need) and their own long-term well-being. Caregiving and care work interfered with the time and energy they had for meeting their own health needs, meeting parole requirements (such as mandatory programming), and searching for employment. While Damian was still in prison, his adult son pled for him to move in with him and his mother (Damian's ex-wife) because she had suffered multiple strokes and they were struggling financially. They needed not only another income but also someone who could help with basic tasks of daily life as well as managing medical appointments and medicines. Yet Damian had his own health problems, including glaucoma, high blood pressure, hypertension, and "a bad back." Before prison, he was a heavy drug user. Although he moved in to help his ex-wife and his son, he ended up frustrated and feeling taken advantage of: "They're relying on me at this point. But it's hard for me to get my thing together when I'm dealing with their things more so than mine." He explained that he believed his ex-wife was faking her ailments and that he was being taken advantage of to help with the rent. He was paying their portion of the rent for their Section 8 subsidized housing with his social security income. His relationship with his stepson, who suffers from bipolar disorder, became increasingly stressful also. The son was struggling to launch his own business and was involved in a conflict in which he ended up a stabbing victim. Damian was arrested and put in jail after borrowing his son's car (without a license), which turned out to be stolen. When he returned home from jail, he found his ex-wife and son using drugs heavily. The situation had become intolerable, and he moved out and into a shelter for formerly incarcerated individuals. "Right now, it's all about me," he explained, "until I get me straight." He felt relieved to be free of his caretaking responsibilities and—despite his unstable housing situation—looked forward to restarting his music career, buying a house, and completing parole.

The Power of Informal Social Control

A pillar of Sampson and Laub's age-graded theory of informal social control is that close social bonds help people monitor and supervise one another to enforce mutual obligations and restraints. Although the literature emphasizes the capacity of spouses (particularly wives) as agents of social control, similar processes are common in other family relationships, such as parent-child, grandparent-grandchild, or even child-parent relationships. The risk posed to important social bonds can motivate returning citizens to avoid substance abuse and criminal behavior and encourage prosocial behavior such as searching for employment or persisting in an unpleasant work situation. Moreover, family relationships provide important forms of identity and prosocial roles for individuals who face otherwise spoiled identities. These identities and roles are symbolically important to those who face challenges achieving other forms of social status such as employment or education. Inhabiting the role of spouse or parent provides the opportunity for symbolic affirmation and reinforcement of postprison identities, especially when other potentially affirming roles— such as successful worker or student—are unattainable.

Although the restrictions and restraints that family members impose can often benefit returning citizens in their reintegration efforts, in other circumstances family members can channel such influence to encourage or coerce one another into remaining active in crime, substance use, or other forms of antisocial behavior (Colvin, Cullen, and Vander Ven 2002). Coercion can thus be viewed as the negative counterpart to the protective effects of family-based informal social control. Moreover, family members may actively or passively approve of criminal behavior when it provides benefits to them (such as money for the household or access to drugs). Moreover, family relationships can put individuals at risk for domestic violence and other forms of emotional or physical abuse, all of which can interfere with other aspects of reintegration, such as residential stability, employment, and community involvement.

It Keeps Me Straight

For both men and women, relationships curtailed offending by providing both an identity that was incompatible with continued offending and direct monitoring and supervision that helped keep negative impulses and behaviors in check. Though these processes are usefully identified as distinct for analytic purposes, they were often intertwined.

James described "messin' with women" as an important part of his "wild" past. He described a lonely and difficult childhood in which his father had passed away as a result of hepatitis and his mother had been incarcerated twice for crimes related to her drug addiction. Having never received the love he needed from family, he had sought it out with women, and these relationships had often led to poor choices. Yet this time the relationship he formed seemed different. About six months after his release, he became involved with a nurse with four children. He describes the positive role the relationship played in his life: "It's forcing me to man up. That's one thing." Being in this relationship encouraged him to take on the responsibilities of a new social role, one incompatible with his past irresponsible behaviors. Further he described: "It's keeping me out of trouble. I got somebody to come home to I can say is mine, ain't nobody else. So I'm all right.... The other night, shoot, this is recent, my friend wanted to go to this little bar down here, this little club, and she didn't want to go. She was with me. I didn't go. So we left, then what happened? Somebody got killed. Three people.... Yeah, I probably would have got in trouble."

Not only did his partner keep James out of risky situations, but the relationship also provided a positive role and an emotional connection that he found orienting. Although he credited his girlfriend with helping him stay out of trouble and maintain employment, he also occasionally chafed at this informal social control, attributing it to unreasonable suspicion of cheating, jealousy, and a lack of trust. Echoing a sentiment voiced by other men, James explained: "I get stressed sometimes. You know how women get jealous. Sometimes she don't trust me.... [Some women] think you want to go out and cheat." Still, he viewed his girlfriend positively and, notably, reported no substance use or criminal activity during the study period.

A common form of informal social control resulting from family relationships was the motivation to stay away from crime and drugs that maintaining the relationship provided. Returning to substance use or criminal activity might jeopardize the relationship or, at the very least, result in further prolonged separation from loved ones. This was initially the case for DeAngelo, who explained how his first relationship after prison functioned to control his behavior: "My girl and her mom, she's been more of a mother to me than my mother ever have. And they just good people. They never judge me because of my past. They never looked at me and perceived me as a hoodlum or a thug.... She just been there for me, and I never had that before. So it feels good. And I really can't let them down." He also describes how his girlfriend's supervision helped keep him safe, although initially he had seen it differently:

I used to think that she was being controlling, but she was really looking out for me, and I guess my pride and my ego was getting in the way, that's why we clashed a lot.

Interviewer: What was she trying to get you to do?

I would be like, "I'm going to Detroit with such and such." She'd be like, "No I don't want you going with him. You know that dude always carries guns with him," Or, "You're going to Detroit looking like that? Somebody might try and rob you or something." "Man ain't nobody going to rob me, and he ain't got no gun. He ain't going to put me in that situation." But really she was just thinking about the what-if factor and I shouldn't be taking that risk. She just wanted to see me do right, man. I need to do right, and I'm not going to say I'm weak and I can't do it on my own, but it's always good to have somebody that's there with you to kind of help keep you on your toes.

Over time, his perception of his girlfriend's controlling behavior changed; he came to see it as supportive of his goals. For DeAngelo and others, these processes of informal social control encouraged conventional behavior because continuing to engage in criminal offending could spell the end of these valued relationships, which for some was simply not worth the risk.

Children can provide a similar motivation. Indeed, among those participants who had children, almost all mentioned in their prerelease interviews that rebuilding their relationships with them and being a better parent were key motivators for staying out of prison. This was the case for Jennifer, whose primary motivation to stay sober was her children. She recognized that her past substance abuse had negatively affected her children, and she held onto significant guilt about her past. Moving forward, she thought she could do things differently. She continued to make her children a primary focus of her life and her recovery and maintained a strong belief that she must stay sober for them. Moreover, taking care of her son structured her day and helped her avoid past mistakes. Her daily routine revolved around her son's school schedule—making sure he got up in the morning, ate breakfast, and got on the bus, then getting him off the bus, ensuring he did his homework, preparing dinner, and putting him to bed. When she suffered a bout of depression, being accountable to her son seemed to help her recover from it:

I know I gotta get him off to school. There was three days I didn't. [Her girlfriend] got up and got him out to school. I slept. Three days in a row, and I said I can't do that. It's making it worse for me, and it's not good for [my son]; he's my responsibility. Just knowing that he counts on me helps me so much. Know-

ing that he knows what to expect every morning and the same routine. And if I
don't expect him to break it, how can I? You know I've got to set examples for
him, so we're doing it. It's working.

While women in our sample did experience supervision and monitoring
within their relationships as well, their partners' criminal involvement and/
or addictions often meant either that they were weakly positioned to exert
conventionalizing control or that other aspects of the relationship (such
as providing criminal opportunities) overrode their regulatory efforts. Because most women's offending was tightly linked to their drug and alcohol
abuse, a drug- or alcohol-involved partner was unlikely to play a purely
supervisory role, as we discuss further below.

Coercion and Negative Social Control

Although the restrictions and restraints that family members impose can
often benefit reintegration efforts, in other circumstances family members
can channel such influence to encourage or coerce one another to remain
active in crime, substance use, or other forms of antisocial behavior. Coercive or negative social control was present in Jada's relationship. Jada,
thirty-one, lives in a working-class Detroit suburb. Prior to her incarceration she had held a steady job as a home health aide for eleven years
while caring for her two daughters. At our initial in-prison interview, she
was completing a two-year prison term for smuggling drugs into a men's
prison. She explained that, when she was finally caught, she had been
smuggling drugs into the prison for months at her boyfriend's request.
At the time of this crime, she had been on probation for drug dealing and
firearm possession, the same offenses for which her boyfriend had been
incarcerated. Her boyfriend, the father of her younger daughter, was a
partner in each of her crimes. This relationship directly contributed to her
criminal involvement as many of her crimes were facilitated by her boyfriend and often benefited him.

Romantic partners also provided our participants with opportunities
for drug relapse, which served as pathways to crime. In the lingo of AA,
exposure to "old places and old faces" is an easy route to relapse, which
can then renew the cycle of criminal offending. This was the case for Kristine. She was able to establish sobriety in prison, but Pete, a past boyfriend
and former partner in heroin use, remained on the streets. Although she
had avoided seeing or talking to him initially following her prison release,

after three months on parole she changed her mind: "He called me and asked me how I was doing. I told him everything, and I said, 'Well, I want to come and see you.' And he's like, 'Well,' he said, 'are you sure?' I said, 'Yeah, yeah, you know, I'm okay.' And we ended up going out there and, you know, looking for Pete, finding Pete, and then I ended up getting high being around everyone." While it may have been that deciding to meet him indicated a desire to use again, seeing him also directly facilitated her relapse. Following this relapse, Kristine absconded from parole and began supporting herself and her drug habit by shoplifting and selling stolen goods. Soon thereafter, she was arrested for retail fraud and sentenced to a year in jail. The facilitation of recidivism by romantic partners was particularly common among female participants who partnered with criminal or drug-using men. It is important to note that we did not see this pathway among our male participants, largely because men's female partners were simply not as criminally involved as were women's male partners.

It is not only romantic partners who can enable or encourage substance use and criminal behavior, as can be seen with Randall, discussed above. Some of his past crimes were committed with one of his brothers, and on his release family members presented him with opportunities to engage in crime again. When he did some odd jobs for a cousin in the hopes of making some extra spending money, that cousin paid him in marijuana and told him to sell it. His brother, with whom he lived for a few months immediately after his return to prison, demanded a cut of the marijuana for his own personal use in exchange for living in his house and provided the opportunity to sell marijuana to friends for whom he cut hair in his basement on weekends. Another brief foray into drug selling was prompted by another cousin who enlisted Randall to help him sell heroin. Randall did so for a week and then quit. This behavior was never detected by his parole officer.

An example of outright coercion comes from Kristine. Kristine received significant instrumental support from her mother and siblings, including housing, transportation, clothing, and assistance navigating medical appointments. She viewed her family as a motivation to stay clean and reported that they were helping her work to achieve this goal. She described how her siblings offered her encouragement and her mother specifically talked her through her substance abuse issues. Despite this ongoing support, she struggled mightily with her addiction and continued to engage in criminal behavior during the study period.

A key contributor to Kristine's continuing legal troubles appeared to be her nineteen-year-old daughter, Rose. On her release, Kristine reported that she wanted to be a part of her daughter's life—a life she had been "in and out of so much." She did in fact return to living with Rose, who also was living with Kristine's mother. Initially, Kristine reported that Rose helped her with transportation but also became a significant source of stress. She quickly turned to describing Rose in very negative terms as manipulative, an addict, a slob, and routinely having an attitude—"she's just hateful sometimes." Further, Rose directly contributed to Kristine's illegal behavior. Soon after Kristine's release, they went looking for jobs together in the Rose's boyfriend's car. Rose begged Kristine to drive the car because she feared the car's brakes were broken, even though Kristine did not have a license. The police pulled them over, which Kristine attributed to suspicion that the car contained drugs (the police apparently pulled them over for a broken taillight), and Kristine was arrested for driving without a license. Not long after, she reported that her daughter, who was also abusing substances (Vicodin and Xanax), pressured her to engage in shoplifting. Even though Kristine tried to walk away, both were arrested. Following their retail theft case, Kristine again relapsed, which she attributed to stress at home over conflict with her daughter, and again was arrested, this time for driving a stolen car.

Relationships and Emotional Dynamics

Although much of the theoretical and empirical literature on relationships and desistance has focused on the ways in which romantic partnership affects patterns of social interaction and routine activities, other family members can also play critical roles in providing emotional support and buffering returning citizens from stressful life events that could otherwise trigger violence, substance use, or rash decision making (Cohen 2004; Cullen 2004; Umberson, Crosnoe, and Reczek 2010). Such support can be particularly important among returning citizens, given the emotional challenges posed by imprisonment. Men in our qualitative data felt that they had to present a tough, emotionally distant demeanor in order to stay safe, while women felt isolated and lonely. Given the loss of nonfamily social ties and the intensification of family relationships during our participants' time in prison, it is not surprising that they relied heavily and primarily on their family members and romantic partners for emotional support in the challenging and stressful period after release. In many cases, such emotional support proved to be an important buffer against relapse or an encouragement to persevere in a previously unsuccessful job search. On release, returning citizens face a period of emotional upheaval as their high expectations—for themselves and their loved ones—often meet harsh realities. We observed many instances in which family members provided a sympathetic ear to talk through problems or stressful events, affirmation, and confidence boosts in an otherwise lonely time, though this was significantly more common among men than among women.

Yet, just as family relationships can provide support, they can also bring new sources of stress, such as patterns of conflict and disagreement. The stress created by conflict within family relationships can also trigger drug and alcohol use (Mowen and Visher 2015). Because staying sober is one of the greatest challenges of reentry for many formerly incarcerated individuals, avoiding stressful relationships can be one way to protect against potential relapse. Leverentz (2014) shows how the demands of family relationships or family roles can compete with the tenets of addiction-recovery programs, which often emphasize independence and staying away from relationships that can be triggers for use, leading to relapse and reoffending.

Expressive Support: Easing the Transition

Once Jake was paroled, he began a romantic relationship with Anna, a friend of his sister's with whom he had corresponded in prison. Soon he came to rely on Anna emotionally. As discussed above, he felt that the drinking problem that originally landed him in prison had been triggered by his relationship with his ex-wife, who had cheated on him. He was able to talk through the continuing difficulties he experienced interacting with his ex-wife, with whom he had two children: "That's one of the things me and her are good at. We discuss everything and anything. . . . Past relationships aren't a topic that we can't discuss . . . which is good for me. I talk to her about every time my ex comes over." This support has been critical for Jake, who feels his drinking is triggered by emotional stress:

Interviewer: What are you biggest triggers for alcohol or drugs?

When I get off of work I feel entitlement to drink because I just worked for the day, you know. I'm not a very angry person, but I know anger will drive me to drink very quickly. When I get upset, emotions, past relationships are a good trigger for me. Top five probably deal with my ex-wife, the relationship I'm in, how I'm dealing with my family has a lot to do with relationships, my communication with people. But it's almost like my emotions and keeping that in check.

To counteract this urge to drink at night, he made a practice of calling Anna right after work.

However, Anna faced her own struggle with addiction. When Jake first started the relationship, he viewed their shared experience with addiction and incarceration favorably: she understood what he was going through and recognized the signs and triggers that might presage a relapse. However, several months into the relationship, when Anna suffered a relapse of her own, the relationship became more threatening to Jake's sobriety than emotionally supportive, and he ended it.

A second example comes from Leon. Recall that Leon has an eleven-year-old son and was separated from his wife before he was incarcerated. His past relationship was a marriage to a woman who was bipolar, drank heavily, and "kinda" knew about his multiple armed robberies; she had done nothing to dissuade him from crime in the past. Now, with support from his family, Leon was well on his way to achieving independence and economic security one year following his release. Around this time, he met a coworker named Delilah with whom he became romantically involved. He quickly moved in with her, and they began a serious relationship. While Leon had achieved some stability prior to this relationship, Delilah's emotional support became an important stabilizing force in his life.

Delilah had been clean and sober for twenty-one years, and recovery was a huge part of her life. She had a laser-like focus on Leon's substance use. He said: "I might drink two days in a row, and she'll be like, Oh my god, you done had a beer yesterday, and now you're having another one today. I'm like, Whoa, whoa, whoa, I'm not in recovery!" And she also inspired him to better himself: "You know before I was just . . . staying here, staying there, not really wanting more in life. Luckily that's what this relationship has helped me with too is saying that you know I want to do something else with my life."

Not only did Delilah discourage him from falling into the ruts he had in the past—such as becoming socially isolated and spending his free time on the computer—her own education and life goals served as a model for his own. He was impressed by her ongoing schooling and said that she challenged and motivated him to think about what he wanted to do with his life: "You know it's easy just to get out and get into a relationship and shack up with anybody, but you know you want to try and find somebody that at least is better than you or at least has the same type of goals and expectations that you have in life or at least want in life, and that's what she has is definitely a good direction in life." Not only was she working full-time; she was in school, engaged in the community, and involved in church. Leon described this relationship as "turning [him] around"; it had pulled him out of his "cocoon," and together they were socializing and seeing family more often. His father was excited about the positive change he had seen in him since the relationship had begun. In Leon's case, an addiction or a criminal history could actually serve as a point of commonality, so long as the behavior has been left in the past and the partner remained strongly committed to a conventional lifestyle.

Furthermore, Leon says he can be open with Delilah about various stressors, such as his financial situation, in ways that he could not have been in the past with others. When asked whether the relationship caused financial stressors that might lead him to thinking about crime, he said: "You know, maybe before it could have. But now she's actually helped me with that, with just being happy with what you have. You know, and I am happy with what I have. You know, I never knew I could just enjoy life." In the context of this positive relationship, he is able to avoid criminal behavior, instead focusing on looking toward what he wants for his future. This example also makes clear the multiple effects any particular relationship can have as, in addition to emotional support, we see evidence of informal social control via motivation as well as instrumental support through shared living expenses. It also shows how, even where partners shared a history of crime or addiction, the relationship can be beneficial.

Although women faced similar emotional stresses and similar threats to sobriety and desistance, they rarely described emotional support as a benefit of their romantic relationships with men. Relationships with men did not seem to play a similar role for our female participants, as is revealed in the following exchange between Jada and the interviewer:

Interviewer: Do you feel like [your boyfriend is] supportive for you? Can you talk to him, share issues, concerns, stuff like that?

What man do that?

Interviewer: I don't know. Some do.

Oh. Some you know?

Interviewer: Some, yeah. Some.

Oh, yeah? Not none I know.

Interviewer: None you know?

Nope.[2]

While Jada expressed her beliefs most bluntly, no woman in our sample described emotional support as a function of a relationship. Rather, women tended to turn to female friends and relatives or, as was the case with two participants, female partners. Jennifer, for example, had met her girlfriend of two years while incarcerated. Though she struggled to square the relationship with her own religious beliefs and continued to hide it from her children, she found her partner, Robin, deeply emotionally supportive.

The support of her sisters was also critical for Jennifer's material well-being and sobriety. Leaving prison, Jennifer recognized the strong support system she had in her sisters, who provided both instrumental and emotional support: "A lotta people coming home from prison don't have anybody." Indeed, receiving instrumental support may reinforce emotional support as it indicates family members' confidence in one's eventual successful reintegration. Jennifer talked to her sisters frequently after release, ate meals with them, and received a great deal of material aid from them, including a trailer to live in, assistance with transportation, and financial support to help her pay off legal fees and buy things for her son. She said in her first follow-up interview. "My sisters helped me a lot. I call my sisters and let them know what's going on. . . . Both my sisters . . . they're really supportive." While she initially tried to stay busy as one of her strategies to avoid thinking about drugs, she also stayed occupied in part by spending time with her sisters: "Without them I'd be stuck here doing nothing." This is another example of the importance of routine activities with family members.

In her third follow-up interview, Jennifer explained where she would have been without her sisters' support: "I don't know what I would have did. I probably would have ended up relapsing because I would have got overwhelmed by everything." Within her first year of release, she did in fact face significant stressors: a prior romantic partner of eleven years who provided her with material aid during the study period died, her son's father—also a substance abuser—engaged her in a domestic altercation and continued to harass her (leading her to obtain a no contact order), and one of her two brothers who was on parole came to live with her, used drugs in her home, and stole from her neighbors. While the support of her sisters decreased over time as she achieved greater independence and transitioned to relying more on her girlfriend, she continued to recognize the important role they provided as a buffer from the stress of the reentry process as she successfully strived to stay sober.

Relationship Conflict and Stress

Many participants vented to us about the stresses they experienced within their relationships and worried that these everyday strains could trigger a drug or an alcohol relapse. As described previously, our participants' recognition of this possible pathway back to prison was a primary reason why those who were single had planned to stay out of a relationship on release, at least for a time. The role of relationship stress was more salient and was more frequently discussed among our female participants. Drugs and alcohol could be used to escape stressful, frustrating, or discouraging situations, of which family members were a frequent source. While one-time drug use is not recidivism, a sustained relapse poses a substantial threat to desistance. Lenora, fifty-two, noted that romantic relationships could be risky: "They get on your nerves, some guys." Implicit in this reasoning is the idea that being in a relationship requires emotional work, and focusing on men might mean women have fewer emotional resources to expend on their own recovery and reintegration. Stressful, conflict-laden relationships are the negative analogue to emotionally supportive relationships and illustrate how the effects of relationships differ depending on the characteristics of the partnership. Jane's relapse, described above, owing to the stresses of her relationships with her husband and stepdaughter is but one example.

When Michelle—a twenty-five-year-old white woman convicted of drug dealing—left prison, she and Luke had been together on and off for three years, during which time they both cycled through multiple periods of sobriety and relapse. As she explained, they hardly knew each other sober. Nonetheless, as she left prison, she had high hopes for the relationship, describing how they "always came back together." Yet two months following her prison release the couple had broken up, and at six months postrelease they had reunited, gotten engaged again, begun planning the wedding, and once more broken up. Michelle explained that she had broken up with Luke because he returned to drinking and the stress of the relationship endangered her own sobriety. She realized that conflict in the relationship could easily trigger a relapse that might result in her reincarceration. She recounted how breaking up with Luke had changed her life:

> It's a lot of stress out of my life, and I don't think it would have worked. I think we were holding on to something that we just don't have any more. It worked out good, but that's a big adjustment because he was a main source of me getting around. Now I'm taking the bus a lot more.

Interviewer: How did you know [it wasn't going to work]?

> Little arguments since I've been out over the stupidest stuff. And I don't need that stress in my life because it had me thinking, "You know what, I just need to go and relax, go have a drink or something." I can't have myself get to that point because then I'll be in prison. So it worked out for the best.

Despite the material support Michelle gained through this relationship, stressful dynamics threatening to her sobriety came to outweigh the benefits, at least for a time.

Men also described relationship stress as a pathway to relapse. Recall that Jake described his current relationship as the primary emotional support system he had for maintaining sobriety, but he also explained that the continuing stress of interactions with former partners could trigger a relapse. Other men echoed this concern with stressors from prior relationships and their connection to drug and alcohol abuse. For example, DeAngelo traced the roots of his alcoholism, which contributed to three drunk-driving convictions, to a particularly painful ending to his marriage, his wife cheating on him: "I was devastated. Like how could you accept these vows knowing that you was this kinda person, knowing that you can't live up to what these vows are saying? I think that's when I really start drinking. I've always drank, but I think that's when I really started drinking. But like I was just hurt. Man, I felt just like mistreated, like I just felt like something that you just don't even care about, something you throw out. I couldn't feel so low." Particularly for those with a history of addiction, stressors experienced within relationships can be more than those tenuously clinging to sobriety are able to bear.

Family health problems were also significant sources of stress for our participants, leading in some cases to relapse or criminal behavior. Recall that Michelle is a white woman approaching her mid-twenties whose heroin addiction—undeterred by twelve stints in drug rehabilitation—led both to her imprisonment for a probation violation related to check fraud and drug possession and to the loss of custody of her daughter. Following release from prison, she faced a seriously strained relationship with her mother, who had custody of her daughter, but received significant material and emotional support from her father and stepmother. They provided her with housing, paid all the bills, and supplied her with food, transportation, and other necessities. She quickly obtained her first job with the assistance of a referral from her stepmother's sister, and her father instituted a requirement that she pay $150 in rent monthly, $100 of which he kept for her in a savings account. Michelle said that her father and stepmother were "real supportive" and noted: "He [her father] always tells me he's proud of me because I'm, you know, I'm finally doing the right thing." Living with them, she was able to sustain a period of sobriety and maintain employment in several different service-industry jobs.

However, eight months after Michelle was released, her stepmother unexpectedly died owing to complications from routine surgery. With her father facing his own health problems related to a prior heart attack and also experiencing significant grief, she was left to arrange the funeral and provide him with emotional support. Further, her father, who had struggled with substance abuse in the past, returned to abusing prescription drugs. Looking back, she thinks his substance use began to threaten her sobriety: "I think just me watching him and sitting there nodding and I'm think[ing] of that feeling that he's having. You know it started to get to me, and it's like when your mouth waters like if you see pizza or something, that's what it's like, you know." After a particularly negative encounter with her mother over Christmas and the growing stress of her situation with her father, a coworker who was also on parole offered her heroin, which she said was particularly difficult to resist in her circumstances: "It was just like right place, right time, and I fell." Not long after, her father kicked her out of the house when he discovered her relapse and accused her of stealing her stepmother's jewelry. She reported: "[This] just made the addiction even worse, you know, for the next couple of weeks." And she was forced briefly to move to a hotel for shelter. Shortly thereafter, she reconnected with her ex-boyfriend and moved in with him and his mother, focusing on her recovery. While Michelle managed to achieve some stability with her boyfriend, her relationship with her father continued to be a source of stress.

Consider again Randall, who, as explained above, tried to cope with his role strain by providing household labor. Eleven months after his release, he began a romantic relationship with a woman he met at a job-assistance program. His partner suffered from a severe drug addiction and had previously dropped out of college because of it. Despite the challenges that both of them faced, Randall viewed the relationship as mutually supportive and considered asking her to marry him: "I think it'd help both of us. . . . With her, keep her mind straight, and me, keep me from running the streets. . . . Keep my mind right. Keep me focused." The two got engaged, and the girlfriend became pregnant. Randall was looking forward to a new life with his fiancée and their baby and believed that this new role would motivate him to stop drinking and find a job: "I told [my fiancée] that this is basically the deal I made with myself. That as soon as my baby got here I was gonna stop [drinking]. 'Cause I was just gonna be there a hundred percent. And then by me getting a job the same time, that would've cut [the drinking] all the way down, 'cause I wouldn't have had time to do nothing, 'cause I'm the type, I'll work all day."

For the first time since his release, Randall received job offers, one from a fast-food restaurant and one from a light-manufacturing plant, and he felt a new sense of optimism after two years of daily struggle. But, only a few days later, his fiancée experienced a difficult labor, and the baby girl died in neonatal intensive care just days after she was born. Randall worried that his fiancée's pain from the complications of labor coupled with the emotional loss would prompt her to relapse, and he turned down the job offers and struggled to care for her as best he could. He himself began to suffer from severe depression and suicidal ideations owing to his own grief. He dealt with the loss the only way he knew how: "I really been drinking now since my baby passed. . . . I drink like a pint, a fifth, or something like that [every day]."

Conclusion

This chapter reveals the complex and countervailing roles that contemporary family relationships play in formerly incarcerated individuals' desistance processes. Despite the difficulties of these relationships, our participants turned to them for social connection and a sense of belonging as well as for the housing, transportation, and other basic necessities that they had literally no other means of obtaining. With ties to old friends severed and the psychological strain of readjusting to a life outside prison walls alone, they quickly formed relationships, moved in with partners, and even started families within months of leaving prison.

As we reflect on the various complex and countervailing effects of family relationships, we must also recognize the role that our participants themselves play in selecting their romantic partners and the family members with whom they will interact. For example, partners and family members often face similar or related challenges related to substance use, mental health, poverty, and involvement in the criminal justice system as those returning home from prison. And those leaving prison tend to form romantic relationships with others who have experienced similar life events and challenges. Although this did not necessarily entail a criminal history, it often meant that partners had a history of substance abuse or suffered from the same kinds of mental health problems and barriers to employment faced by our participants themselves. This was particularly true for women. Whether by personal choice or simply as a function of the pool of available partners, all our female participants' current partners had a history of drug or alcohol addiction or criminal offending or, as was the case for most, both. While this was less true of men's relationships, seven of fifteen men's partners had a history of substance abuse, and three had also been incarcerated in prison or jail. This may simply reflect the realities of formerly incarcerated individuals' lives, spent as they are moving between substance abuse treatment programs, appointments at the parole office, and group meetings. Other formerly incarcerated individuals and addicts are among those they are most likely to meet.

Some of our female participants even suggested that such partnerships were a conscious choice: they sought out less-conventional partners now and in the past because these were the people with whom they felt most comfortable. Lenora explains how this was true of past relationships: "Well, I was in the lifestyle, so ... the good guys I didn't want to be bothered [with]. My oldest sister tried to introduce me to some guys that work in offices, oh I don't want to be bothered." Likewise, Michelle explained that she scoffed at what her father saw as the right kind of guy for her: "The all-American good-looking handsome Christian boy who's at least got a decent job and a little bit of money." Rather, she saw herself with somebody with more of an edge: "I don't need somebody who's like straight, tough guy, like that, but I don't want no preppy little dork who can't stand up for me or himself." Michelle had been through a great deal in her twenty-two years, from violence to homelessness, and she simply could not see sharing a life with someone who had never experienced some of the same things. Yet, as we saw with Leon, such homogamous pairing need not always be dangerous. Indeed, the fact that he and his partner experienced some of the same life challenges strengthened their relationship and helped him stay on the straight and narrow.

Having identified the complexity inherent in the role of relationships and the diverse pathways through which these social ties served to influence participants' behaviors, are we able to predict when a relationship might facilitate desistance and when it might discourage it? We suggest that we can. Certainly, partners and family members who were actively continuing to abuse drugs and alcohol posed a substantial risk, though, as in the case of Jennifer, a strong personal motivation to sobriety could withstand such assaults. While material support and, to some extent, emotional support were important resources that our participants gained via their romantic pairings and certainly served to ease the reentry transition, they did not on their own help them remain crime free. For such resources could also come at a price—whether that be the role strain of being unable to fill the desired social role or the enabling that resulted when partners provided too much support and acceptance of problematic behaviors, as was the case for Jennifer's, Christopher's, and David's relationships. Even processes of informal social control seemed to have a dark side when partners criminally involved or substance abusing themselves provided opportunities for drug relapse or criminal activity or coercive pressure to make bad choices. For those with a lengthy addiction history, the desire to use was a constant companion, and identifying a reason to relapse could be easier than finding a reason to stay clean. Given this ongoing pressure, relationships, with their many challenges, could easily fit the bill.

Yet for some participants relationships did make a positive difference. In these cases, partners and family members actively discouraged negative behaviors and modeled positive behaviors—inspiring a positive transformation. The importance of the partner as an inspirational figure is beautifully revealed in the words of Lamar: "I've been in relationships where the females I was with, they were doing good things and trying to get places in life, and so me being in a relationship with them, I'd say that that was rubbing off on me. Being a thug and a street guy was not something that they wanted within their life, so that was something that I kind of would put on the back burner, and I was striving in that light in which they were shining." Relationships discouraged his admittedly bad behaviors because they provided a source of hope and the possibility that life could be different.

Even in cases where partners or family members were actively struggling to overcome their own personal challenges, as was true of Michelle's fiancé and most romantic relationships of which women were a part, a sustained commitment to sobriety coupled with negative judgment of the partners' own poor choices could result in a positive change over time.

Thus far we have largely focused on the most micro of contexts, personal relationships with partners and family. In the next chapter, we turn to a more distal context with potential importance for reentry and reintegration, the neighborhood.

CHAPTER FIVE

Navigating Neighborhoods

W hen Christopher paroled to Ann Arbor at the age of thirty-eight, he ended up there almost by chance. With no family that would take him, he was released not back to the Detroit suburb where he was living before prison but into the community of his most recent conviction, a carjacking that had occurred near the campus of the University of Michigan. The state's reentry program placed him first in a temporary hotel in a busy commercial strip on the outskirts of town, then in another hotel downtown before it could secure him a spot in Ann Arbor's downtown homeless shelter.

Although living in a homeless shelter was trying to say the least, with its rigid rules, crowding, and lack of privacy, in many ways downtown Ann Arbor could be considered an ideal community to start the process of reintegration. An affluent college town, it has a low unemployment rate and many social services and supports. There is little street crime and no visible drug selling in public places to test Christopher's fierce addiction to crack cocaine, although, because it was a college town, alcohol-fueled parties were easily accessible, especially on football game days. (Once, when Christopher decided to collect and recycle cans from the frat parties to make a few bucks, the temptation to join the drinking overwhelmed him, and he ended up in a detox program for three days.) From the homeless shelter, Christopher needed to walk only a few blocks to find an AA meeting, a free meal at a church soup kitchen, a bus depot providing transportation in any direction, and a central library where he could search the Internet for jobs or just pass the time reading and listening to music, especially when the winter weather came: "Oh, man, you can be at the library Tuesday through Saturday from nine o'clock in the morning till nine o'clock at night. The malls are really not my scene. The library would probably be the biggest hangout when the weather gets bad. It's perfect to sit there, look at the Internet all day. And tons of other stuff. And they got music, and they got books and everything." When the weather was nice, he could always find a place to hang out on campus: "There's a ton more places to hang out here. One reason is because of the school. It's the funniest thing that you can just go to that Diag up there, or that Bell Tower, throw your backpack right on the grass, just lay on your back, and just go to sleep for two or three hours, and people don't even care."

Yet, although Christopher felt safe, he did not develop social ties in the community, at least at first. He felt strongly the social distance between him and the college students, their professors, and the other professionals in and around Ann Arbor. Neither did he want to develop ties with those who shared some of his own challenges for fear that such companions might lead him back to the alcohol and drugs that bedeviled him every other time he had come out of prison. With no family or friends from his life before prison nearby, he lived a very socially isolated existence:

> I don't kick it with the street people. I don't kick it with the people from the shelter. I hang out by myself.... And there's a lot of rich kids running around here. So I almost feel as I'm below Ann Arbor.... You know, sometimes I just look like I'm not even supposed to be here amongst these people. Or other things I'm thinking to myself, you know, if these cats walking around here actually knew that I just came from prison for robbing people out here on this campus, how would they react to that?

Eventually, Christopher connected with what he described as a vibrant addiction-recovery community in Ann Arbor. This community of former addicts and those struggling to tame their addictions was nurtured by a number of strong institutions dedicated to addiction treatment and recovery, both residential and not. For Christopher, the recovery community was a network of eyes around town—on buses, at the library—that monitored your sobriety, acting as a support when you were clean, but providing informal social control and stern judgment when you had relapsed:

> I've been busted by a couple people [for appearing high or drunk in public], "Hey what the fuck you doing, hey what do you think you're doing, come on man." Other people just kind of look and just, just shook their head, eh, I knew it. Some people are, "Hey man you need to come on back to a meeting, you need to do this, you need to do that." It's stronger in Ann Arbor. Here it's a

monster. . . . There's like four main programs that they have here, and they are
so tight-knit. You cannot hide. . . . Everybody's on the bus. . . . We all get around
the buses, so we're all running into somebody somewhere.

When I'm doing the right thing, to have these people in this town that are
cooperative with recovery and involved with the program, they are awesome.
There is such a support system here it's crazy. . . . That's what makes you run so
far from it when you're not doing the right thing. It's because it's that strong.
I like to talk a lot of shit about it, "Oh these bitches in recovery in Ann Arbor,
they got their nose up in the air." No, they don't. They're doing the right thing.

Christopher met his future wife, Janice, in a recovery program and made a
close friend in another. Although neither of them, nor the larger recovery
community, was able to keep him clean and sober, they provided a pathway back to sobriety when relapse occurred—at least when he did not get
himself into trouble too quickly.

In addition to being far from his prior family and social relationships,
Christopher's Ann Arbor neighborhood was also far from his existing job
networks. Christopher described himself as an auto detailer by trade and
felt that he could easily have found a job in the suburbs north or west of
Detroit, where he had worked in the past. When we asked him why he
did not go back there, he explained that he had nowhere to live in those
suburbs and that the programs and shelters in Detroit itself would challenge his sobriety on a daily basis owing to the visibility and ease of access
of drugs: "To go to Detroit and get the job? And then what? Where am
I going to stay? There's one place to stay that's close to it. It's called the
NSO. It's like Neighborhood Service Organization. Do you think that's a
good place for me to stay? No. It's fucking Crack General. I can't do that.
I will get high. Detroit is not a place for me."

Lenora moved to just such a neighborhood when she was released from
prison. No one in her family would take her in either, and she was assigned
to a residential substance abuse treatment program and halfway house on
the east side of Detroit, where she lived for four months before moving in
with her nephew. In addition to the temptation of drugs, she feared for her
physical safety, doing her best to avoid interactions in the neighborhood,
and staying inside whenever she could. Her fears were first confirmed after
a threatening encounter at a gas station near the halfway house: "This one
guy walked up to me. I was coming out of the gas station, and I was putting
my money up, and he walked up to me and said, 'Do you believe in God?'
And I said, Oh my goodness, I wonder if he, if he seen me do that and he's

trying to conversate with me. I said, 'Yes I do,' and then I turned, and I started walking backward facing him, and I said, 'You have a blessed day, and God bless you.' So that made me a little nervous."

Such encounters seem even more likely when one is new to a neighborhood, as returning citizens typically are. Potentially dangerous people and places are still unknown, and new neighbors cannot be relied on for help. Moreover, new residents are unknown quantities and may be perceived as outsiders or easy prey. Lenora explained how her discomfort was heightened by being a newcomer and how she would feel if she were in a neighborhood closer to where she grew up or closer to family:

> And then I won't be so nervous about where I'm staying 'cause my son's not far from me. And then my son's fiancée, her parents don't stay far from them. . . . The areas like over there, for instance, I was staying [in that] area since I was fifteen. I know everybody over there. And it's got a little rowdier than when I moved over there when I was fifteen. [My son's] area is a little more down. The rent is more there in that area where I'm from than over here. . . . It's not like a lot of ADC [welfare] in here that's laying around smoking weed or getting high.

Lenora attempted to manage both the threat of victimization and the temptations to return to drug use in her new neighborhood as many others do, by isolating herself as much as possible from those threats and from neighborhood-based relationships and interactions more generally. In her case, that meant coming back to the halfway house as soon as she was allowed to in the afternoon (after having conducted her daily job search). She recalled feeling unsafe coming home after dark: "It was dark. . . . I don't know the area that good. I don't know nobody over here. . . . I just watch everything. I just be real observant. And [a fellow resident] was telling me, When you go out, watch your purse. So, when I start working, I got another one up there like this, but it's got the handle like this, and it's smaller."

Nevertheless, Lenora also understood her new neighborhood as holding an advantage when it came to her sobriety. Her old neighborhood would have meant running into old friends with whom she used to drink and use drugs as well as seeing places that she associated with substance abuse, potentially triggering cravings. A new neighborhood made it easier to avoid "wet places and wet faces," a language many of our participants used to justify the strategy of avoidance and isolation that Lenora pursued.

It's like I'm outta town, which is OK, better for me anyway.... Because if I was in the old neighborhood I would see people I know.... Because, it's not healthy for me. A lot of people that I used to go over to they house and drink with and get high with. What am I gonna go see them for? 'Cause I did that before. That's how I know, when I messed up before, going to wet places and wet faces. Soon as you go around there and they drinking, they smoking crack, and they using heroin, and they ask you for some money 'cause they need some drugs. So, no, I learned that in [the prison residential substance abuse treatment program] to stay away from wet places, wet faces, and it's working.

Lenora also came to terms with her new neighborhood by reasoning that anywhere she could afford to live would likely be just as dangerous. Her only option was to make the best of where she was: "Anywhere is what you make it; you just might have to secure your door of your house more."

While the last two chapters focused on the family as a context for reentry and reintegration, in this chapter we turn to more distal contexts, neighborhoods and communities. Christopher's and Lenora's early experiences in Ann Arbor and Detroit highlight many of the key themes that emerged from our analysis of the experiences of our interview participants as they navigated the new places in which they found themselves after prison. Why might places matter for reintegration? Places and the people one interacts with in them present opportunities to connect to employment, social services, friends, and community groups. Social networks embedded within neighborhoods can exert social control, but they can also facilitate a return to drugs and crime. Neighborhoods also present different chances for victimization. The availability of public transportation can prove critical to accessing jobs and social services, while avoiding the people and places deemed risky often leads to strategies of social isolation from the neighborhood and community that lessen their direct impact. Although both Christopher's and Lenora's stories highlight key themes, it is important to note that Christopher's proximity to affluence is relatively unusual among returning citizens; Lenora's experience is more typical. Because many formerly incarcerated people move initially into poor neighborhoods, and because such neighborhoods appear to increase recidivism and reduce employment, avoiding or escaping them may be a critical dimension of formerly incarcerated people's successful reintegration.

We first describe the types of neighborhoods to which returning citizens move after prison and in subsequent years. We then turn to the potential effects of these neighborhoods on reintegration, focusing on how they are related to substance use, criminal activity, and labor market out-comes.[1] Here, we make a distinction between neighborhoods as venues for social interaction and social network formation and neighborhoods as places embedded in larger geographies of economic opportunity or isola-tion. Understanding the degree to which neighborhoods are venues for social interaction and social network formation requires us to examine how our participants engaged—and did not engage—with others in their neighborhoods, including how they perceived the dangers and opportuni-ties present in those neighborhoods. Understanding the degree to which neighborhoods structure access to economic opportunities in the labor market requires us to examine how our participants navigated geographic spaces within and beyond their neighborhoods.

Prior research suggests that neighborhood contexts are indeed associ-ated with recidivism and employment after prison. Most studies that have been able to access residential information in administrative records on returning prisoners—including those conducted in California (Hipp, Pe-tersilia, and Turner 2010), Florida (Mears et al. 2008), and Multnomah County, Oregon (Kubrin and Stewart 2006)—have found that the risk of recidivism (measured by arrests, felony convictions, parole violations, or returns to prison) was greater for those living in more disadvantaged neighborhoods or counties.[2] A study of returning prisoners in Iowa (Tillyer and Vose 2011) found no relationship between county-level disadvantage and recidivism, but living in a county where fewer people have moved recently was associated with a lower risk of recidivism. Our own analyses of our administrative data also find strong associations between neigh-borhood context and formal employment (Morenoff and Harding 2011).[3] However, two questions that are important to understanding the role of neighborhood context in reintegration remain largely unaddressed: What are the determinants of living in a high-poverty neighborhood, both after release and over time, and how do neighborhood effects on reintegration come about? We turn next to the first of these questions.

Postrelease Neighborhoods and Neighborhood Attainment over Time

Figure 5.1 shows the poverty rates of the census tracts where a typical individual in our administrative data lived, month by month, for the first two years after release.[4] This figure shows results separately for African

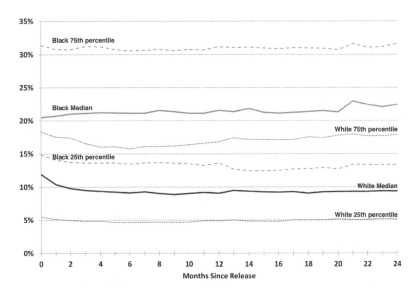

FIGURE 5.1. Tract poverty rate by race and months since release

Americans and for whites, and for each racial group we show the median tract poverty rate (solid lines) and the twenty-fifth and seventy-fifth percentiles of the tract poverty rate (dashed or dotted lines). This figure shows four important facts about the neighborhoods that formerly incarcerated people return to initially and live in over time after release. In this section, we explore the explanations for and implications of these stylized facts.

First, the neighborhoods where formerly incarcerated individuals live right after release (month 0 on figure 5.1) are characterized by relatively high poverty rates. Among African Americans, the median poverty rate is just over 20 percent, the threshold often used by social scientists to designate high-poverty neighborhoods. Among whites, the median poverty rate is about 12 percent. This is consistent with prior research, which shows that formerly incarcerated people typically return to very disadvantaged neighborhoods, ones characterized by poverty, joblessness, and high rates of crime and disorder (Cadora, Swartz, and Gordon 2003; Lynch and Sabol 2004; Solomon, Thomson, and Keegan 2004).

Second, we see very little change in the types of neighborhoods that formerly incarcerated individuals experience over time for both African Americans and whites as the lines in the graph are all very close to horizontal. On the surface, this seems to be inconsistent with the high residential mobility we documented in chapter 3. However, we can understand this apparent discrepancy by noting that most of the residential mobility is between neighborhoods of similar socioeconomic status. Of course, these median values could mask a great deal of variation across individuals in their neighborhood attainment over time. A more sophisticated analysis based on latent class trajectory models shows that this is not the case. Only 9 percent of whites and 10 percent of African Americans experienced either upward or downward mobility in terms of the socioeconomic status of their neighborhoods over time, while the vast majority of formerly incarcerated people remained in similar neighborhood environments (Lee, Harding, and Morenoff 2017).

Preprison neighborhood and first postprison neighborhood are the strongest predictors of later postprison neighborhood context for both African Americans and whites (Lee, Harding, and Morenoff 2017). Formerly incarcerated people who lived in less disadvantaged neighborhoods before incarceration or are from rural areas tend to start their postprison lives in relatively more advantaged neighborhoods. Not surprisingly, given its closer proximity in time, the first postprison neighborhood is an even stronger predictor of the neighborhood disadvantage level of later residences than is the preprison neighborhood. Those who restarted their community lives after prison in poor neighborhood conditions are likely to stay in those poor conditions, while those who entered into more advantaged places tended to remain in similar neighborhood conditions over the subsequent two-year period. This path-dependency pattern is similar for African Americans and whites.

Why are formerly incarcerated people concentrated in the most socioeconomically disadvantaged neighborhoods, both initially and over time? We argue that three processes are particularly important: affordability, family and other social support, and institutional constraints imposed by parole and the ubiquity of criminal background checks. With regard to affordability, we know from the wider literature on neighborhood attainment—which examines how and why different families come to live in neighborhoods of different social and economic composition—that characteristics common among formerly incarcerated people tend to be generally associated with living in poorer, more disadvantaged neighborhoods. One challenge in avoiding or escaping disadvantaged neighborhood contexts is formerly incarcerated people's low levels of human capital (job skills, as typically measured by education and work experience); empirical research shows that individuals are likely to move to better neighborhoods when they have greater human capital and therefore greater income, meaning that they can afford to live in more advantaged neighborhoods (e.g., South and Crowder 1997).

Another possible explanation for the concentration of formerly incarcerated individuals in the poorest neighborhoods relates to the importance of social ties, particularly ties to family, which we discussed in chapters 3 and 4. Since formerly incarcerated people are unlikely to have the resources to live alone after prison, their first residence after prison depends substantially on individuals who can provide housing or financial support, and such ties may also prevent formerly incarcerated people from moving later as well. In the general population, strong social relationships with people living nearby tend to provide local resources that would be lost by moving. The strength of social ties in the neighborhood may, therefore, deter residential mobility (Kan 2007).

There are also institutional aspects of prisoner reentry that may also make moving to lower-poverty neighborhoods more difficult, at least for some formerly incarcerated people. The criminal justice system may exert an independent influence on neighborhood choice through aspects of supervision such as intermediate sanctions and regulations concerning residential location. For instance, supervision conditions may prohibit living near schools or near where past victims live. Institutional constraints based on criminal history and type of crime are another obstacle formerly incarcerated people may encounter in finding housing in more desirable neighborhoods. In the housing market, landlords often require disclosure of criminal history and are reluctant to rent to those with a criminal record (Helfgott 1997), and public housing may similarly be unattainable (Geller and Curtis 2011). Parolees subject to electronic monitoring may also be precluded from moving from officially allowed areas.[5]

Third, figure 5.1 also shows that African Americans return, on average, to much more disadvantaged neighborhoods than do whites. This reflects the larger racial geography of neighborhoods in Michigan and the United States more generally (Massoglia, Firebaugh, and Warner 2013), a product of higher poverty rates among African Americans and segregation by race and income (Massey and Denton 1993). Indeed, formerly incarcerated African American individuals are no more likely than the typical African American resident of Michigan to live in a high-poverty neighborhood. The census tract poverty rate of the median African American Michigander was 22 percent in the 2000 census, very similar to the rate for the median African American parolee in our data (21 percent). However, there is a stark difference among whites. Whereas the first postrelease neighborhood of the typical formerly incarcerated white individual has a poverty rate of 12 percent, the census tract poverty rate of the typical white Michigander is 6 percent. In other words, going to prison does not seem to have a negative effect on the neighborhood poverty rate of an African American individual in Michigan.[6]

Fourth, figure 5.1 also shows that, even within racial groups, there is a great deal of variation in the poverty rates of neighborhoods. One-quarter of African Americans return to neighborhoods where the poverty rate is at least 32 percent (see the dashed line indicating the black seventy-fifth percentile), while another quarter of blacks return to neighborhoods where the poverty rate is less than 15 percent (dashed line indicating the black twenty-fifth percentile). There is somewhat less variation among whites, but it is still considerable. One-quarter of whites return to neighborhoods where the poverty rate is at least 17 percent (see the dotted line indicating the white seventy-fifth percentile), while another quarter of whites return to neighborhoods where the poverty rate is less than 6 percent (dotted line labeled indicating the white twenty-fifth percentile).

What might explain within-race variation in neighborhood poverty after prison? There are important differences between African Americans and whites in terms of the roles of human capital, social ties, and institutional factors in explaining such within-race variation. Among whites, institutional residence, such as treatment facilities, homeless shelters, and other short-term correctional institutions, resulted in exposure to more disadvantaged neighborhoods after prison release, reflecting the fact that these institutional residences tend be located in areas that are more disadvantaged than the typical white neighborhood. Among African Americans, lack of human capital is associated with entering more disadvantaged neighborhoods, and social ties (specifically, being married) appear to protect against living in disadvantaged neighborhoods (Lee, Harding, and Morenoff 2017).[7]

Safety and Connectedness in Postrelease Neighborhoods

Variation in the neighborhoods where formerly incarcerated individuals live means that there is considerable potential for neighborhoods to play an important role in explaining differences in prisoner reentry and reintegration. In order to understand how neighborhoods were experienced by our participants, we need to characterize neighborhoods by the features that were most salient in their day-to-day lives. Two key dimensions of variation in neighborhood experiences among our participants were safety versus disorder and connection versus isolation. The distinction between safety and disorder primarily revolved around the degree to which the neighborhood presented two types of threats, violent victimization and proximity to drugs and drug users. These two types of threats tended to be concentrated together in the poorest neighborhoods, places that our participants described as *chaotic*. The distinction between connection and isolation revolved around the degree to which our participants felt socially connected with others in the neighborhood and the potential they perceived for such connections based on the connections they saw between their neighbors, or what sociologists typically call *social cohesion*. Neighborhoods where our participants experienced isolation rather than social cohesion or interaction with neighbors made them feel detached and separated. We emphasize that the detached versus connected distinction is based as much on our participants' history and experiences in the neighborhood as on some objective measure of the neighborhood as a whole. On the basis of these two dimensions, we can characterize neighborhood environments as experienced by returning citizens into four types: *safe detached*, *chaotic detached*, *safe connected*, and *chaotic connected*.

Safe Detached

Those returning to safe detached neighborhoods described quiet, peaceful locales that nonetheless presented little in the way of community or social connection. Participants returned to homes where they had grown up, some living with their parents in working-class suburbs of Detroit. A subset of those moving to safe detached neighborhoods moved to areas that were new to them, living either on their own or with a romantic partner. They experienced their neighborhoods as peaceful and their neighbors as polite but had no sense of social connection to the neighborhood. For them, social networks could be forged over time via jobs or substance abuse treatment or recovery groups, as was the case for Christopher, whose early neighborhood experiences were discussed above. Our participants lived about 25 percent of their time in our study in neighborhoods considered to be safe detached (36 percent for whites and 15 percent for African Americans).[8]

Those residing in safe detached neighborhoods knew some of their neighbors but had very little interaction with them. And, while dangers in the form of violence or drug selling were not present, neither was there a sense of community or shared place. Participants often stayed inside, spending time watching television, talking on the phone, or with family. When they did go outside, it was most often to get into a car and head elsewhere. While our participants professed concern as to what their neighbors thought of their actions, they did not necessarily think that neighbors could get together to solve a problem. Thus, those residing in these neighborhoods seemed to experience social control via their neighborhood contexts but not a sense of collective efficacy. Safe detached neighborhoods seem to be what Janowitz (1952) called *communities of limited liability*, in which people are invested in the neighborhood as a whole not because of close connections with neighbors but because the neighborhood meets particular needs—here, the need for a safe, peaceful environment. As Leon put it when describing the neighborhood where he lived with his sister in a wealthy suburb north of Detroit: "I rarely see these people [his neighbors]. No one sees anyone here. You know how those places are. Everybody just goes to work and comes back."

Chaotic Detached

Participants returning to chaotic detached neighborhoods most often returned to residences on their own or with romantic partners in high-poverty neighborhoods where drug selling and violence were common. These neighborhoods differed from those characterized as connected either because participants were new to the neighborhood and therefore knew no one or because the dominance of neighborhood violence undermined the possibility for social cohesion as neighbors tended to keep to themselves in their houses in order to avoid being victimized by crime.[9] To stay safe and away from criminal and drug opportunities, our participants largely adhered to the same strategy as Lenora, remaining inside to steer clear of neighborhood social networks, gathering places, and interactions. This meant that those returning to chaotic detached neighborhoods were generally quite isolated; dependent on family and employment for social connectivity. Our participants lived about 43 percent of their time in our study in neighborhoods they considered to be chaotic detached neighborhoods (25 percent for whites and 61 percent for African Americans).

Participants returning to chaotic detached neighborhoods felt no connection or responsibility to their neighborhood or their neighbors. And, when asked whether they cared what their neighbors thought of their actions, they responded no. Indeed, they saw their postprison trajectories as unaffected by their neighborhood context. Echoing the language of treatment programs, they tended to voice narratives that it made no difference where they were, that what mattered were their own thoughts, decisions, and actions. Perhaps unsurprisingly, these participants had the most negative views of their neighborhoods, aware only of the dominant street culture and unaware of the decent families who also called the neighborhood home (Anderson 1990). Participants described these neighborhoods as, "lost," "a pit," "terrible," and, when asked about their neighbors, explained, as one put it: "I don't be paying no attention because I don't care." They remained disconnected from neighborhoods they viewed as containing nothing but problems.

Jennifer found herself in a chaotic detached neighborhood after she decided to move out of her fiancé's house, both to avoid his substance use and to secure a place where she could live with her son. After she inherited a trailer from an aunt, her sisters found a location for it in a trailer park in Ypsilanti. Soon thereafter, she expressed misgivings about her neighborhood context, not primarily for herself, but for her thirteen-year-old son, whom she feared would be enticed into the same sort of troubles with drugs and crime that engulfed her life and that of her older son:

> I can't believe I chose this place. Out of all places I could have moved this trailer to. I just was so scatterbrained.... This place is full of drugs.... It's full of pills. It's full of crack. Alcohol, for sure.... The kids over here are fourteen, fifteen years old, and their parents allow them to smoke pot. That's one of the reasons I got [my son] in therapy because he was over there experimenting with marijuana with them kids. I was like, "Oh, hell no." I went over there. I threatened them with the cops. Give them cigarettes, the little boy over here. And I've spoken to [his mother] before about it. I said, "I don't know what you allow your son to do, and it's none of my business, and, frankly, I don't care. But I care about my son, what he's doing, and your son's a little bit too old to be hanging around with my [son] and especially giving him cigarettes." And I ain't had a problem with them since.

Like Lenora, Jennifer has nowhere else to go (even if she could find another trailer park, she could not afford to have the trailer moved), so she adapted to this environment by isolating herself and her son from its perceived dangers by staying indoors and avoiding interactions with neighbors.

In Jennifer's case, some of her neighbors were former drug buddies and therefore posed a special danger:

> I don't care about these people or what they think. I just stay to myself. [*Laughs.*] I don't want to associate with these people because I'm not getting into that trailer park drama. I stay to myself. And I go out of this trailer, I go look for [my son] and bring him in the house, or we're in the van leaving. Because you see on the weekends they are out here partying.... All that drama going on after dark, and I'm glad the blinds and the doors are closed and I'm in here and not out there. Because, if I was using, I'd be right along with them.

Safe Connected

The few participants who returned to safe connected neighborhoods were those returning to live with middle- or upper-middle-class families in a diverse set of neighborhood contexts, from gated communities within Detroit to apartment buildings in Ann Arbor. For these participants, street life was present but neither threatening nor tempting, and neighbors were not just friendly but also important resources. They mentioned community organizations of which they were (often only tenuously) a part, from churches to martial arts clubs. Embedded within safe, supportive neighborhood contexts, they were able quickly to begin laying the foundation for a successful reintegration, undistracted by street life and public drug selling or drug use, and feeling a sense of belonging in the community. Our participants lived about 18 percent of their time in our study in neighborhoods they characterized as safe connected spaces (23 percent for whites and 12 percent for African Americans).

For example, Daniel is thirty-two-year-old white man who served twelve years in prison for involuntary manslaughter, an incident in which he shot a fellow drug dealer in the back of the head. On release, he moved in with his father and stepmother in a white, rural area outside a small town northwest of Ann Arbor, living there for a year and a half before his burgeoning career as a personal fitness trainer allowed him to afford his own apartment in town. He described the friendliness of the community and the ease he had in establishing social networks. "Oh, I love it out here. I love it. The people are nice, I went to my nephew's, he had a Christmas concert over at [the] high school. I get in there, and there's just families, crowd, you know family are everywhere. I just like that family togetherness you know and coming to support their children. Man this is great; I like it. People out here are nicer, friendlier."

Others who came to live in safe connected neighborhoods were new to that environment. Because networks had not been established previously, they enjoyed the proximity to jobs and the safety of their neighborhoods, but it took them a few months to establish neighborhood networks and a sense of community. For instance, after a few days in a hotel and months in Ann Arbor's homeless shelter, Lamar had saved enough money from his various service-sector jobs to afford a room in a transitional rooming house in Ypsilanti run by the local prisoner reentry program. He explained how friendly people in the neighborhood were to him and the other residents and how that had bred confidence and a sense of belonging for him and the other reentrants:

> It's a very peaceful neighborhood. Quiet, family oriented.... And which I think works out good for us [returning citizens] because it helps to keep us in a particular state of mind to where we're constantly trying to achieve and move forward and not be into anything negative.... Although they know that people here are pretty much newly released from prison and they're trying to make their way back into society, a lot of people in the neighborhood are friendly; they speak to us if they see us walking toward the store.... It's very comforting to see and know that members of society are willing to allow a chance for those who have been convicted, trying to make their way back.

Chaotic Connected

Finally, participants returning to chaotic connected neighborhoods were largely moving in with family members who lived in impoverished neighborhoods in Detroit or the surrounding suburbs. These participants knew many of their neighbors, classifying them largely as "working people" or "settled people." While drug dealing and violence were pervasive, there was a sense that it could be avoided by staying inside at night or away from certain blocks or houses. These participants tended to agree with the statement, "I care what my neighbors think," but tended to disagree with the statement, "If there's a problem in my neighborhood, we can get it solved." Thus, while there was a sense of community and connection that exerted some amount of social control, the dangers of the street kept these participants inside and limited the extent to which neighborhood networks could be leveraged for positive ends. Our participants lived about 14 percent of their time in our study in neighborhoods they considered to be chaotic connected (15 percent for whites and 13 percent for African Americans).

For example, recall that Randall experienced a great deal of residential instability in the year after his release before finally finding a semipermanent home with his stepsister and her father on the east side of Detroit. He perceived many of the residents of his new neighborhood as similar to the man he lived with: retired or soon-to-be retired working-class people who did their best to care for their homes and maintain community. Nonetheless, he also recognized a dangerous element of the neighborhood that he needed actively to avoid:

> As far as the neighbors, the neighbors [are] straight because I've been knowing them for years too . . . basically a lot of older people. It's a lot of old working people over there. . . . I'm talking about as far as the daytime, that how it be all day beside at night when these dummies be outside shooting, it's stupid. . . . They just be drunk, they're drunk, and then a lot of them guys be over there on them pills, they be on them ecstasy pills, and they be just going crazy over there; that's why I stay in the house at night. . . . I don't mess with nobody in the neighborhood. I just stay in the house.

For Randall, avoiding the neighborhood's more chaotic elements meant that he was unable to take advantage of neighborhood social networks or social supports.[10]

Risk, Temptation, Isolation, and Opportunity

How might we understand the effects of neighborhood context on prisoner reintegration? Sociologists and other social scientists have offered many different but related perspectives on how neighborhood effects operate. To organize our discussion, we first discuss neighborhoods as sites of social interaction and network embeddedness and then discuss the spatial or geographic dimensions of neighborhoods (Sampson 2012). As suggested by many of the examples we have considered thus far, the majority of our interview participants in high-poverty neighborhoods actively avoided interacting with their neighbors, limiting their ability to leverage any local sources of social support or network connectedness outside the family. In addition, the geographic location and spatial dimensions of their neighborhoods often proved to be particularly important as they struggled to find employment and access services, especially with limited options for transportation.

We first discuss the theoretical underpinnings of the first perspective—neighborhoods as networks of social interaction—and examine how our participants understood and navigated their neighborhoods as they tried to avoid the twin potential dangers of high-poverty neighborhoods: temptations to return to drugs and crime and victimization by violence. In the final section of the chapter, we turn to the second theoretical perspective—neighborhoods as geographic locales—and consider how the geography of opportunity affected our participants' access to employment and social services.

Social Interactions and Social Organization

Thinking of neighborhoods as networks of social interaction leads us to consider three processes through which neighborhoods may affect returning citizens. First is the opportunity to become involved with crime or drug use. Crutchfield and his colleagues (Crutchfield, Matsueda, and Drakulich 2006; Drakulich et al. 2012) argue that neighborhoods where many residents have weak attachment and commitment to conventional jobs are likely to expose returning prisoners to social situations that are conducive to crime. Differential opportunity theory (Cloward and Ohlin 1960) suggests that, if disadvantaged neighborhoods provide former prisoners with more opportunities to engage in crime and substance abuse, the result will be greater recidivism and less employment. Disadvantaged neighborhoods have higher concentrations of former prisoners (Clear 2007b), and rates of alcohol use and use of hard drugs are higher in poorer neighborhoods (Freisthler et al. 2005; Hill and Angel 2005). Such neighborhoods can make staying away from crime and substance abuse more difficult, especially for those with a weak cognitive commitment to desistance (Berg and Cobbina 2017).

Second, a social organization perspective focuses on how neighborhood poverty and residential instability can undermine residents' capacity to exercise informal social control by impeding the creation and maintenance of local social networks, community organizations, and a shared sense of cohesion and trust among neighbors (Sampson 1999; Sampson, Morenoff, and Earls 1999; Sampson, Raudenbush, and Earls 1997). Rose and Clear (1998) theorized that these problems are especially pernicious in disadvantaged neighborhoods where residents' ties to one another become attenuated by high levels of cycling in and out of prison. Such neighborhood conditions, they argue, undermine systems of private and parochial control, thus diminishing the capacity of the neighborhood to exert collective supervision and surveillance and creating a climate in which it is difficult to foster norms of mutual obligation and trust among neighbors. Former prisoners who return to neighborhoods with lower levels of informal social control may face fewer sanctions for deviant behavior and more opportunities to return to crime. As we discussed in chapter 3, returning prisoners also tend to have very unstable living situations, potentially making it more difficult for them to build local social networks and participate in local organizations (Swaroop and Morenoff 2006). One corollary of the social organization perspective is that neighborhoods with low capacity for informal social control will have higher rates of crime and violence than neighborhoods where social cohesion and trust can be leveraged to maintain public spaces as peaceful and orderly (Sampson 1999; Sampson, Morenoff, and Earls 1999; Sampson, Raudenbush, and Earls 1997).

A third perspective on how neighborhoods can influence returning prisoners' ability to reintegrate focuses on cultural environments. Shaw and McKay (1969, 170) argued that socially disorganized slum neighborhoods contain a wide array of "competing and conflicting moral values," both conventional and unconventional, creating a breakdown of social control and a cultural environment in which "delinquency has developed as a powerful competing way of life." More recently, Rose and Clear (1998, 450) argued that high levels of prison cycling "open opportunities for entrance of newcomers (with potentially different norms and values) into the neighborhood" and "increase opportunities to be socialized into prison subcultures." Normative environments may also be important for understanding how returning prisoners are treated by community members. For example, research has shown that there is variance across communities in prevailing narratives about the nature of crime, who is responsible for it, and who is victimized by it (Leverentz 2011). Also, the degree of mistrust and antagonism toward agents of the law (termed *legal cynicism*) in a community can influence residents' willingness to cooperate with one another and the police (Kirk and Matsuda 2011; Tyler and Fagan 2008).

These processes also suggest that, when formerly incarcerated individuals return home to areas where they lived prior to prison and may still have strong local network ties, neighborhoods may have an especially important impact on recidivism and employment. People who return home after prison may renew ties with friends and acquaintances who helped facilitate their criminal lifestyles by influencing their motivation to offend and engaging them in activities that lead to criminal opportunities (Kirk 2009,

2012). Also, the environmental stimuli that former prisoners encounter when returning to places that they associate with prior drug use could trigger a "cue-reactivity" process (Carter and Tiffany 1999) that can lead to drug cravings and increase the risk of relapse.[11] On the other hand, returning to one's preprison neighborhood may mean greater access to social support.

Risk and Temptation

All three of these processes—criminal opportunity, social organization and informal social control, and cultural environment—are premised on some degree of social interaction in the neighborhood, and thus evaluating whether they can help us explain postprison reintegration requires first understanding how formerly incarcerated individuals understand their neighborhoods and interact with their neighbors. Many of our participants—particularly those who did not live in safe connected neighborhoods—understood their neighborhoods as sites of risk and temptation: risk of victimization by crime (including violence) and temptation to use drugs and alcohol. Recall Lenora's discussion above of the risks she faced in her Detroit neighborhood. The risk of violence was especially salient for James, who paroled to a chaotic detached neighborhood on Detroit's east side to live with his mother. He explained how he is "on guard" whenever he leaves his house and does his best to avoid neighbors who approach him on the street as he expects most are either drug sellers or drug users: "You just got to be careful, be on guard. I don't even come outside, even in the block; I don't really mess with nobody. Don't know nobody, so. . . . Aw, man, lost, a pit, terrible. It's really crazy everywhere in Detroit. It depends on how you carry yourself, see. People sell dope down on the street and this and that. Poor people come approach me. I'm like, 'Nah man, I cut hair. But I can't cut your hair because you sell dope and shit.'" James emphasized that the risk of violent victimization is especially high after dark and described the following incident to illustrate the danger he faces outside his home:

> But at night it gets crazy, like I'll peek out the window, take out the trash, and I'll see some shit like the other night. I hear something, "Pop, pop," Oh, I ducked. She like, "That ain't no thing, no thing." I'm like, "Yes, it was. It might have been a little gun, but it was a gun, I know a gun." We just go on the porch. This guy's talking like, "Yeah, he tried to shoot me," and this and that. But

when I heard the . . . before I heard the two gunshots, I saw the guy get out the
car, because I was like, "Who's this parked in front of my house on the one way,
going the wrong way?" He walked out, and I went away from the window, and
I heard, "Pop, pop."

For our female participants, the high risk of victimization in their neighborhoods included not only being robbed or shot but also being sexually
assaulted. Some had previous experience of the latter. Jennifer, who as we
have seen described the dangers of her chaotic detached neighborhood in
a trailer park in Ypsilanti, had been raped prior to her imprisonment while
trying to buy drugs:

I lived down the street from my mother on a very bad street and walking to
my mom's to get money for drugs. I was going to lie to my mom and tell her I
needed this and that at the house and it was getting dark, and a guy grabbed
me by razor point to my neck and threw me in the car and took me to a field
and raped me. And I don't remember a lot of it. I just remember the knife, and
I remember fighting and crying and trying to run from him. . . . That's another
thing I deal with, you know, with my addiction and stuff. I made bad choices.
Every choice I ever made because of my addiction was bad. . . . If I wouldn't
have been going to get drugs, I wouldn't have got raped. I wouldn't have been
out there walking in that area that time of night.

Although we should question the way Jennifer blames herself for the incident, for being out alone in a dangerous neighborhood, it is clear that she
associates certain neighborhoods with the risk of rape.

Similarly, Jane, a forty-eight-year-old white woman who also had a long
history of drug addiction, linked neighborhoods where drug selling is especially common to the risk of sexual assault. She had also been raped while
attempting to buy drugs off the street and been lured into an abandoned
building by two young men. She carried this fear of violence with her following her release from prison. For instance, when she and her sister-in-
law took walks in the morning, they would take a baseball bat with them
for protection.

Other participants emphasized the role that risky neighborhoods might
play in their own involvement in crime or drug use, echoing criminal opportunity theory. For example, once Lamar could afford to move out of
the reentry rooming house and into his own apartment, he carefully considered the type of neighborhood where an apartment was located before

moving. Working with a housing counselor from the reentry program in his search, he chose an apartment in Ypsilanti near Ann Arbor in part because the neighborhood would not tempt him to return to old behaviors that had gotten him into trouble in the past:

> And she says, "Well, I got a place you know, and it's within the range and all this." Because she had had other places but they were mostly in Ypsi in an Ypsi area which I didn't want to be because it was too vulnerable, put me in a vulnerable position.... It was a position I didn't want to be in because I feel like I'm still kind of weak, so I don't want to be put in a position where I fall prey to old behaviors and stuff. She told me she had a place, she said where it was at, and I said, "Well, let's go look at it." And she says not real deep in Ypsi, close to Ann Arbor, plus both of my jobs was out in Ann Arbor.

Similarly, when DeAngelo was released from prison for a second time during our study (having been given a parole violation for driving without a license and having an open container in the car), he favorably compared his new Ann Arbor neighborhood to where he had lived in Ypsilanti: "It's a little different than Ypsi. It's just more of a chance that you might get involved in some trouble [in Ypsilanti] than it is here because of the kind of people that's out there. But I mean it was pretty laid back, but, if I wanted to find trouble, I knew it was right there." Later, he and his girlfriend moved to a safe connected neighborhood in one of Detroit's racially diverse northern suburbs. It was there that he felt most comfortable, not only because he felt safe but also because he felt a connection to his neighbors:

> The neighborhood is wonderful. It's clean; everybody keep they property up. The people are super friendly. Like, if I'm sitting on the porch and somebody's driving past, they wave. The kids aren't bad. You know how in certain neighborhoods the teenagers, like the preteens, will be out there bad and breaking bottles in the street and throwing rocks at cars and stuff like that. The kids not bad. Go to the store, and you get friendly service. It's just wonderful. It makes you wanna be happy. It brings out the positive energy in you. It's a beautiful thing. You all through the neighborhood at two o'clock in the morning, and it's peaceful outside. All the neighbors, when we first moved here, within a week all the neighbors came over and introduced theyselves to us. ... We was just like wow. It was crazy. It was real crazy. Good crazy, though.

Drugs and Violence Are Everywhere

When participants like DeAngelo, Lamar, and Jennifer had a choice of
neighborhoods to live in, or when they had previously had exposure to
neighborhoods they would not characterize as ridden with crime, drug use,
and violence, they tended to focus on risk and temptation as a core feature of neighborhoods and a potential danger to their goals of social and
economic reintegration. In contrast, other participants who did not have
this larger perspective discounted the effects that negative aspects of their
neighborhood could have on their own behaviors. Instead, they explained
away the risks and temptations the neighborhood presented.

One common refrain was that drugs and to some extent violence are
pervasive in modern society even if they are not always occurring in public
(see also Leverentz 2010). For example, participants residing in high-crime
areas where open-air drug selling was common voiced a belief that drugs
are everywhere, that the buying and selling of drugs was a common feature
of all neighborhoods and could not be avoided. As Damian explained:
"There's no neighborhood where you can live in the world, from the best
ones to the worst ones, where there are no drugs. . . . The war on drugs,
we lost." These individuals, who were struggling with their sobriety amid
temptation on every corner, turned inward to views that emphasized will-
power or personal choice while simultaneously dismissing the importance
of accessibility to drugs in shaping their decisions.

Similarly, for the majority of our participants, violence was understood as a normal part of everyday life in their neighborhoods and the
threat of violence as routine. Although they described hearing gunshots
multiple times per week, being the victim of street or home robberies,
and seeing people killed in their neighborhoods, they seemed to distance
themselves emotionally from these risks by claiming that violence was
pervasive. This view suggests that neighborhood context is irrelevant to
one's experience of violence or feeling of safety. Viewed through this
lens, the ongoing stress of violence in one's immediate surroundings is
an unavoidable part of life, and those subject to it are not disadvantaged
relative to those residing in other neighborhoods. Henry voiced this belief in discussion of his neighborhood. As he explained, no matter where
you live you have to deal with violence, so it is up to each person to avoid
victimization: "It's basically everywhere. You just have to have enough
common sense to know not to fool with it. You've got a lot of drugs in
the suburbs. A lot of people like to deal with the suburbs because there's
more money there."

Interview participants often adhered closely to narratives that emphasized their own individual agency rather than the role of contexts and institutions in shaping their social and economic reintegration. For instance, despite the dangers of her neighborhood, Jennifer nevertheless felt considerable agency over the risks it posed (at least for herself, the risks her son potentially faced causing her considerable stress). Although she initially worried about returning to Ypsilanti (where she used to buy and use drugs), a conversation with her sister convinced her otherwise. She came to see her sobriety as ultimately a choice she needed to make regardless of her neighborhood:

> I had no intentions on coming back to Ypsilanti ever. Even to see my family. I said they could come see me; I can't come back to that town because that's where I spent all my life using. And my sister said that it's not going to do me any more good to move out of Ypsilanti or try to stay away. My sister told me that it's going to be wherever I go, and it's true. It's going to be wherever I go. If I want it, I'll find it, and, if I choose not to want it, then I'll be OK. And I said in my head, That's true. . . . I know there are going to be days that some are going to be badder than others, I'll just have to work through it as they come.

A closely related response was to acknowledge that risks and temptations were nearby but to think of them as spatially distant and therefore not to worry about them unduly. While violence or the sound of gunshots might be common across the neighborhood as a whole, participants emphasized that such things did not occur on their own block, for instance, highlighting the relative safety of their own homes. Henry, for instance, indicated: "[Drug dealing is] all over. Every now and then [the police] are pulling people over, so that's nothing new. You may hear some shots, but not drive-by. You, well, every once a week or every twice a week you may hear some shots, but they're not right around in the hood; you can just hear them." Jane voiced similar sentiments: "[The neighborhood] has ups and downs. But for the most part, in a lot of areas of Detroit, you'll have streets that are very good, and then you have streets that are not. We're on one of the good streets."

Finally, some participants were simply resigned to the threat of violence. Because violence was pervasive, random, and unpredictable, they believed that fearing it was useless. While they stayed inside as much as possible, they also adopted a fatalistic attitude toward the risk of violence. Randall expressed this view when he described his reaction to a threat he experienced walking home to his uncle's house one night:

Guys be looking at you like they got a problem. Like last night I'm walking, mad, I don't know what these guys were doing, but they were following me last night. I'm walking around coming towards here, and they just came from nowhere. They followed me all the way down [my street] throwing rocks at me.... Like teenagers.... I can sense when somebody's following; I don't know what the hell they were doing, but I was so damn mad that night I just slowed the walk, let 'em catch up. You gonna do what you're going to do when you're going to do it.... It was like six of them. Ain't no lights on [my street] at night. Whatever's going to happen's going to happen. That's all I kept saying. I didn't know if they had a gun or not on them. That's why I ain't really turn around. I just slowed up. If they're going to do it, do it.

Like others, he chose to live his life and simply accept what came.

Isolation as a Strategy for Avoiding Neighborhood Risks and Temptations

Most of our participants found themselves at some point in chaotic neighborhoods that presented risks of violence or other victimization or temptations to become involved again in crime or substance use. Rather than dismissing these threats as ubiquitous, by far the dominant strategy was one of intentional social isolation. Because so many of our participants isolated themselves from even casual contact or interaction with neighbors, there was little room for the social organization or cultural environment of the neighborhood to play a strong direct role in their behaviors or experiences. Staying at home was one way to isolate oneself from the risks and temptations the neighborhood presented, as Randall explained:

I stay confined to the house. If I ain't looking for no job, I'm at home. I stay away from anything that's negative. Any time I'm not putting money in my pocket. I don't trust the streets. I might be an innocent bystander. 'Cause I heard gunshots all last night.... All you hear is, Boom, boom. I thought I heard a car crash. Then I heard the ambulance, and I heard gunshots and all kinda stuff. [*Laughs.*] I been up all night.... Every day you hear the ambulance or the fire truck around through there.... That's why I stay in the house. I'm not about to come out and get affiliated with nobody.

However, everyone must leave home and traverse the neighborhood at some point. Parole agents must be visited, programs attended, food bought, services received, jobs searched for, work done. For those who could not access private transportation (those without access to a car, rides from friends and family, or the legal right to drive), traversing the neighborhood on foot, as Randall described, or waiting for the bus was an inevitable part of daily life. Participants limited their risk of victimization by carrying themselves as confidently as they could, avoiding carrying valuables (recall Lenora's discussion of purses above), and avoiding going out at night. These strategies did not protect them, however, from the temptations that neighborhood friends could present. Avoiding these temptations was more difficult as they required shunning even causal social contact with people one knows personally and might see quite often. One set of existing social connections in the neighborhood was often to individuals enmeshed in criminal activities or actively using drugs and alcohol, which posed a risk in terms of weakening one's resolve to stay on the straight and narrow.

In negotiating these encounters, our participants often drew on lessons learned in substance abuse treatment programs (either in prison or in the community), which emphasize the dangers of "wet faces and wet places," a phrase that, as we have seen, came up repeatedly in our interviews (see also Leverentz 2010). This means that certain people or places could be triggers for substance use because of their cognitive associations with prior drug or alcohol use. The strategy that such programs recommended was to simply say, "Hi and bye." Instead of snubbing former friends or family, which could provoke confrontations or bad feelings, interactions were to be kept limited by acknowledging the individual, finding an excuse to end the conversation quickly, and moving on (e.g., a waiting family member, a pending appointment). Several participants directly quoted lessons learned in treatment to support this strategy, such as, "I'll just say hi and bye," and, "Avoid wet places, wet faces," as Jennifer explained when she discussed how she isolated herself from drug-involved acquaintances in her neighborhood. Jennifer further explained how she avoided former drug dealers who lived nearby:

> My drug dealers.... They haven't seen me. I just avoid them. At first, I was worried about it, but I just know what I gotta do. In my heart I know I gotta avoid them. I'm not strong enough to meet them, talk to them face-to-face. So I just go if I see them coming, I'll go the other direction. And then just change my thoughts real fast. I won't let myself think a negative thought about drugs or alcohol or violent behavior. You know, nothing to do with my old past me that took me to prison.

Thus, the neighborhood quickly came to be understood as place of many potential dangers, a place to be navigated rather than a place of opportunity or social cohesion. Linked closely to this framing of the neighborhood as rife with risks and temptations was the idea that, if not intended to achieve some other purpose such as a ride or a job lead, social interaction itself carried a negative connotation. Because the community that they knew was largely either criminal or substance using, social engagement was associated with those activities and therefore better avoided. In other words, socializing—on the street, on the bus, or anywhere outside the home—came to be understood as "doing dirty." Lamar, Randall, and Jocelyn provide three examples of this way of thinking:

> Lamar: I'm in the house, by six, seven o'clock. Unless I'm out specifically doing something like work. I'm not out socializing like that in the evening, after dark. People that I know that is on another train, I just pretty much say "Hi" and "Bye" to. I pretty much stay by myself or with family. Socialization is very minimal, unless at work. But, like, me going over to somebody's house and sitting down, watching a football game with 'em and stuff like that, no, it's not gonna happen.

> Randall: I ain't doing nothing dirty, so . . . I do the housework. I'm cutting the grass, wash the cars or whatever, help the neighbors out. And I'm back in the house.

> Jocelyn: All my bills are paid. I got clothes. I got food. I got cable. There's nothing else out there. I don't go to bars. I don't go to clubs, and I don't visit people and hang out and get high and do all that stuff. I don't do that stuff no more. I'm forty-one years old now. I'm just a homebody.

Some participants also deliberately avoided neighborhoods where they would be likely to come into contact with those from their past, as Lamar described. Yet this strategy was difficult for many to execute because they often had little direct control over where they lived. Relying on family or institutional housing meant they had to take what they could, where they could. Moreover, being a newcomer to the neighborhood posed its own risks for safely navigating a dangerous neighborhood, and moving to a new neighborhood to avoid problematic social networks could have the unintended consequence of also severing supportive social ties, especially those to nearby family (on the tension between isolation strategies and the need for social support, see also Leverentz [2014]).

Finding Community

Given that most formerly incarcerated people return to chaotic detached neighborhoods and that strategies of isolation were common, in what forms of community were our participants involved? First, it bears emphasizing that the vast majority of our participants had no consistent community or organization involvements, formal or informal. They socialized primarily with family and romantic partners and, when not busy simply meeting their daily needs for food and shelter (working, looking for work, or accessing social services and programs), remained inside and engaged in independent pursuits like watching television or housecleaning. Also important was the idea that social interactions or involvements outside the home with people other than family were often perceived as "doing dirty," as discussed above. This pattern is itself an important statement about the difficulty of social reintegration after prison, at least in the short term.

Although they were few, those who were consistently involved in their communities during the early period of reintegration covered by our study most commonly focused on either church or addiction-recovery communities (and these communities overlapped when churches provided addiction-recovery programs). For example, as we have seen, Christopher explained the role of the local Ann Arbor addiction-recovery community in his own social reintegration, providing both companionship and a source of informal social control. Similarly, Damian found support at a halfway house made up of sex offenders and other serious offenders, some of whom were still on electronic monitoring. The program managers were formerly incarcerated individuals themselves and ran the house on an egalitarian model, which was, in Damian's opinion, a key aspect of its success. The community was bound together by shared goals, "all making a fair attempt to better ourselves," which he found inspirational.

Participants who attended church regularly discussed feeling both embedded in their religious community as well as deeply nourished spiritually by their church membership. Their church was central to their understanding of whom they were and with whom they belonged. For instance, Damian described attending church with others in recovery and explained that watching their success was inspiring. For him, church was a place where congregants "are more concerned with [their] futures" than with their pasts:

This here is total creation from the beginning to the end. We're creating something new. We created something that's never been done before. . . . So I try to continue that. I go because I like the music. . . . And the people that's there [from the Salvation Army program], some are there because they have to be, but the majority from the outside are there because they want to be. . . . I'm encouraged by the graduations and the elevations of the ex-offenders of alcohol and drugs. All that's inspiring. You're not just outside looking in; you're inside looking out . . . and seeing success. . . . They don't care about our backgrounds. They are more concerned with our futures and . . . and what we have to offer. You know we have experiences to offer that they are not aware of.

For Damian, this church-based addiction recovery was an important form of community and belonging. Involvement in this community oriented him toward the future and its possibilities and thereby helped him deal with the daily challenges of reentry.

Neighborhoods and the Geography of Opportunity

Thus far we have considered neighborhoods as networks of social interaction. We have argued that, because most formerly incarcerated individuals return to neighborhoods they understand as presenting considerable risk and temptation, they attempt to avoid social interactions with neighbors, preferring to spend time with family or, in a minority of cases, in formal organizations such as churches or recovery programs. As a result of these isolation strategies, there is little chance for neighborhood social networks to influence their behavior directly, either positively or negatively. We now turn to neighborhoods as geographic locales, embedded in larger spatial, institutional, and economic contexts. Here, we see much more evidence for a role of neighborhoods as these explanations hinge not on local interactions with neighbors but on the spatial location of the neighborhood, access to transportation, and access to jobs and social services.

To the extent that disadvantaged neighborhoods are located in labor markets with high unemployment rates, returning to them will reduce employment and thereby potentially increase recidivism. County unemployment rates are associated with the employment prospects and recidivism of former prisoners (Raphael and Weiman 2007; Sabol 2007). Moreover, disadvantaged neighborhoods tend to be located far from available jobs (Mouw 2000; Wilson 1987), creating a spatial mismatch between job seekers and job openings and making finding employment more difficult. In a study of California parolees, Raphael and Weiman (2007) found that being released to a county with a lower unemployment rate was associated with a lower risk of being returned to custody. Wang, Mears, and Bales (2010) found similar results for a sample of returning prisoners in Florida.[12] County unemployment rates were also negatively associated with employment outcomes in a study of returning prisoners in Ohio (Sabol 2007).

Different communities have differential access to local social services from which formerly incarcerated individuals can benefit. Neighborhoods with a greater density of middle-class families are thought to have stronger community institutions and greater resources as such families disproportionately sustain community institutions and organizations (Wilson 1987). Small and McDermott (2006) found that, on average, poorer neighborhoods actually have slightly more commercial establishments such as pharmacies, grocery stores, and child-care centers but that poor African American neighborhoods with declining populations—which would characterize most of Michigan's African American urban neighborhoods—have fewer such establishments. Hipp et al. (2009b) found considerable variation across parolees in the local availability of social services in California, with African American and Hispanic parolees and parolees who have been in prison longer living in neighborhoods with fewer services or services that are in greater demand (see also Hipp et al. 2009a). Because formerly incarcerated individuals may especially need employment assistance, drug and alcohol treatment, and help meeting basic needs for food and shelter, their concentration in low-resource neighborhoods with many other residents who also have significant needs may overtax available services. In a study set in California, low proximate availability of social services was found to be predictive of parolee recidivism (Hipp, Petersilia, and Turner 2010).

Another approach to understanding the role that neighborhood context might play in prisoner reintegration is rooted in ideas about how institutional reactions to deviance can vary across communities. Prior research suggests that police practices vary considerably across neighborhoods in such a way that "disadvantaged areas are both overpoliced and underpoliced" (Lerman and Weaver 2014, 204). On the one hand, poor and nonwhite jurisdictions tend to have less police protection per recorded crime (Thacher 2010). On the other hand, in more disadvantaged, higher-crime neighborhoods, police are more likely to arrest suspects they encounter and use coercive force and less likely to provide citizens with assistance and information or file incident reports (Smith 1986; Sun, Payne, and Wu 2008). Lerman and Weaver (2014) argue that the heavy use of stop-and-frisk tactics, especially when suspects are not engaged in illicit activity, is likely to have a "chilling effect" on the willingness of residents to reach out to the police and engage in other forms of civic life.[13] Those on parole may be especially targeted by law enforcement for surveillance and arrest.

Accessing and Using Public Transportation

A crucial aspect of one's neighborhood from a geographic location perspective is the way its location and access to reliable transportation facilitate or hinder mobility. For those fortunate enough to live in geographic areas well served by safe and efficient public transportation, the bus proved to be an easy way to take care of the necessities of daily life (grocery shopping, doctor visits, and other errands) as well as to access services and look for jobs (see also chapter 6). Given the many obligations of being on parole (see chapter 2), efficient transportation to and from parole officer appointments, mental health and substance abuse programs, job-readiness programs, and other social services was critical to accomplishing these tasks and still having time for job search and family responsibilities. Such safe and efficient public transportation was generally available only to participants who lived in wealthier areas of southeast Michigan, either the Ann Arbor–Ypsilanti area (particularly those neighborhoods adjacent to the bus depots in each city) or the middle-class suburbs north of Detroit. For example, Paul lived in downtown Ann Arbor with his wife, and, even though his driver's license was suspended owing to drunk-driving convictions, he was able to accomplish all his daily tasks as well as get to and from school and work easily on the bus: "I have my month bus pass. It takes me anywhere I need to go from parole to the mall to the doctor's office. I can walk to my dentist. So living in downtown Ann Arbor has some huge advantages for me and being on the bus line. But I can go to the grocery story, the pharmacy, wherever I need to go I can get to on the bus, with the exception of say friends who live in the country."

Though Paul's experience with the bus was not unique, it was also not typical. For some, the bus was yet another site of risk and temptation, like the neighborhood as a whole. Detroit's bus system was uniformly perceived to be dangerous, not to mention inefficient, with slow and infrequent or unreliable service. Waiting for the bus or walking home from the bus stop, particularly in Detroit's poorest and most depopulated neighborhoods, meant risking victimization. Recall how Lenora worried about her safety getting to and from the bus, especially at night. Even the bus itself could be dangerous; Lenora also worried about people she called "rowdies" on the bus.

Riding the bus also meant the potential for exposure to "wet places and wet faces." For some, the bus was understood as endangering their sobriety or their commitment to desistance from crime. The chances were high of running into someone from their past lives of drug abuse or criminal behavior and therefore a potential trigger. Moreover, our participants worried that even talking to such individuals could be interpreted as violating one's conditions of parole as it is forbidden to associate with other felons on probation or parole, many of whom are also riding the bus. DeAngelo, for instance, strategized about how to deal with chance meetings with former associates. He needed a way both to avoid snubbing such individuals and to keep the interaction short as a social snub could be interpreted as a sign of disrespect and thus prompt an altercation. Such altercations could easily result in contact with the police, especially if they occurred on the bus or in the bus depot while waiting for a bus. To avoid this result, DeAngelo developed a bus-specific version of "hi and bye": "I gotta catch the bus to the transit [depot]. So I run into them all the time. I stand there and kick it with them till my bus come. When my bus come, you know, 'cause I don't wanna be rude, make it all obvious that I'm not trying to kick it with them 'cause that creates a problem."

Some participants avoided the bus altogether whenever possible, even when it was available. For example, Jennifer preferred to risk missing appointments or waiting for a day when family could give her a ride. In her first interview after her release, she recalled a stressful encounter she experienced on the bus many years in the past: "There might be times I will have to take buses, but hopefully not because I'm scared to ride the bus.... I rode it one time before, the city bus in Ypsilanti, and there was bums on the bus trying to get money off us, me and [my son] when [he] was little. He took me on the bus, I wouldn't let him ride the city bus to school no more because it was dangerous."

Still other participants simply had little or no access to public transportation because they lived in rural or exurban areas with limited or no bus service and were totally dependent on family for transportation. Without cars or valid driver's licenses, they had trouble meeting the basic requirements of their parole, such as regular attendance at AA or NA meetings or searching actively for work. After a relapse and new arrest, Kristine was offered the opportunity to participate in a drug court rather than go to jail. Living again with her mother in the outer Detroit suburbs, she had trouble complying with the treatment requirements of drug court:

So then when I went to see [my agent] yesterday she said you have to see your therapy before you come get me, you have to go to a meeting every single day, and I'm like, Well, how am I supposed to do all this? The only one I have is my mom. My sister will help as much as possible, but she has a family, she works a full-time job. As long as I do what I'm supposed to do they're there to help me. . . . There's no buses out here. It's freezing outside. Who wants to go stand outside and wait for a bus or walk to a bus stop? If I was to walk to the bus stop, it's a mile away, plus it only goes like down Grand River, and that's not where I have to go. I have to go to Pontiac, so there's no bus lines here for me. So [my parole officer is] like, "Well, I have plenty of people that make it here, da, da, da, that gets rides, whatever, they do what they have to do." Yeah, drug court don't give you a break, or they don't try to help you at all, to me. At all.

Similarly, Jennifer also skipped substance abuse treatment because she did not have transportation. Recall that, when she was first released, she lived with her fiancé, Fred, in a small town between Detroit and Ann Arbor (before moving to the trailer park in Ypsilanti). In this small town she had no access to public transportation and no money for gas. More importantly, even if she could borrow Fred's car, she was not legally allowed to drive owing to a suspended license, and reinstating her driver's license was a costly roadblock, one that almost all our participants experienced.

Suspended Driver's Licenses as Collateral Punishment

One of the reasons access to safe and efficient public transportation was important to our participants is that almost none were legally allowed to drive. The reasons were myriad, complex, and overlapping but were the result of restrictions imposed by parole, suspended licenses owing to impaired-driving convictions, unpaid past fines, tickets, driver responsibility fees, and lack of insurance. Those whose prior crimes involved automobiles (drunk driving, auto theft, using a car in a crime) could be prohibited from driving while on parole. Those with histories of addiction typically had at least one conviction for impaired driving, and periods of sustained and active drug addiction meant that past fees and fines went unpaid, only to accumulate in ways that made them very expensive to pay off. Driver responsibility fees were the most common barrier.

Michigan, like other states, has a driver responsibility law that imposes fees on drivers who either commit specific offenses (driving while intoxicated, driving while impaired, driving with a suspended license, driving without proof of insurance, driving with an expired license) or who accrue a certain number of points on their license for moving violations. Points accrue and then drop off over time, and maintaining one's license requires keeping current on those fees. The stated purpose of the law is to encourage traffic safety.[14] For our participants, however, it typically meant that they would never be able to drive legally again as fees quickly ballooned to thousands of dollars. For example, each driving-while-intoxicated conviction carries a $1,000 per year fee that must be paid for two years. Driving while impaired or with a suspended license carries a $500 fee, again for two years in a row. Having seven points on one's license carries a yearly fee of $100, with an additional $50 for each point. Once a license has been suspended for nonpayment of fees, another fee of $125 is required for reinstatement. Although it is possible to have one's license reinstated after setting up an installment payment plan, the maximum length of time for such installments is twenty-four months, meaning that monthly payments would still be prohibitively expensive for someone recently released from prison. And fees continue to accrue while an individual is in prison.

Jennifer's circumstances illustrate the challenges our participants faced in paying off these fees. Owing to past drunk-driving convictions and other violations, her fees were over $5,000 at release. This increased to over $6,000 the next year. Once those fees had been paid, Jennifer could get a restricted license that would allow her to drive for only specific purposes (like work and child care). She was fortunate that her sisters gradually paid down these fees for her, but she still had to wait another year to have her license reinstated owing to her past drunk-driving convictions. Like most of our participants, Jennifer drove anyway as she had no other practical way to meet her daily needs and, in her case, care for her son: "It's like telling the poor people that they'll never get outta debt, you know, you'll never get your license back. Because a lotta people in my situation don't have jobs. They don't have money to pay off things like that. You try to learn from your mistakes, but how in the hell do you get ahead when they're doing this to you?"

Jennifer and many others felt caught in a catch-22. They cannot access jobs and services because they cannot drive, but they cannot pay their driver's fees without a job. This is similar in many ways to the role of monetary sanctions in the criminal justice system, in which fees and fines serve to trap individuals who cannot pay them in states of surveillance and monitoring (Harris 2016). An inability to drive also presented problems for meeting family responsibilities, taking care of children, and accessing medical care. Jennifer, for example, had no other way of regularly visiting her older son in prison.

Most participants continued to drive illegally and without insurance, though doing so posed obvious risks. Jennifer worried that being caught driving without a license could be a felony that would land her back in prison. (This is technically incorrect as driving without a license is a misdemeanor, albeit one that can result in a sentence of up to ninety-three days in jail and a $500 fine. However, for someone on parole, a misdemeanor conviction could technically result in a parole violation that could be punished by a return to prison.) She continued to drive, trying to limit her driving to absolute necessities like groceries or taking her son to appointments. Her worst fears almost came true when she was pulled over. She imagined being returned to prison and losing custody of her youngest son:

> I'm not supposed to be driving, and I got a ticket.... Thank god, the officer was real nice to me. I broke out crying, and I told him, I said, "Oh my god." I said, "I only drive when I have to, and I don't have a license, and I'm sorry." I said, "You're gonna look at my record. I was recently, a few years back, released from prison, but I said it was a life-learning experience. I said it's totally changed my life. I have custody of my child." And he sat there, and he listened to me for about fifteen minutes. And he said, "I'm going to give you a big break today." He said, "I want to congratulate you on your sobriety." And he said, "No need to cry." I was hyperventilating and everything. I was freaking out. I got home, I had chest pains all night. I thought for sure I was going to lose my license forever, end up in jail, lose [my son].

DeAngelo provides another example. At one point he owed over $8,000 after he was caught driving on a suspended license with an open container in the vehicle, an arrest that also resulted in a parole violation and a return to prison. Although at one point he had hopes of going to barber college so he could turn his experience cutting hair informally for friends and neighbors into a real career, he needed a car to make regular trips to and from the college: "I need a car. If I had my license, I'd be able to drive to a barber's college that's twenty-five, thirty minutes away." He talked about getting a motorized bicycle, which doesn't require a license to drive but would have limited range and utility. In the meantime, he kept driving without a license and was again pulled over. After going to court, he had all but given up on ever getting a driver's license again for the rest of his life, owing to both the fees and his history of driving under the influence and with a suspended license: "[The police officer] let me come home. But he wrote me a ticket. The judge looked at my driver's record. And he was like, 'Honestly, I don't think you're ever going to get your license back. You've got five pages with predominantly suspensions.' And I can pay the money off. But, then, I have to go in front of, like, a board, meet the board or something, and they're gonna decide whether they want to give me my license back or not."

Not everyone decided to risk driving without a license. Some had no car to drive, and others felt close enough to paying off fees or fines that they did not want to risk the consequences. How did those faced with limited public transportation and no ability to drive cope? In addition to rides from family, some simply did they best they could, combining limited available public transportation with walking or biking long distances, essentially employing a grit approach to getting around. They were willing to ride the bus for hours each way to and from work or appointments or walk or bike for miles through Michigan's harsh winters and even if it meant waking at four in the morning to arrive on time.

Christopher, Leon, Randall, and Lenora relied on the grit approach to transportation at various times throughout the study. Such strategies reveal how hard some of our participants were willing to work just to keep a low-wage job and the barriers they had to overcome to keep those jobs. Yet such strategies require an investment in time and physical energy that was simply impossible for others with health problems, serious caretaking responsibilities, or the need for intensive participation in substance abuse treatment. Thus, the grit approach to getting around reveals as much about the challenges created by lack of access to transportation as it does about the perseverance of those who could make it work.

Conclusion

This chapter has considered the neighborhood as a context in the reintegration of formerly incarcerated individuals. Returning citizens tend to live in disadvantaged neighborhoods and experience little improvement in neighborhood conditions over time. The concentration of formerly incarcerated individuals in high-poverty neighborhoods is particularly strong among African Americans, owing to the larger social patterns of residential segregation by race and income in American society. Two characteristics of neighborhoods that were most salient to our research participants are safety and connectedness as most described their neighborhoods in terms of risk and temptation and experienced few interactions with their neighbors.

As a result, we saw little evidence that interactions with neighbors played a role in employment or recidivism outcomes. Most of our participants socialized largely with family, while some were involved in community or addiction recovery communities. In contrast, neighborhoods play a larger role as geographic locations, structuring access to jobs and social services. Transportation plays a critical role in overcoming the challenges of geographically isolated neighborhoods. With public transportation typically either unsafe, unreliable, or inefficient, driving proved to be the main option for many, despite the risks associated with driving with a suspended license. The challenges presented by the combination of dangerous and geographically isolated neighborhoods and poor access to reliable transportation illustrates one way that contexts and individual characteristics interact to influence reintegration outcomes. In the next chapter, we turn to an in-depth examination of the labor market as another critical context for reintegration.

CHAPTER SIX

Finding and Maintaining Employment

Lamar represents one end of the continuum of employment outcomes after prison. Immediately after his release from prison, he embarked on an intense job search that involved looking for job postings in the newspaper, taking the bus around Ann Arbor and Ypsilanti to apply for those jobs in person, and also applying for jobs at any neighboring business—mostly stores and restaurants—that would take an application. Each morning he left the homeless shelter in downtown Ann Arbor, walked a few blocks to a church that provided free breakfast for the homeless and the poor, and then walked a few more blocks to the city's bus depot. Waiting for the bus he would chat up other riders who were on their way to work about whether there were openings with their employers. He estimated that he applied at over two hundred businesses in the first few weeks after his release. After walking into a fast-food restaurant to buy a soda and deciding to fill out an application, he managed to talk to the manager in person. A few days later he called back and was told he had a part-time job at the minimum wage, then $7.15 an hour. About the same time, his stepsister told him that a discount store was hiring stock clerks, and he put in an application—without mentioning the referral—and was hired there, also part-time and also at the minimum wage. He suspects that his felony record may have actually helped him land both these jobs as both employers seemed to be interested in hiring people—like felons and former welfare recipients—who made them eligible for federal tax credits.

Juggling two variable part-time schedules without a car was challenging, so Lamar continued to search for jobs on his days off. From his brother he heard that a new chain restaurant that was under construction was interviewing for employees, and he filled out an application and waited for an interview. While waiting for his own interview, he overheard the questions the interviewers asked other applicants and practiced his answers in his head. Neither the application nor the interviewer asked about a felony record, and he was hired as a prep cook full-time at $9.00 per hour when the restaurant opened. He also found another part-time job working the night shift at a different fast-food restaurant, which also paid $9.00 per hour, although he quit that job after his full-time job began giving him overtime hours. After two months in the full-time job, he was fired after a dispute with his boss over accommodations for his epilepsy, which was exacerbated by the heat of the kitchen. He hit the pavement again and was hired as a taxi driver, taking home whatever fares and tips he earned after paying for the lease on the taxi. He lost that job when he was arrested, jailed, and eventually returned to prison on a parole violation. He had skipped appointments with his parole officer when they conflicted with his taxi shifts, purchased a stolen money order for a fraction of its face value, using it to pay a utility bill, and was accused of stealing jewelry by his sister-in-law (although the jewelry accusation was eventually withdrawn).

Randall's experience in the labor market stands in stark contrast to that of Lamar, although in many ways their prerelease trajectories were similar. Even though Randall had some experience working in fast food and as a prep cook at a restaurant before he was first incarcerated, he struggled to secure any sort of employment and often ended up doing odd jobs for family, friends, and neighbors, like cleaning, yard work, and washing cars. On two occasions he also briefly returned to selling drugs—acts of desperation, he explained—but quickly stopped. At first he looked for jobs by talking to family and friends, but referrals never yielded anything. He suspects this was because of his criminal record, but he was never explicitly told this. Over time he sought help securing a job through a temporary labor firm, three social service providers, and Michigan Works! the state employment agency, but none of these attempts paid off. Because there were few opportunities in his neighborhood, he often resorted to walking downtown, which could take an hour and a half each way, another example of the grit approach to transportation discussed in the previous chapter. A retired stepuncle he was living with occasionally drove him to the suburbs to look for work, but applications he submitted there never resulted in a callback. A year after his release, Randall estimated that he had applied for about fifty jobs. Finally, three years after his release and after moving to the suburbs with his new wife, he was hired as a short-order cook and dishwasher in a chain restaurant, earning $9.00 an hour and working full-time. He explained that the woman who hired him knew about his criminal record but had a record of her own and was sympathetic to his struggles.

As discussed in the previous chapter, Lamar's success in the labor market relative to Randall's might be attributed in part to the local geographic context in which each searched for work. Labor markets where there is lower unemployment and more construction and manufacturing employment are associated with better employment and recidivism outcomes for formerly incarcerated people, particularly for first-time offenders and those who were employed after prison (Bellair and Kowalski 2011; Bushway, Stoll, and Weiman 2007; Nguyen, Morenoff, and Harding 2014; Schnepel 2014; Wang, Mears, and Bales 2010). Lamar found that his search strategy worked particularly well in Ann Arbor and Ypsilanti, where a comparatively readily available system of public transportation and a more vibrant economy meant many low-skill service-sector job openings to which he had access. Randall, in contrast, was looking for work in Detroit, where the official unemployment rate approached 15 percent in 2008 (according the Bureau of Labor Statistics) and mobility without reliable access to a car is challenging. (Note, however, that the official unemployment rate understates joblessness because it excludes those not actively searching for work, so prospects for employment in Detroit are even worse than this figure suggests.) As we will discuss further below, Lamar was also comparatively advantaged by what seemed to be better interviewing skills and a high school diploma rather than a GED.

Yet perhaps the most striking difference between Lamar and Randall is that, despite his relative success in the labor market, Lamar ended up back in state prison while Randall did not. Lamar was returned to prison for multiple parole violations, including failure to report to his parole officer and accusations of burglary and theft, while Randall successfully discharged from parole about two years after his release (although he did spend a few weeks in the county jail for petty theft of a cell phone). This contrast illustrates one case that challenges our conventional wisdom and social science theory about the importance of employment for recidivism or desistance. For example, Sampson and Laub (1995) argue that employment creates stakes in conformity by increasing the costs of reincarceration, reduces the material motivations for crime, and structures one's time and social networks. Yet prior research clearly shows that, although employment is a statistically significant predictor of recidivism (Engelhardt 2010; Hagan 1993; Sampson and Laub 1995; Tanner, Davies, and O'Grady 1999; Thornberry and Christenson 1984; Uggen 2000), employment is far from determinative, and the evidence is decidedly mixed (Crutchfield 2014; Petersilia 2003). For example, there is some evidence that employment merely delays recidivism rather than preventing it, and in some samples employment and recidivism are only weakly associated (Tripodi, Kim, and Bender 2010). We will also show below that—like Randall—many formerly incarcerated individuals who never appear to be employed in the formal labor market also never return to prison while many who do find formal employment nevertheless end up back in prison, like Lamar.

We view postprison employment as important not simply for its role in affecting recidivism but for the fact that it is a key indicator of—and prerequisite for—social and economic reintegration after prison more generally. Prior chapters revealed the importance of employment for successfully negotiating and maintaining family roles and responsibilities (particularly but not exclusively for men) as well as for residential stability and escaping from or avoiding the most disadvantaged neighborhood environments. Moreover, steady and gainful employment can be viewed as a foundation for full participation in other domains of society, such as political participation, community involvement, and civil society.

The comparison between Lamar and Randall illustrates a number of important features of the postprison labor market experiences of formerly incarcerated people that we elaborate on below, including challenges securing and maintaining employment, the types of industries in which formerly incarcerated people do find employment, and the volatility of employment for many formerly incarcerated people. Our analysis of postprison employment highlights several key aspects of the theoretical framework outlined in the introduction, including the importance of contexts like parole supervision and the larger criminal justice system, institutions that preserve and reinforce stigma, families and broader social networks, and the precarious nature of work in the low-wage labor market. It also highlights the mismatch between the resources and health of formerly incarcerated individuals and the job requirements of contemporary employers.

The Nature of Postprison Employment

We begin by documenting and describing key features of the postprison labor market on the basis of prior research and our own data from Michigan. Rates of employment among formerly incarcerated people are very low and do not improve over time. Figure 6.1 shows mean rates of

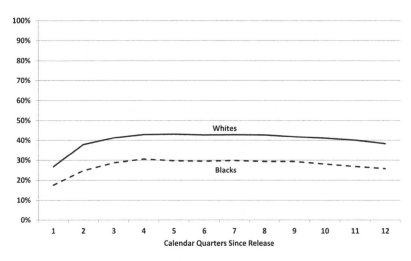

FIGURE 6.1. Percentage of parolees in the community who are employed in the formal labor market

holding any job in the formal labor market in a calendar quarter over time since release, figures based on administrative data collected from employers by the state unemployment insurance system.[1] We focus on formal employment in this analysis largely because that is what our administrative data are able to measure. This means that work under the table (whether legal or illegal) is not included. Many of the forms of self-employment we discuss further below would also not be captured in these data. However, we would argue that formal employment is often preferred as it indicates a stronger tie to the labor market, greater job security, and access to social protections such as unemployment insurance, workers' compensation, and the like. Quarter 1 is the first full quarter after the quarter of release from prison, so it represents the first quarter for which we observe parolees in the community for an entire quarter. The horizontal axis extends from quarter 1 until quarter 12, or three years after release.

Formal employment among both African American and white employees increases through the fourth quarter, or one year after release, and then levels off and even declines slightly toward the end of the time period. White employment peaks at around 43 percent, African American employment at about 29 percent. We note also that this figure includes only individuals who at any given point in time are still in the community and have not been returned to prison. This makes the leveling off of employment rates even more pronounced as we might otherwise assume that those returning to prison would have been less likely to be employed had they remained in the community. By that logic, removing individuals from the data when they go back to prison should have pushed employment rates upward over time. The fact that we do not observe this suggests both the profound challenges of finding and maintaining employment after prison and the absence of a tight link between employment and recidivism.[2]

When they do find formal employment, formerly incarcerated people tend to work in what is called the *secondary labor market*, jobs that are characterized by lower wages, greater turnover, poor working conditions, and fewer possibilities for upward mobility (Kalleberg and Sørensen 1979; Piore 1975; Weiman, Stoll, and Bushway 2007; Western 2007). For example, Western (2002) shows that incarceration not only reduces employment and wages in the short term but also lowers wage growth over the long term, suggesting that formerly incarcerated people may be relegated to the secondary labor market as a result of their incarceration. However, to our knowledge, no prior research has directly examined the types of jobs in which formerly incarcerated people are employed.

Table 6.1 shows the industries in which formerly incarcerated people worked during the first three years after their release and compares the composition to all Michigan workers.[3] The table sorts industries by the percentage of employed parolees working in them. At the top of the list are what are called *administrative and support industries*. Among parolees, these mostly include temporary labor positions (the *employment services industry* in table 6.1), which accounted for almost 19 percent of all person-quarters, and janitorial and maintenance work (3.7 percent). The second largest category is *manufacturing*, owing in part to the importance of manufacturing in the Michigan economy. Almost 16 percent of Michigan workers hold jobs in manufacturing industries, while manufacturing accounts for 20 percent of employed quarters among Michigan parolees. Rounding out the top of the list for parolees is *accommodation and food services*, mostly fast-food restaurants (8.1 percent) and full-service restaurants (5.7 percent), construction (9.6 percent), retail (7.8 percent), health care and social assistance (4.2 percent), and a category called *other services* that is dominated by auto repair and maintenance (3.0 percent).

Table 6.1 also shows that parolees tend to be more concentrated in these industries than the Michigan workforce as a whole (see the parolee/worker ratio column, which is the ratio of Michigan parolee employment percentage to that for all Michigan workers) and that the industries in which parol-

TABLE 6.1 **Employment by industry, Michigan parolees versus all Michigan workers**

Industry (NAICS code)	Michigan parolees[a] (%)	All Michigan workers[b] (%)	Parolee/ worker ratio	Payroll per employee among all workers[b] ($)
Administrative and support (56)	25.1	8.4	3.0	31,782
Employment services (5613)	19.3	5.3	3.6	32,139
Services to buildings/dwellings (5617)	3.7	1.1	3.5	24,842
Manufacturing (31–33)	20.0	15.7	1.3	51,701
Fabricated metal product manufacturing (332)	4.9	2.1	2.4	43,196
Transportation equipment manufacturing (336)	4.8	4.6	1.1	62,035
Accommodation and food services (72)	16.5	9.1	1.8	12,531
Limited-service eating places (7222)	8.1	3.4	2.4	12,768
Full-service restaurants (7221)	5.7	4.0	1.4	10,584
Construction (23)	9.6	3.8	2.5	52,000
Retail trade (44–45)	7.8	12.9	0.6	21,663
Health care and social assistance (62)	4.2	14.9	0.3	39,203
Other services (81)	4.4	4.6	1.0	23,921
Automotive repair and maintenance (8,111)	3.0	0.8	3.6	28,209
Wholesale trade (42)	3.1	4.5	0.7	56,147
Professional, scientific, and technical (54)	1.9	7.3	0.3	63,859
Transportation and warehousing (48–49)	1.8	2.9	0.7	42,891
Arts, entertainment, and recreation (71)	1.0	1.5	0.7	30,044
Real estate and rental and leasing (53)	0.8	1.6	0.5	30,990
Education services (61)	0.6	1.8	0.4	24,265
Information (51)	0.6	2.1	0.3	56,604
Agriculture, forestry, fishing, hunting (11)	0.5	0.1	6.4	31,746
Finance and insurance (52)	0.4	4.6	0.1	54,498
Mining (21)	0.1	0.2	0.7	57,050
Management of companies/enterprises (55)	0.1	3.4	0.0	90,959
Utilities (22)	0.0	0.6	0.0	84,496
Other/unclassified	1.6	0.0	N.A.	N.A.
All industries				40,935

Note: NAICS = North American Industry Classification System. N.A. = not applicable.
[a]Source: Michigan Study of Life after Prison, unemployment insurance records, quarterly employment weighted by number of employers per quarter in the three-year period following release.
[b]Source: US Bureau of the Census, 2007 County Business Patterns.

ees are concentrated tend to be some of the lowest-paying in the economy (see the rightmost column, "Payroll per Employee among All Workers"). For example, while median payroll per worker across all industries is $40,935, parolees commonly work in administrative and support, accommodation and food services, and retail, where median payroll is $31,782, $12,531, and $21,663 per year, respectively. The two exceptions where parolees are concentrated in higher-wage industries are manufacturing and construction, which tend to have mean wages above the state average, although we cannot know from these data what hourly wages parolees in these industries are being paid.

Table 6.2 examines parolee employment and earnings by industry broken down by race, revealing stark racial disparities in the labor market for formerly incarcerated people, with African American parolees even more concentrated in low-paying industries than white parolees. For example, slightly over a quarter of employed person-quarters among African American parolees occur in the temporary labor industry (employment services), whereas the comparable figure for white parolees is just under 14 percent. In contrast, African Americans are far less likely to be employed in construction and slightly less likely to be employed in manufacturing. They are also more likely to be employed in fast food (limited-service eating places). Moreover, in almost every industry, mean quarterly earnings are lower for African Americans than whites (it is impossible to know from these data whether this reflects fewer work hours or lower hourly wages). This implies that the persistent racial difference in the probability of employment of about 14 percentage points observed in figure 6.1 is compounded by racial differences in the type of work that African American and white parolees are able to find when they are working and the amounts they earn. These racial differences do not appear to be due simply to differences in human capital or other preprison characteristics. In regression analyses published elsewhere, we find that racial differences in employment and earnings are robust to education, preprison employment, substance abuse history, age, marital status, county unemployment rates, and measures of criminal history (Morenoff and Harding 2011).[4]

The employment rates in figure 6.1 obscure another important feature of involvement in the labor market among formerly incarcerated people, the high degree of volatility in employment from quarter to quarter among individuals (see also Cook 1975; and Sugie and Lens 2017). Of those who are employed in a calendar quarter, 23 percent of those who remain in the community (i.e., have not been returned to prison) are no longer employed in the following calendar quarter. This does not include changing employers, a further form of volatility in employment but one that could be viewed as positive if the employee is changing to a better job. Of those unemployed in a particular calendar quarter, only 13 percent of those who remain in the community have any employment in the following calendar quarter. Both finding and keeping jobs appear to be very difficult for many formerly incarcerated people.

TABLE 6.2 **Michigan parolee industry of employment and mean quarterly earnings by race**

Industry (NAICS code)	Employment (%)		Mean quarterly earnings ($)	
	Whites	Blacks	Whites	Blacks
Administrative and support (56)	19.42	32.15	2,852	1,862
Employment services (5613)	13.81	26.34	2,550	1,681
Services to buildings/dwellings (5617)	4.04	3.11	3,654	2,334
Manufacturing (31–33)	21.08	18.58	5,473	5,240
Fabricated metal product manufacturing (332)	5.36	4.15	5,245	5,017
Transportation equipment manufacturing (336)	4.42	5.42	6,342	6,783
Accommodation and food services (72)	15.69	17.54	2,271	1,927
Limited-service eating places (7222)	7.04	9.65	1,908	1,622
Full-service restaurants (7221)	6.08	5.11	2,526	2,319
Construction (23)	14.42	3.35	4,962	4,341
Retail trade (44–45)	8.48	6.88	4,113	2,729
Health care and social assistance (62)	2.05	6.97	2,274	2,087
Other services (81)	5.01	3.67	3,971	3,209
Automotive repair and maintenance (8111)	3.74	2.08	4,161	3,660
Wholesale trade (42)	3.49	2.57	5,538	4,938
Professional, scientific, and technical (54)	2.00	1.73	5,628	6,875
Transportation and warehousing (48–49)	2.10	1.53	5,846	5,051
Arts, entertainment, and recreation (71)	1.27	0.52	3,384	1,951
Real estate and rental and leasing (53)	0.96	0.71	3,823	4,892
Education services (61)	0.34	1.03	3,434	4,076
Information (51)	0.67	0.47	3,637	3,354
Agriculture, forestry, fishing, hunting (11)	0.85	0.16	3,414	3,139
Finance and insurance (52)	0.28	0.47	6,469	6,064
Mining (21)	0.21	0	5,907	N.A.
Management of companies/enterprises (55)	0.11	0.08	5,736	4,310
Utilities (22)	0	0.02	N.A.	2,619
Other/unclassified	1.30	0.95	3,293	2,276

Source: Michigan Study of Life after Prison, unemployment insurance records, quarterly employment weighted by number of employers per quarter in the three-year period following release.
Note: NAICS = North American Industry Classification System. N.A. = not applicable.

In order to explore employment volatility further, we conducted what is called a *sequence analysis* of quarter-to-quarter employment for the first three years after release from prison.[5] This method of analysis deploys a descriptive, data-driven algorithm that sorts individuals into groups based on their quarterly employment trajectories. Seven groups of parolees emerged from this analysis. An examination of these groups, their employment experiences, and their characteristics sheds light on the nature of employment volatility among formerly incarcerated people (see tables 6.3 [on employment experiences] and 6.4 [on group characteristics]). For each group, we graphed the probability of employment by quarter since release (similar to figure 6.1, although in this case those who are reincarcerated are counted as not employed).

TABLE 6.3 **Employment trajectory groups and their employment experiences**

Group	Individuals (%)	Quarters employed (%)	Employment-unemployment transition rate (%)	Unemployment-employment transition rate (%)	Three-year reincarceration rate (%)
Overall	100	33	23	13	39
No employment	18	0	N.A.	0	0
High instability	27	16	63	11	45
Late bloomers	3	32	27	19	19
Slow starters	6	52	25	35	3
Reincarcer-ation	25	32	38	21	100
Trouble maintaining	4	48	30	22	8
Steady employment	17	83	8	61	9

Note: N.A. = not applicable.

Common industries	Mean quarterly wages when employed ($)	Employment probability over time
Manufacturing (20%), temp labor (19%), construction (10%), fast food (8%), retail (8%)	4,029	
(none)	N.A.	
Temp labor (27%), manufacturing (14%), construction (10%), fast food (8%), retail (8%)	1,738	
Temp labor (42%), manufacturing (11%), restaurants (7%), retail (7%), wholesale (7%)	3,009	
Temp labor (23%), fast food (21%), manufacturing (17%), retail (10%), restaurants (8%), construction (8%)	3,247	
Temp labor (28%), manufacturing (14%), fast food (13%), construction (10%), retail (7%)	2,503	
Manufacturing (21%), temp labor (20%), fast food (13%), fast food (13%)	2,863	
Manufacturing (21%), temp labor (21%), retail (9%), fast food (8%), restaurants (8%)	5,266	

TABLE 6.4 **Employment trajectory group characteristics**

Group	Mean age at parole	Black (%)	Female (%)	First prison sentence (%)	Mean prison years	Alcohol or drug abuse history (%)	Preprison employment (%)
Overall	35	54	8	48	2.9	49	17
No employment	39	62	10	58	2.8	40	9
High instability	35	59	8	45	2.6	55	15
Late bloomers	34	50	8	56	2.7	42	24
Slow starters	35	43	10	63	3.0	39	23
Reincarceration	34	54	6	27	2.8	63	16
Trouble maintaining	34	47	9	57	3.4	45	22
Steady employment	35	41	8	65	3.8	35	27

High school or greater (%)	GED (%)	Release to central city (%)	Mean tract unemployment rate of first residence (%)	Employment probability over time
26	31	53	10.3	
28	23	61	11.4	
21	33	58	10.8	
28	26	55	10.0	
31	27	50	9.3	
21	38	51	10.6	
24	33	47	9.6	
37	26	41	8.6	

One group that we isolated first was those individuals who never found employment but also never returned to prison. This group is most important because it suggests that the link between employment and recidivism is not as strong as one might intuitively expect. This group includes almost one-fifth (18 percent) of the individuals in our sample. Compared to the overall sample, they are four years older, more likely to be African American, released to a central city, have very low rates of preprison employment, are more likely to be on their first prison sentence, are least likely to hold a GED, and have lower than average rates of substance abuse prior to prison. These characteristics suggest that individuals in this group generally have less of a criminal history than the rest of the sample but are also otherwise disadvantaged in the labor market owing to their employment history, education, and race. The size of this group raises questions about how these individuals manage to get by day-to-day without employment and without returning to criminal activity (or at least getting caught). Given our analysis in chapter 3, we believe that assistance from family is playing a critical role here.

A second conceptually important group to emerge from the analysis, accounting for 27 percent of individuals, is a group we label *high instability*. Individuals in this group are employed in only 16 percent of the quarters observed and experience very high rates of transition out of employment when they do have a job (63 percent) and average rates of finding employment when they do not have a job (11 percent). In quarters in which they do have a job, their earnings are very low, which may reflect part-time work, work for only part of the quarter, and/or particularly low-paying jobs. Forty-five percent of this group eventually return to prison. The group is fairly typical of the sample as a whole on the individual characteristics we can observe in our data. Its size suggests that employment volatility, driven substantially by job loss from quarter to quarter, is an important aspect of the labor market experience of formerly incarcerated people.

The second largest group to emerge from the analysis is one in which all members are reincarcerated within three years. It is labeled *reincarceration* and includes 25 percent of all individuals. It is composed largely of repeat offenders as only 27 percent were serving their first prison sentence, compared to 48 percent for the sample as a whole, and its members have high rates of histories of substance abuse problems (63 percent as compared to 49 percent for the sample as a whole). Members of this group are about as likely as the sample as a whole to be employed in any given quarter but have high rates of both job loss and finding a job, frequent employment in temp services, as well as low mean quarterly earnings, suggesting that they also experience a great deal of employment volatility.

A fourth sizable group, accounting for 17 percent of our sample, is one we label *steady employment*. These individuals have the highest employment rates, and their employment tends to persist over time. When they are working in a calendar quarter, they transition to unemployment in the next calendar quarter less than 10 percent of the time, while they transition to employment from a quarter with no employment 61 percent of the time. They also have a very low rate of return to prison. These individuals are characterized by multiple advantages in the labor market. They are most likely to be white, to be serving their first prison sentence, to have low rates of substance abuse, to have the highest rates of preprison employment, and to have a high school degree, are least likely to exit prison into an inner city, and tend to move immediately after prison to neighborhoods with lower-than-average unemployment rates. In quarters in which they were employed, they had the highest average quarterly earnings.

Finally, the last three groups that the sequence analysis distinguished— *trouble maintaining*, *slow starters*, and *late bloomers*—each represent a very small portion of the sample (4, 6, and 3 percent, respectively). They contain individuals whose employment prospects changed most dramatically during the three-year period. In the case of trouble maintaining, they exhibited high rates of employment initially but then did not sustain this employment over time despite having low rates of reincarceration. Slow starters and late bloomers struggled initially with employment but then tended to find and maintain employment later (slow starters tended to recover earlier in the three-year period than late bloomers, whose employment prospects improved much later). These groups are important to consider precisely because their members are relatively rare. Postprison trajectories characterized by fundamental change in employment prospects over time, either positive or negative, are atypical. This suggests that initial outcomes and experiences are very likely to continue over time, a fact that we will return to in the next chapter as we discuss the importance of the period immediately after release and the notion of turning points in life trajectories.

In sum, our analysis of postrelease employment among Michigan parolees and the prior literature show the following. First, rates of employment in the formal labor market are very low among formerly incarcerated people, and African Americans fare considerably worse than whites.

Second, when formerly incarcerated people do find employment, they are disproportionately concentrated in certain industries in the secondary labor market where wages are low, turnover is high, working conditions are unpleasant, and there are fewer career ladders for upward advancement (Kalleberg 2011; Newman 2009). Third, partly related to their relegation to the secondary labor market, employment instability is very high among formerly incarcerated people, even by our crude measure of quarter-to-quarter transitions between employment and unemployment. This suggests that a simple story about how the stigma of a felony record makes getting a job extremely difficult cannot be the entire explanation for low rates of employment.

These key facts suggest three interrelated questions that we pursue in the remainder of this chapter on the basis largely of our qualitative interview sample. First, given the low rates of employment among formerly incarcerated people and the high proportion of them who never find employment in the formal labor market in the first three years after release, what are the main barriers? Second, how do some formerly incarcerated people manage to find jobs despite the stigma of their felony record, and why are these jobs concentrated in the secondary labor market? Third, what explains the high rates of job loss among formerly incarcerated people?

Barriers to Employment among Formerly Incarcerated People

Why are employment rates so low among formerly incarcerated people? The literature provides a number of explanations, all of which probably contribute somewhat to the rates of employment we see in figure 6.1. One important explanation is that individuals who serve time in prison tend to have poor labor market prospects before they even enter prison owing to low human capital (Kurlychek, Brame, and Bushway 2007). Indeed, the most consistent predictors of postprison employment among formerly incarcerated people, in addition to criminal history, are preprison employment and preprison education levels (Bushway, Stoll, and Weiman 2007). This is reflected in our administrate data (table 6.3), which show high rates of substance abuse, high rates of prior involvement in the criminal justice system, low levels of education, and low rates of employment in the year before prison.

This means that, even had they not been incarcerated, many formerly incarcerated people would have been unlikely to have been employed outside the low-skill labor market, where real incomes across all workers have fallen over the last few decades. The nature of the contemporary low-wage labor market is critical. Weiman, Stoll, and Bushway (2007) argue that larger-scale changes in our political economy have created a low-wage labor market that has made employment challenging for formerly incarcerated people and other disadvantaged workers, particularly the shift to the knowledge economy and the decline in manufacturing, falling rates of unionization, a decline in the real value of the minimum wage, movement of jobs out of central cities, and declines in the enforcement of antidiscrimination and minimum wage laws.

Poor health may also be a significant barrier to labor market success among formerly incarcerated people, who have high rates of what are often called *behavioral health problems* (mental illness, substance abuse) and associated problems such as homelessness (Visher and Travis 2003). An aging prison population (Carson and Golinelli 2013) also means that the physically demanding work available to low-skill workers is not possible for a growing share of formerly incarcerated people. We saw many examples of health problems posing barriers to employment in our qualitative interviews. Kristine suffered severe pain from a back injury that made physically demanding jobs difficult, even those involving standing for long periods of time such as waitressing or retail work, which she had worked in the past. Jocelyn suffered from chronic obstructive pulmonary disease (COPD) and was effectively unable to work. Lamar lost a job in part because his boss would not allow accommodations for his epilepsy, which was exacerbated by the hot work environment of a restaurant kitchen. Jennifer could not lift heavy objects owing to a back injury from a car accident. DeAngelo suffered from anxiety, bipolar disorder, and depression that, if untreated, sapped his motivation to work and made social encounters stressful. We will discuss further below the important role of substance use and addiction in job losses. Moreover, as we discussed in chapter 4, health problems among family members and the need to help care for them interfered with work as well.

Another set of explanations focuses on the effects of incarceration on readiness for the labor market. Human capital may erode while in prison, the conditions of prison may lead to problems with physical health, mental health, and substance abuse, and soft skills may be damaged by the harsh social environment of prison (Bushway, Stoll, and Weiman 2007). With regard to soft skills, Caputo-Levine (2013) argues that the strategies and interaction styles that men develop to deal with the interpersonal violence

of prison life become internalized and persist after release, making it difficult to perform well in job interviews or in a hectic work environment. For
instance, formerly incarcerated people may be more sensitive to confining physical spaces, perceive accidental bodily contact as threatening, be
resistant to making small talk, and be hesitant to display outward signs of
friendliness such as smiling. These problems are likely to be most serious
immediately after release and seem to dissipate as the formerly incarcerated have time to adjust to their new social environment (see chapter 2).

A third set of explanations is the intensity of complying with parole
requirements, especially in the early period after release. In chapter 2,
we discussed the ways in which being on parole can feel like a full-time
job, especially when transportation to and from the required meetings, appointments, and check-ins is taken into account. These requirements tend
to become less onerous after the first month or two on parole, but other
requirements persist. Parole conditions can also limit the types of jobs a
parolee can hold. Certain industries may be off-limits because they tend
to pay workers under the table and parole officers want to see a pay stub
as proof of formal employment (although not all parole offices or parole
officers were strict about this rule). When Randall was asked about his
troubles finding a job at his second follow-up interview, he explained that
he could not work in the bars or car washes near his Detroit neighborhood
that might otherwise have been willing to hire an ex-con: "They don't want
me working at no car wash. I can't work at no bar. I think that's against
parole guidelines. . . . You can't get paid under the table, basically. . . . They
want to see the check stub for verification of a job. There got to be a check
stub."

Electronic monitoring can also make finding a job more challenging.
Recall that Leon was placed on GPS electronic monitoring for the first
three months of his parole, which kept track of whether he was at home
during prescribed times. This precluded him from working at a temp
service—the most common source of employment for formerly incarcerated people according to our administrative data—owing to the irregular
nature of temporary labor employment: "I went to the temp service. [My
parole officer] told me . . . I got to work like a three week, thirty times,
and then he can change the [electronic] monitor, but he ain't going to be
changing it every day. . . . He ain't going to come out to the house, reset
the monitor, or call Lansing and say, 'Set it for this time every day,' switch
it. But if I get a job, a regular job, they'll switch it for me. But shit, I can't
find no regular job."

Finally, our participants also worried about employment-verification checks by parole officers, fearing that such contact would annoy their bosses or prove to be a continual reminder of their status as formerly incarcerated people on parole. Jane explained how this might affect her ability to get an office job like the one she had before her most recent incarceration. It also forced her to reveal her criminal record even to employers who might not otherwise do record checks:

> They might not run [my record] in an office job. But, see, that's the chance you take. 'Cause if you lie they will guarantee that they will fire you.

> *Interviewer: And does your parole officer check with your job?*

> Well, they are supposed to. Now when I had my job in a law firm before, it was my cousin's law firm. There's like fifty people that work there. So I put her down as the contact person, as my boss. So they would contact just her, not someone else. And [my parole officer] says to me one day when I was in there, doesn't other people in the office know you came from prison? I said, no. She said, Well they should. I said, No, the person that hired me is the one that knows. The people that sit next to me in an office don't need to know. She said, Why wouldn't you tell? Why would I tell? I said; this way I have a better chance of them getting to know who I am first. And you make a judgment call on who I am instead of what I've done. When she called, she still saying she was "Agent Washington." Thanks.

Results from regression analyses regarding the likelihood of finding a job using our administrative data are largely consistent with the employment barriers identified in the prior literature and in our qualitative interviews. Formerly incarcerated people who have higher levels of education, who have preprison work experience, and who return to whiter, suburban neighborhoods have the highest probability of finding a job in the formal labor market. Those with a history of mental illness, those released onto electronic monitoring, those who are African American, and those who are older are less likely to find a job. We see no effect of substance abuse history or recent positive substance use tests on *finding* a job, but we will see below that recent substance use nonetheless plays an important role in job *loss*.

A fourth set of explanations for low employment after release from prison—and probably the most researched—is the stigma of a felony record and incarceration. We can distinguish between two types of stigma: formal and informal. Formal stigma prevents individuals with a criminal record or a record of certain types of crimes from working certain types of jobs or from obtaining the licenses or other certifications needed for whole classes of jobs.[6] Although variation across states and the sheer number of occupations involved make an exact count all but impossible, those with a criminal record are barred from working in a very large number of occupations, even long after they have completed their sentences (Petersilia 2003).[7]

Informal stigma affects employment prospects when employers prefer not to hire those with felony or prison records. A series of recent audit experiments employed testers with fictitious résumés that vary in terms of whether they signal a recent prison term. They are trained to pose as job applicants for real job openings. They show that having a criminal record reduces one's chance of a callback after applying for a job, ranging from 17 percentage points for a job applicant with a felony conviction and prison sentence to 4 percentage points for a misdemeanor arrest (Pager 2003, 2007a; Pager, Western, and Bonikowski 2009; Uggen et al. 2014).[8] A critical aspect of this informal stigma is the use of criminal background checks by employers. With the computerization of criminal records and easier access to them online through both private companies and public records searches, the use of criminal background checks among employers has been steadily increasing (Holzer, Raphael, and Stoll 2002, 2007).

To fully understand the role of stigma in the labor market experiences of formerly incarcerated people, we must also consider the ways in which a criminal record affects the types of jobs that formerly incarcerated people are able to obtain and which formerly incarcerated people are most likely to be affected. Audit studies and surveys of employers show that different types of firms are more or less likely to conduct background checks. Smaller firms are less likely to conduct background checks than larger firms and those with separate human resources departments. Firms covered by formal bans on hiring ex-offenders are more likely to conduct background checks, as are those that hire for jobs with child contact, cash handling, or customer contact (Holzer, Raphael, and Stoll 2007). Restaurants are among those employers least likely to conduct background checks (Pager 2007a), likely because they are small firms with high job turnover. Thus, it was not surprising that Lamar found some of his first jobs in that industry.

Surveys of employers also suggest that characteristics of the formerly incarcerated person play a role in how information about a criminal record is used in hiring decisions. Employers say they are most open to hiring drug offenders, then property offenders, and finally violent offenders. They also consider mitigating circumstances like work history since conviction or release, enrollment in rehabilitation programs, and time since release (Pager 2007a). Indeed, there is some evidence that firms that use background checks are more willing to hire ex-offenders than are those that do not, although this applies only to those using private background check companies and not public records checks (Holzer, Raphael, and Stoll 2007). This also suggests than such firms may use background checks to exclude only offenders with particular criminal histories or to exclude them from only particular types of jobs.

As discussed above, racial differences in postprison employment among formerly incarcerated people cannot be explained simply by preprison characteristics. One explanation is discrimination in the labor market against African Americans in general. Another is the heightened stigma attached to felony conviction and incarceration experienced by African American as compared to white formerly incarcerated people (Pager 2003, 2007a). Pager (2007a) finds that restaurants, which tend not to do background checks, are an industry most likely to hire whites with criminal records but least likely to hire African Americans with criminal records. This suggests that, when employers do not do background checks, race may stand in as a proxy for criminal record, disadvantaging African American applicants in general (although it might also simply result from greater discrimination in this industry). Pager also finds some evidence that formal disqualification from jobs based on a criminal record is more common among jobs typically occupied by African Americans, such as employment in the public sector. The racial difference we observe in figure 6.1 could also reflect greater reliance on informal employment among African Americans, although, if that were the case, we would view that as a further indicator of racial differences in outcomes as our qualitative interview participants almost universally expressed a preference for formal employment.

Although the evidence on the importance of stigma is powerful, it is still unclear how stigma in the labor market translates into lower employment rates. For example, Bushway, Denver, and Kurlychek (2015) point out that, if only relatively few employers in an industry do background checks or refuse to hire formerly incarcerated people, the effect could be small if most job seekers are applying for many jobs and need to be hired into only one. Second, stigma may also affect employment by discouraging formerly incarcerated people from looking for jobs or looking as actively. Sugie (2018) finds that some formerly incarcerated people observed for the first three months after release stop looking for work after a period of unsuccessful job searching, particularly older formerly incarcerated people, namely, those in their thirties and forties. Third, stigma may affect not just whether and where one finds a job but also whether one can keep a job, for instance, whether formerly incarcerated people are subject to greater scrutiny or are the first to be laid off when layoffs occur. Moreover, interviews with formerly incarcerated people suggest that they worry about background checks done after hiring, perhaps after a probationary period or before one's first pay raise (Harding 2003).[9] However, as we discuss below, we find little evidence of this effect of stigma on job loss among our interview participants.

Finding a Job with a Criminal Record

The job search strategies that formerly incarcerated people use can have important consequences for whether they are effectively able to manage the stigma of their criminal records and whether they eventually find a job (Smith and Broege 2012). Different search strategies are differentially effective in general, with social networks, labor market intermediaries, temporary labor firms, and direct application being generally more effective than placing or responding to ads or using public employment offices.

Given the employment barriers discussed above, how do those with a criminal record manage to find jobs? How do they manage the stigma of a felony and a prison term? And what are the consequences of these strategies for the type of work they do secure and their ability to maintain employment? We analyzed the job search experiences of our interview participants to answer these questions.[10] The results indicate that conventional means of looking for jobs—by responding to advertisements or walking in to fill out applications—were successful only under very special circumstances. Working with what Smith and Broege (2012) call *labor market intermediaries*—placement services, job-training programs, or employment coaches—seemed to result in only short-term employment. Instead, participants who were successful tended to target industries that are particularly friendly to those with a criminal record, such as temp firms and restaurants, but these types of jobs also exposed them to all the downsides of the secondary labor market: irregular hours and pay, high turnover, poor working conditions, and few opportunities for advancement. Other participants, frustrated by lack of success in the formal labor market and desperate for income, turned to working on their own, everything from yard work to plumbing to cutting hair, finding customers through their social networks and referrals. This strategy provided them with an income, but it was also irregular and uncertain and left them without the protections of the formal labor market, such as workers' compensation and unemployment insurance. Consistent with Berg and Huebner (2011), who find that those with strong family ties are more likely to find employment, our most successful participants leveraged their family networks to find jobs outside the secondary labor market. Yet few of our participants had family members who could provide this sort of assistance.

Jennifer is one example. Without a GED, with no real work history, and unable to lift more than four to six pounds owing to a car accident injury, she faced many obstacles to finding employment after her release from prison. Like Randall, she tried a combination of walk-in job applications, responding to advertisements, and applying for jobs online as well as trying to leverage her family's social networks, primarily those of her two sisters, both of whom were employed. She applied to retail stores, gas stations, and packaging plants but never received so much as a callback or an interview. She persisted in applying for jobs but eventually gave up when her application for disability benefits was approved. She supplemented this income by babysitting for family members, although they only occasionally paid her for this work.

Randall and Jennifer were not alone in struggling to find work through conventional job search strategies. Only rarely were such strategies successful and then only under particular circumstances. Lamar, discussed above, was probably the most successful at using these strategies. Further details of his experiences are instructive. He managed to secure multiple part- and full-time jobs in retail, fast food, and restaurants using this strategy but was able make this strategy work only because he applied for many jobs. This was possible because he had no other obligations, such as caring for family members or going to treatment programs and because he paroled to Ann Arbor, where the labor market was relatively strong—at least prior to the onset of the Great Recession—and public transportation was comparatively readily available. Just as importantly, however, he was skilled at impression and stigma management. He explained in detail his strategies for securing job interviews (e.g., always asking to speak with the manager, pretending he had been called for an interview), for impressing interviewers (e.g., listening in on other job interviews and practicing his answers, staying on topic and not talking too much, never saying anything negative about a prior employer), and directly addressing his prior record. On this issue he would be sure to provide potential employers with information about federal tax breaks for hiring formerly incarcerated people and would list only a very old felony when asked if he had a criminal record:

> Now when they ask have you ever been convicted of a felon before, I mark yeah, but I give them one way back from 1984. . . . You can't say I lied, so even if you look up and you say well you got one in 2011, yeah so? You just asked me have I ever been convicted. I told you yeah, and then I gave you one.

> *Interviewer: Has that worked?*

> Yeah, it actually has.

One possible way to overcome the stigma of a criminal record is to use a labor market intermediary, such as a job-training or apprenticeship program that places graduates in jobs, a job-placement service, or an on-the-job training program. Such programs might provide an opportunity to demonstrate one's dependability or a positive credential that could be an effective voucher. Although many of our participants tried to enter these programs and some did manage to do so, they never resulted in long-term employment. Consider Randall, whose many unsuccessful attempts to find work were discussed at the beginning of this chapter. Again, further details are instructive. After a few months of unsuccessfully looking for a job on his own, Randall sought the help of a vocational services organization in downtown Detroit. He took classes there on how to look for a job, write a résumé, and conduct himself in an interview and received individual help with writing a résumé. He used the organization's computers to apply for jobs and put his résumé on the Michigan Talent Bank (an online system for matching employers and potential employees and applying for jobs run by the state). He was placed in an eight-week culinary arts training course that would have provided him with one three-hour session a week and, as he reported, guaranteed a job after successful completion of the program. Unfortunately, his girlfriend had a miscarriage right before he was set to begin the class, and he missed the class to care for her. Once he was ready to look for a job again, he went to another similar organization, which also provided him with a course on job search, résumé writing, and interviewing and gave him access to computers to look for and apply for jobs online. A counselor at this organization helped him find a two-day temporary job at a church helping set up and clean up after a weekend-long event, but his hopes that this would become a permanent janitorial job did not materialize. He then tried a third service provider and attended its classes. A counselor there arranged for an interview with a light-manufacturing company in the suburbs, but he was not selected for the job. He then returned to the second organization, at one point going to its offices three or four days a week to use its computers to look for jobs.

Christopher and Jada provide other examples. Christopher paroled to the Salvation Army residential program in Detroit and worked there full-time sorting donations in exchange for room and board. He was asked to leave the program after he was accused of stealing some cash that was accidentally left in an item that was donated. Later, he was placed by the state's prisoner reentry program in a temporary job at an auto parts plant, but, after the ninety-day trial period, he was not hired for a permanent position. Jada secured a temporary position doing data entry at a financial firm through a state-funded social service provider, but, when the three-week position ended and there was no more work to be done, she returned to being unemployed. In all these cases, the service providers did indeed help our participants get job interviews or temporary jobs, but these never translated into long-term employment. We suspect that the weak labor market saturated with low-skill workers in southeastern Michigan, coupled with the criminal records and poor work histories of our participants, made helping them secure long-term employment extremely difficult. This would be consistent with prior research that shows that local labor market conditions play an important role in the employment outcomes of formerly incarcerated people (Raphael and Weiman 2007; Sabol 2007; Wang, Mears, and Bales 2010). Moreover, the tax breaks that Lamar told potential employers about are short-term, providing an incentive for employers to churn through formerly incarcerated people given the sizable pool of such available workers.

Felon-Friendly Industries and the Secondary Labor Market

Certain industries did prove to be more welcoming to our participants than others. Consistent with the evidence from the administrative data presented above, these tended to be restaurants and fast food, retail, construction, and automobile repair and maintenance. Of the twenty-two formal jobs our participants obtained, sixteen were in restaurants or fast food, three were in construction, three were automobile related, and three were in retail stores.[11] Our participants reported that employers in these industries—especially restaurants and fast food—were less likely to ask about criminal records and were more forgiving of past mistakes. While these industries provided our participants with an entry point into the labor market, they also tended to exhibit the hallmarks of the secondary labor market discussed above: low wages, monotonous and physically demanding work, high turnover, constantly changing schedules, irregular hours, and fluctuating earnings. To this dispiriting list we would add difficult and at times abusive supervisors and coworkers with their own drug and alcohol problems.

DeAngelo's job search and work experiences illustrate the challenges of certain industries in the secondary labor market, restaurants in his case. On release, DeAngelo targeted the restaurant industry, particularly full-service chain restaurants in Ypsilanti and Ann Arbor that were within a reasonable commute by bus, although he also applied for retail jobs. Working for tips appealed to him because it could mean higher income than a minimum wage position, despite his long-term social anxieties. He described how he started looking for jobs:

> Well, at first it took ... you know, I had to gather up my courage, dealing with my anxiety and my depression and everything to even go start looking for a job. But I had to psyche myself up mentally, to think positive about everything and just get out there and do it. And I sat for about a week after that and I did a lot of follow-up calls. And after that I was just getting calls to come do interviews. And that made me feel good, just to get that call. So when I went in there, I was real optimistic and enthusiastic too. So I think that played a good part. It made me look better in the interview because of how good I was feeling. I pretty much knew that I had the jobs once I left the interviews.
>
> [The interviews] were pretty tough, but I bounce back real quick. One of the interviews, the lady grabs out a ketchup, "Sell that to me." [*Laughs.*] So I had to come up with something real quick. But for the most part, typical questions ... "Why would we hire you for our company? What are your strengths? What are your weaknesses?" Pretty typical stuff. So I knocked them out.

Interviewer: Did your criminal record come up at all in any of these?

I put "yes" on every last [application]. Everybody told me I should, so I did it.... I put down what I was locked up for [a third driving under the influence], and everything, and they never brought it up. They didn't even ask me about it. It's right there on the front page of the application.... And that made me feel real good. I was honest, and I still got the job. Because I've worked a lot of restaurant jobs. I think they looked at that more than my conviction.... I worked [before], and I think that they decided to give me a chance off of that.

DeAngelo believed that his strategy of targeting the restaurant industry worked because of his prior experience working in restaurants. He quickly found a job working part-time as a server, making about $15.00 an hour with tips, but he lost that first job when his hours changed and he missed a shift:

My last job I was terminated because the schedule is put up . . . from Thursday till Wednesday, that's the week's schedule.... And I pretty much had a set schedule; I never worked Wednesdays. But when I come in on Thursday the new schedule is up, but I don't come in until four every Thursday, that's the set schedule. So one day I come in at Thursday at four, like I always do. The manager had changed the schedule, where I was supposed to have been there at twelve on Thursday.... And they fired me off of that. How am I supposed to know that all of a sudden they was going to change it on me like that without informing me.

He then began searching again for restaurant jobs and landed another one at another chain restaurant. After several weeks of making a similar income from tips, he reenrolled in community college to resume his studies in custom collision and paint, with the hope of eventually working on customizing cars. Although both work and school were part-time, juggling them (along with child-care obligations and maintaining his mental health treatments) proved unwieldy. Restaurant shifts, which at his new job were even more irregularly scheduled, conflicted with his courses, and management would not work with his scheduling needs. He tried to have others fill in for him, but, when they did not show up, he was held responsible. He ultimately lost the job after missing too many shifts and decided to focus on school and live off financial aid and a girlfriend's public benefits.

After DeAngelo was reincarcerated for a parole violation (driving with an open container and without a license) and later returned to the community again, he soon moved in with his Ypsilanti girlfriend in Oakland

County, north of Detroit. There he struggled to find work with his criminal record. Whether this was because employers in this area were less forgiving of those with a record, or because the economy had since slid into recession, or because a less readily available public transportation system made it harder to search for jobs, we cannot say for certain. For a time, DeAngelo and his girlfriend lived off her disability benefits, money from her family, and odd jobs DeAngelo did such as cutting hair, moving lawns, and selling Avon products. He eventually landed another restaurant job, this time as a prep cook at a family-owned business, but lost it when his work schedule shifted to Sundays, conflicting with his child-care responsibilities and causing transportation problems. The two buses he needed to take to get to work did not run on Sundays. When we last saw DeAngelo, three years after we first met him, he was scraping by on food stamps and odd jobs and trying to enroll in school again to develop the work skills to lift himself out of the secondary labor market.

Jane also found work in the restaurant industry despite a long criminal record and also experienced the difficulties of work in the secondary labor market as a result. She had worked many different legitimate jobs in the past as well, including clerical work in an office, as a waitress, a hairdresser, and a paralegal. She has two years of college but no degree to show for it. She lost her cosmetology license owing to her criminal convictions. She entered a work-readiness program a month after her release but was unable to find a job through it when it ended. Her goal is to get an office job, secretarial or clerical, and she applied to over seventy-five positions in her first few months after release. Although she managed to get interviews for a secretarial position and at an auto plant, she was not hired for either.

After posting her résumé on the Michigan Talent Bank and on a commercial hiring website, Jane landed a waitress position at a diner in Detroit. The work was usually part-time, twenty to twenty-five hours a week, although it fluctuated depending on whether she was able to fill in for others when they missed their shifts. Because the restaurant was not very busy and the food was inexpensive, she made only $40–$50 each five- to seven-hour shift. She was paid in cash under the table, so her parole officer did not count it as employment and insisted that she still report to the parole office every other week (because she had no proof of steady employment). Working as a server was physically demanding, but she stuck with the job for several months, using that time to try to update her computer skills, still hoping eventually to find a clerical or secretarial job that would provide a more pleasant work environment and better and more stable pay. She looked into a training program in information technology but decided against it when she was told that her criminal record would be seen as too much of a security risk. For Jane, probably the worst part of the restaurant job was the abusive boss: "The restaurant I work at, the guy is like really arrogant, and he talks to you really nasty, and it's like it makes it even harder. He'll call you stupid. . . . Another lady, he called her a bitch and everything, oh he's horrible. But, you know, it's a job, and a few times I've had to swallow my words and not say nothing."

Jane lost the restaurant job after a fight with her husband led to a heroin relapse. She then turned to prostitution, using an online escort website to find clients. After she completed another job-readiness program for formerly incarcerated women, the program found her a minimum wage job at a fast-food restaurant. She kept that job for two months but quit after another verbally abusive boss turned physical, pushing her, and she walked out of the restaurant and never returned:

> The manager there, I just couldn't work with him. He was just very degrading, insulting. You know, racist comments, everything. "I'm not having no more whites after you and . . . you and [this other white girl that worked there]. Because it must be in the color because you're very slow." He'd say we're stupid. Just keep insulting me. And one day I was at the drive-through window, and they have, like, a thirty-second thing. But, if the person does not come to the window and give you the money in their car, I can't make them give it to me. And he'd be screaming in the back at me, "Get their money. Get their money." Customers even be looking at me, like, "What's his problem?" And so then he got irritated, and he's like, "Just get away from here. Just go. Just go." So I went away because he had did that to me before. And I just went in the back and sat a minute and then came back and went back to work. And this day, when I came back, he literally pushed me. "No, just get out of here. Go. Get away from here. Go clean the bathroom if you think you can do that." So I went to the bathroom, and I was in there, and I was thinking, "You know what, I don't even need to listen to him no more today," and then went and got my coat and left. I know jobs are tough and they're hard to get, but that doesn't mean you abuse people.

As our study follow-up period ended, Jane was planning on returning to the job program to see whether they could help her find another job at a different franchise of the same fast-food chain.

Informal and Self-Employment

As a result of challenges they faced finding and maintaining employment in the formal labor market, some of our participants turned to informal, though not illegal, work arrangements or started their own businesses (see also Sugie 2018). For example, Christopher opened a car-detailing business with his wife, and James rented a chair at a barber shop and cut hair. Morgan—a thirty-three-year-old white man convicted of larceny after embezzling money to support his gambling addiction—tried to make money by leveraging his former career as a car salesman by wholesaling used cars (buying them in Michigan and selling them to an auto dealer in the South, where used cars command a higher price). And Jada worked as a home health aide for an elderly client under the table. Others did occasional work, cutting hair, babysitting, or mowing lawns.

Geoffrey was the participant who most embraced this strategy, and his experiences illustrate both the potential promise of such a strategy and its pitfalls. Geoffrey left prison eager to begin plumbing work again and confident that his drug-using days were behind him. He planned to rely on his self-proclaimed high skill level and network of colleagues who could hire him or help him find work. Yet he struggled to find stable employment. He called all the plumbers he knew but could not find anyone willing to hire him. He also applied for plumbing and remodeling jobs advertised in the newspaper. He attributed these struggles to a general lack of work for plumbers and contractors owing to the weakness of the economy. An additional potential barrier for formal construction work was his lack of a driver's license, which was suspended during his last prison spell for overdue fines and fees and past drunk-driving offenses. When asked for a driver's license number on job applications, he hoped the potential employer would not check his driving record.

Geoffrey quickly turned to working informally doing short-term jobs for friends and acquaintances at relatively low wages or for in-kind exchange, usually rent. He did plumbing and remodeling for a family friend, then repaired a damaged roof in exchange for $4,000 and a chance to live in the house rent free for four months. He then began distributing flyers advertising his services and trying to recruit customers by word of mouth, all the while continuing to search for formal work in the newspaper and on the Internet. He landed a position as an independent contractor with a company that maintains foreclosed homes but quit when the costs and uncompensated time of driving left him with little net pay and he developed health problems owing to the mold in many of the homes. He then moved in with another friend in exchange for performing home repairs. After a customer responded to an advertisement he placed in the newspaper, he did some plumbing and remodeling work at the man's house and some additional work for his small business. A hand injury sustained while working and a month-long hospitalization owing to an infection and hepatitis C put him in an even more precarious situation, and he soon had to disconnect his phone and sell his tools to afford food. Because he was not formally employed when he sustained the hand injury, he was ineligible for worker's compensation, and he applied for disability when he lost much of the use of the injured hand. He continues to work occasional short-term jobs that he finds through his social networks, but these are few and far between and allow him only barely to scrape by.

The prevalence of this sort of informal work may help explain two interrelated puzzles about the labor market experiences of formerly incarcerated people. One puzzle is simply why employment rates are so low (see figure 6.1); the other is why incarceration seems to decrease the probability of searching for work. Dissuaded and disheartened by the challenges of finding a job, some formerly incarcerated people like Geoffrey, Jada, Morgan, and Christopher turn to self-employment to make ends meet. Such self-employment is typically informal and not reflected in data on formal employment, though Christopher's business with his wife may be the exception.

Upward Mobility

Despite the challenges that most of our participants faced either finding employment or escaping the secondary labor market, four of our participants were able to secure jobs that held significant promise for long-term economic security and a middle-class lifestyle. How did they do so? We find that strong and sustained social support, usually from family or a romantic partner with considerable social and economic resources, was the primary path to upward mobility. For example, family or partners who could harness the social capital of their own job networks were able to help these participants connect to better-paying jobs with possibilities for career advancement. Resource-rich family or partners also give formerly incarcerated people access to communities and institutions that may provide a path to a better job. The comparison between Randall and Leon illustrates the importance of family assistance for finding a job and establishing a career.

Recall that, leaving prison, Randall had few family resources to rely on. Prior to his release he endured sleepless nights worrying about how to stay away from his brothers and the bad influence they might have on him. He had not seen his mother since he was just eleven, and his father had run off when he was very young. The woman who took him and his brothers in thereafter had fourteen children of her own, and resources were stretched thin. During his incarceration he had received mail only once, from his grandmother. He had more frequent contact with a cousin, Keshawn, who he hoped might provide a job connection on his release. But, although Keshawn was doing well—he was in school and working as an engine repair technician—at twenty-eight he still lived at home and had a limited capacity to provide the kind of support that could make a real difference. In fact, while he was able to offer Randall a few odd jobs, he would sometimes also pay him for his work in marijuana rather than cash—suggesting that Randall might sell it for a profit.

While Randall was able to find a more permanent home for about a year with a half sister and her father, this family was also struggling. The father was a retired blue-collar worker, and the half sister was not employed. The family had little food in the refrigerator, and the electricity was turned off for a time. Not only was Randall's family poorly positioned to provide the long-term support he needed to stabilize, his closest relatives were marginally criminally involved themselves, and, contrary to the hopes he had voiced while incarcerated, no one was able to help him land a job. Nearly three years after his release from prison and with the help of his fiancée in completing online job applications, he finally landed a job as a line cook at a restaurant.

Leon also received considerable social support from relatives, but, in contrast to Randall's experience, the form and extent of that support helped him relatively quickly secure a stable job that led to upward mobility. When paroled, he moved in with his father, then to a halfway house to enable him to qualify for a rent subsidy in the future. After a conflict with the halfway house manager, he moved in with his sister. His job search was frustrating at first as he applied for over forty jobs with little response. Those that did respond were difficult to get to or were not jobs in which he was interested. Then his uncle connected him with a friend who ran a nonprofit organization, and he landed a temporary job. After three months on this provisional status, he became a regular full-time employee with benefits and then rose further up the ranks in the organization to a position of greater responsibility and slightly higher pay. With this job security, he and his girlfriend, who worked for the same organization, moved into an apartment of their own. Leon saw his son every week and voluntarily contributed $300 a month in child support. He was constantly on the look-out for an even better job and, when the study concluded, was starting to think about returning to college to finish his degree.[12] Leon's experience illustrates the power of social support to launch a formerly incarcerated person on an upward trajectory. His father and sister met his basic needs while his job search began, which allowed him the flexibility to await a better job offer. More importantly, his uncle used his social networks to find him a job that was appropriate for his level of education and provided the opportunity for upward mobility.

A second comparison that reveals the importance of family social support and job networks for upward mobility is that between Daniel and Jake. After serving twelve years for manslaughter, Daniel moved in with his father and stepmother, who were both retired and living on social security benefits. He lived at this residence for close to a year and a half. While he made some attempts to look for other housing during this period, he was not pressured to move or to contribute rent or household expenses until after he found a job, at which point he was asked to contribute $75 per month. Beyond the advantages posed by his social network, he en-joyed the benefits of a high school diploma and freedom from the addic-tions that hindered many of our other participants. Further, although prior to prison he made the majority of his income selling drugs, he had also had legitimate work experience as a forklift operator.

With a stable residence and his basic needs met, Daniel was able to take the time needed to seek out a job with long-term career prospects. While he remained willing to work at low-wage jobs and had applied to a few, he also scoured his social network, trying to find job opportunities through his neighbors, brothers, and friends. More than six months after release, he started his first job, which he located through a family friend. He worked full-time for a janitorial supply company—eventually receiv-ing benefits—while he also pursued his longer-term career goal, employ-ment as a physical trainer.

Once Daniel became a full-time personal trainer, he was able to move into his own apartment. Stably employed, he applied for grants to further his education in nutrition and personal training. While he benefited from a number of advantages not shared by most other participants, he also benefited every step of the way from family support and a social network that provided him with the resources to pursue his interests. His family paid for his initial gym membership. His sister drove him to appointments. His father let him take his car to drive to his first job. He found the job at the gym through a friend. His mother put him on her credit card so that he could improve his credit score. And his cousin helped him find his first apartment.

In contrast, although Jake ultimately achieved a level of basic economic security, he did not have a social network that could be leveraged into a stable, lucrative job. On release, he moved into his father's house, where he lived for over a year. He actually gained full-time employment (at a restaurant) much more quickly than Daniel, largely because he had worked at the restaurant prior to his imprisonment. His next job (with a car mechanic) was found through a job search and application process. Although he initially thought that a restaurant where his sister was a manager might yield a job, he never ended up working there. He also believed that he might get a job at an automobile manufacturer through his father, but he would have had to move to Tennessee, and the certainty of this opportunity was unclear. Furthermore, he contributed a significant amount to his parents' households. By the time he had his second job, he was living alone in his father's house and paying $525 per month in rent, an amount similar to what he would have paid for an apartment of his own. While his mother initially provided him with transportation, he did not receive much else in terms of support from family.

Moreover, the people in Jake's social network faced many adversities of their own, making it difficult for them to provide much in the way of support. His only romantic partner during this period was introduced to him while she was in prison, and Jake later separated from her because she relapsed after being diagnosed with cervical cancer. One of his three sisters was on probation and married his prison bunk mate, causing tension in their relationship. He had a good relationship with his mother, but she was diagnosed with cancer and later moved out of state. Thus, while Jake was able to secure a job, his social network did not provide him with the resources to be upwardly mobile.

Keeping a Job

Our statistical analysis of the administrative data and many of the experiences of our participants indicate that low rates of employment among formerly incarcerated people are as much a result of the difficulty of keeping a job as of the difficulty of finding one. How and why do formerly incarcerated people have trouble keeping jobs? According to our administrative data, workers who are otherwise advantaged in the labor market—either because of their skills or because of their social supports—are least likely to experience a job loss. Those with higher levels of education, those who are married, those working for the same employer for whom they worked prior to prison, and those who are older are less likely to lose a job. Conversely, workers with mental health problems experience high rates of job loss. Those who have a history of mental illness or substance abuse before prison are more likely to lose a job, as are those who have recently tested positive for drug or alcohol use. The industry in which one is employed matters greatly as well, net of individual characteristics. Among those industries where formerly incarcerated people commonly find employment, we observe the highest rates of job loss (and job change) among workers employed in temporary labor, construction (likely owing to the seasonal nature of this industry in Michigan), restaurants and fast food, janitorial services, retail, and automotive repair and the lowest rates in manufacturing, health care, and the wholesale industries. This suggests that employment in the secondary labor market is highly associated with job instability, both losing one's job and moving to a different one.

These statistical findings suggest that the high rates of job loss among formerly incarcerated people are the combined product of three factors: (1) their long-standing structural and social disadvantages (such as low levels of education), (2) their ongoing behavioral health problems (particularly but not exclusively substance abuse), and (3) the types of jobs that they are able to find when they do find work. Our qualitative data are also consistent with this explanation. We analyzed all the job losses experienced by our participants during the course of the study, whether voluntary or involuntary, to understand how and why they were losing jobs. Because we do not have the employer's side of the story, we can discuss these issues only from the perspectives of the participants themselves, and we focus on what participants deemed the most important reason for a job loss. However, as will become clear below, most of our participants placed the blame on themselves in one fashion or another.

The most common reason for a job loss was some sort of health problem; ten of the thirty-two job losses we analyzed were health related. Recall from above that Lamar lost his job as a line cook at a restaurant when he had trouble negotiating accommodations for his epilepsy, which was exacerbated by the hot work environment of the kitchen. Geoffrey quit a job maintaining foreclosed homes because he could not tolerate the mold in the residences. However, the remaining eight were all substance abuse related. For instance, as discussed above, Jane lost a waitress job after she relapsed and stopped going to work, and Christopher stopped working for the business he started with his wife after he was incarcerated for trying to rob a bank while extremely drunk. In only two cases did we observe someone lose a job owing to incarceration that was not due to substance abuse problems. Lamar lost his position as a taxi driver when he was returned to prison on a technical violation for receiving stolen property and theft, and Morgan lost a job as a car salesman when he was arrested for absconding out of state and returned to prison. The second most common reason for job loss was a temporary position terminating without converting into a permanent hire (eight instances). As we discussed above, such temporary positions never led to long-term employment in our sample even when they were secured through job-readiness or job-placement programs.

Other common reasons for job losses stem from the unstable nature of employment relations, the treatment of employees, and work environments in the secondary labor market. One reason is conflicts with difficult supervisors or experiencing verbal or physical abuse from supervisors (four instances). Experiencing abusive supervisors tended to happen to women, as Jane's experience illustrates (Michelle provides another example; see below). Problems with fluctuating work hours and changing work schedules were another common reason for job losses (four instances). Particularly when coupled with low wages, juggling other obligations, and the challenges of finding transportation to and from work, shifting work schedules and fluctuating work hours sapped our participants' motivation to keep working and/or made it difficult to avoid missing work. Recall, for example, DeAngelo's job losses both when his work shift changed without notice and when he was assigned to work on a Sunday when buses did not run and he had to care for his son.[13]

Michelle's labor market experiences illustrate the ways in which job loss results from the compounding of problematic individual and job characteristics. Michelle had over $15,000 in medical debt and also owed back child support, court fees, and driver's responsibility fees when she left prison, so she focused on working, usually multiple jobs at once, both to pay off those debts and to establish economic independence and regain custody of her daughter. Young, female, and white, she did not fit the stereotype of a formerly incarcerated person, and she had little trouble finding low-wage service-sector jobs in the suburbs north of Detroit where she lived with her father and stepmother after prison. She left the criminal record question on job applications blank, and the topic never came up in interviews. Her long-term plan was to return to school to get credentialed in a medical field, perhaps medical records or nurse's assistant.

Michelle's first job after prison was a minimum wage position at a fast-food restaurant, secured after a relative recommended her. Because that job was part-time, she continued to look for work, later finding a full-time job as a server in a full-service restaurant. She quit the job at the fast-food restaurant after her paycheck was repeatedly shorted. At the full-service restaurant, she made considerably more from tips (about $500 a week working full-time) but had to endure a boss who was verbally abusive. After a few months, she was one of the most senior employees, nearly everyone else having quit, and then she quit too:

> On a Wednesday, he just started going off on me. I can't even remember [why] to be honest with you. . . . He started yelling at me and called me a bitch, and I went off on him. He did it right in front of my customers. And it was so bad that my one table . . . I had a four top, and they tipped me $65. They're like, You shouldn't have to deal with that, and gave me a $65 tip. . . . And you know as I was getting ready to punch out because I was like fuck this, I'm out of here, whatever, I finished my tables. I didn't just walk out; I at least did my work and then punched out. [A customer] grabbed my arm, and he's like, "My sister is a manager at the place at the mall that does surveys. . . . I guarantee you'll have a job." I was like, "OK." So the very next day I had a [new] job.

Michelle's new job collecting customer satisfaction surveys at a shopping mall started out part-time, so she found an additional job waitressing at a banquette hall and a third part-time job at a grocery store. When the mall job became full-time, she was earning about $500 a week and quit the grocery store job. Then she relapsed after a new coworker offered her heroin after work one day:

> This guy, he started working at the mall. He was older, and he had just did like thirty-five years for murder. And that's basically what my boss does is hired ex-felons and stuff like that, you know, give them another chance. . . . Well in the meantime I find out he knew me from the parole office, I knew him, you know just from face. So we started talking, and I find out that he's using and offers it to me, and I was having the shittiest day. I can't remember what exactly all happened, but it was just like right place, right time, and I fell. And it was just bad. I felt so shitty after, but I continued to do it. . . . It was about almost three weeks, about two and a half weeks. . . . Nobody had a clue because you know I know

how to play it. You know, it's really sick and sad that I can do that. I know how to do just enough dope to make my eyes still dilate so you can't do that test, which is what cops do to see. And, because I hadn't used in so long, my tolerance wasn't high, so I wasn't using a lot at first. So then it starts getting in your head, well nobody knows, I could do this forever. But then it started to show.

During this time, her stepmother had passed away, her father—also a former addict—had relapsed, and Michelle started a new relationship. She quit her jobs and moved in with her boyfriend and his mother to try to regain her sobriety: "I've always been close with his mom. And then I ended up quitting my job when I moved in with him. And I just said you know what, screw this, and I just talking to [my boyfriend] and his mom and his mom said, 'If you need a couple months,' she's like, 'you just do whatever makes you happy right now as long as it's not using. Just get yourself together.' And I had never done that before."

At first, Michelle worried about returning to work, to the stress and the coworkers who might also be addicts, but she quickly grew bored sitting at home, which seemed like more of a threat to her sobriety than working. She found two jobs again, one in a cafeteria at a senior center and then another at a diner as a waitress. Later, after another relapse, she lost those jobs when she was sentenced to six months in jail for possession of a controlled substance. When she was released, she returned to live with her boyfriend. At our final interview, she was pregnant and in her first trimester. She was doing some informal work cleaning a neighbor's apartment and was considering getting a part-time job.

Notably, none of our participants reported losing a job because an employer discovered their criminal record after they were hired. Although when they were searching for jobs they often expressed fears that this would happen, it never did, even among those who did not disclose their records. Informal stigma, then, seems to play a role primarily in limiting hiring opportunities and channeling formerly incarcerated people into sectors of the economy clustered in the secondary labor market.

Conclusion

In this chapter, we have explored the experiences of formerly incarcerated people in the labor market. We view employment not just as important for the material well-being of former citizens or for its effects on recidivism but as an indicator of their social and economic reintegration more generally. Stable employment and the resulting income security is a critical foundation for full and effective participation in other life domains, including family, community, and polity. As a result of their generally low levels of education and work experience, resource-poor social networks, the stigma of a felony conviction, and their high rates of health problems, formerly incarcerated people struggle mightily to support themselves through work. These struggles involve not just trouble finding jobs but difficulties maintaining jobs as well. The stigma of a criminal record poses a particular challenge when searching for work. Parole supervision, including restrictions on types of employment and onerous parole reporting and program requirements, also complicates finding and keeping a job.

Success in the labor market after prison requires a particularly strong set of social and cultural skills in order to interact with potential employers as well as the resources to seek out and apply for many jobs. Formerly incarcerated people often turn to short-term positions, such as temporary labor arrangements or job programs, to self-employment (either formal or informal), or to industries that are particularly open to hiring those with a criminal record. Such industries, such as restaurants, construction, retail, and automotive, mostly provide jobs in the secondary labor market, which is characterized by few opportunities for promotion or significant wage growth, poor working conditions, irregular hours, low pay, few benefits, and shifting work schedules (see also Crutchfield 2014). The labor market struggles of formerly incarcerated people mirror those of many other low-skill, low-wage workers in the contemporary US labor market, as elaborated by other scholars (e.g., Kalleberg 2011; Newman 2009) and are further exacerbated by the mark of a criminal record and the mental health and substance abuse problems that, in many cases, led to their incarceration in the first place.

Yet some formerly incarcerated people do secure good jobs that lead to economic stability and upward mobility over time. Our analyses suggest that they do so largely with the help of family members who can connect them with employment opportunities outside the secondary labor market. While the family members of many formerly incarcerated people work hard to help them reintegrate into the labor market after release—for example, by providing transportation to look for work, money for interviewing clothes, or information about job leads—few formerly incarcerated people return to families with the social capital needed to connect them to better-paying jobs with stability, benefits, and career ladders.

   These findings illustrate not just the importance of individual characteristics such as low human capital or health problems but also the role of
contexts and institutions—such as families and their social networks, labor
market intermediaries, employment relations in the low-skill labor market, stigma-preserving institutions, and supervision by the criminal justice
system—thus leading to an obvious further question. What might be done
to better integrate formerly incarcerated people into the labor market? We
take up this question in the next chapter as part of a larger discussion of
strategies for improving the reintegration of formerly incarcerated people.

Conclusion

In the introduction, we proposed that postprison reintegration could be broadly conceptualized as a product of three factors: the characteristics and social positions of the formerly incarcerated individuals themselves (particularly race, gender, and health status), the context of reintegration, and the fit between the two (recall that this framework is adopted from the literature on immigrant incorporation). We also suggested that reintegration is not a single event or a short-term episode but a process that unfolds over time, often in a nonlinear and bidirectional pattern, with many formerly incarcerated individuals experiencing reintegration in fits and starts and with periods of progress and setback. Indeed, most of our participants failed to reintegrate completely over the time period we observed them, given our metric of securing steady employment at a living wage, discharging from parole and staying free of the criminal justice system, forging stable family relationships, and securing stable housing. Recall, for example, that employment rates are only approximately 30–40 percent and that residential mobility is extremely high. In this book we have documented and analyzed the challenges, failures, and successes of our participants and Michigan parolees more generally along these lines. Here, we step back to summarize what we have learned about how the factors identified in this framework contribute to postprison reintegration. We then discuss the notion of prison as a turning point in the lives of our participants and what might be done to support their social and economic reintegration.

We begin with individual characteristics and social positions. Race looms large as a key social determinant of postprison outcomes. For example, chapter 6 showed that African Americans are about 10 percentage points less likely than whites to be employed at any point in time in the first three years after release. Similarly, they experience greater residential instability and neighborhood poverty. These racial disparities cannot be explained by other individual attributes like education, preprison employment, mental health, or substance abuse history. As we discussed in the introduction, the experiences of the formerly incarcerated individuals we have discussed in this book are tied to larger systems of racial domination in US society and institutions, and the criminal justice system is a key part of these systems. For instance, racial threat has played a critical role in the expansion of incarceration and other aspects of the criminal justice system, and blackness has become closely associated with the stigma of criminality. The negative effects of involvement in the criminal justice system are exacerbated for African Americans by other features of racial domination, including concentrated-poverty neighborhoods, social networks that are less able to help in finding low-skill jobs outside the secondary labor market, and greater health problems in the families to which they return. In this sense, racial disparities in outcomes related to prisoner reentry and reintegration reflect long-standing and pervasive racial inequalities in US society.

Health—particularly mental health and substance abuse—is another critical factor in reintegration (and health is itself related to both race and gender). By our estimates, at least a fifth of formerly incarcerated individuals have a history of mental health problems, and at least half have substance use disorders and addictions to alcohol or hard drugs (i.e., not including marijuana) known to the criminal justice system, though this is certainly an underestimate. The role of health problems in reintegration came through far more forcefully in the detailed accounts of our participants. For Jennifer and Jane, physical health problems limited their ability to work in jobs that required any lifting of heavy objects, and Jocelyn was essentially permanently disabled by chronic obstructive pulmonary disease. Lamar's epilepsy contributed to job loss on one occasion. Christopher's drinking and drug problems led him into harm's way multiple times, including two stints of reincarceration (once in jail and once in prison). Incidents of relapse interfered with work for Lenora, Jane, and Michelle. Craig was reincarcerated for drunk driving. Many more saw their substance use cause problems with partners and family members.

These experiences indicate that drug and alcohol dependence played a significant role in the well-being of many of our participants. Indeed, all but one of those who struggled with homelessness and constant economic instability suffered from significant substance use disorders. Episodes of relapse often derailed attempts to find or maintain employment or re-connect with family, and behavior while under the influence of drugs or alcohol was sometimes responsible for severing the social ties that had provided important social support prior to prison. Substance abuse prob-lems resulted in access to fewer resources and made it more challenging for participants to take full advantage of the resources to which they did have access. However, we also emphasize that the struggle of reintegra-tion is not merely a substance abuse story. Some participants with histories of substance abuse did achieve stability and upward mobility, and not all problems with employment, social support, and criminal justice contact could be traced back to drug and alcohol abuse.

Our data also suggest, however, that we must be careful not to over-medicalize our understanding of mental health and substance use among formerly incarcerated individuals.[1] It is tempting to fall back on individ-ualistic accounts that frame the poor and their health problems as pa-tients merely in need of treatment and ignore how social structures and relationships affect substance use and addiction relapse. Our participants' accounts show that their problems with substance abuse were strongly so-cially patterned, often sparked by the challenges of reintegration as much as contributing to them. Heavy drinking and returns to drug use often fol-lowed from stressful social relationships and living arrangements, unstable housing, and struggles in the labor market.

Moreover, these health problems reflect the trauma that our partici-pants experienced even before their incarceration, experiences that were in part structured by gender and race (Burton and Lynn 2017; Richie 2012). Our participants' accounts of their lives suggest that these health problems—particularly mental health and related substance use—stem from early life experiences. Sexual, physical, and emotional abuse figured prominently in the life stories of those who struggled with depression, anx-iety, or related mental health problems—problems that they often treated by self-medicating with alcohol or drugs, leading to addictions. This was the case for both men and women, but it appears to be even more common among women. Christopher, Randall, and David were all sexually abused as children, for example, and Christopher and David linked those experi-ences directly to their addictions, while Randall experienced depression as a result and drank heavily at times. DeAngelo suffered emotional abuse at home, including being locked in his room and kicked out of the house as a teenager, experiences he felt contributed to his anxiety and depression and resulting alcoholism. Lenora experienced severe domestic violence as a teenager from an older, criminally involved romantic partner. Kristine, Michelle, and Jane were all molested as very young children and related these experiences to their substance use in later life. Families who refused to believe that abuse had occurred or pretended that it had never happened heightened the long-term negative emotional impact of the abuse. For instance, when Jane was twelve, her parents forced her to go on a trip to Florida to visit the uncle who had molested her when she was four. Her father did not want to believe her because, as she explained, "he loved his brother," while her mother felt that sexual abuse was simply "what men did sometimes." Moreover, women in our study found themselves at particularly high risk of victimization after release in multiple contexts, from neighborhoods to workplaces to their own homes.

Human capital also has the potential to play a key role as well. Only about a fifth of Michigan parolees have a high school diploma, and only about 6 percent have more than a high school education. Rates of pre-prison employment are also very low, with only about 17 percent having any employment in the formal labor market in the year before entering prison. The absence of human capital translates directly into either difficulties finding a job or securing employment only in the brutal secondary labor market. This in turn leads to instability in other domains, particularly housing. And, without stable housing to provide a foundation for reentry, other problems like family instability and family conflict related to doubling up often follow. Lack of stable housing and insecure employment exacerbate stress, which then makes sustaining sobriety all the more challenging. However, because so few formerly incarcerated individuals leave prison with even a high school education or any sustained work experience, human capital does not go very far in explaining variation in postprison reintegration.

In our analysis, we have highlighted the role of four social contexts in the process of prisoner reintegration: neighborhoods, the labor market, the criminal justice system, and, most importantly, families. Although neighborhood contexts figure prominently in the literature on crime and recidivism, we found that our participants tended not to participate in the social lives of their neighborhoods, particularly when they returned to high-poverty neighborhoods. This is in part because they are more often than not returning to different high-poverty neighborhoods than the ones they lived in before prison and in part because they sought to avoid the problems that the streets had generated in the past. However, when stresses mount and drugs and drug users are nearby, opportunities for relapse are heightened.

Neighborhoods were also important for our participants in terms of limiting opportunities for employment. In addition, those who returned to high-poverty neighborhoods—particularly in Detroit—were physically far from job opportunities and had little access to individuals who could help them find jobs. Like our participants, many formerly incarcerated individuals—particularly African Americans—are returning to neighborhood environments in which it is very difficult for those leaving prison to succeed. Despite this, formerly incarcerated individuals return to these neighborhoods because they are where their families live and where institutional housing tends to be located.

The labor market is a second critical context for reintegration and one in which the fit between the characteristics of formerly incarcerated individuals and the characteristics of the context is particularly poor. Almost all our participants aspired to work when they walked out the prison door, and almost all did work at some point in the three years after their release, though not always in the formal labor market. They wanted to contribute to the economic well-being of their families, to demonstrate their moral reform, to stake a claim as a full member of US society, and to avoid returning to crime. Work was also a requirement of parole for those without a disability or full-time enrollment in school. Yet, with low levels of education, few skills, and often little work experience, our participants typically had to settle for work in the secondary labor market. As documented by many other scholars, today's low-skill secondary labor market is a brutal institution that demands much of its desperate workers and offers little in return. It features wages too low to live off of, work hours that are often part-time, irregular, and unstable, difficult working conditions, and few, if any, benefits like paid sick days or vacation days that those in high-skill or middle-class occupations take for granted. Owing to the stigma of a felony conviction, low human capital, lack of social support, and mental health problems, formerly incarcerated individuals enter this discouraging labor market at the bottom. Particularly for African American formerly incarcerated individuals, the stigma of a criminal record and the lack of social network connections to blue-collar job opportunities outside the secondary labor market make the low-skill labor market an inhospitable context for reintegration. These characteristics of the labor market, coupled with other substantial challenges, make for considerable employment volatility, which makes building an economic foundation for successful reintegration in other domains even more difficult.

A third core context that shapes the reintegration outcomes of formerly incarcerated individuals is the criminal justice system itself. Alongside the rise in incarceration in prison has come a shift in community corrections from a social work model focused on rehabilitation and reintegration to a law enforcement model focused on surveillance, control, and capture. We saw this most clearly in the experiences of our participants with the intensity of parole supervision requirements in the early period after release, the use of short-term custodial sanctions such as brief periods of incarceration in jail or parole violator centers in response to relatively minor violations of parole requirements (see also Harding, Siegel, and Morenoff 2017), and returns to prison for technical violations of parole conditions. Indeed, the rise of incarceration was in part fueled by such parole revocations. Whereas, in 1980, 18 percent of individuals entering prison did so for a parole violation, that figure was 34 percent in 2000 (Travis 2007). In 2014, still over one-quarter of prison admissions were for technical parole violations (Carson 2015).

We found that minor forms of criminal activity and the criminal justice sanctions that could result were closely tied to our participants' economic instability and uncertainty. (We characterize them as *minor* because they were not crimes or behaviors that would result in incarceration in prison for someone who was without a criminal record or who was not on parole or probation.) Although certainly less detrimental than simply returning parole violators to prison, such sanctions can nonetheless have long-term effects on employment and material well-being more broadly. For example, even short periods of incarceration in jail, technical rule violator centers, or custodial treatment programs could lead to eviction and loss of material possessions, complicate applications for public benefits, and result in job loss. Moreover, the stigma of involvement in the criminal justice system is heightened by the largely unregulated use of computer technology to disseminate criminal records, which can affect not only employment opportunities but also and increasingly the ability to find rental housing.

Finally, our findings show that the family, broadly defined, is a key context for reintegration. As shown in chapter 2, the period of incarceration in prison tends to result in the loss of weak ties and the strengthening of strong ties, particularly those to family members and romantic partners. This is due in part to the signal that going to prison sends to family members about the extent of the recent struggles faced by their loved one, the prisoner's need for family support to live in prison with any measure of comfort, and reflection on the importance of family relationships that prison brings. Once released, formerly incarcerated individuals rely on their families for basic material support, including housing, food, and often transportation. Returning to a family home avoids the need to transition to institutional housing, such as shelters and treatment programs. Those who are able to find work outside the secondary labor market were able to do so largely through the social networks of their more advantaged family members. Family members, including romantic partners, also provided emotional support and served as enforcers of informal social control. Moreover, family relationships provide important forms of identity and prosocial roles for individuals who face otherwise spoiled identities. These identities and roles are symbolically important to those who face challenges achieving other forms of social status, such as employment or education. Particularly roles as spouses and parents provide the opportunity for symbolic affirmation and reinforcement of postprison identities.

At the same time, however, family roles and responsibilities can create role strain that leads to further criminal behavior, stressful relationships can challenge sobriety, and family members who are themselves involved in criminal activity can enable or coerce criminal behavior. An important corollary is that the well-being of most formerly incarcerated individuals is closely tied to that of the families and partners to which they return. Among our participants, those who returned to families with greater social and economic resources were clearly better off in both the long and the short term. Formerly incarcerated individuals without access to social support face greater challenges in meeting their basic needs, attaining economic security and residential stability, recovering from mental health problems, and avoiding substance use and criminal behavior.

Another implication of our findings is that our participants' families are bearing most of the burden of meeting the material needs of their loved ones leaving prison, particularly in the immediate postrelease period, before formerly incarcerated individuals can secure their own employment or public benefits, but often in the medium or long term as well. This burden falls disproportionately on those families with the fewest resources, creating material strain that affects not just formerly incarcerated individuals but many others as well (Braman 2004). This represents a further collateral consequence of mass incarceration and reentry and an abdication of state responsibility for individuals on community supervision. As Megan Comfort (2008, 2012) has argued, families are taking on social work and social welfare functions that in prior times would have been the responsibility of parole officers, who are now primarily tasked with monitoring and controlling an unprecedentedly large reentry population.

Our focus on contexts of reintegration as well as individual characteristics makes clear that the challenges of prisoner reentry and reintegration are closely related to the challenges that the poor and increasingly the working and middle classes face in the contemporary society and economy of the United States. Some of these challenges are long-standing features of American life, such the connection between race and concentrated poverty. Others reflect changes in the political, cultural, and institutional logics that occurred alongside the rise in incarceration over the last four decades, such as changes to the labor market and employment conditions of low-skill workers and the increasing punitiveness of the social welfare state. At the same time, the burden of supporting and reintegrating formerly incarcerated individuals falls on the same largely poor and working-class families already struggling in our neoliberal society and economy.

Prison as a Turning Point?

Conceptualizing reintegration as a social, cultural, and economic process that unfolds over time leads naturally to a discussion of the role of prison and prisoner reentry in the life course of those who find themselves imprisoned. Here, it is useful to return to the life-course framework discussed in the introduction, a developmentally informed theoretical perspective that emphasizes the connections between different stages in the life course. As Sampson and Laub (1992, 64) note: "The life-course perspective highlights continuities and discontinuities in behavior over time and the social influences of age-graded transitions and life events." A central underlying assumption of this framework is that outcomes and events (e.g., marriage, employment, school completion) are linked over time and that, instead of viewing events in isolation, the researcher must examine their sequences and patterns over time (Elder 1998). The question, then, is what role prison plays in structuring an individual's sequence of future life events.

Trajectories and *transitions* are the two primary concepts that link individual experiences over the life course and structure key life outcomes (Sampson and Laub 1992, 1995). Trajectories are long-term patterns or sequences of behaviors and social roles. The notion of state dependence captures the idea that inhabiting a particular state decreases the probability of transition to a new state. For example, intensive work during adolescence or young adulthood may decrease the time and energy one has to devote to schooling, preventing the accumulation of resources necessary to improve one's education level and transition to higher-wage work (Staff and Mortimer 2008). Transitions are discrete changes in roles and behaviors connected to "salient life events" (Elder 1998) such as marriage, school completion, or military service. For instance, children are able to accumulate human capital while parents provide for their basic material needs, allowing them to successfully transition to work and establish their own households. Life-course research attempts to understand variations in trajectories and transitions, focusing on the intergenerational transmission of disadvantages, the effects of historical events such as the Great Depression or the Second World War (Elder 1974), and structural positions such as gender, race, and class (Hogan and Astone 1986; Sampson and Laub 1992).

The life-course perspective has been fruitfully employed by criminologists to understand desistance from crime, a central, though not exclusive, aspect of prisoner reintegration. Desistance from crime can be understood as a life-course transition that changes one's long-term behavioral trajectory.[2] Informal social control is a product of both interpersonal ties and participation in wider social institutions, emerging from "the role reciprocities and structure of interpersonal bonds linking members of society to one another and to wider social institutions such as work, family, and school" (Sampson and Laub 1995, 18). Adult social bonds—particularly those resulting from marriage, employment, and military service—determine adult criminality through informal social control (Laub, Nagin, and Sampson 1998; Sampson, Laub, and Wimer 2006). Transitions, or turning points, occur when social ties are changed in such a way as to increase social control (e.g., marriage or employment), increasing the likelihood of desistance. In short, life events change social bonds, which in turn affect informal social control, which in turn affects criminal behavior. Institutions are a key source of social control in this theory as they structure and stabilize social roles and constrain daily routines. In the case of marriage and the military, they may also separate individuals from criminal peers (Laub and Sampson 2001; Warr 1993).

Recently, scholars have also paid close attention to the role of cognitive change in desistance from crime and turning points in the life course. In other words, life events do not just happen to us; we act to bring them about, so cognitive change—motivations and ways of thinking—are important as well. One theory of the process by which cognitive changes occur and their role in desistance is developed by Giordano, Cernkovich, and Rudolph (2002), who argue that cognitive transformation is a four-step process. (1) Openness to change leads to (2) exposure and receptivity to "hooks for change" provided in the environment, such as prison or treatment, religion, employment, parenthood, or marriage. "Latching onto" these hooks for change leads to (3) identity transformation, which in turn leads to (4) a change in the meaning and desirability of deviance and crime. Possible hooks for change vary in their "transformative potential" based on their capacity to provide a "clear prosocial cognitive blueprint," a new identity, a template for future behavior, a link to "positively valued themes," and access to nondeviant others who can reinforce the new identity. Applying this view of desistance to the life-course framework suggests that turning points will occur when hooks for change are readily available in the contexts and institutions in which the individual is embedded and when latching onto successfully leads to identity transformation.

How do our findings inform theories of desistance in the context of the life course? First, as we noted in the introduction, many of the sources of informal social control emphasized in prior research, such as marriage, the military, and steady employment, are simply not available to contemporary returning prisoners—even those motivated to desist. Job opportunities are scarce and steady employment even more rare, military service is closed to most convicted felons, and marriage is uncommon among them. This implies that, for those who desist, alternative institutions are providing sources of informal social control. Our results suggest that relationships with families—romantic partners, parents, children, and other close relations—are playing key roles in providing such informal social control for many formerly incarcerated individuals.

Second, from the perspective of the cognitive transformation framework, new roles and identities must be developed, reinforced, and maintained over time in these family and household contexts as other prosocial roles and identities developed through work or school are very difficult for the typical formerly incarcerated individual to achieve and maintain. Families often became the basis for new prosocial identities, for example, as caregivers and providers. In other words, while many leave prison with plans for further education and rewarding careers, such family roles are often what formerly incarcerated individuals end up latching onto, although not always successfully. Fulfilling these roles successfully, and thereby cementing new identities, proved very difficult for our participants given the challenges of maintaining sobriety and—particularly for men— the absence of steady employment.

Third, we might ask whether prison and the moment of reentry can be a turning point that puts an individual on a new life trajectory, either positive or negative. Two views in the literature on incarceration speak to this point. A more classical view is that prison can be a positive turning point. Most prisoners were on a downward life trajectory before they were incarcerated, and prison at least has the potential to change that trajectory in a more positive direction either through specific deterrence (the threat of further incarceration) or through rehabilitative prison programs (for reviews, see Lipsey and Cullen [2007]; and Nagin, Cullen, and Jonson [2009]). A more contemporary view, stemming from the literature on mass incarceration and its role in creating and maintaining inequality, suggests that prison either has little potential to act as a positive turning point or is actually a negative turning point, putting prisoners on a downward trajectory by cutting off employment opportunities, fracturing families, and undermining community cohesion and social support (e.g., Western 2006). Although the very difficult experiences of our participants make us sympathetic to the contemporary/mass incarceration view, we see neither view as sufficiently nuanced. Instead, the appropriate questions are for whom and under what circumstances prison is (or might be) a positive turning point.

Our findings reveal some reasons for optimism about prison as a turning point, but they have little to do with the deterrence or rehabilitation potential of the prison emphasized by the classical view. First, as is clear from the stories of our focal participants presented in chapter 1, prison provides an opportunity for cooling out and reflection, a break from the challenges of daily survival and drug addiction that so many of our participants faced before their incarceration. For Lenora, Christopher, DeAngelo, and Jennifer, it provided a halt from intense substance abuse and the accompanying criminal behavior required to support their habits. For Randall, prison ended a period of running from the law after absconding from parole after a previous imprisonment, a situation that left him unable to build a conventional life. For Leon, his arrest and incarceration represented the end of a spree of armed robberies, which he described as a relief from a pattern from which he could not seem to break free (he was "glad it was over").

In addition, most of our participants left prison surprisingly optimistic about their prospects after release (see also Irwin and Owen 2005). Almost universally, our participants imagined new, prosocial roles and identities for themselves. DeAngelo developed a more nuanced understanding of his mental health problems and their role in his drinking as well as a plan for finding treatment and social support after release. Jennifer focused on being a mother to her son and turned to family and public benefits for the resources to do so. Lenora left prison with a plan to return to school and use the financial aid money to fix and sell houses in Detroit. In the language of cognitive transformation theory, our participants had begun the process of cognitive change and identified hooks for change.

Finally, as we discussed in chapter 2, prison largely served to strengthen ties to family and weaken ties to others, including those with whom crimes had been committed or substance use engaged in. This means that there is considerable potential for the experience of incarceration in prison to help sever procriminal ties and foster prosocial ties.[3] In the language of social control theory, the experience of incarceration in prison has the potential to increase prosocial informal control by severing ties to negative influences and building ties to those with positive influences, those who can provide opportunities for developing prosocial identities and roles, even if these are not the conventional roles of husband or wife, breadwinner, or worker. For example, DeAngelo separated himself from family members who had been unsupportive in the past or who had encouraged his drinking while connecting with a new romantic partner who provided both emotional and material support. Jennifer broke ties with the people she had once used drugs with and rekindled ties to her two sisters, who were leading more conventional lives and could provide her with emotional and material support.

Yet, consistent with the mass incarceration perspective, our participants' experiences also reveal that these potentially positive features of prison and the moment of reentry were often (but not always) overwhelmed by the challenges of reentry documented throughout this book: the struggle of addiction, the stigma of a criminal record and features of the low-wage secondary labor market that await formerly incarcerated individuals after release, families too overwhelmed by their own challenges or too economically disadvantaged to provide more than the minimal social support required for daily survival, and families, households, and romantic partners that prove to be sources of stress and conflict rather than social support and residential stability that proved elusive for many. While Leon was able to translate his middle-class social ties into a job lead and the start of a career in the nonprofit social services sector and eventually establish an independent household with a new girlfriend, Christopher was again foiled by his addictions despite a seemingly positive start with a new wife, a baby, and a family business. DeAngelo managed to keep his mental health problems and alcohol addiction mostly at bay but faltered in the secondary labor market and in maintaining a long-term romantic relationship. Randall struggled just to survive on a daily basis but managed to discharge from parole—despite a few forays back into crime, both detected and undetected—and marry, move to the suburbs, and find a low-wage job. While Jennifer stayed focused on her motherhood role and maintained her sobriety for the first time in her life, Lenora fell back on old habits when residential stability remained elusive and her efforts in school and the labor market failed to provide any economic stability, let alone a new life. In short, the potential of a turning point was squandered by many as postrelease plans met the harsh realities of reentry and few supports were available to help formerly incarcerated individuals realize those plans.

Thus, our findings suggest that prison can serve as a turning point away from crime and substance abuse only when an individual has the social and material resources to capitalize on the moment of optimism at release. Because these social and economic resources largely came from family members and romantic partners (as opposed to participants' own human capital or social programs, e.g.), we conclude that effective family support is critical for realizing the transformative potential of the reentry moment. Indeed, those who struggled to find or maintain social supports had considerably more difficulty desisting from crime or avoiding relapse. This raises the question of what might be done to help ex-offenders better capitalize on the reentry moment and reintegrate into conventional society.

Policy Recommendations

What can be done to facilitate the successful reintegration of formerly incarcerated individuals? How can we make prison a turning point away from crime and criminal justice system involvement for more individuals leaving prison? The first and most important step is incarcerating fewer people in the first place so that the billions of dollars spent on prisons every year can be better spent on prevention, treatment, and reintegration.

Incarcerate Fewer People

If nothing else, the experiences of the interview participants documented in this book have demonstrated just how difficult it is to leave prison and find a new, more conventional place for oneself in society. It is worth reminding ourselves that the fact that the United States is the world's leader in incarceration is the result of a long series of policy decisions. As we discussed in the introduction, the increase in the rate of incarceration over the last four decades occurred not because of a sharp increase in crime but because we are now sentencing to prison people who would not have been so sentenced in the past. Presumably, we as a society believe that incarcerating ever more people makes us safer, but the evidence actually shows the opposite: that at best the experience of prison does not change at all the probability that the typical offender will commit a new crime after release and that at worst going to prison actually makes the typical offender more likely to commit a new crime. The long-term implications of imprisonment for the individuals sentenced, for their families, and for their communities more broadly are difficult to overstate.

The question of how going to prison affects criminal behavior is challenging to answer correctly because finding the right comparison group—those otherwise similar to people who have been sentenced to prison but who stayed in the community—is difficult. The average prisoner is very different from the average person sentenced to probation (supervision in the community). Recently, however, social scientists have begun to leverage natural experiments to provide better answers to this question. These studies compare prisoners to others who were convicted of a crime but received a nonprison sentence by isolating variation in sentence type due to factors unrelated to the characteristics of the individuals being sentenced. The most common strategy is to compare individuals sentenced by a harsh judge to those sentenced by a lenient judge in settings where judges are randomly assigned to defendants. Those on the margin between prison and another type of sentence like probation for whom the judge randomly assigned makes a difference provide a research design that mimics many of the properties of a randomized experiment. According to these studies, going to prison either does not affect the probability of reoffending (Berube and Green 2007; Harding, Morenoff, et al. 2017a; Loeffler 2013) or increases offending (Mueller-Smith 2014) after release, and additional time in prison does not reduce the probability of reoffending (Abrams 2012; Green and Winik 2010).

One might also argue that, at the very least, incarcerating people in prison prevents them from committing crimes against people in the community while they are in prison, what criminologists call the *incapacitation effect*. Yet it is easy to overestimate the incapacitation effect by focusing solely on the fact that someone in prison can harm only fellow inmates and prison staff. We also need to know how many prisoners would have committed crimes again had they remained in the community, for example, had they been sentenced to probation. Here, again, the natural experiment design can help. Such studies show that incapacitation effects reduce an individual's probability of being convicted of a new felony by 15 percentage points in the first three years after sentencing for the typical offender on the margin between prison and remaining in the community on probation (Harding, Morenoff, et al. 2017a). The incapacitation effect is smaller— only 4–7 percentage points—if we consider only violent crime (Harding, Morenoff, et al. 2017b).

Recent evidence from California's prison realignment also suggests that incarceration rates can be reduced with minimal effects on public safety (Lofstrom and Raphael 2015). Citing unconstitutional overcrowding in its prisons, a federal court ordered California to reduce prison populations, which it did starting in October 2011 using four mechanisms: (1) by sentencing nonviolent, nonsexual, and nonserious offenders to probation or county jail instead of state prison, (2) by putting parole and probation technical violators in county jails for short stays rather than returning them to prison (analogous to what we have called *intermediate sanctions* in this book), (3) by supervising low-level parolees less intensely in county probation departments, and (4) by reducing the maximum amount of time parole and probation violators spend in prison from one year to six months. The result was a dramatic decrease in prison incarceration in the first year, from 431 to 355 inmates per 100,000 residents, with only about one-third of that drop made up for by individuals incarcerated in county jails rather than in prison. The Public Policy Institute of California estimates that violent crime rates were unaffected in the first two years following the reforms, but there was a slight increase in property crime rates, driven entirely by an increase in auto thefts (Lofstrom and Raphael 2015).

There are basically two pathways to reducing the rate of incarceration: (1) changes to so-called front-end sentencing, such as reducing the number of individuals sentenced to prison when they commit a new crime or reducing how much time they serve in prison, and (2) changes to so-called back-end sentencing, such as reducing incarceration in prison for parole and probation violators. Both these pathways are included in California's justice realignment. Although there are many possible ways to change front-end sentencing, including shortening prison sentence lengths and removing mandatory minimum sentences, the main alternative—which avoids sentencing to prison entirely—is to sentence offenders to community supervision, called *probation* in most states. Probation is similar to parole supervision but is typically less intense, with fewer community corrections staff supervising more individuals. Probation avoids the life disruptions of a prison term and is also far less expensive than prison; in Michigan, for example, the cost of probation is about one-sixth that of prison. Research that we have presented elsewhere suggests that we can actually reduce offending while saving money by sentencing lower-level offenders not to prison but to intensive probation (see Harding, Morenoff, et al. 2017a).

The danger of placing more people on probation is what criminologists call the *net widening effect* of probation (Phelps 2013). Individuals being supervised on probation are at considerable risk of being sent to prison on a technical violation or for a new crime because they are under considerably more scrutiny and surveillance from law enforcement than the typical citizen. Thus, the danger is that a probation sentence can merely be a delayed prison sentence in its effect. A similar dynamic is at play for those on parole after prison, leading to more back-end sentencing, or what has been termed the *revolving door* of prison (Harding, Morenoff, et al. 2017a)—those released are returned quickly because of the greater scrutiny and surveillance faced by individuals on parole and because of the challenges of reentry and reintegration. This is especially important because the literature suggests that short prison terms may be especially criminogenic (Loughran et al. 2009; Meade et al. 2013). We suspect that those individuals cycling in and out of prison for six months to a year at a time may experience all the disruptive effects of prison without the opportunity for a sufficient period of cooling out, reflection, or any rehabilitative or educational programming.

One way to dampen the net widening effect of probation, slow the revolving door, and cut down on back-end sentencing is to punish individuals on parole or probation who commit technical violations or minor property crimes with intermediate sanctions rather than incarceration in prison (Jacobson 2005). Some such sanctions are custodial but shorter than prison. These are alternatives to prison that remove violators from the community for a very short period of time and ideally also provide them with services or supports that address the root causes of the violation behavior, such as drug addiction, and continue those supports after the end of the sanction. In Michigan, such sanctions involve residential drug treatment, short jail stays, or other forms of custody with programming, such as technical rule violator centers. However, intermediate sanctions themselves can be disruptive, especially with regard to employment and residential stability (Harding, Morenoff, and Herbert 2013; Harding, Siegel, and Morenoff 2017; Herbert, Morenoff, and Harding 2015). In addition to using them more sparingly, another option is to sanction parolees who have committed minor parole violations to jail on weekends or overnight, as some states have, so that the sanction is less likely to interfere with employment or job search or create a long-term rift with one's household or eviction for non-payment of rent. Other sanctions such as community service or intensive outpatient treatment for substance abuse may similarly serve to address the root causes of criminal behaviors while not wholly disrupting the individual's life. The costs and benefits of using various intermediate sanctions and the situations in which they are effective warrant future research and policy evaluation.[4] We need a better set of more effective but less punitive and disruptive intermediate sanctions in order reduce back-end sentencing and thus incarceration (Jacobson 2005; Laub and Sampson 2003).

What are the prospects for making such radical changes to sentencing, parole, and probation? Ten years ago, before the Great Recession and still in the grips of tough-on-crime politics, there would have been ample reason for pessimism. However, the passage of California's Proposition 47, opinion polling evidence of the public's distaste for harsh punishments (Simon 2007), and recent emphasis on state budget cuts suggest that the time may be ripe for "justice reinvestment" (Clear 2011), moving public funds from prisons to community supervision and preventative services (see also Jacobson 2005; Petersilia and Cullen 2014). The Great Recession put significant strains on state budgets, and ever-increasing incarceration in prison came to be seen as unsustainable. As one of the top line items in the discretionary budgets of most states, cutting corrections costs is now arguably on the table across the country. And policies designed to reduce reliance on incarceration are touted as smart on crime by legislators of all political affiliations. As many have before, we argue that we can improve public safety, improve the lives of those caught up in the criminal justice system and their families, and save money by reinvesting prison dollars in high-quality, effective services in prison and, for ex-offenders, in the community (e.g., Irwin 2005; Jacobson 2005). The election of President Trump and his appointment of Jeff Sessions as attorney general threaten to shift the momentum back toward more punitive criminal justice policies, but reform is still afoot in many state capitals. We now turn to some of the ways reinvestments might be made to improve the lives of ex-offenders and their families.

Reduce Collateral Punishments Related to Stigma

As we discussed in chapter 6, ex-offenders coming out of prison face a severe stigma in the labor market, both formally, through bans on certain occupations, and informally, through employer preferences for hiring employees without a criminal record. Recall as well that this stigma is much more severe for African American ex-offenders. With the ubiquity of background check technology, a similar stigma now likely extends into the realm of rental housing as well, although the evidence here is not as complete. In addition, many states also impose other restrictions on those with a criminal record, from voting to living in public housing to receiving certain social welfare benefits (Godsoe 1998; Pinard 2010; Rubinstein and Mukamal 2002; Travis 2005). In short, these collateral punishments mean that those with a felony record actually experience much more punishment than is formally assigned them at sentencing, what Uggen and Stewart (2015) call *piling on*. This represents a further escalation of what scholars of crime, punishment, and social control have called *the culture of control*. Gradually, and without conscious, democratic deliberation, we have increased the collateral punishment of a felony conviction to the point where the stigma of a felony record arguably is a harsher punishment than the sentence itself, a form of punishment that lasts far longer than a term in prison or jail or a period of probation supervision. Arguably, this punishment is more severe for those sentenced to prison because (1) it is harder for prisoners to conceal their felony record and because (2) going to prison may signal to employers, landlords, and welfare bureaucrats a more serious crime and therefore create a more severe stigma.

What can be done to reduce the harms that stem from a felony record? In an abstract sense, the answer is simple. We can treat the actual sentence imposed by a judge in a court of law as the only legitimate form of punishment imposed on an individual convicted of a crime and the completion of that sentence as the full extent of the punishment. Once one has paid one's debt to society, it should really be paid. The current system of a virtual lifetime of punishment is like a corrupt bill collector who will never stop harassing a debtor for payment, even when the debt has been paid. In practice, this means lifting the formal bans on employment in certain occupations after one's sentence has been completed as long as no new offenses have been committed in the meantime, restoring access to social welfare benefits, education grants and loans, and public housing, and doing more to protect an individual's criminal record from public scrutiny or at least disallowing the use of a criminal record in hiring and renting conditions after some reasonable period of time has elapsed.

The barriers to and arguments against some of these changes will make them a difficult sell to lawmakers and the public and difficult to implement effectively. Some would argue that employers and landlord have a right to know about or consider a criminal record when making a hiring or renting decision. Yet it is unclear whether it makes sense to conceive of information about a prospective employee's or renter's criminal past as a right. There are many other statuses or types of information that we regularly disallow from hiring or renting decisions, such as family composition, health status, or race, even when there is a statistical association between these characteristics and outcomes employers and landlords care about. We do so (1) because we believe that individuals should be treated as individuals and not as stereotypical representations of the social groups they belong to and (2) because these generalizations are often incorrect or misunderstood. This latter point is critical for understanding the stigma of a criminal record because criminological research shows that, by three to nine years after a crime has been committed (depending on the type of crime and age at first arrest), the probability of an ex-offender committing a new crime is little different than that of the average person of the same age committing a crime (Blumstein and Nakamura 2009; Kurlychek, Brame, and Bushway 2006, 2007). Moreover, prohibiting employers or landlords from using criminal records in hiring or firing decisions could protect them from negligence lawsuits based on the behavior of employees or tenants with a criminal record.

Some local governments have passed "ban-the-box" laws that prohibit employers from asking about a criminal record until a hiring decision has been made. Typically, they do not prohibit criminal records from influencing hiring decisions, but they do limit their use until later in the hiring process so that individuals with a criminal record cannot be excluded from consideration outright. These laws vary in that sometimes it is only public employers who are covered, and there has been little research on their impact. However, one study of recidivism before and after the implementation of a ban-the-box law in Honolulu County, Hawaii, found a 57 percent drop in the proportion of prosecutions that were for repeat offenders (D'Alessio, Stolzenberg, and Flexon 2015). This suggests that even relatively mild stigma remediation measures can substantially improve outcomes for formerly incarcerated individuals. The question of whether such measures help formerly incarcerated individuals escape the secondary labor market is not well understood, however. In addition, there is some evidence that ban-the-box measures in particular harm the overall employment of demographic groups that have high incarceration rates, such as low-skill minority men, through statistical discrimination as employers use group stereotypes regarding imprisonment when individual information is not available (Doleac and Hansen 2016).

One practical barrier is that criminal records are currently a matter of public record and that the businesses that collect and sell such information to landlords and employers collect it from public records. Criminal records are currently sealed only for juveniles, and the expungement of records from publicly available databases is limited in most states because the circumstances under which a criminal record can be expunged is very limited, often to single, first offenses (Love 2003). One option is to expand the opportunities for expungement of criminal records, although this would not help those just released from prison as even more liberalized expungement rules would likely require a waiting period without a new conviction. A related problem is that the little available research on such privately held arrest records suggests that this information is often inaccurate (Bushway, Briggs, et al. 2007). Currently, companies maintaining publicly available criminal record databases are subject to fewer regulations than are those maintaining publicly available credit score databases.[5]

Another option is to develop ways for those with a criminal record to signal their reform or rehabilitation positively, that is, to allow them some control over how a criminal record is interpreted or understood by employers and landlords. Bushway and Apel (2012) develop what they call a *signaling perspective* on stigma remediation. They argue that the completion of specific programs, such as job-training programs, can signal to employers a commitment to staying away from crime as demonstrated by the effort involved in completing the programs. They then extend this idea more generally to propose that a "positive credentialing" system for those with a criminal record could be used to counteract the stigma of widely available criminal record information. As certifications, time milestones, and/or education, training, or treatment programs are completed; an individual with a criminal record could earn a formal certification of good conduct in the community or progress toward rehabilitation. This would signal not only intent to desist from crime but more importantly effort and accomplishments in that direction. It would also provide a goal toward which formerly incarcerated individuals could work in the community, even if they struggle in the short term with finding employment or stable housing. To be effective, such a system would need to be relatively simple for employers to understand, well publicized, and national (or at least statewide) in scope so that employers have ready access to straightforward information. Such formal credentialing systems may also help reduce racial disparities in employment outcomes after prison. For instance, a study of drug testing and employment outcomes found that, when employee drug testing was implemented, African American employment and wage outcomes actually improved, presumably because it allowed individuals who were not using drugs to prove that to employers, thereby negating the (incorrect) stereotype associating African Americans with drug use (Wozniak 2015).

Finally, we note that the experiences of our participants suggest that aspects of the way the criminal justice system supervises, surveils, and controls parolees may serve to intensify the stigma of a criminal record for parolees, especially with regard to employment. One example is that efforts to verify employment or employment search can make the criminal records of employees or prospective employees more salient. That is, contact with parole or probation agents attempting to verify employment may color views of the employee or even inform an employer of the parolee's criminal record. Michigan parole officers tended to rely on pay stubs whenever possible, but individuals paid in cash under the table could not demonstrate their employment in this way. Another example is restrictions on cell phone ownership or bank account use that can make job search more difficult or pay by direct deposit impossible. A third example is that intermediate sanctions for parole violations can signal instability to employers or cause someone to lose a job while in short-term custody, not to mention interfering with job search. Where practical, such intermediate sanctions could be better tailored to avoid disrupting employment or job search, and officers could be more cautious about revealing supervision status to employers.

Use Time in Prison to Prepare for Release

Even if we successfully reduce incarceration rates to levels last seen four decades ago, we will still be incarcerating and subsequently releasing significant numbers of people. Time spent in prison can and should be used more effectively. Our participants' accounts of their incarceration indicate that much of the time they spend in prison is idle and could be better used to prepare for release. Part of this seemed to be because work assignments and programming in prison often covered only short periods of time each day. Part also stemmed from the need to wait for opportunities to participate in programming owing to lack of capacity. Both these reasons underscore a point made above, but here we state it in a slightly different way: given the high cost of simply keeping someone in prison, improving the prison experiences of those we do incarcerate is going to be next to impossible unless we reduce the number of people we incarcerate. We cannot afford significantly better rehabilitative programming any other way.

Education is one way to take better advantage of time spent in prison. Recall the challenges formerly incarcerated individuals face in finding employment and their concentration in the worst low-wage jobs in the secondary labor market, a result partly due their low levels of education and work experience. As we became more and more punitive in our approach to corrections, fewer and fewer prisons offered anything more than basic literacy and numeracy (also called *adult basic education*) and GED programs, although life-skill programming has increased. For example, like many other states, Michigan does not allow the use of state funds for the postsecondary education of state prisoners. Whereas, in 1990, about 60 percent of prisons offered college programs, only about 35 percent did so by 2005 (Stephan 1992, 2008). Estimates suggest that today only about 6 percent of prisoners are participating in postsecondary education, the vast majority in vocational or certificate programs rather than college degree programs (Gorgol and Sponsler 2011). Simply allowing prison inmates to access the same federal education grants and loans as those in the community could significantly increase access to higher education in prison.[6]

The evidence suggests that we could significantly improve postprison outcomes by expanding access to education in prison. On the basis of reviews of the evaluation literature, both Mackenzie (2006) and Petersilia (2003) find that in-prison academic and vocational education programs effectively reduce recidivism. Limiting access to education in prison seems particularly shortsighted given the importance of human capital for success in the labor market and the opportunity that time in prison might provide for focusing on education. There is some evidence that inmate higher education decreases the probability of return to prison (Lockwood et al. 2012), although this is an important area for further research.[7] For such programs to be effective, they need to improve outcomes beyond the GED. The available evidence suggests that a GED itself provides little labor market benefit for formerly incarcerated individuals (e.g., Tyler and Kling 2006), but it may be an effective stepping-stone to higher education.

The importance of social support from family, friends, and romantic partners for the well-being of formerly incarcerated individuals, both before but especially after release, suggests that family reunification should also be a priority for the time spent in prison. Some of the difficulties of prisoner reentry faced by those without social support might be mitigated by prison programs that aim to help inmates rebuild relationships with family members and others or improve on prisoners' relationship and communication skills. Our participants' accounts suggest that the incarceration of a loved one serves as a crisis moment for some families and as a result presents opportunities for reconciliation and renewal. However, a number of aspects of prison management can unintentionally make such reconciliation more difficult, including the location of prisons far from the population centers from which most prisoners are drawn, the high cost of telephone calls to and from prisons, and restrictive visitation policies that limit the amount of time allowed for visitation or the individuals who can visit prison inmates (Comfort 2008). These systems are designed to serve the interests of the overburdened corrections bureaucracy rather than facilitate the reintegration of prisoners after release. Information technology like video conferencing could be better leveraged to increase contact and communication with family during prison. However, we would not recommend the complete replacement of in-person visitation with video conferencing and must be wary of attempts by for-profit companies to charge high rates for low-quality video visitation services, as is increasingly being done with jail visitation (Rabuy and Wagner 2015). Instead, video conferencing should be used as a venue for increased frequency of prisoner-family contact.

One potential solution is to move prisoners to prisons close to home in the months before release, although the evaluation of New York's Project Greenlight casts doubt on the effectiveness of such strategies (Wilson et al. 2005). Efforts to improve family relationships must also be sensitive to histories of family conflict, domestic violence, and the stresses of separation for both the inmate and the family (Bobbit and Nelson 2004). Two well-known examples of in-prison parenting and family reunification programs are operated in New York's Sing Sing and Bedford Hills prisons. While there are many examples of family reunification programs (Bobbit and Nelson 2004), few, if any, have been rigorously evaluated. Finally, we must do more to allow prisoners to assist family members while they are incarcerated as a way to rebuild relationships. Donald Braman (2004) suggests, for example, that material support, however minor, has symbolic value for both families and prisoners, potentially increasing or at least maintaining the strength of family bonds. Work in prison at fair wages that could be directed to supporting family on the outside might have both economic and social benefits for prisoner reintegration.

The findings in this book have also highlighted the importance of health—particularly mental health and substance abuse—for the postprison experiences and outcomes of ex-offenders. The extent of substance abuse and other mental health problems within this population and the ability of some participants to overcome them suggest that improved access to substance abuse and mental health treatment has the potential to improve the well-being of formerly incarcerated individuals significantly (Mackenzie 2006). Time in prison seems like an especially opportune moment to engage in substance abuse treatment because access to drugs and alcohol is much more limited (although not impossible), the environment is otherwise more easily controlled, and there are fewer triggers and distractions. Some even argue that in-prison treatment is more cost-effective than residential treatment programs in the community as housing and food are already being provided (McCollister 2008). However, not all programs are created alike. It is the intensive programs that isolate patients in their own units that appear to be the most effective in prison—such as therapeutic community programming and residential substance abuse treatment—rather than brief group therapy sessions or programs that educate prisoners about addictions and addictive substances while keeping them in the general inmate population (Wexler, Falkin, and Lipton 1990). A quasi-experimental study of one therapeutic community program found reductions in recidivism and determined that these reductions were proportional to time in the program (Wexler, Falkin, and Lipton 1990). Again, the costs of such programs are high, and providing them for sufficient time periods to all who could benefit from them will require a greater investment in resources than current levels of incarceration allow. We also caution that, without effective follow-up treatment in the community after release that is aligned and coordinated to continue in-prison treatment (so-called continuity of care), addiction relapse will continue to be a major challenge for many formerly incarcerated individuals.

We are less optimistic about treatment for other mental health problems in prison because of what psychologists and psychiatrists describe as, for example, an "inherent tension between the security mission of prisons and mental health considerations" (Fellner 2006, 391). The conditions of confinement in prison, at least in its current form (see, e.g., the discussion of prisonization in chapter 2), are more likely to exacerbate mental health problems than provide an environment conducive to treatment. These conditions include overcrowding, violence, lack of privacy, lack of meaningful activities, isolation, and conflictual relationships with guards and staff. Common punishments for prison misconduct, often the product of mental health problems, are likely only to further aggravate mental health problems. Such punishments include isolation, removal of privileges, or moving cells or cell blocks. For these reasons, the mental health treatment profession typically argues, for example: "The ultimate solution to this problem [concentrated mental illness behind bars] is to maintain a functioning public mental health treatment system so that mentally ill persons do not end up in prisons and jails" (Torrey et al. 2014, 8).

Support Prisoners and Their Families during Reintegration

No matter how much we prepare prisoners for release, if they do not continue to receive supports during the period of reintegration, they will continue to struggle. Currently, their families are providing most of this support, so efforts to improve reintegration must take into account the support that families need as well. At the most basic level, we must acknowledge the material support families are providing for their loved ones leaving prison, often at significant sacrifice to their own well-being. We saw multiple examples of families and romantic partners stretching public benefits intended for some family members (e.g., Temporary Assistance for Needy Families, supplemental security income, Section 8) to cover the needs of formerly incarcerated individuals as well. This suggests that the rise in incarceration and the accompanying increase in reentering citizens are placing additional burdens on public benefits that are invisible to policy makers but have important consequences for the well-being of the low-income children and families they are intended to support. Evaluations of reentry programs that provide material resources such as transitional housing, subsidized employment, or transportation directly to the ex-offender should also take into account the effects of such resources on the well-being of his or her family or household. In addition, programs that directly involve families in the reentry process, such as La Bodega de la Familia or the Osborne Association's FamilyWorks program in New York City, can help support families struggling to assist a returning family member while also increasing the chances of family reunification (Sullivan et al. 2002). Moreover, the magnitude of the social support that our participants' families do provide suggests that prisoner reentry programs have much to make up for when serving those formerly incarcerated individuals without family social support.

Given the number of prisoners beset by mental health and substance abuse problems, treatment in the community after prison is critical. Yet not all treatment is created alike. Most of our participants were able to access only what we might call *low-dosage* treatment—AA and NA meetings or perhaps group therapy sessions with a trained therapist. We suspect that higher-dosage treatments like intensive outpatient or residential treatment and access to medication-assisted therapies (e.g., methadone, buprenorphine, acamprosate) would have better served at least some of our participants, especially if care could be continued for longer than is currently typical. There is some reason to be optimistic that better treatment may now be available, given the passage and implementation of the Affordable Care Act (ACA). Not only does the ACA provide for parity of mental health and substance abuse care (Beronio et al. 2013), but, more importantly, it increases access to health care for many formerly incarcerated individuals through Medicaid expansion, at least in states that adopt the expansion. Prior to the ACA, there were few eligibility categories under which formerly incarcerated individuals—particularly those who were not caring for children and were not disabled—could qualify for Medicaid (Hammett, Roberts, and Kennedy 2001), but Medicaid expansion has expanded eligibility to anyone under 138 percent of the poverty line (Beronio et al. 2013; Ogundimu et al. 2012). If program capacity eventually expands to meet this new demand, substance abuse treatment programs may help stop the downward spiral of addiction before it leads to criminal behavior. Because some states have elected not to participate in Medicaid expansion, there is an opportunity for researchers to study the impact of health care coverage and utilization among formerly incarcerated individuals, including mental health and substance abuse treatment.

Employment-related programs were a close competitor with mental health and substance abuse treatment for the most common programs utilized by our participants. These included both employment counseling and transitional jobs, and, as discussed in chapter 6, most of our participants seemed to benefit little from them, at least directly in terms of employment outcomes. While a number of such programs have been held up as successful models in recent years, including those run by the Center for Employment Opportunities in New York, the Texas Re-integration of Offenders project, and the Safer Foundation of Chicago, recent reviews of the literature disagree about their general effectiveness (Bushway and Apel 2012; Raphael 2011). The experiences of our participants are consistent with the mixed results of these programs. Given the current state of the low-skill labor market, characterized by poverty-level wages, high turnover, schedule volatility, and unpleasant work and working conditions, and the low human capital and health challenges of our participants and their families, it is no surprise that short-term jobs or employment counseling does not measurably improve the employment or recidivism outcomes of formerly incarcerated individuals. The problems are too large and the solutions too small.

Another strategy for improving labor market outcomes on release is building human capital, and some of our participants did indeed attempt to pursue further education or training. Only those with considerable material social support were able to take advantage of education opportunities; the others simply did not have the resources to support themselves while enrolled in school. For others, disruptions of jail stays, relapse, or employment conflicted with school schedules and demands, and few of our participants who started programs completed them. This suggests that education or training programs may also need to make better provisions for the basic material needs of their students, especially for those with low levels of social support. This might be achieved through earnings supplements, paid on-the-job training, employment subsidies, or the provision of housing assistance in order to serve most formerly incarcerated individuals effectively (Bloom 2006). Otherwise, meeting short-term material needs may interfere with effective program participation, simply turning financial aid into accumulated debt. It may also be that such programs need to be more closely coupled with other services such as mental health and substance abuse treatments (Bloom 2010) or—in our view—need to be better linked to jobs outside the secondary labor market that pay a living wage and offer opportunities for further skill acquisition and career advancement.

We close by emphasizing a more general point that we have discussed in various ways throughout this chapter: that improving the reintegration of formerly incarcerated individuals requires changing the institutional and economic systems that govern their choices and behaviors rather than treating each formerly incarcerated individual individually. Our current system of recording, managing, and disseminating information in criminal records leaves the typical formerly incarcerated individual with little recourse in terms of navigating the labor market with a criminal record other than gravitating toward the most felon-friendly industries, which are often those in the secondary labor market. The current nature of the low-wage labor market, with its concentration of secondary labor market jobs, creates steep barriers to employment stability and upward mobility for all low-wage workers, including formerly incarcerated individuals. The surveillance and control apparatus of community supervision leaves little room for error and generates its own forms of instability and heightened stigma. The lack of in-prison opportunities for acquiring real education credentials or participating in the intensive treatment programs where the probability of success is highest—the result of overincarceration—leaves released prisoners no better prepared to take on the roles and responsibilities of conventional social life than they were when they entered prison. In sum, improving prisoner reintegration requires reducing our reliance on incarceration so that the vast resources dedicated to confining and managing prisoners can be redirected toward improving our institutions and economic systems.

Appendix: Data and Methodology

The findings reported in this book were drawn from data compiled in the Michigan Study of Life after Prison, a mixed-method study designed to understand the processes, dynamics, and experience of prisoner reentry and reintegration in the age of mass incarceration. The data are composed of a qualitative sample of twenty-two formerly incarcerated individuals, interviewed intensively over a three-year period following release from prison, and a quantitative sample of Michigan Department of Corrections (MDOC) administrative records composed of the entire population of Michigan prisoners released to parole in 2003 and followed through 2009.

A. Qualitative Data Collection and Analysis

Sampling Strategy and Interview Processes

A sample of sixteen male and eight female interview participants was selected from MDOC administrative records on the basis of their expected release date (those who would be released within two months of the baseline interview) and release county (four counties in southeast Michigan). Because statistical representativeness across multiple participant characteristics is impossible in a study with a small sample size, we instead pursued a sampling strategy common in qualitative research called *sampling for range* (Small 2009). Our goal in selecting participants was to ensure racial and gender diversity, diversity of local geographic context, and diversity of services and supervision provided by MDOC. Accordingly, the sample was stratified by gender, race (white vs. black), reentry county (urban vs. suburban), and type of release (receiving services from Michigan Prisoner Re-entry Initiative [MPRI], not receiving MPRI services, or being released without parole [i.e., maxing out]).[1] Within these categories, potential participants available at the time of recruitment were selected at random. This sampling strategy ensures that theoretically important categories are present and that conclusions drawn are not particular to the largest group of formerly incarcerated individuals in the population (minority males released to central cities). Our sample is not representative of the population of formerly incarcerated individuals released in Michigan during this time period in a statistical sense. For example, the inclusion of a sampling cell for white males released to suburban areas resulted in an overrepresentation of drunk-driving offenses in our sample.

Three males in our sample refused to participate in the study, and one female participant was discontinued from the study after she was denied parole after the first in-prison interview. They were replaced by additional randomly selected individuals with the same sampling characteristics, resulting in a response rate for in-prison prerelease interviews of 86 percent (twenty-four of twenty-eight).

We intentionally chose to study a small number of participants intensively over a relatively long period of time for three reasons. First, a longitudinal design is necessary in a study of formerly incarcerated individuals owing to the rapidly changing nature of their lives. Reentry is a period of significant flux, and individuals' experiences immediately after release can be very different from their experiences months and years later. Second, a longer follow-up allows for the observation of outcomes that take time to develop. Third, frequent interviews are required to capture the processes driving change over time as well as to increase participant retention in this hard-to-study population (we discuss strategies used to prevent participant attrition below).

Interview Timing and Details

In-prison interviews were conducted in private rooms (often those used by lawyers visiting their clients). MDOC regulations forbid recorders within prisons, so field notes were used to document in-prison interviews. Postrelease interviews were conducted primarily in the participants' residences but also occasionally in the researchers' offices or in a public location. These interviews were recorded and transcribed. Interviews covered a diverse array of topics, both researcher and participant driven, but focused on the participants' community context, family roles and relationships, criminal activities and experiences, labor market experiences, life in prison, service use, and health and well-being, including drug and alcohol abuse. Interviews were unstructured, meaning that we prepared a detailed interview protocol with a lengthy list of questions and follow-up probes but let the conversation follow the interests and experiences of the participant. When a particular conversation thread was complete and the list of probes exhausted, we returned to the next topic in the protocol. Initial in-prison interviews lasted roughly ninety minutes, follow-up interviews usually one to two hours. Interview protocols are available on request.

Individuals involved in criminal activity, the criminal justice system, and substance abuse are challenging to study. Although we began the study with prerelease interviews with twenty-four participants, two—one male and one female—left the study immediately following their prison release. These individuals were younger than our average participant, and both were subsequently convicted of new crimes. All remaining twenty-two participants were interviewed once before release and then repeatedly during the three years following release for a total of 154 interviews. The first two postrelease interviews were targeted for the first and second months after release in order to capture the challenges and instability of the immediate postrelease period. Following the initial interviews, most participants followed a fairly regular interview schedule: roughly every three months through the first year and every six months thereafter unless incarceration, residential treatment, or absconding made it impossible to stay on schedule (for detailed interview timing, see table A.1). Interviews with participants who got off schedule were conducted at a later date, including follow-ups in prison with three participants, and the missed time period was covered. One participant was shot and killed by a burglar during the second year of the study. Another achieved stable employment and marriage one year after release, and, owing to the consistency in his responses across his five postrelease sessions, we discontinued his interviews.[2] We kept in touch with him informally throughout the study period, however, and monitored his parole agent's case notes for arrests or other indications of reoffending, of which there were none. Finally, in some cases our interviews extended past the three-year mark, either because the participant was recently released from jail or prison or because of continued instability, which required further follow-up to understand desistence and recidivism. For all but two of our participants who committed new crimes, we were able to interview the participant at some point afterward, sometimes after the three-year period that is the main focus of this study. The number of postrelease interviews per participant ranged from 2 (two

TABLE A.1 **Timing of follow-up interviews (months since release)**

	Interview number											
Participant	2	3	4	5	6	7	8	9	10	11	12	
Christopher	1	2	7	11	16	23						
Damian	1	3	9	12	17	23						
Geoffrey	1	2	8	9	11	22						
James	1	2	6	9	a							
Daniel	1	4	9	14	21							
Henry	1	1	**19**	21	b							
Jake	1	3	8	12	c							
Leon	2	3	8	11	16	23						
Randall	3	4	6	8	11	13	19	22	25	33	38	
David	1	9d	b									
Lamar	1	2	6	16d	**21**	23	24					
DeAngelo	1	2	5	9	16	18	21	25	36			
Paul	1	2	5	9	13	e						
Morgan	2	3	15d	b								
Craig	1	2	f	b								
Jennifer	2	3	7	10	13	19	25	33	39			
Kristine	1	2	9	14	17	**26**	31	g				
Michelle	1	2	5	9	12	18	30	**44**				
Jocelyn	1	2	6	8	11	17	24	32	38			
Lenora	1	2	6	13	20	c						
Jane	1	2	6	8	12	**29**	38					
Jada	1	2	7	9	11	18	25	36				

Note: Bold type indicates that the interview occurred after a new release from prison.
[a] Deceased.
[b] In prison at end of study.
[c] Dropped out of study.
[d] In-prison interview.
[e] Interviews discontinued owing to saturation.
[f] Interview refused while incarcerated.
[g] In jail at end of study.

participants who were returned to prison not long after release) to 11, with a mean of 5.8 and a median of 6.

We used a number of strategies to maintain contact with participants in this difficult-to-track population. The most important was access to parole agents' records, which allowed us to maintain contact with participants whenever parole agents knew how to find them. For all but two participants, we obtained consent to access their MDOC records, allowing us to view their parole agents' case notes for updated contact information, substance use tests, parole violations, and arrests. This was particularly useful for tracking residential moves, periods of incarceration in jail, and periods of confinement to residential treatment. A second strategy was to elicit from participants at the initial interview and regularly thereafter the names of and contact information for three individuals who would be likely to know how to reach them. A third strategy was to provide incentive payments of $60 per interview. Finally, we believe, though we cannot independently verify, that the rapport we were able to develop with participants over repeated interviews also contributed to our lower attrition rate than was seen in some earlier studies of formerly incarcerated individuals. Three participants attritted during the course of the study—at two, twelve, and twenty months.

Sample Description

Half the male sample is white and half black.[3] At the initial interview, the men ranged in age from twenty-two to seventy-one, with most participants in their late twenties and early thirties. Crimes for which they were convicted range from armed robbery to driving under the influence (multiple convictions can lead to imprisonment) to manslaughter. Five of these participants were being released from prison for the first time; all the others had experienced multiple prison spells.[4] The female sample is also half white and half black. The women ranged in age from twenty-two to fifty-two at the initial interview, with most participants in their late thirties and early forties. Their crimes ranged from felony firearm possession to retail fraud to drug selling. Three were leaving prison on their first release; the other four had served previous prison terms. We assigned pseudonyms to all participants and to any other individuals mentioned by name.

All but four of the fifteen men and two of the seven women in our study engaged in some form of illegal behavior other than drug use (including behavior not known to law enforcement authorities) during the study. Drug and alcohol addiction was also common among them. Our interviews made clear that conventional measures of involvement in drugs, such as whether a participant has been convicted of a drug-related crime, understate the prevalence and significance of these addictions. The majority of participants' crimes were committed while under the influence of drugs or alcohol or motivated by drugs. Six of our fifteen male participants characterized themselves as alcoholics, five as both drug abusers and alcoholics, and three as drug abusers solely; only one reported no addiction to drugs or alcohol. Of seven female participants, four characterized themselves as drug addicted, one as drug and alcohol addicted, and one as formerly drug addicted; only one did not describe a serious current or past problem with drugs or alcohol.

Our analysis and results depend on the collection of potentially sensitive data from participants, so cultivating a rapport with them and gaining their trust were critical. Participants were matched with interviewer on the basis of gender, and the same interviewer conducted all interviews/ interactions with each participant throughout the study. The longitudinal nature of the study was also essential to building rapport and trust as participants revealed more and more information as time passed, occasionally including information that was intentionally withheld in earlier interviews. One potential barrier to trust was the recruitment of participants in prison with the cooperation of MDOC. However, consent forms clearly stated that no individual information from the study would be shared with MDOC or any other law enforcement agency unless there was indication of imminent harm to participants or others, and we secured a certificate of confidentiality prior to the initial interviews in order to protect study data from law enforcement and the courts. All study procedures were also approved by the University of Michigan's Institutional Review Board.

Data Analysis

The open-ended portion of the interviews was digitally recorded and professionally transcribed. Completed documents were reviewed for accuracy. The coding and analysis of the field notes and transcripts were conducted using Atlas TI qualitative software. Our analysis strategy alternated between inductive and deductive approaches to the data. For instance, in the investigation of job search and stigma management strategies, we brought a very specific research question and analytic lens to the data, one shaped by substantial prior reading on the topic. In other cases, such as the role of romantic relationships in the reentry processes, findings emerged inductively from the data themselves. An initial list of codes was generated prior to analysis on the basis of theoretically motivated categories and concepts, and additional descriptive codes were generated during the course of the analysis (Braun and Clarke 2006; Lofland and Lofland 1995). Where possible, we cross-checked specific facts with those recorded in parole agents' case notes.

B. Quantitative Research Design and Data Collection

Sample

The data for the quantitative portion of this study are the population of individuals paroled from Michigan prisons to Michigan communities in 2003 ($N = 11,064$), although some analyses are based on a one-third sample (N

= 3,689) of this population. To ensure adequate variation in both the geographic locations and the characteristics of neighborhoods represented in the sample, a two-stage clustered sampling design (in which parolees are clustered within census tracts) with probabilities proportionate to size was employed, a sampling scheme for selecting individuals with equal probability when clusters are of unequal sizes (Groves et al. 2004). In the first stage, census tracts were sampled with probability proportionate to their size (i.e., the number of parolees who returned to each tract). In the second stage, individuals within each selected tract were sampled with probability inversely proportionate to the tract selection rate. When the first- and second-stage selection rates are multiplied together, the sampling probability is equal for all individuals (Groves et al. 2004). This approach also ensures that the final sample size remains the same no matter which tracts were sampled in the first stage. More details on the methods used to draw the sample are provided in Morenoff and Harding (2011). Basic descriptive statistics on the population are provided in table A.2.

Data Sources

The most novel aspect of the data collection for this project is the use of parole agent narrative case notes to collect data on the residences and living arrangements of parolees. Our research team developed essential expertise in reading and coding case notes (which include many abbreviations and terminology particular to MDOC) in the process of collecting data on each parolee's first residential address after prison for sampling purposes. A coding system was designed and tested using multiple coders and multiple iterations to ensure adequate inter- and intracoder reliability. Customized data-entry screens were designed (using Microsoft Access) to minimize error, resulting in dynamically linked databases that track every mention in the case notes of a change in the parolee's residence or the composition of the household (in the case of private residences). In addition, the address where each sample member lived immediately prior to the prison term that led to their parole in 2003 was obtained from hard copies of presentence investigation reports, in which addresses are usually verified by the MDOC agent preparing the report, as well as from parole violation reports and parole agent case notes (for those who were on parole prior to their sampled prison term). When a person was discharged from parole but subsequently imprisoned for a new crime and placed back on parole, the research team did resume collecting residence data. Although most case note records were collected only on the one-third sample, the

Variables	
County of first neighborhood	
MSA, central city (urban)	53.1
MSA, non–central city (suburban)	38.5
Non-MSA (rural)	8.3
Age in 2003	
18–25	18.7
26–30	16.7
31–35	18.3
36–40	16.1
41–45	14.2
46–50	9.7
51–89	6.4
Race	
White	44.7
Black	53.5
Other	1.8
Female	7.8
Marital status	
Never married	66.3
Married	12.4
Divorced or separated	20.2
Widowed, common law, unknown	1.1
Number of dependents (mean)	1.24
Education in 2003	
8 years or less	7.2
Some high school	35.4
GED	31.0
High school graduate	20.1
Some college or more	6.2
Formal employment in year before prison entry	14.3
Sex offender	7.4
Known mental illness status	20.6
Prior prison commitments	
0	47.5
1	26.8
2 or 3	19.7
4 or more	5.9
Years in prison, prior spell (mean)	2.94
Type of most serious offense	
Assaultive	28.5
Drug	25.7
Nonassaultive	45.8
Substance abuse history (self-report)	
None	50.9
Alcohol only	4.2
THC only	7.8
Hard drugs only	5.0
Alcohol and THC	6.5
Hard drugs and alcohol/THC	25.6
Year of release	
2000–2001	1.0
2002	5.9
2003	93.1
Conditions of release	
Released to center	10.1
Released on electronic monitoring	7.7

project team coded the first postprison residential address for all 11,064 parolees in the population so that baseline neighborhoods could be identified and used in the two-stage cluster sampling procedure described above.

It is important to note some of the limitations of the case note data. Although all parole agents are required to report information on changes of address/living arrangements, arrest (which must be verified by cross-checking with police records), and parole violations, in practice there may be variability across agents in how completely this information is recorded. Some of the variation could be due to county-specific norms of what parole agents are required to record, and this could result in more missing data for some counties than others.

The project team also collected a wide range of data on all 11,064 parolees in the cohort from administrative databases and documents. Through a collaboration with MDOC, the project was able to extract records from MDOC databases, which cover all time periods during which a person in the cohort was under MDOC supervision or custody, either in a custodial facility or on parole or probation in the community. The MDOC databases contain records dating back to 1980, including information on prior criminal history, demographics, marital status, number of minor children, education, services received in prison, recommitments, behavior violations in prison, and MDOC assessments of health, substances use, security level, recidivism risk, and mental health. They also contain longitudinal data (updated weekly or monthly throughout the parole period) on residential addresses, employment, drug and alcohol tests, arrests, parole violations and revocations, the issuance of absconding warrants, changes in the conditions of supervision (either in custodial facilities or on parole/probation, including electronic monitoring), and transit movements in and out of MDOC facilities or supervisory locations. MDOC also provided data from the basic information report (BIR), a section of the presentence investigation report written by MDOC agents each time someone is convicted of a felony in Michigan courts. The BIR includes the multiple dates associated with each case as it moves through the court system (e.g., the date of the offense, arrest, bond, conviction, and sentencing) as well as information about the sentence and the background characteristics of the individual.

The Michigan State Police (MSP) also agreed to link all individuals in the population with records of every arrest they had as an adult in Michigan (through January 2011). Arrests are reported regularly by all police departments and other law enforcement agencies to MSP. The records included dates of the incident, arrest, charging of the offense, and judicial action as well as details about the charged offenses, their dispositions, and the resulting sentences. MSP matched its records with the study population using social security numbers, names, dates of birth, MSP identification numbers, and MDOC identification numbers (which are permanently assigned to each person and thus do not vary over time).

Linked data from unemployment insurance records for the entire population were obtained from a data-sharing agreement between MDOC and the Michigan Unemployment Insurance Agency (MUIA). These records track employment status and gross wages of cohort members over every calendar quarter since the release from prison that coincided with their 2003 parole (some people were released to residential centers before being paroled in 2003) and for the calendar quarter before they went to prison (for the prison spell that ended in their 2003 parole). The unemployment insurance records are based on employer reports of the gross wages they paid during a calendar quarter. These records also contain information on each employer who paid the individual wages, including their North American Industry Classification System code and a multiunit code for distinguishing multiple establishments (if applicable). The MUIA data exclude temporary or under-the-table employment. MUIA matched its records to the study population using social security numbers, names, and, where possible, employer names.

Administrative records from all sources were cleaned to check for duplicated records and logical inconsistencies both within and across data sets. When necessary, parole agent case notes were consulted to resolve discrepancies and other errors detected.

Key Measures

Space limitations preclude us from describing the measurement of all variables in the data here. We refer the reader to published papers and reports (Harding, Morenoff, and Herbert 2013; Harding, Morenoff, et al. 2016; Harding, Siegel, and Morenoff 2017; Herbert, Morenoff, and Harding 2015; Lee, Harding, and Morenoff 2017; Morenoff and Harding 2011). This section provides details on how the data sources described above were used to construct key measures from the administrative data, including (1) residential histories and neighborhood characteristics, (2) recidivism, and (3) employment and earnings.

1. RESIDENTIAL HISTORIES AND NEIGHBORHOOD CONTEXT MEASURES. As the role of neighborhood context in prisoner reentry was an important theme of the project, a concerted effort was made to collect postprison

residential histories of sampled parolees from parole agent case notes. All parolees are required to report changes of address to their parole officers, who in turn are supposed to verify the address and record it in the OMNI database. It is a technical parole violation to fail to keep one's parole agent informed of one's address, and parole agents are required to verify residence information provided by parolees, so parolees have a strong incentive to provide address information. Parolees also provide an address to MDOC before their release, and these residences are visited by parole agents for approval prior to the parolee's release and recorded in MDOC databases.

Residential histories, including move dates, residence types, and addresses, were assembled from the case notes, beginning on the day of parole from prison in 2003 (or earlier for those who were released to correctional centers before they were paroled) and ending on or before August 17, 2009, the date on which parole agent case notes were downloaded (only 3.6 percent of sample members were still on parole on this date). About 15 percent of sample members were released from prison before their parole date because they were moved to a correctional center where they had community exposure or placed on electronic monitoring (although technically not yet considered to be on parole).[5] Residential histories were censored when the parolee discharged from parole and was therefore no longer observed (49 percent of the sample members discharged). About 2 percent of sample participants died during the observation period before their discharge from parole or a return to prison. The median number of residence records was 5 and the mean was 7.6, but there was considerable variation. For example, 15.7 percent of participants resided in the same residence for the entire observation period, and 25 percent had 10 or more residence records, indicating at least nine moves during the observation period. The mean length of a sample member's observation period was 700 days, with a median of 731 days and a standard deviation of 494 days.

Determining exact move-in and move-out dates for residences was particularly challenging. Approximately one-quarter of move-in and move-out dates were estimated on the basis of inexact information in the case notes. When there was insufficient information to identify an address in a given period, including periods when the parolee was absconding, the time period was coded as one with an unknown address. Parole agents are careful to document all absconding periods as the issuance of an absconding warrant signals that the parolee is no longer being supervised by the agent and thus that the agent cannot be held responsible for the parolee's behavior. One-third of the sample had at least one unknown residence, and about 9 percent of the average parolee's time was spent in unknown residences.

For sampling purposes (to implement the two-stage cluster sampling design), it was necessary to code the first postprison address for all 11,064 parolees in the population. Thus, the entire population is used in analyses of the effect of first postprison neighborhood characteristics on subsequent outcomes. The first postprison neighborhood was defined as the first place where an individual stayed for at least one night and had some community exposure, meaning that he or she had unsupervised access to people and places outside the residence. Less than 1 percent of the parolees in the study cohort stayed in their first address for only one night. Those who were paroled to institutions offering no exposure to the community, such as hospitals, inpatient treatment centers, or county jails, were assigned the first subsequent noninstitutional address. Homeless individuals were assigned the census tract of the shelter or mission where they were staying (no parolees were living on the streets immediately after their release as a prisoner must have a place to live before being paroled).

Although all parole agents are required to report information on changes of address or living arrangements, employment status, arrest (which must be verified by cross-checking with police records), and parole violations, in practice there may be variability across agents in how completely this information is recorded. Our analysis suggests, however, that the addresses in the case notes are surprisingly accurate. We used our qualitative sample to test the accuracy of the notes. For eighteen of the interview participants, it was possible to compare self-reported residential histories from researcher interviews for the first few months after release with those recorded in MDOC administrative data. Fourteen (78 percent) of these residential histories matched exactly, and the remaining four had one missing address each. Overall, thirty-three of thirty-seven addresses were correctly recorded by MDOC parole agents. Missing addresses were either brief stays or short periods of living on the streets, and those with missing addresses tended to be more residentially mobile, suggesting that the administrative data will understate mobility slightly for some parolees. While two of the participants experienced periods in which they were moving quickly between multiple addresses (staying with multiple friends or family members to avoid living on the streets or in a shelter), these periods were very short (only a few weeks).

Preprison addresses were collected for the one-third sample from hard copies of presentence investigation reports, in which addresses are usually

verified by the MDOC agent preparing the report, as well as parole violation reports and parole agent case notes (for those who were on parole
prior to their sampled prison term). Preprison addresses were successfully
identified and geocoded for approximately 99 percent of the sample. Forty-
nine of the identified addresses, or 1.5 percent, were outside Michigan.
Preprison addresses were linked to census tract characteristics for the
year in which the individual entered prison. Tract characteristics for years
between censuses were assigned values created by linear interpolation.

All pre- and postprison residential addresses were geocoded (i.e., assigned latitude and longitude) using ArcGIS software and the Street-
Map database and matched to census tracts. Postrelease neighborhoods
were linked to tract- and county-level data from the 2000 Census and
the American Community Survey (ACS). Tract-level data from the 1980,
1990, and 2000 Censuses as well as the 2005–9 ACS were assembled for
all Michigan tracts.

2. RECIDIVISM.   These data track recidivism measured in multiple ways,
including violations (of criminal law or parole guidelines) that result in
(1) arrest, (2) felony conviction, (3) recommitment to prison for a new
crime, (4) recommitment for a technical parole violation, (5) issuance of
an absconding warrant, or (6) issuance of any other technical violation of
parole or probation. Dates of commitments to prison, absconding, and
technical violations were obtained from MDOC records.

3. EMPLOYMENT.   Records for the study population were matched with
unemployment insurance records using the following procedures. First, all
social security numbers available in MDOC databases for the population
were sent to MUIA and the Workforce Development Agency for matching. In some cases, more than one social security number was available
for each participant. MDOC had no social security number for thirty-two
individuals, so they have no unemployment insurance data. Returned unemployment insurance records were matched with names from MDOC
databases, including aliases, to eliminate incorrect social security numbers.
Sixteen percent of the population, or 1,758 individuals, had no unemployment insurance data match their social security number, indicating that
they never had any formal employment in Michigan between 1997 and
2010. If more than one social security number that MDOC had recorded
for the same person matched records in the unemployment insurance data,
project staff selected the best match by comparing employer names listed

in the unemployment insurance records with those listed in the MDOC records (from parole agent reports). This procedure resulted in one-to-one matches of individual records between MDOC and unemployment insurance records for all but 199 parolees (2 percent of the population), for whom a single social security number could not be selected after matching on the parolee's name and the name(s) of that person's employer(s). In such cases, unemployment insurance data were retained for all social security numbers listed in the MDOC records for a given individual, under the assumption that such people worked under multiple social security numbers.

The advantage of the unemployment insurance records is that they cover the entire population, provide complete coverage of the postprison period, even when a person has been discharged from parole, and contain preincarceration data on employment and wages. They also provide information on employers. Some important limitations of the unemployment insurance data are that they exclude under-the-table employment, they are aggregated into three-month increments (they do not have precise dates of employment), they are based on employer reports, and they require matching by social security number and name, which may not be accurate in MDOC records for the entire population.

The analysis of labor market outcomes based only on the unemployment insurance data thus covers only employment in the formal labor market, meaning legal employment reported to the state government's unemployment insurance system by the employer, whether paid by cash or by check. In addition to capturing employment status and wages in the period after the 2003 parole (or earlier release from prison), the matched unemployment insurance records also provided employment status and wages immediately prior to the prison spell that ended in 2003 (unemployment insurance records were examined for both the calendar quarter preceding that incarceration spell and the quarter that the incarceration spell began). All wage data were adjusted to 2010 dollars using the consumer price index (CPI-U-X1).

Notes

Introduction

1. The term *mass incarceration* has been critiqued by some scholars as being a mischaracterization of the transformative change in the American criminal justice system. Wacquant (2010) argues that it implies that incarceration has been used in a widespread and indiscriminate manner with regard to class, race, and place and prefers the term *hyperincarceration of (sub)proletarian African American men*. Weisberg and Petersilia (2010) are critical because *mass incarceration* suggests a conspiratorial view of state action and implies that "there is inherent value in reducing the size of the mass," which undermines the legitimate goals of incarceration. They prefer the term *unnecessary* or *inefficient incarceration*. Still other scholars refer to the new system of law and order as the *carceral state* (Gottschalk 2008; Weaver and Lerman 2010), although this term is also used more generally as a reference to modes of government emphasizing surveillance, security, and punishment.

2. For example, there is some evidence that black applicants for disability benefits are more likely to be turned down than white applicants (General Accounting Office 1992).

Chapter One

1. In contrast, an estimated 13.5 percent of women and 2.5 percent of men in the general population report experiencing childhood sexual abuse (Molnar, Buka, and Kessler 2001). According to the National Longitudinal Study of Adolescent Health, 28.4 percent of US young adults interviewed in 2001–2 reported experiencing physical assault, 11.8 percent reported physical neglect, and 4.5 percent reported contact sexual abuse in the past (Hussey, Chang, and Kotch 2006). Among a representative Canadian sample, 31 percent of men and 21 percent of women reported childhood physical abuse (MacMillan et al. 1997).

2. Other studies find similar or higher figures. A study of long-term prison inmates in Alaska found that 70 percent of women and 17 percent of men reported experiencing sexual abuse in childhood. Over 80 percent of inmates reported physical abuse, almost 50 percent reported severe violence, and almost 25 percent reported experiencing neglect during childhood (Langworthy, Barnes, and Curtis 1998).

3. DeAngelo's struggles were not anomalous within his family. Of the six siblings, one had become a severe alcoholic following his service in Iraq, another had been incarcerated and was an addict, and two had died.

Chapter Two

1. On the effects of incarceration on physical health, see Binswanger, Krueger, and Steiner (2009) and Schnittker, Massoglia, and Uggen (2011).

2. On the long-term impacts of parental incarceration on children, see also Wakefield and Wildeman (2013).

3. Ten of the 11,064 parolees died in the first two weeks, which corresponds to a rate of 2,350 deaths per 100,000 person-years. By one month, 15 had died, corresponding to a rate of 1,626 deaths per 100,000 person-years. By six months, 50 had died, corresponding to a rate of 900 deaths per 100,000 person-years.

4. Fines, court costs, and restitution were also paid during prison through prison work and through a tax on transfers to prisoner commissary accounts from family and friends. For those who owed restitution, half of any amount over $50 transferred could be confiscated and applied to restitution. The frequency of fees, fines, and restitution obligations after prison appears to vary from state to state. On the basis of survey data from the Urban Institute's Returning Home study, McLean and Thompson (2007) report that 58 percent of recently released prisoners in Ohio are required to pay supervision fees and 17 percent owe court costs and other fines. In Texas, 39 percent were required to pay supervision fees, and 6 percent owed court costs and other fines.

5. The seeming arbitrariness of bureaucratic rules and procedures that govern the poor and the implementation and application of those rules is not unique to parole offices; the same patterns can be seen in other state bureaucracies that serve or govern the poor. For example, on a public emergency room in Los Angeles, see Lara-Millán (2014), and, on state bureaucracies in Argentina, see Ayero (2012).

6. There was considerable variation across our participants in how concerned they were with these obligations, however. In addition, there were widely varying understandings of the nature of these debts and the repercussions of not paying them, in terms of both parole supervision and credit history.

Chapter Three

1. Prior research on families and incarceration has focused mainly on the impact of the incarceration of parents (mostly fathers) on children and their mothers (e.g., Harris and Miller 2003). One set of consequences is economic. Half of fathers in prison were the primary breadwinner in the family before their incarceration (Wakefield and Wildeman 2013). The incarceration of a parent can also interfere with the nonincarcerated partner's economic stability, increasing the risk that the partner will become unemployed, experience housing insecurity, and receive public assistance (National Research Council 2014; Wakefield and Wildeman 2013). Families must deal with these economic hardships while also supporting their incarcerated loved one (Braman 2004; Comfort 2007). Additional expenses include commissary accounts, care packages, and the cost of prison phone calls and visits (Grinstead et al. 2001).

The incarceration of a father also has profound health and developmental consequences for children. Mothers experience greater depression and anxiety when the father of their children goes to prison (Wildeman, Schnittker, and Turney 2012) and exhibit more neglect and harsh parenting (Turney 2014). The incarceration of a father can trigger feelings of shame and embarrassment in children and erode trust between children and fathers (National Research Council 2014). Paternal incarceration is associated with higher rates of learning disabilities, attention deficit disorder, behavioral or conduct problems, developmental delays, and speech or language problems (Haskins 2015; Turney 2015; Wildeman and Turney 2014; Turney 2014). Children of incarcerated fathers enter school less prepared to learn, are more likely to be placed in special education, and are more likely to be held back (Haskins 2014; Turney and Haskins 2014). On the other hand, the incarceration of a father with a severe substance addiction or pattern of violent behavior can benefit children (National Research Council 2014). Another key finding is that incarceration tends to lead to reduced contact between fathers and children after release. Turney and Wildeman (2013) show that much of this reduction can be explained by the dissolution of relationships between mothers and incarcerated fathers and by the formation of new romantic relationships among the mothers. In addition, Turney (2014) shows that paternal incarceration leads to less child contact with paternal but not maternal grandparents.

2. The decline in availability of single-room-occupancy hotels (SROs) has further constrained housing options for those, like formerly incarcerated individuals, seeking very low-cost housing. SROs historically were utilized by returning prisoners or others leaving institutions, the elderly, and casual laborers (Blau 1992). These single-room rentals shared a bathroom and kitchen facility and were available for weekly or monthly rental (Rossi 1989). But, as urban areas gentrified, SROs were increasingly converted into high-cost rental units for urban professionals returning to the city (Blau 1992).

3. Some studies have used national surveys of state prisoners to examine their housing status prior to imprisonment. One such study (Hughes, Wilson, and Beck 2001) found that 12 percent of state prisoners had been homeless at the time of their arrest, while another (Ditton 1999) reported that 9 percent had been living on the street or in a shelter at some point during the year prior to their arrest. In one of the few studies to use postincarceration data on a large sample of returning prisoners, Metraux and Culhane (2004) analyzed longitudinal data on all persons released from New York State prisons and paroled to New York City counties between 1995 and 1998 ($N = 48,424$) and found that 11.4 percent entered a New York City homeless shelter within two years of release. There have been fewer studies of housing instability and residential mobility among returning prisoners. One study, using survey data collected on 145 Illinois prisoners returning to the city of Chicago (La Vigne and Parthasarathy 2005), found that roughly 72 percent of the sample members stayed in the same residence throughout the observation period of the study (which varied by individual but lasted between one and two years). In a study offering a much less sanguine view of housing security among formerly incarcerated men, Geller and Curtis (2011) analyzed housing instability among fathers from the Fragile Families and Child Wellbeing sample ($N = 2,768$) and found that men who had been incarcerated faced significantly higher odds of being homeless or experiencing some form of housing insecurity within the last year compared to men with no history of incarceration.

4. Sometimes economic factors manifested directly in eviction or foreclosure. For example, Lenora was living with a cousin but had to move when his house was foreclosed on. When his brother's rental home was foreclosed on, Randall moved with his brother and his family to another house. Jada was evicted after a conflict with her landlord but quickly found another house to rent nearby. Geoffrey (to be introduced shortly) was living with his girlfriend in her house until it was foreclosed on, forcing them to move to a rental house. In addition, two participants (DeAngelo and Lamar) were evicted from their own apartments and lost all their possessions, but this was after they were arrested and returned to prison, not because they had been unable to pay the rent. On another occasion, after his second release from prison during our study, Lamar voluntarily left his apartment and moved into a homeless shelter after losing his job. On the importance of eviction for residential instability and the perpetuation of poverty, see Desmond (2016).

5. For example, Leon—who as we have seen worried about finding stable housing and rebuilding his relationship with his son after release—lived with his father, his sister and her girlfriend, in a homeless shelter, and in transitional housing for formerly incarcerated individuals before saving enough money to rent an apartment with a girlfriend he met at work. They moved in together about fourteen months after he was released from prison, and having his own apartment made it easier to have regular visits from his son. Similarly, with the help of her sisters, Jennifer was able to move out of her preprison residence with her drug-abusing fi-

ancé, purchase a trailer, and establish a stable residence in a trailer park. Here, she could provide a home for her son that was stable and positive so long as the two avoided the dangers of the neighborhood. Unable to work, she scraped by on food stamps, her son's SSI benefits, and help from her sisters.

6. We are unaware of any national data on parole conditions, types of violations, or rates of absconding.

7. An additional seven participants had household members with some kind of health problem, disability, or substance abuse problem, and nearly all the participants had health issues of their own, ranging from addiction to epilepsy to diabetes to depression.

8. Jennifer, like nearly all our participants, did regularly drive without a license or car insurance. In the rural setting where her trailer park was located, there was no public transportation, and she had no alternative.

Chapter Four

1. While domestic violence was an important feature of past relationships, only one participant revealed suffering from it in a current partnership. In our final interview, Jane revealed that her husband had struck her three years previously and that he continued to occasionally feint as though he would strike her when they argued.

2. This exchange is especially revealing of the class and cultural differences between the authors and our participants.

Chapter Five

1. An equally important but separate question is how a concentration of former prisoners affects disadvantaged communities. For a recent review, see Morenoff and Harding (2014).

2. Similar results were found in an unpublished study of Ohio (Huggins 2009) and a published study of delinquent male juveniles in Philadelphia (Grunwald et al. 2010). Two studies have found no relationship between neighborhood disadvantage and recidivism. One was a study of former prisoners returning to select Baltimore neighborhoods (Gottfredson and Taylor 1988) that summarized but did not report results from statistical models. Another was a study with a much different sampling frame, offenders with felony convictions (mostly probationers) in Wayne County, Michigan (Wehrman 2010).

3. As with other neighborhood effects studies, a concern is that unobserved factors could simultaneously determine the neighborhoods people live in and their outcomes of interest, thereby confounding causal inferences about neighborhood

context. This problem becomes even more worrying in the case of returning prisoners because of the critical role played by criminal justice and social service institutions in determining where former offenders are able to live and find work, the type of supervision they will face, and the nature of their encounters with police. In some states, a parolee must return to the county where he or she was prosecuted, but this is not the case in Michigan.

4. These data are based on addresses coded from parole agent case notes and then geocoded to census tracts. On data quality, see Morenoff and Harding (2011) and Harding, Morenoff and Herbert (2013). Each monthly time point is based on where an individual was living at the end of the specific month since release. Residences without community exposure, such as hospitals, jails, or other custodial institutions, are excluded from the figure, as are time points after an individual was either discharged from parole or returned to prison.

5. The importance of a criminal record may depend on type of crime and parole conditions. Sex offenders, e.g., are legally restricted from moving into certain areas near parks, schools, and day-care centers. Empirical evidence from a California parolee study shows that sex offenders are released into more disadvantaged neighborhoods and tend to move into more disadvantaged neighborhoods (Hipp, Turner, and Jannetta 2010).

6. This result is confirmed by comparing the median preprison and postprison neighborhood poverty rates. Although neighborhood poverty falls following prison (from 26 percent to 21 percent, respectively), a closer examination of our data shows that this decline reflects initial institutional residences such as halfway houses, which tend to be located in neighborhoods with lower poverty rates than the typical African American neighborhood in Michigan. As can be seen in figure 5.1, the neighborhood poverty rate of formerly incarcerated African Americans increases slightly over time, reflecting movement out of institutional residences. In contrast, whites appear to be slightly negatively affected by going to prison when it comes to neighborhood poverty, as the median preprison tract poverty rate among whites is 9 percent, compared to 12 percent for the first neighborhood after prison (see also Harding, Morenoff, and Herbert 2013; Massoglia, Firebaugh, and Warner 2013; and Warner 2014). After release, the neighborhood poverty rate of the median white falls in the first few quarters. This also reflects movement out of institutional residences, which tend to be located in neighborhoods with a higher poverty rate than the typical white neighborhood in Michigan. After that, there is no change over time in the median neighborhood poverty rate of whites.

7. These effects are robust to controls for preprison and initial postprison neighborhood conditions, suggesting that they are not due simply to selection based on time-constant unmeasured variables as such variables should be highly correlated with preprison and initial postprison neighborhood characteristics.

8. This calculation and others like it below exclude time spent in prison, jail, residential treatment, or any custodial residence without exposure to the neighborhood.

9. Urban sociologists have long documented the effects of street violence on local social networks, social control, and social cohesion (e.g., Harding 2010; Sampson 2012; and Anderson 1990).

10. Three caveats should be mentioned regarding these neighborhood classifications. First, consistent with the high rates of residential mobility we see in the administrative data, many of our interview participants moved repeatedly over the course of our study and as a result had the opportunity to experience multiple neighborhoods. However, for most of them, the neighborhoods they moved between tended to be of a similar type. When neighborhoods differed, they tended to do so on just one dimension, such as moving from a chaotic connected to a chaotic detached neighborhood. Second, whether participants had lived in the neighborhood previously influenced (though did not completely determine) the extent to which they experienced that neighborhood as connected or not. For instance, those returning to neighborhoods where they had lived previously and knew their neighbors tended to characterize their neighborhoods as populated by working people and settled people. They saw disturbances as reflecting only a part of the neighborhood (occurring only at night, prompted by "knuckleheads," or at a distance) rather than characterizing the neighborhood as a whole. Those returning to suburban contexts where they had lived before were less likely to see their neighborhoods as connected, however. For instance, Kristine and Michelle both returned from prison to live with their parents in neighborhoods familiar to them but nonetheless remained isolated from neighbors and did not leverage neighborhood ties or supports. Third, our participants' own characteristics influenced the way they perceived their neighborhoods. Specifically, those who characterized themselves as loners (as Jake did) were less likely to experience their neighborhoods as being connected, while those more externally oriented were more likely to give accounts of community or networks within their neighborhoods.

11. In the only study to leverage quasi-experimental conditions to address concerns about neighborhood selection, Kirk (2009, 2012) used the destruction of housing by Hurricane Katrina as an exogenous determinant of residential options for parolees in New Orleans. He found that parolees who returned to different places from where they were living before prison had a substantially lower risk of reincarceration (Kirk 2009) that persisted throughout the three-year observation period (Kirk 2012). Using a different approach to study a similar phenomenon, Stahler et al. (2013) found that prisoners returning to Philadelphia neighborhoods were more likely to recidivate when they lived nearby higher concentrations of other ex-offenders who recidivated. To analyze contagion they constructed a measure of the percentage of ex-offenders living within one mile of each participant who recidivated within three years. We caution against interpreting this as evidence of contagion, however, because their spatial concentration measure was based on preprison addresses and they did not address the issue of endogeneity bias introduced in their spatial model because they used one measure of recidivism to predict another.

12. Wang, Mears, and Bales (2010) used race-specific contextual variables and ran race-specific models. They found that, among African Americans, county unemployment was associated with a higher risk of violent recidivism and that, among whites, violent recidivism was lower in counties with higher rates of manufacturing employment.

13. Potentially equally important to understanding the reentry process—though rarely studied—is how neighborhood context influences the behavior of parole and probation officers. Grattet, Lin, and Petersilia (2011) offer a framework for studying the formal and informal features of what they call *supervision regimes*. The formal side of supervision regimes refers to laws and policies regarding supervision that are usually determined at the state level and shaped by the political and historical context in which criminal justice institutions developed and operate. More salient to understanding neighborhood effects are the informal features of supervision regimes, i.e., how agents use their discretion over reporting and sanctioning deviance and can be influenced by local professional norms, workload management pressures, and other resource constraints. Grattet, Lin, and Petersilia (2011) also define three measureable dimensions of supervision regimes: (1) the *intensity* of parolee supervision, referring to how closely parolees are monitored (e.g., frequency of reporting and drug testing), (2) the system's *capacity* to supervise parolees and detect deviant behavior, which is determined by human resources (e.g., caseload size and type) and the laws and policies that constitute the official procedures for supervision, and (3) parole agents' *tolerance* for deviance, as manifested in how they use their discretion in reporting and sanctioning parole violations.

Lin, Grattet, and Petersilia (2010) studied institutional reactions to parolee deviance by modeling the risk of being returned to prison as a sanction for a parole violation among returning prisoners in California. Among those who had parole violations, the risk of being returned was greater in counties with more punitive political environments (based on election results from two punishment-oriented ballot propositions). A separate study of California parolees (Hipp, Petersilia, and Turner 2010) found that living near a higher density of social service organizations was associated with a lower risk of recidivating, but living in areas with a higher "potential demand" for social services increased the risk of recidivism. In another study of this kind, Wallace and Papachristos (2014) conducted a zip-code-level analysis of the association between the presence of health care organizations (HCOs) and firearm-related felonies in Chicago. Although measures of HCO density and its change over time did not significantly predict recidivism rates, there was an interaction whereby HCO loss was associated with higher recidivism rates in more disadvantaged areas.

14. See http://www.michigan.gov/driverresponsibility.

Chapter Six

1. For a full description of these data, including information on data quality, coverage, and matching to parolee records, see Morenoff and Harding (2011).

2. Other studies have documented that formerly incarcerated people experience temporary employment increases after their release relative to their employment status just before going to prison, which may be partially attributable to the effects of postprison parole supervision and reentry programs (Bloom et al. 2007; Loeffler 2013; Pettit and Lyons 2007; Tyler and Kling 2006).

3. Ideally, we would also observe occupation, but such detail is not available in the unemployment insurance records.

4. Further analyses show that African Americans are less likely to find a job when they are unemployed and more likely to be fired or laid off when they are employed, net of these same factors (tables available from the authors).

5. Sequence analysis methods originated in biology for genomic sequencing (Sankoff and Kruskal 1983) and were introduced into sociology to study sequences of occupations or jobs in careers (e.g., Abbott 1990; Abbott and Hrycak 1990; Stovel, Savage, and Bearman 1996). The methodology is based on sequences of events over time, in this case employment or unemployment in the twelve calendar quarters following release from prison (with incarcerated quarters treated as unemployment). Sequence analysis uses an optimal matching algorithm to create a measure of the difference (or distance) between any pair of sequences by determining the minimum combination of insertions, deletions, and substitutions that are required to change one sequence into another. Each insertion, deletion, or substitution carries a cost that is added to the total distance. With a measure of distance between every pair of individuals in the data having been determined, cluster analysis is then used to sort individuals into categories based on similarities and differences in their sequences. We use the Stata SQ package written by Ulrich Kohler, Magdalena Luniak, and Christian Brzinsky-Fay with insertion, deletion, and substitution costs all set to one (because there are two events in the sequences). Cluster analysis was conducted using Ward's linkage, although the results are robust to other choices of linkage.

6. Another potential barrier to hiring ex-offenders is so called negligent hiring lawsuits. If an employer is sued over the behavior or actions of an employee and it is demonstrated that he or she should reasonably have known that the employee was likely to engage in such behavior, he or she can be liable for negligent hiring. An employee's past criminal record can be used against the employer in such cases, though only if the crime is directly related to job responsibilities (Holzer, Raphael, and Stoll 2002; Petersilia 2003). One question is whether employers are actually aware of these legal issues. Pager's (2007a) employer surveys suggest that most are not.

7. According to the American Bar Association, there are over thirty thousand state laws, provisions, and exclusions from employment related to criminal records across the United States (National Research Council 2014). Another estimate suggests that over eight hundred occupations are closed to those with a criminal record somewhere in the United States (Bushway and Sweeten 2007).

8. For an earlier generation of audit studies on the effect of a criminal record, see Boshier and Johnson (1974), Buikhuisen and Dijksterhuis (1971), and Schwartz and Skolnick (1964). These studies were conducted before the large increase in incarceration that started in the mid-1970s and the technology that allowed for fast and inexpensive record checks.

9. It is also unclear whether stigma is attached to the criminal record, incarceration, or both. Audit studies and employer surveys tend to focus on felony criminal records (though, on misdemeanors, see Uggen, Vuolo, Lageson, Ruhland, and Whitham 2014). One might hypothesize that incarceration amplifies the impact of a criminal record because it signals a more serious crime, because employers worry about prisonization and other effects of prison, or because incarceration makes it harder to conceal a criminal record (owing to resume gaps).

10. To conduct this analysis, we cataloged all the job search strategies of our participants individually, their experiences attempting to use these strategies, and the types of jobs they managed to secure. We then categorized the job search strategies of all our participants collectively and whether and how those strategies worked in the labor market.

11. The overrepresentation of restaurant and fast food jobs likely reflects the overrepresentation of women in our sample compared to formerly incarcerated people in general as well as the overrepresentation of formerly incarcerated people living in the suburbs in our sample.

12. Leon's employment history evokes what has been termed *the professional ex* (Ebaugh 1988), individuals who leverage expertise and experiences in their old roles (ex-prisoner) into new professional identities. Leon's work in the nonprofit organization—providing services to formerly incarcerated people—was based on his identity as a formerly incarcerated person who had been successful at staying away from crime and finding steady employment. Another example is Paul, who built a professional ex identity as a formerly incarcerated person now teaching about crime and the criminal justice system. Although such role transformations are interesting from a theoretical perspective, we do not believe that they play much of a role in the labor market experiences of formerly incarcerated people, both because employment in such positions is relatively rare and because few formerly incarcerated people are likely to have the human and cultural capital to develop such identities and secure such jobs.

13. The remaining four job losses were attributable to being accused of theft, absenteeism not related to substance use or scheduling problems, quitting work to focus on school, and an expensive commute relative to the pay.

Conclusion

1. For a more general discussion of the medicalization of poverty, especially as it relates to the receipt of social welfare related to diagnosed permanent mental illness, see Hansen, Bourgois, and Drucker (2014).

2. Sampson and Laub (1995) develop what they term an *age-graded theory of informal social control* to explain changes in delinquency and criminality over the life span. Such antisocial behavior continues into adulthood in part because of the weak personal and institutional ties that result from earlier delinquency. Sampson and Laub argue that structural circumstances in childhood and adolescence (opportunities related to class, race, and family background) affect informal family and school social controls that in turn affect delinquency.

3. There are theoretical perspectives that suggest that prisons are "schools of crime" or serve to reinforce criminal identities or ties to others who were involved in crime, but we did not see any evidence of these processes in the experiences of our subjects.

4. Although intermediate sanctions have been included in policy initiatives such as the Serious and Violent Offender Reentry Initiative (Lindquist, Hardison, and Lattimore 2004), their independent effects are difficult to assess when bundled with many other interventions. We do know from cognitive psychology and the evaluation of the Hawaii Opportunity Probation and Enforcement program, however, that the swiftness and certainty of the sanction is usually a more valuable deterrent than the severity of the sanction (Hawken and Kleiman 2009).

5. The issues around criminal record accuracy and predictive ability are more complex than we can treat fully here. Use of criminal records by employers is currently governed by both the Fair Crediting Reporting Act and the Equal Employment Opportunity Commission as well as various state laws and regulations, although it is unclear the extent to which such guidelines are followed and by which employers. Court records of convictions are thought to be more accurate than arrest records, which are subject to incorrect links to identities and lack of information on case adjudication or dismissal. The time after which an arrest or conviction is no longer predictive of future criminal behavior may depend heavily on age. There are also complicated normative arguments about how public criminal records should be used for background checks. For a recent discussion, see DeWitt et al. (2017).

6. Because prisoners became ineligible for federal Pell Grants in 1994, funding for postsecondary education in prison comes in large part from federal funds through the incarcerated youth offender block grant, but those funds can be used to serve only specific categories of inmates, categories based on age and type of offense. States that enroll many inmates in postsecondary education are able to do so currently only through the use of state funds (Erisman and Contardo 2005).

7. We need to understand not just program impacts but the processes through which they occur. Although we may assume that they operate primarily through credentialing and job skills, they may also affect moral and social psychological developments (Ubah and Robinson 2003), or what we have called *cognitive change*.

Appendix

1. MPRI was a statewide policy effort to reduce crime and incarceration by providing additional services to parolees and by implementing a regime of graduated sanctions for technical parole violations. During the period when we were conducting our research, it was still being phased in, and not all parolees received services. During participant recruitment, MPRI parolees tended to be those classified as high risk or medium risk by MDOC. This research is not an evaluation of MPRI.

2. This participant reached a saturation point (Bowen 2008) after three consecutive interviews revealed little new information about his circumstances, plans, or perspectives.

3. Latinos and Asians make up a very small proportion of the Michigan population generally and of individuals released from Michigan prisons.

4. This does not include time in jail. Whereas jails are run by local cities and counties and hold individuals with sentences less than one or two years or awaiting trial, prisons are run by the states or the federal government and hold individuals who have longer sentences.

5. This policy, in place in 2003, was discontinued soon after with the passage of truth-in-sentencing legislation in Michigan, which required that the entire minimum sentence be served in prison.

References

Abbott, Andrew. 1990. "A Primer on Sequence Methods." *Organization Science* 1, no. 4:375–92.

Abbott, Andrew, and Alexandra Hrycak. 1990. "Measuring Resemblance in Sequence Data: An Optimal Matching Analysis of Musicians' Careers." *American Journal of Sociology* 96, no. 1:144–85.

Abrams, David S. 2012. "Estimating the Deterrent Effect of Incarceration Using Sentencing Enhancements." *American Economic Journal: Applied Economics* 4, no. 4:32–56.

Agnew, Robert. 1992. "Foundation for a General Strain Theory of Crime and Delinquency." *Criminology* 30, no. 1:47–87.

Alexander, Michelle. 2010. *The New Jim Crow: Mass Incarceration in the Age of Colorblindness*. New York: New Press.

Anderson, David A. 1999. "The Aggregate Burden of Crime." *Journal of Law and Economics* 42, no. 2:611–42.

Anderson, Elijah. 1990. *Streetwise*. Chicago: University of Chicago Press.

Apel, Robert. 2016. "The Effects of Jail and Prison Confinement on Cohabitation and Marriage." *Annals of the American Academy of Political and Social Science* 665, no. 1:103–26.

Ayero, Javier. 2012. *Patients of the State: The Politics of Waiting in Argentina*. Durham, NC: Duke University Press.

Bassuk, Ellen L., John C. Buckner, Linda F. Weinreb, Angela Browne, and Shari S. Bassuk. 1997. "Homelessness in Female-Headed Families: Childhood and Adult Risk and Protective Factors." *American Journal of Public Health* 87, no. 2:242–48.

Beck, Allen J., and Laura L. Maruschak. 2001. *Mental Health Treatment in State Prisons, 2000*. Washington, DC: US Department of Justice, Bureau of Justice Statistics.

Beckett, Katherine. 1999. *Making Crime Pay: Law and Order in Contemporary American Politics*. New York: Oxford University Press.

Beckett, Katherine, and Steve Herbert. 2010. *Banished: The New Social Control in Urban America*. New York: Oxford University Press.

Bellair, Paul E., and Brian R. Kowalski. 2011. "Low-Skill Employment Opportunity and African American–White Difference in Recidivism." *Journal of Research in Crime and Delinquency* 48, no. 2:176–208.

Berg, Mark T., and Jennifer E. Cobbina. 2017. "Cognitive Transformation, Social Ecological Settings, and the Reentry Outcomes of Women Offenders." *Crime and Delinquency* 63, no. 12:1522–46.

Berg, Mark T., and Beth M. Huebner. 2011. "Reentry and the Ties That Bind: An Examination of Social Ties, Employment, and Recidivism." *Justice Quarterly* 28, no. 2:382–410.

Beronio, Kirsten, Rosa Po, Laura Skopec, and Sherry Glied. 2013. "Affordable Care Act Will Expand Mental Health and Substance Use Disorder Benefits and Parity Protections for 62 Million Americans." ASPE Research Brief. Washington, DC: US Department of Health and Human Services.

Berube, Danton, and Donald P. Green. 2007. "The Effects of Sentencing on Recidivism: Results from a Natural Experiment." Paper presented at the second annual Conference on Empirical Legal Studies, New York.

Binswanger, Ingrid A., Patrick M. Krueger, John F. Steiner. 2009. "Prevalence of Chronic Medical Conditions among Jail and Prison Inmates in the United States Compared with the General Population." *Journal of Epidemiology and Community Health* 63:912–19.

Binswanger, Ingrid A., Marc F. Stern, Richard A. Deyo, Patrick J. Heagerty, Allen Cheadle, Joann G. Elmore, and Thomas D. Koepsell. 2007. "Release from Prison—a High Risk of Death for Former Inmates." *New England Journal of Medicine* 356, no. 2:157–65.

Blau, Joel. 1992. *The Visible Poor: Homelessness in the United States.* New York: Oxford University Press.

Bloemraad, Irene. 2006. *Becoming a Citizen: Incorporating Immigrants and Refugees in the United States and Canada.* Berkeley: University of California Press.

Bloom, Dan. 2006. "Employment-Focused Programs for Ex-prisoners: What Have We Learned, What Are We Learning, and Where Should We Go from Here?" New York: Manpower Demonstration Research Corp.

———. 2010. *Transitional Jobs: Background, Program Models, and Evaluation Evidence.* Washington, DC: National League of Cities.

Bloom, Dan, Cindy Redcross, Janine Zweig, and Gilda Azurdia. 2007. "Transitional Jobs for Ex-prisoners: Early Impacts from a Random Assignment Evaluation of the Center for Employment Opportunities (CEO) Prisoner Reentry Program." New York: Manpower Demonstration Research Corp.

Blumstein, Alfred, and Allen J. Beck. 2005. "Reentry as a Transient State between Liberty and Recommitment." In *Prisoner Reentry and Crime in America*, ed. Jeremy Travis and Christy A. Visher, 50–79. Cambridge: Cambridge University Press.

Blumstein, Alfred, and Kiminori Nakamura. 2009. "Redemption in the Presence of Widespread Criminal Background Checks." *Criminology* 47, no. 2:327–59.

Bobbit, Mike, and Marta Nelson. 2004. *The Front Line: Building Programs That Recognize Families' Role in Reentry*. New York: Vera Institute of Justice, State Sentencing and Corrections Program.

Boshier, Roger, and Derek Johnson. 1974. "Does Conviction Affect Employment Opportunities?" *British Journal of Criminology* 14, no. 3:264–68.

Bowen, Glenn A. 2008. "Naturalistic Inquiry and the Saturation Concept: A Research Note." *Qualitative Research* 8, no. 1:137–52.

Bradley, Katherine H., R. B. Michael Oliver, Noel C. Richardson, and Elspeth M. Slayter. 2001. *No Place like Home: Housing and the Ex-prisoner*. Policy Brief. Boston: Community Resources for Justice.

Braman, Donald. 2004. *Doing Time on the Outside: Incarceration and Family Life in Urban America*. Ann Arbor: University of Michigan Press.

Braun, Virginia, and Victoria Clarke. 2006. "Using Thematic Analysis in Psychology." *Qualitative Research in Psychology* 3, no. 2:77–101.

Brayne, Sarah. 2014. "Surveillance and System Avoidance Criminal Justice Contact and Institutional Attachment." *American Sociological Review* 79, no. 3:367–91.

Buikhuisen, Wouter, and Fokke P. H. Dijksterhuis. 1971. "Delinquency and Stigmatisation." *British Journal of Criminology* 11, no. 2:185–87.

Burgard, Sarah A., Kristin S. Seefeldt, and Sarah Zelner. 2012. "Housing Instability and Health: Findings from the Michigan Recession and Recovery Study." *Social Science and Medicine* 75, no. 12:2215–24.

Burke, Peggy, and Michael Tonry. 2006. "Successful Transition and Reentry for Safer Communities: A Call to Action for Parole." Silver Spring, MD: Center for Effective Public Policy.

Burton, Susan, and Cari Lynn. 2017. *Becoming Ms. Burton: From Prison to Recovery to Leading the Fight for Incarcerated Women*. New York: New Press.

Bushway, Shawn. 2003. "Reentry and Prison Work Programs." Urban Institute Reentry Roundtable. New York: New York University Law School.

Bushway, Shawn D., and Robert Apel. 2012. "A Signaling Perspective on Employment-Based Reentry Programming." *Criminology and Public Policy* 11, no. 1:21–50.

Bushway, Shawn, Shauna Briggs, Faye Taxman, Meredith Thanner, and Mischelle Van Brakle. 2007. "Private Providers of Criminal History Records: Do You Get What You Pay For?" In *Barriers to Reentry? The Labor Market for Released Prisoners in Post-industrial America*, ed. Shawn Bushway, Michael A. Stoll, and David F. Weiman, 174–200. New York: Russell Sage.

Bushway, Shawn, Megan Denver, and Megan Kurlychek. 2015. "Estimating the Mark of a Criminal Record." Paper presented at the meeting of the Association for Public Policy Analysis and Management (APPAM), Albuquerque, November 6.

Bushway, Shawn D., Alex R. Piquero, Lisa M. Broidy, Elizabeth Cauffman, and Paul Mazerolle. 2001. "An Empirical Framework for Studying Desistance as a Process." *Criminology* 39, no. 2:491–516.

Bushway, Shawn, Michael A. Stoll, and David F. Weiman, eds. 2007. *Barriers to Reentry? The Labor Market for Released Prisoners in Post-industrial America.* New York: Russell Sage.

Bushway, Shawn D., and Gary Sweeten. 2007. "Abolish Lifetime Bans for Ex-felons." *Criminology and Public Policy* 6, no. 4:697–706.

Cadora, Eric, Charles Swartz, and Mannix Gordon. 2003. "Criminal Justice and Health and Human Services: An Exploration of Overlapping Needs, Resources, and Interests in Brooklyn Neighborhoods." In *Prisoners Once Removed: The Impact of Incarceration and Reentry on Children, Families, and Communities*, ed. Jeremy Travis and Michelle Waul, 285–311. Washington, DC: Urban Institute Press.

Caputo-Levine, Deirdre D. 2013. "The Yard Face: The Contributions of Inmate Interpersonal Violence to the Carceral Habitus." *Ethnography* 14, no. 2:165–85.

Carlson, B., and M. Shafer. 2010. "Traumatic Histories and Stressful Life Events of Incarcerated Parents: Childhood and Adult Trauma Histories." *Prison Journal* 90, no. 4:475–93.

Carson, Elizabeth Ann. 2015. "Prisoners in 2014." Bureau of Justice Statistics Bulletin, NCJ 248955. Washington, DC: US Department of Justice, Bureau of Justice Statistics.

Carson, E. Ann, and Daniela Golinelli. 2013. "Prisoners in 2012—Advance Counts." Bureau of Justice Statistics Bulletin, NCJ 242467. Washington, DC: US Department of Justice, Bureau of Justice Statistics.

Carter, Brian L., and Stephen T. Tiffany. 1999. "Meta-analysis of Cue-Reactivity in Addiction Research." *Addiction* 94, no. 3:327–40.

Chesney-Lind, Meda, and Marc Mauer, eds. 2002. *Invisible Punishment: The Collateral Consequences of Mass Imprisonment.* New York: New Press.

Clear, Todd R. 2007a. "The Impacts of Incarceration on Public Safety." *Social Research: An International Quarterly* 74, no. 2:613–30.

———. 2007b. *Imprisoning Communities: How Mass Incarceration Makes Disadvantaged Neighborhoods Worse.* New York: Oxford University Press.

———. 2011. "A Private-Sector, Incentives-Based Model for Justice Reinvestment." *Criminology and Public Policy* 10, no. 3:585–608.

Cloward, Richard A., and Lloyd E. Ohlin. 1960. *Delinquency and Opportunity: A Theory of Delinquent Gangs.* New York: Free Press.

Cohen, Lawrence, and Marcus Felson. 1979. "Social Change and Crime Rate Trends: A Routine Activity Approach." *American Sociological Review* 44, no. 4:588–608.

Cohen, Sheldon. 2004. "Social Relationships and Health." *American Psychologist* 59:676–84.

Colvin, Mark, Francis T. Cullen, and Thomas Vander Ven. 2002. "Coercion, Social Support, and Crime: An Emerging Theoretical Consensus." *Criminology* 40, no. 1:19–42.

Comfort, Megan. 2003. "In the Tube at San Quentin: The 'Secondary Prisonization' of Women Visiting Inmates." *Journal of Contemporary Ethnography* 32, no. 1:77–107.

———. 2007. "Punishment beyond the Legal Offender." *Annual Review of Law and Social Science* 3:271–96.

———. 2008. *Doing Time Together: Love and Family in the Shadow of the Prison.* Chicago: University of Chicago Press.

———. 2012. "It Was Basically College to Us: Poverty, Prison, and Emerging Adulthood." *Journal of Poverty* 16, no. 3:308–22.

Cook, Philip J. 1975. "The Correctional Carrot: Better Jobs for Parolees." *Policy Analysis* 1, no. 1:11–54.

Crutchfield, Robert D. 2014. *Get a Job: Labor Markets, Economic Opportunity, and Crime.* New York: New York University Press.

Crutchfield, Robert D., Ross L. Matsueda, and Kevin Drakulich. 2006. "Race, Labor Markets, and Neighborhood Violence." In *The Many Colors of Crime: Inequalities of Race, Ethnicity and Crime in America*, ed. Ruth D. Peterson, Lauren Joy Krivo, and John Hagan. New York: New York University Press.

Cullen, Francis T. 2004. "Social Support as an Organizing Concept for Criminology: Presidential Address to the Academy of Criminal Justice Sciences." *Justice Quarterly* 11, no. 4:527–738.

D'Alessio, Stewart J., Lisa Stolzenberg, and Jamie L. Flexon. 2015. "The Effect of Hawaii's Ban the Box Law on Repeat Offending." *American Journal of Criminal Justice* 40, no. 2:336–52.

Dance, Lory J. 2002. *Tough Fronts: The Impact of Street Culture on Schooling.* New York: Routledge Falmer.

Danziger, Sandra K. 2010. "The Decline of Cash Welfare and Implications for Social Policy and Poverty." *Annual Review of Sociology* 36:523–45.

Demleitner, Nora V. 2002. "Collateral Damage: No Re-entry for Drug Offenders." *Villanova Law Review* 47, no. 4:1027–54.

Desmond, Matthew. 2012. "Disposable Ties and the Urban Poor." *American Journal of Sociology* 117, no. 5:1295–335.

———. 2016. *Evicted: Poverty and Profit in the American City.* New York: Crown.

DeWitt, Samuel E., Shawn D. Bushway, Garima Siwach, and Megan C. Kurlychek. 2017. "Redeemed Compared to Whom? Comparing the Distributional Properties of Arrest Risk across Populations of Provisional Employees with and without a Criminal Record." *Criminology and Public Policy* 16, no. 3:963–97.

Ditton, Paula M. 1999. "Mental Health and Treatment of Inmates and Probationers." Special Report, NCJ 174463. Washington, DC: US Department of Justice, Bureau of Justice Statistics.

Doleac, Jennifer L., and Benjamin Hansen. 2016. "Does 'Ban the Box' Help or Hurt Low-Skilled Workers? Statistical Discrimination and Employment Outcomes When Criminal Histories Are Hidden." Working Paper no. 22469. Cambridge, MA: National Bureau of Economic Research.

Donley, Amy M., and James D. Wright. 2008. "Cleaning Up the Streets: Community Efforts to Combat Homelessness by Criminalizing Homeless Behaviors."
Homelessness in America 3:75–92.

Donovan, Shaun. 2011. Letter to Public Housing Authority Executive Directors.
June 17, 2011. https://www.usich.gov/resources/uploads/asset_library/Rentry
_letter__HUD_Secretray_to_PHAs_June_2011.pdf.

Drakulich, Kevin, Robert Crutchfield, Ross Matsueda, and Kristin Rose. 2012. "Instability, Informal Control, and Criminogenic Situations: Community Effects of
Returning Prisoners." *Crime, Law and Social Change* 57, no. 5:493–519.

Ebaugh, Helen Rose Ruchs. 1988. *Becoming an Ex: The Process of Role Exit*. Chicago: University of Chicago Press.

Edin, Kathryn, and Timothy J. Nelson. 2013. *Doing the Best I Can: Fatherhood in
the Inner City*. Berkeley: University of California Press.

Elder, Glen H. 1974. *Children of the Great Depression: Social Change in Life Experience*. Chicago: University of Chicago Press.

Elder, Glen H., Jr. 1998. "The Life Course as Developmental Theory." *Child Development* 69, no. 1:1–12.

Engelhardt, Bryan. 2010. "The Effect of Employment Frictions on Crime." *Journal
of Labor Economics* 28, no. 3:677–718.

Erisman, Wendy, and Jeanne Bayer Contardo. 2005. "Learning to Reduce Recidivism: A 50-State Analysis of Postsecondary Correctional Education Policy."
Washington, DC: Institute for Higher Education Policy.

Feeley, Malcolm M., and Jonathon Simon. 1992. "The New Penology: Notes on
the Emerging Strategy of Corrections and Its Implications." *Criminology* 30,
no. 4:449–74.

Fellner, Jamie. 2006. "Corrections Quandary: Mental Illness and Prison Rules."
Harvard Civil Rights–Civil Liberties Law Review 41, no. 2:391–412.

Fox, Kathryn J. 2015. "Theorizing Community Integration as Desistance-
Promotion." *Criminal Justice and Behavior* 42, no. 1:82–94.

Freisthler, Bridget, Elizabeth A. Lascala, Paul J. Gruenewald, and Andrew J. Treno.
2005. "An Examination of Drug Activity: Effects of Neighborhood Social Organization on the Development of Drug Distribution Systems." *Substance Use and
Misuse* 40, no. 5:671–86.

Freudenberg, Nicholas, Jessie Daniels, Martha Crum, Tiffany Perkins, and Beth E.
Richie. 2005. "Coming Home from Jail: The Social and Health Consequences
of Community Reentry for Women, Male Adolescents, and Their Families and
Communities." *American Journal of Public Health* 95, no. 10:1725–36.

Ganem, Natasha M., and Robert Agnew. 2007. "Parenthood and Adult Criminal
Offending: The Importance of Relationship Quality." *Journal of Criminal Justice* 30, no. 1:47–87.

Garland, David. 2001. *The Culture of Control: Crime and Social Order in Contemporary Society*. Oxford: Oxford University Press.

Geller, Amanda, and Marah A. Curtis. 2011. "A Sort of Homecoming: Incarceration and the Housing Security of Urban Men." *Social Science Research* 40, no. 4:
1196–213.

General Accounting Office. 1992. "Racial Difference in Disability Decisions Warrants Further Investigation." Washington, DC.

Giordano, Peggy C., Stephen A. Cernkovich, and Jennifer L. Rudolph. 2002. "Gender, Crime, and Desistance: Toward a Theory of Cognitive Transformation."
American Journal of Sociology 107, no. 4:990–1064.

Glueck, Sheldon, and Eleanor Glueck. 1950. "Unraveling Juvenile Delinquency."
New York: Commonwealth Fund.

———. 1968. *Delinquents and Non-delinquents in Perspective.* Cambridge, MA:
Harvard University Press.

Godsoe, Cynthia. 1998. "The Ban on Welfare for Felony Drug Offenders: Giving a
New Meaning to Life Sentence." *Berkeley Journal of Gender, Law and Justice*
13, no. 1:257–67.

Goffman, Alice. 2014. *On the Run: Fugitive Life in an American City.* Chicago:
University of Chicago Press.

Goffman, Erving. 1961. *Asylums: Essays on the Social Situation of Mental Patients
and Other Inmates.* Garden City, NY: Anchor.

Gorgol, Laura E., and Brian A. Sponsler. 2011. "Unlocking Potential: Results of
a National Survey of Postsecondary Education in State Prisons." Issue Brief.
Washington, DC: Institute for Higher Education Policy.

Gottfredson, Stephen, and Ralph B. Taylor. 1988. "Community Contexts and
Criminal Offenders." In *Crime and Community Context,* ed. Time Hope and
Margaret Shaw, 62–82. London: HM Stationery Office.

Gottschalk, Marie. 2008. "Hiding in Plain Sight: American Politics and the Carceral
State." *Annual Review of Political Science* 11:235–60.

Gowan, Teresa. 2002. "The Nexus: Homelessness and Incarceration in Two American Cities." *Ethnography* 3, no. 4:500–534.

Gowan, Teresa, and Sarah Whetstone. 2012. "Making the Criminal Addict: Sub-
jectivity and Social Control in a Strong-Arm Rehab." *Punishment and Society*
14, no. 1:69–93.

Gramlich, Edward, Deborah Laren, and Naomi Sealand. 1992. "Moving into and
out of Poor Urban Areas." *Journal of Policy Analysis and Management* 11, no. 2:
273–87.

Grattet, Ryken, Jeffrey Lin, and Joan Petersilia. 2011. "Supervision Regimes, Risk,
and Official Reactions to Parolee Deviance." *Criminology* 49, no. 2:371–99.

Green, Donald P., and Daniel Winik. 2010. "Using Random Judge Assignments to
Estimate the Effects of Incarceration and Probation on Recidivism among Drug
Offenders." *Criminology* 48, no. 2:357–87.

Greenberg, Greg A., and Robert A. Rosenheck. 2008. "Jail Incarceration, Homelessness, and Mental Health: A National Study." *Psychiatric Services* 59, no. 2:170–77.

Greenfeld, L. A., and T. L. Snell. 1999. "Women Offenders." Special Report, NCJ 175688. Washington, DC: US Department of Justice, Bureau of Justice Statistics.

Grieger, Lloyd D., and Jessica Wyse. 2013. "The Impacts of Welfare Reform on Federal Assistance to Persistently Poor Children." *Journal of Children and Poverty* 19, no. 2:71–89.

Grinstead, Olga, Bonnie Faigeles, Carrie Bancroft, and Barry Zach. 2001. "The Financial Cost of Maintaining Relationships with Incarcerated African American Men: A Survey of Women Prison Visitors." *Journal of African American Men* 6, no. 1:59–70.

Groves, Robert M., Jr., Floyd J. Fowler, Mick P. Couper, James M. Lepkowski, Eleanor Singer, and Roger Tourangeau. 2004. *Survey Methodology*. Hoboken, NJ: Wiley.

Grunwald, Heidi E., Brian Lockwood, Philip W. Harris, and Jeremy Mennis. 2010. "Influences of Neighborhood Context, Individual History and Parenting Behavior on Recidivism among Juvenile Offenders." *Journal of Youth and Adolescence* 39, no. 9:1067–79.

Hagan, John. 1993. "The Social Embeddedness of Crime and Unemployment." *Criminology* 31, no. 4:465–91.

Halushka, John. 2016. "The Runaround: Criminal Justice and Welfare Bureaucracies in the Daily Lives of Formerly Incarcerated Men." Typescript, New York University.

Hammett, Theodore M., Mary Patricia Harmon, and William Rhodes. 2002. "The Burden of Infectious Disease among Inmates of and Releasees from US Correctional Facilities, 1997." *American Journal of Public Health* 92, no. 11:1789.

Hammett, Theodore M., Cheryl Roberts, and Sofia Kennedy. 2001. "Health-Related Issues in Prisoner Reentry." *Crime and Delinquency* 47, no. 3:390–409.

Haney, Craig. 2003. "The Psychological Impact of Incarceration: Implications for Post-prison Adjustment." In *Prisoners Once Removed: The Impact of Incarceration and Reentry on Children, Families, and Communities*, ed. Jeremy Travis and Michelle Waul, 33–66. Washington, DC: Urban Institute Press.

Haney, Lynne A. 2010. *Offending Women: Power, Punishment, and the Regulation of Desire*. Berkeley: University of California Press.

Hansen, Helena, Philippe Bourgois, and Ernest Drucker. 2014. "Pathologizing Poverty: New Forms of Diagnosis, Disability, and Structural Stigma under Welfare Reform." *Social Science and Medicine* 103:126–33.

Harding, David J. 2003. "Jean Valjean's Dilemma: The Management of Ex-convict Identity in the Search for Employment." *Deviant Behavior* 24, no. 6:571–95.

———. 2010. *Living the Drama: Community, Conflict, and Culture among Inner-City Boys*. Chicago: University of Chicago Press.

Harding, David J., Jeffrey D. Morenoff, Cheyney C. Dobson, Erin R. Lane, Kendra Opatovsky, Ed-Dee Williams, and Jessica J. B. Wyse. 2016. "Families, Prisoner Reentry, and Reintegration." In *Boys and Men in African American Families*, ed.

Linda M. Burton, Derrick Burton, Susan M. McHale, Valerie King, and Jennifer Van Hook. New York: Springer.

Harding, David J., Jeffrey D. Morenoff, and Claire W. Herbert. 2013. "Home Is Hard to Find: Neighborhoods, Institutions, and the Residential Trajectories of Returning Prisoners." *Annals of the American Academy of Political and Social Science* 647, no. 1:214–36.

Harding, David J., Jeffrey D. Morenoff, Anh P. Nguyen, and Shawn D. Bushway. 2017a. "Short- and Long-Term Effects of Imprisonment on Future Felony Convictions and Prison Admissions." *Proceedings of the National Academy of Sciences.*

Harding, David J., Jeffrey D. Morenoff, Anh P. Nguyen, Shawn D. Bushway, and Ingrid A. Binswanger. 2017b. "Effects of Imprisonment on Violence in the Community: Evidence from a Natural Experiment." Typescript, University of California, Berkeley.

Harding, David J., Jonah A. Siegel, and Jeffrey D. Morenoff. 2017. "Custodial Parole Sanctions and Earnings after Release from Prison." *Social Forces* 96, no. 2: 909–34.

Harding, David J., Jessica J. B. Wyse, Cheyney C. Dobson, and Jeffrey D. Morenoff. 2014. "Making Ends Meet after Prison." *Journal of Policy Analysis and Management* 33, no. 2:440–70.

Harlow, C. W. 1999. "Prior Abuse Reported by Inmates and Probationers." *Alcohol* 75, no. 29:24.

———. 2003. "Education and Correctional Populations." Special Report, NCJ 195670. Washington, DC: US Department of Justice, Bureau of Justice Statistics.

Harris, Alexes. 2016. *A Pound of Flesh: Monetary Sanctions as a Permanent Punishment for Poor People.* New York: Russell Sage.

Harris, Alexes, Heather Evans, and Katherine Beckett. 2010. "Drawing Blood from Stones: Legal Debt and Social Inequality in the Contemporary United States." *American Journal of Sociology* 115, no. 6:1753–99.

Harris, Othello, and R. Robin Miller. 2003. *Impacts of Incarceration on the African American Family.* New Brunswick, NJ: Transaction.

Haskins, Anna R. 2014. "Unintended Consequences: Effects of Paternal Incarceration on Child School Readiness and Later Special Education Placement." *Sociological Science* 1, no. 1:141–58.

———. 2015. "Paternal Incarceration and Child-Reported Behavioral Functioning at Age 9." *Social Science Research* 52:18–33.

Hawken, Angela, and Mark Kleiman. 2009. "Managing Drug Involving Probationers with Swift and Certain Sanctions: Evaluating Hawaii's HOPE." Report submitted to the US Department of Justice, Grant Award 2007-IJ-CX-0033. https://www.ncjrs.gov/pdffiles1/nij/grants/230444.pdf.

Helfgott, Jacqueline. 1997. "Ex-offender Needs versus Community Opportunity in Seattle, Washington." *Federal Probation* 61, no. 2:12–24.

Herbert, Claire W., Jeffrey D. Morenoff, and David J. Harding. 2015. "Homelessness and Housing Insecurity among Former Prisoners." *Russell Sage Foundation Journal of the Social Sciences* 1, no. 2:44–79.

Hill, Terrence D., and Ronald J. Angel. 2005. "Neighborhood Disorder, Psychological Distress, and Heavy Drinking." *Social Science and Medicine* 61, no. 5:965–75.

Hipp, John R., Jesse Jannetta, Rita Shah, and Susan Turner. 2009a. "Parolees' Physical Closeness to Health Service Providers: A Study of California Parolees." *Health and Place* 15, no. 3:679–88.

———. 2009b. "Parolees' Physical Closeness to Social Services: A Study of California Parolees." *Crime and Delinquency* 57, no. 1:102–29.

Hipp, John R., Joan Petersilia, and Susan Turner. 2010. "Parolee Recidivism in California: The Effect of Neighborhood Context and Social Service Agency Characteristics." *Criminology* 48, no. 4:947–79.

Hipp, John R., Susan Turner, and Jesse Jannetta. 2010. "Are Sex Offenders Moving into Social Disorganization? Analyzing the Residential Mobility of California Parolees." *Journal of Research in Crime and Delinquency* 47, no. 4:558–90.

Hirschi, Travis. 1969. *Causes of Delinquency.* Berkeley: University of California Press.

Hogan, Dennis P., and Nan Marie Astone. 1986. "The Transition to Adulthood." *Annual Review of Sociology* 12:109–30.

Holzer, Harry J. 1996. "Employer Hiring Decisions and Antidiscrimination Policy." Madison: University of Wisconsin, Institute for Research on Poverty.

Holzer, Harry J., Steven Raphael, and Michael A. Stoll. 2002. *Will Employers Hire Ex-offenders? Employer Preferences, Background Checks, and Their Determinants.* Discussion Paper no. 1243-02. Madison: University of Wisconsin, Institute for Research on Poverty. https://www.ssc.wisc.edu/irpweb/publications/dps/pdfs/dp124302.pdf.

———. 2007. "The Effect of an Applicant's Criminal History on Employer Hiring Decisions and Screening Practices: Evidence from Los Angeles." In *Barriers to Reentry? The Labor Market for Released Prisoners in Post-industrial America,* ed. Shawn Bushway, Michael A. Stoll, and David F. Weiman, 117–50. New York: Russell Sage.

Huggins, Christopher M. 2009. "Returning Home: Residential Mobility, Neighborhood Context and Recidivism." PhD diss., Ohio State University.

Hughes, T. A., D. J. Wilson, and A. J. Beck. 2001. "Trends in State Parole, 1990–2000." Special Report, NCJ 184735. Washington, DC: US Department of Justice, Bureau of Justice Statistics.

Hussey, J. M., J. J. Chang, and J. B. Kotch. 2006. "Child Maltreatment in the United States: Prevalence, Risk Factors, and Adolescent Health Consequences." *Pediatrics* 118, no. 3:933–42.

Irwin, John. 2005. *The Warehouse Prison: Disposal of the New Dangerous Class.* Los Angeles: Roxbury.

Irwin, John, and Barbara Owen. 2005. "Harm and the Contemporary Prison." In *The Effects of Imprisonment*, ed. Alison Liebling and Shadd Maruna, 94–117. Cullumpton: Willan.

Jacobs, David, and Ronald Helms. 2001. "Toward a Political Sociology of Punishment: Politics and Changes in the Incarcerated Population." *Social Science Research* 30, no. 2:171–94.

Jacobson, Michael. 2005. *Downsizing Prisons: How to Reduce Crime and End Mass Incarceration*. New York: New York University Press.

James, Doris J., and Lauren E. Glaze. 2006. "Mental Health Problems of Prison and Jail Inmates." Special Report, NCJ 213600. Washington, DC: US Department of Justice, Bureau of Justice Statistics.

Janowitz, Morris. 1952. *The Community Press in an Urban Setting: The Social Elements of Urbanism*. New York: Free Press.

Johnson, Elizabeth Inez, and Jane Waldfogel. 2004. "Children of Incarcerated Parents: Multiple Risks and Children's Living Arrangements." In *Imprisoning America: The Social Effects of Mass Incarceration*, ed. Mary E. Pattillo, Bruce Western, and David Weiman, 97–131. New York: Russell Sage.

Kalleberg, Arne L. 2011. *Good Jobs, Bad Jobs: The Rise of Polarized and Precarious Employment Systems in the United States, 1970s–2000s*. New York: Russell Sage.

Kalleberg, Arne L., and Aage B. Sørensen. 1979. "The Sociology of Labor Markets." *Annual Review of Sociology* 5:351–79.

Kan, Kamhon. 2007. "Residential Mobility and Social Capital." *Journal of Urban Economics* 61, no. 3:436–57.

Kaufman, Nicole. 2015. "Prisoner Incorporation: The Work of the State and Nongovernmental Organizations." *Theoretical Criminology* 19, no. 4:534–53.

Kirk, David S. 2009. "A Natural Experiment on Residential Change and Recidivism: Lessons from Hurricane Katrina." *American Sociological Review* 74, no. 3: 484–505.

———. 2012. "Residential Change as a Turning Point in the Life Course of Crime: Desistance or Temporary Cessation?" *Criminology* 50, no. 2:329–58.

Kirk, David S., and Mauri Matsuda. 2011. "Legal Cynicism, Collective Efficacy, and the Ecology of Arrest." *Criminology* 49, no. 2:443–72.

Kubrin, Charis E., and Eric A. Stewart. 2006. "Predicting Who Reoffends: The Neglected Role of Neighborhood Context in Recidivism Studies." *Criminology* 44, no. 1:165–97.

Kurlychek, Megan C., Robert Brame, and Shawn D. Bushway. 2006. "Scarlet Letters and Recidivism: Does an Old Criminal Record Predict Future Offending?" *Criminology and Public Policy* 5, no. 3:483–504.

———. 2007. "Enduring Risk? Old Criminal Records and Predictions of Future Criminal Involvement." *Crime and Delinquency* 53, no. 1:64–83.

Langworthy, Robert H., Allan R. Barnes, and Richard W. Curtis. 1998. "Results from the Long-Term Inmate Survey: Focus on Child Abuse Histories." Anchorage: University of Alaska, Anchorage, Justice Center.

Lara-Millán, Armando. 2014. "Public Emergency Room Overcrowding in the Era of Mass Imprisonment." *American Sociological Review* 79, no. 5:866–87.

Laub, John, Daniel Nagin, and Robert Sampson. 1998. "Trajectories of Change in Criminal Offending: Good Marriages and the Desistance Process." *American Sociological Review* 63, no. 2:225–38.

Laub, John H., and Robert J. Sampson. 2001. "Understanding Desistance from Crime." *Crime and Justice: A Review of Research* 28:1–69.

——. 2003. *Shared Beginnings, Divergent Lives: Delinquent Boys to Age 70.* Cambridge, MA: Harvard University Press.

La Vigne, Nancy, and Barbara Parthasarathy. 2005. "Prisoner Reentry and Residential Mobility." Returning Home Illinois Policy Brief. Washington, DC: Urban Institute, Justice Policy Center.

Lee, Barrett A., Kimberly A. Tyler, and James D. Wright. 2010. "The New Homelessness Revisited." *Annual Review of Sociology* 36:501–21.

Lee, Hedwig, Christopher Wildeman, Emily Wang, Niki Matusko, and James S. Jackson. 2014. "A Heavy Burden? The Health Consequences of Having a Family Member Incarcerated." *American Journal of Public Health* 104, no. 3:421–27.

Lee, Keun Bok, David J. Harding, and Jeffrey D. Morenoff. 2017. "Neighborhood Attainment after Prison." *Social Science Research* 66:211–33.

Lerman, Amy E., and Velsa M. Weaver. 2014. *Arresting Citizenship: The Democratic Consequences of American Crime Control.* Chicago: University of Chicago Press.

Leverentz, Andrea M. 2006. "People, Places, and Things: The Social Process of Reentry for Female Ex-offenders." PhD diss., University of Chicago.

——. 2010. "People, Places, and Things: How Female Ex-prisoners Negotiate Neighborhood." *Journal of Contemporary Ethnography* 39, no. 6:646–81.

——. 2011. "The Neighborhood Context of Attitudes towards Crime and Reentry." *Punishment and Society* 13, no. 1:64–92.

——. 2014. *The Ex-prisoner's Dilemma: How Women Negotiate Competing Narratives of Reentry and Desistance.* New Brunswick, NJ: Rutgers University Press.

Liebow, Elliot. 1967. *Tally's Corner: A Study of Negro Streetcorner Men.* With a foreword by Hylan Lewis. Boston: Little, Brown.

Lin, Jeffrey, Ryken Grattet, and Joan Petersilia. 2010. "'Back-End Sentencing' and Reimprisonment: Individual, Organizational, and Community Predictors of Parole Sanctioning Decisions." *Criminology* 48, no. 3:759–95.

Lin, Nan. 1986. "Conceptualizing Social Support." In *Social Support, Life Events, and Depression*, ed. Nan Lin, Alfred Dean, and Walter Edsel, 17–30. Orlando, FL: Academic.

Lindquist, Christine, Jennifer Hardison, and Pamela K. Lattimore. 2004. "The Reentry Court Initiative: Court-Based Strategies for Managing Released Prisoners." *Justice Research and Policy* 6, no. 1:93–118.

Lipsey, Mark W., and Francis T. Cullen. 2007. "The Effectiveness of Correctional Rehabilitation: A Review of Systematic Reviews." *Annual Review of Law and Social Science* 3:297–320.

Lipton, Douglas S., Robert Martinson, and Judith Wilks. 1975. *The Effectiveness of Correctional Treatment.* New York: Praeger.

Lockwood, Susan, John M. Nally, Taiping Ho, and Katie Knutson. 2012. "The Effect of Correctional Education on Post-release Employment and Recidivism: A 5-Year Follow-Up in the State of Indiana." *Crime and Delinquency* 58, no. 3:380–96.

Loeffler, Charles E. 2013. "Does Imprisonment Alter the Life Course? Evidence on Crime and Employment from a Natural Experiment." *Criminology* 51, no. 1: 137–66.

Lofland, John, and Lyn H. Lofland. 1995. *Analyzing Social Settings: A Guide to Qualitative Observation and Analysis.* New York: Wadsworth.

Lofstrom, Magnus, and Steven Raphael. 2015. "Realignment, Incarceration, and Crime Trends in California." San Francisco: Public Policy Institute of California.

Loughran, Thomas A., Edward P. Mulvey, Carol A. Schubert, Jeffrey Fagan, Alex R. Piquero, and Sandra H. Losoya. 2009. "Estimating a Dose-Response Relationship between Length of Stay and Future Recidivism in Serious Juvenile Offenders." *Criminology* 47, no. 3:699–740.

Love, Margaret C. 2003. "Starting Over with a Clean Slate: In Praise of a Forgotten Section of the Model Penal Code." *Fordham Urban Law Journal* 30, no. 5: 1705–42.

Lutze, Faith E., Jeffrey W. Rosky, and Zachary K. Hamilton. 2014. "Homelessness and Reentry: A Multisite Outcome Evaluation of Washington State's Reentry Housing Program for High Risk Offenders." *Criminal Justice and Behavior* 41, no. 4:471–91.

Lynch, James P., and William J. Sabol. 2004. "Assessing the Effects of Mass Incarceration on Informal Social Control in Communities." *Criminology and Public Policy* 3, no. 2:267–94.

Lynch, Mona. 1998. "Waste Managers? The New Penology, Crime Fighting, and Parole Agent Identity." *Law and Society Review* 32, no. 4:839–70.

———. 2000. "Rehabilitation as Rhetoric." *Punishment and Society* 2, no. 1:40–65.

Mackenzie, Doris Layton. 2006. *What Works in Corrections: Reducing the Criminal Activities of Offenders and Delinquents.* Cambridge Studies in Criminology. Cambridge: Cambridge University Press.

MacMillan, Harriet L., Jan E. Fleming, Nico Trocmé, Michael H. Boyle, Maria Wong, Yvonne A. Racine, William R. Beardslee, and David R. Offord. 1997. "Prevalence of Child Physical and Sexual Abuse in the Community: Results from the Ontario Health Supplement." *Journal of the American Medical Association* 278:131–35.

Mallik-Kane, Kamala, and Christy A. Visher. 2008. "Health and Prisoner Reentry: How Physical, Mental, and Substance Abuse Conditions Shape the Process of Reintegration." Research Report: Washington, DC: Urban Institute, Justice Policy Center.

Manza, Jeff, and Christopher Uggen. 2008. *Locked Out: Felon Disenfranchisement and American Democracy*. New York: Oxford University Press.

Maruna, Shadd. 2001. *Making Good: How Ex-offenders Reform and Reclaim Their Lives*. Washington, DC: American Psychological Association.

Massey, Douglas S., and Nancy A. Denton. 1993. *American Apartheid: Segregation and the Making of the Underclass*. Cambridge, MA: Harvard University Press.

Massoglia, Michael, Glenn Firebaugh, and Cody Warner. 2013. "Racial Variation in the Effect of Incarceration on Neighborhood Attainment." *American Sociological Review* 78, no. 1:142–65.

McCollister, Kathryn E. 2008. "Cost Effectiveness of Substance Abuse Treatment in Criminal Justice Settings." Substance Abuse Policy Research Program Policy Brief. Princeton, NJ: Robert Wood Johnson Foundation.

McLean, Rachel L., and Michael D. Thompson. 2007. "Repaying Debts." Report of the Council of State Governments Justice Center. New York. https://csgjusticecenter.org/wp-content/uploads/2012/12/repaying_debts_summary.pdf.

Meade, Benjamin Dane, Benjamin Steiner, Matthew Makarios, and Lawrence Travis. 2013. "Estimating a Dose—Response Relationship between Time Served in Prison and Recidivism." *Journal of Research in Crime and Delinquency* 50, no. 4:525–50.

Mears, Daniel P., Xia Wang, Carter Hay, and William D. Bales. 2008. "Social Ecology and Recidivism: Implications for Prisoner Reentry." *Criminology* 46, no. 2: 301–40.

Metraux, Stephen, and Dennis P. Culhane. 2004. "Homeless Shelter Use and Reincarceration Following Prison Release." *Criminology and Public Policy* 3, no. 2:139–60.

Metraux, Stephen, Caterina G. Roman, and Richard S. Cho. 2008. "Incarceration and Homelessness." In *Toward Understanding Homelessness: The 2007 National Symposium on Homelessness Research*, ed. Deborah Dennis, Gretchen Locke, and Jill Khadduri, 9-1–9-33. Washington: US Department of Housing and Urban Development.

"Michigan Department of Corrections Annual Report." 2008. https://www.michigan.gov/documents/corrections/2008_Annual_Report_329486_7.pdf.

Molnar, Beth E., Stephen L. Buka, and Ronald C. Kessler. 2001. "Child Sexual Abuse and Subsequent Psychopathology: Results from the National Comorbidity Survey." *American Journal of Public Health* 91, no. 5:753–60.

Morenoff, Jeffrey D., and David J. Harding. 2011. "Final Technical Report: Neighborhoods, Recidivism, and Employment among Returning Prisoners." Report Submitted to the National Institute of Justice, Grant Award 2008-IJ-CX-0018. https://www.ncjrs.gov/pdffiles1/nij/grants/236436.pdf.

———. 2014. "Incarceration, Prisoner Reentry, and Communities." *Annual Review of Sociology* 40:411–29.

Morenoff, Jeffrey D., David J. Harding, and Amy B. Cooter. 2009. "The Neighborhood Context of Prisoner Reentry." Paper presented at the annual meeting of the Population Association of America, Detroit.

Mouw, Ted. 2000. "Job Relocation and the Racial Gap in Unemployment in Detroit and Chicago, 1980 to 1990." *American Sociological Review* 65, no. 5:730–53.

Mowen, Thomas J., and Christy A. Visher. 2015. "Drug Use and Crime after Incarceration: The Role of Family Support and Family Conflict." *Justice Quarterly* 32, no. 2:337–59.

———. 2016. "Changing the Ties That Bind." *Criminology and Public Policy* 15, no. 2:503–28.

Mueller-Smith, Michael. 2014. "The Criminal and Labor Market Impacts of Incarceration." Typescript, University of Michigan, Department of Economics.

Mumola, Christopher. 1999. "Substance Abuse and Treatment State and Federal Prisoners, 1997." Special Report, NCJ 1728171. Washington, DC: US Department of Justice, Bureau of Justice Statistics.

Nagin, Daniel S., Francis T. Cullen, and Cheryl Lero Jonson. 2009. "Imprisonment and Reoffending." *Crime and Justice: A Review of Research* 38:115–200.

National Research Council. 2014. *The Growth of Incarceration in the United States: Exploring Causes and Consequences*. Edited by Jeremy Travis, Bruce Western, and F. Stevens Redburn. Washington, DC: National Academies Press.

Nelson, Marta, Perry Deess, and Charlotte Allen. 1999. "The First Month Out: Post-incarceration Experiences in New York City." New York: Vera Institute of Justice.

Newman, Katherine S. 2009. *No Shame in My Game: The Working Poor in the Inner City*. New York: Vintage.

Nguyen, Anh, Jeffrey Morenoff, and David Harding. 2014. "The Effect of Labor Market Conditions on Employment among Former Prisoners in Michigan." Paper presented at the annual meeting of the American Sociological Association, San Francisco, CA.

Ogundimu, Tomi, Joshua Fangmeier, Karen Stock, and Marianne Udow-Phillips. 2012. "Medicaid Eligibility in Michigan: 40 Ways." Ann Arbor, MI: Center for Healthcare Research and Transformation.

Osgood, D. Wayne, Janet Wilson, Patrick O'Malley, Jerald Bachman, and Lloyd Johnston. 1996. "Routine Activities and Individual Deviant Behavior." *American Sociological Review* 61, no. 4:635–55.

Pager, Devah. 2003. "The Mark of a Criminal Record." *American Journal of Sociology* 108, no. 5:937–75.

———. 2007a. *Marked: Race, Crime, and Finding Work in an Era of Mass Incarceration*. Chicago: University of Chicago Press.

———. 2007b. "Two Strikes and You're Out: The Intensification of Racial and Criminal Stigma." In *Barriers to Reentry? The Labor Market for Released Prisoners in Post-industrial America*, ed. Shawn Bushway, Michael A. Stoll, and David F. Weiman, 151–73. New York: Russell Sage.

Pager, Devah, Bruce Western, and Bart Bonikowski. 2009. "Discrimination in a Low-Wage Labor Market A Field Experiment." *American Sociological Review* 74, no. 5:777–99.

Paternoster, Ray, and Shawn Bushway. 2009. "Desistance and the 'Feared Self': Toward an Identity Theory of Criminal Desistance." *Journal of Criminal Law and Criminology* 99, no. 4:1103–56.

Pedraza, Silvia, and Ruben Rumbaut. 1996. *Origins and Destinies: Immigration, Race, and Ethnicity in America.* Belmont, CA: Wadsworth.

Petersilia, Joan. 1999. "Parole and Prisoner Reentry in the United States." *Crime and Justice: A Review of Research* 26:479–529.

———. 2003. *When Prisoners Come Home: Parole and Prisoner Reentry.* Oxford: Oxford University Press.

Petersilia, Joan, and Francis T. Cullen. 2014. "Liberal but Not Stupid: Meeting the Promise of Downsizing Prisons." *Stanford Journal of Criminal Law and Policy* 2:1–43.

Pettit, Becky, and Christopher J. Lyons. 2007. "Status and Stigma of Incarceration: The Labor-Market Effects of Incarceration, by Race, Class, and Criminal Involvement." In *Barriers to Reentry? The Labor Market for Released Prisoners in Post-industrial America*, ed. Shawn Bushway, Michael A. Stoll, and David F. Weiman. New York: Russell Sage.

Pettit, Becky, and Bruce Western. 2004. "Mass Imprisonment and the Life Course: Race and Class Inequality in U.S. Incarceration." *American Sociological Review* 69, no. 2:151–69.

Pew Center on the States. 2008. "One in 100: Behind Bars in America, 2008." Washington, DC: Pew Charitable Trusts.

———. 2009. "One in 31: The Long Reach of American Corrections." Washington, DC: Pew Charitable Trusts.

Phelps, Michelle S. 2013. "The Paradox of Probation: Community Supervision in the Age of Mass Incarceration." *Law and Policy* 35, nos. 1–2:51–80.

Pinard, Michael. 2010. "Collateral Consequences of Criminal Convictions: Confronting Issues of Race and Dignity." *New York University Law Review* 85, no. 2: 457–534.

Piore, Michael J. 1975. "Notes for a Theory of Labor Market Stratification." In *Labor Market Segmentation*, ed. Richard C. Edwards, Michael Reich, and David M. Gordon, 125–50. Lexington, MA: Heath.

Portes, Alejandro, and Jozsef Borocz. 2007. "Contemporary Immigration: Theoretical Perspectives on Its Determinants and Modes of Incorporation." *International Migration Review* 23, no. 3:606–30.

Portes, Alejandro, and Ruben G. Rumbaut. 2006. *Immigrant America: A Portrait.* Berkeley: University of California Press.

Rabuy, Bernadette, and Peter Wagner. 2015. *Screening Out Family Time: The For-Profit Video Visitation Industry in Prisons and Jails.* Northampton, MA: Prison Policy Initiative.

Raphael, Steven. 2011. "Incarceration and Prisoner Reentry in the United States." *Annals of the American Academy of Political and Social Science* 635, no. 1: 192–215.

Raphael, Steven, and Michael A. Stoll. 2009. "Why Are So Many Americans in Prison?" In *Do Prisons Make Us Safer? The Benefits and Costs of the Prison Boom*, ed. Steven Raphael and Michael A. Stoll, 27–72. New York: Russell Sage.

———. 2013. *Why Are So Many Americans in Prison?* New York: Russell Sage.

Raphael, Steven, and David F. Weiman. 2007. "The Impact of Local Labor-Market Conditions on the Likelihood That Parolees Are Returned to Custody." In *Barriers to Reentry? The Labor Market for Released Prisoners in Post-industrial America*, ed. Shawn Bushway, Michael A. Stoll, and David F. Weiman, 304–32. New York: Russell Sage.

Richie, Beth E. 2012. *Arrested Justice: Black Women, Violence, and America's Prison Nation.* New York: New York University Press.

Roman, Caterina G., and Jeremy Travis. 2006. "Where Will I Sleep Tomorrow? Housing, Homelessness, and the Returning Prisoner." *Housing Policy Debate* 17, no. 2:389–418.

Rose, Dina R., and Todd R. Clear. 1998. "Incarceration, Social Capital, and Crime: Implications for Social Disorganization Theory." *Criminology* 36, no. 3:441–80.

Rossi, Peter H. 1989. *Down and Out in America: The Origins of Homelessness.* Chicago: University of Chicago Press.

Rubinstein, Gwen, and Debbie Mukamal. 2002. "Welfare and Housing—Denial of Benefits to Drug Offenders." In *Invisible Punishment: The Collateral Consequences of Mass Imprisonment*, ed. Marc Mauer and Meda Chesney-Lind, 37–49. New York: New Press.

Ryken, Grattet, and Jeffrey Lin. 2016. "Supervision Intensity and Parole Outcomes: A Competing Risks Approach to Criminal and Technical Parole Violations." *Justice Quarterly* 33, no. 4:565–83.

Sabol, William J. 2007. "Local Labor Market Conditions and Post-prison Employment Experiences of Offenders Released from Ohio State Prisons." In *Barriers to Reentry? The Labor Market for Released Prisoners in Post-industrial America*, ed. Shawn Bushway, Michael A. Stoll, and David F. Weiman, 257–303. New York: Russell Sage.

Sampson, Robert J. 1999. "What 'Community' Supplies." In *Urban Problems and Community Development*, ed. Ronald F. Ferguson and William T. Dickens. Washington, DC: Brookings Institution Press.

———. 2012. *Great American City: Chicago and the Enduring Neighborhood Effect.* Chicago: University of Chicago Press.

Sampson, Robert J., and John H. Laub. 1992. "Crime and Deviance in the Life Course." *Annual Review of Sociology* 18:63–84.

———. 1995. *Crime in the Making: Pathways and Turning Points through Life.* Cambridge, MA: Harvard University Press.

————. 2016. "Turning Points and the Future of Life-Course Criminology: Reflections on the 1986 Criminal Careers Report." *Journal of Research in Crime and Delinquency* 53, no. 3:321–35.

Sampson, Robert J., John H. Laub, and Christopher Wimer. 2006. "Does Marriage Reduce Crime? A Counterfactual Approach to Within-Individual Causal Effects." *Criminology* 44, no. 3:465–508.

Sampson, Robert J., and Charles Loeffler. 2010. "Punishment's Place: The Local Concentration of Mass Incarceration." *Daedalus* 139, no. 3:20–31.

Sampson, Robert J., Jeffrey D. Morenoff, and Felton Earls. 1999. "Beyond Social Capital: Spatial Dynamics of Collective Efficacy for Children." *American Sociological Review* 64, no. 5:633–60.

Sampson, Robert J., Stephen W. Raudenbush, and Felton Earls. 1997. "Neighborhoods and Violent Crime: A Multilevel Study of Collective Efficacy." *Science* 277, no. 5328:918–24.

Sankoff, David, and Joseph B. Kruskal. 1983. *Time Warps, String Edits, and Macromolecules: The Theory and Practice of Sequence Comparison.* Edited by David Sankoff and Joseph B. Kruskal. Reading: Addison-Wesley.

Schnepel, Kevin. 2014. "Good Jobs and Recidivism." Economics Working Paper no. 2014-10. Sydney: University of Sydney, School of Economics.

Schnittker, J. 2014. "The Psychological Dimensions and the Social Consequences of Incarceration." *Annals of the American Academy of Political and Social Science* 651, no. 1:122–38.

Schnittker, Jason, Michael Massoglia, and Christopher Uggen. 2011. "Incarceration and the Health of the African American Community." *DuBois Review* 8, no. 1:133–41.

————. 2012. "Out and Down: Incarceration and Psychiatric Disorders." *Journal of Health and Social Behavior* 53, no. 4:448–64.

Schwartz, Richard D., and Jerome H. Skolnick. 1964. "Two Studies of Legal Stigma." In *The Other Side: Perspectives in Deviance*, ed. Howard S. Becker. New York: Free Press.

Seefeldt, Kristin S. 2015. "Constant Consumption Smoothing, Limited Investments, and Few Repayments: The Role of Debt in the Financial Lives of Economically Vulnerable Families." *Social Service Review* 89, no. 2:263–300.

Seim, Josh. 2016. "Short-Timing: The Carceral Experience of Soon-to-Be-Released Prisoners." *Punishment and Society* 18, no. 4:442–58.

Seiter, Richard P., and A. D. West. 2003. "Supervision Styles in Probation and Parole: An Analysis of Activities." *Journal of Offender Rehabilitation* 38, no. 2: 57–75.

Shaw, Clifford R., and Henry D. McKay. 1969. *Juvenile Delinquency and Urban Areas: A Study of Rates of Delinquency in Relation to Differential Characteristics of Local Communities in American Cities.* Chicago: University of Chicago Press.

Shaw, Mary. 2004. "Housing and Public Health." *Annual Review of Public Health* 25:397–418.

Shlay, Anna B., and Peter H. Rossi. 1992. "Social Science Research and Contemporary Studies of Homelessness." *Annual Review of Sociology* 18:129–60.

Shover, Niel. 1996. *Great Pretenders: Pursuit and Careers of Persistent Thieves.* Boulder, CO: Westview.

Siegel, Jonah A. 2014. "Prisoner Reentry, Parole Violations, and the Persistence of the Surveillance State." PhD diss., University of Michigan.

Simon, Jonathan. 1993. *Poor Discipline: Parole and the Social Control of the Underclass, 1890–1990.* Chicago: University of Chicago Press.

———. 2007. *Governing through Crime: How the War on Crime Transformed American Democracy and Created a Culture of Fear.* Oxford: Oxford University Press.

Small, Mario Luis. 2009. "'How Many Cases Do I Need?' On Science and the Logic of Case Selection in Field-Based Research." *Ethnography* 10, no. 1:5–38.

Small, Mario Luis, and Monica McDermott. 2006. "The Presence of Organizational Resources in Poor Urban Neighborhoods: An Analysis of Average and Contextual Effects." *Social Forces* 84, no. 3:1697–724.

Smith, Douglas A. 1986. "Neighborhood Context of Police Behavior." *Crime and Justice: A Review of Research* 8:313–41.

Smith, Sandra S., and Nora C. R. Broege. 2012. "Searching for Work with a Criminal Record." Berkeley: University of California, Berkeley, Institute for Research on Labor and Employment.

Social Security Administration. 2016. "Monthly Statistical Snapshot, July 2016." *Research, Statistics, and Policy Analysis, Social Security.* https://www.ssa.gov/policy/docs/quickfacts/stat_snapshot/2016-07.html.

Solomon, Amy L., Gillian L. Thomson, and Sinead Keegan. 2004. "Prisoner Reentry in Michigan." Washington, DC: Urban Institute, Justice Policy Center.

South, Scott J., and Kyle D. Crowder. 1997. "Escaping Distressed Neighborhoods: Individual, Community, and Metropolitan Influences." *American Journal of Sociology* 102, no. 4:1040–84.

Soysal, Yasmin. 1995. *Limits of Citizenship: Migrants and Post national Membership in Europe.* Chicago: University of Chicago Press.

Staff, Jeremy, and Jeylan T. Mortimer. 2008. "Social Class Background and the School-to-Work Transition." *New Directions for Child and Adolescent Development* 119:55–69.

Stahler, Gerald J., Jeremy Mennis, Steven Belenko, Wayne N. Welsh, Matthew L. Hiller, and Gary Zajac. 2013. "Predicting Recidivism for Released State Prison Offenders: Examining the Influence of Individual and Neighborhood Characteristics and Spatial Contagion on the Likelihood of Reincarceration." *Criminal Justice and Behavior* 40, no. 6:690–711.

Stemen, Don, Andres Rengifo, and James Wilson. 2005. "Of Fragmentation and

Ferment: The Impact of State Sentencing Policies on Incarceration Rates, 1975–2002." Report Submitted to the National Institute of Justice, Grant Award NIJ 2002-IJ-CX-0027. https://www.ncjrs.gov/pdffiles1/nij/grants/213003.pdf.

Stephan, James. 1992. "Census of State and Federal Correctional Facilities, 1990." NCJ 137003. Washington, DC: US Department of Justice, Bureau of Justice Statistics.

———. 2008. "Census of State and Federal Correctional Facilities, 2005." NCJ 222182. Washington, DC: US Department of Justice, Bureau of Justice Statistics.

Stovel, Katherine, Michael Savage, and Peter Bearman. 1996. "Ascription into Achievement: Models of Career Systems at Lloyds Bank, 1980–1970." *American Journal of Sociology* 102, no. 2:358–99.

Sugie, Naomi F. 2018. "Work as Foraging: A Smartphone Study of Job Search and Employment after Prison." *American Journal of Sociology* 123, no. 5:1453–91.

Sugie, Naomi F., and Michael C. Lens. 2017. "Daytime Locations in Spatial Mismatch: Job Accessibility and Employment at Reentry from Prison." *Demography* 54, no 2:775–800.

Sullivan, Eileen, Milton Mino, Katherine Nelson, and Jill Pope. 2002. "Families as a Resource in Recovery from Drug Abuse: An Evaluation of La Bodega de la Familia." New York: Vera Institute of Justice.

Sun, Ivan Y., Brian K. Payne, and Yuning Wu. 2008. "The Impact of Situational Factors, Officer Characteristics, and Neighborhood Context on Police Behavior: A Multilevel Analysis." *Journal of Criminal Justice* 36, no. 1:22–32.

Swaroop, Sapna, and Jeffrey D. Morenoff. 2006. "Building Community: The Neighborhood Context of Social Organization." *Social Forces* 84, no. 3:1665–95.

Tanner, Julian, Scott Davies, and Bill O'Grady. 1999. "Whatever Happened to Yesterday's Rebels? Longitudinal Effects of Youth Delinquency on Education and Employment." *Social Problems* 46, no. 2:250–74.

Thacher, David. 2008. "The Rise of Criminal Background Screening in Rental Housing." *Law and Social Inquiry* 33, no. 1:5–30.

———. 2010. "The Distribution of Police Protection." *Journal of Quantitative Criminology* 27, no. 3:275–98.

Thornberry, Terence P., and Robert L. Christenson. 1984. "Unemployment and Criminal Involvement: An Investigation of Reciprocal Causal Structures." *American Sociological Review* 49, no. 3:398–411.

Tillyer, Marie Skubak, and Brenda Vose. 2011. "Social Ecology, Individual Risk, and Recidivism: A Multilevel Examination of Main and Moderating Influences." *Journal of Criminal Justice* 39, no. 5:452–59.

Tonry, Michael. 1996. *Sentencing Matters*. New York: Oxford University Press.

Torrey, E. Fuller, Mary T. Zdanowicz, Aaron D. Kennard, H. Richard Lamb, Donald F. Eslinger, Michael C Biasotti, and Doris A. Fuller. 2014. *The Treatment of Persons with Mental Illness in Prison and Jails: A State Survey*. Arlington, VA: Treatment Advocacy Center.

Travis, Jeremy. 2003. "Invisible Punishment: An Instrument of Social Exclusion." In *Invisible Punishment: The Collateral Consequences of Mass Imprisonment*, ed. Marc Mauer and Meda Chesney-Lind. New York: New Press.

———. 2005. *But They All Come Back: Facing the Challenges of Prisoner Reentry.* Washington, DC: Urban Institute Press.

———. 2007. "Back-End Sentencing: A Practice in Search of a Rationale." *Social Research: An International Quarterly* 74, no. 2:631–44.

Travis, Jeremy, Amy L. Solomon, and Michelle Waul. 2001. *From Prison to Home: The Dimensions and Consequences of Prisoner Reentry.* Washington, DC: Urban Institute, Justice Policy Center.

Travis, Jeremy, and Michelle Waul, eds. 2003. *Prisoners Once Removed: Impact of Incarceration and Reentry on Children, Families, and Communities.* Washington, DC: Urban Institute Press.

Tripodi, Stephen J., Johnny S. Kim, and Kimberly Bender. 2010. "Is Employment Associated with Reduced Recidivism? The Complex Relationship between Employment and Crime." *International Journal of Offender Therapy and Comparative Criminology* 54:706–20.

Turney, Kristin. 2014. "Stress Proliferation across Generations? Examining the Relationship between Parental Incarceration and Childhood Health." *Journal of Health and Social Behavior* 55, no. 3:302–19.

———. 2015. "Hopelessly Devoted? Relationship Quality during and after Incarceration." *Journal of Marriage and Family* 77, no. 2:480–95.

Turney, Kristin, and Anna R. Haskins. 2014. "Falling Behind? Children's Early Grade Retention after Parental Incarceration." *Sociology of Education* 87, no. 4: 241–58.

Turney, Kristin, and Christopher Wildeman. 2013. "Redefining Relationships Explaining the Countervailing Consequences of Paternal Incarceration for Parenting." *American Sociological Review* 78, no. 6:949–79.

Tyler, John H., and Jeffrey R. Kling. 2006. "Prison-Based Education and Re-entry into the Mainstream Labor Market." Working Paper no. 12114. Cambridge, MA: National Bureau of Economic Research.

Tyler, Tom R., and Jeffrey Fagan. 2008. "Legitimacy and Cooperation: Why Do People Help the Police Fight Crime in Their Communities?" *Ohio State Journal of Criminal Law* 6, no. 1:231–76.

Ubah, Charles B. A., and Robert L. Robinson Jr. 2003. "A Grounded Look at the Debate over Prison-Based Education: Optimistic Theory versus Pessimistic Worldview." *Prison Journal* 83, no. 2:115–29.

Uggen, Christopher. 2000. "Work as a Turning Point in the Life Course of Criminals: A Duration Model of Age, Employment, and Recidivism." *American Sociological Review* 65, no. 4:529–46.

Uggen, Christopher, and Michael Massoglia. 2003. "Desistance from Crime and Deviance as a Turning Point in the Life Course." In *Handbook of the Life*

Course, ed. Jeylan T. Mortimer and Michael J. Shanahan, 311–29. New York: Kluwer Academic/Plenum.

Uggen, Christopher, and Robert Stewart. 2015. "Piling On: Collateral Consequences and Community Supervision." *Minnesota Law Review* 99:1871–910.

Uggen, Christopher, Mike Vuolo, Sarah Lageson, Ebony Ruhland, and Hilary Whitham. 2014. "The Edge of Stigma: An Experimental Audit of the Effects of Low-Level Criminal Records on Employment." *Criminology* 52, no. 4:627–54.

Uggen, Christopher, Sara Wakefield, and Bruce Western. 2005. "Work and Family Perspectives on Reentry." In *Prisoner Reentry and Crime in America*, ed. Jeremy Travis and Christy A. Visher, 209–43. Cambridge: Cambridge University Press.

Umberson, Debra, Robert Crosnoe, and Corinne Reczek. 2010. "Social Relationships and Health Behavior across the Life Course." *Annual Review of Sociology* 36:139–57.

"Unmarried Childbearing." 2016. National Center for Health Statistics. http://www .cdc.gov/nchs/fastats/unmarried-childbearing.htm.

US Department of Agriculture. 2018. "Supplemental Nutrition Assistance Program." https://www.fns.usda.gov/snap/supplemental-nutrition-assistance-pro gram-snap.

Visher, Christy A., and Jeremy Travis. 2003. "Transitions from Prison to Community: Understanding Individual Pathways." *Annual Review of Sociology* 29: 89–113.

Wacquant, Loïc. 2001. "Deadly Symbiosis: When Ghetto and Prison Meet and Mesh." *Punishment and Society* 3, no. 1:95–133.

———. 2009. *Prisons of Poverty*. Minneapolis: University of Minnesota Press.

———. 2010. "Class, Race and Hyperincarceration in Revanchist America." *Daedalus* 139, no. 3:74–90.

Wakefield, Sara, and Christopher Uggen. 2010. "Incarceration and Stratification." *Annual Review of Sociology* 36:387–406.

Wakefield, Sara, and Christopher Wildeman. 2013. *Children of the Prison Boom: Mass Incarceration and the Future of American Inequality*. New York: Oxford University Press.

Wallace, Danielle, and Andrew V. Papachristos. 2014. "Recidivism and the Availability of Health Care Organizations." *Justice Quarterly* 31, no. 3:588–608.

Wang, Xia, Daniel P. Mears, and William D. Bales. 2010. "Race-Specific Employment Contexts and Recidivism." *Criminology* 48, no. 4:1171–211.

Warner, Cody. 2014. "Incarceration and Residential Mobility between Poor and Non-poor Neighborhoods." Paper presented at the 2014 annual meeting of the American Sociological Association, San Francisco.

Warr, Mark. 1993. "Parents, Peers, and Delinquency." *Social Forces* 72, no. 1:247–64.

———. 1998. "Life-Course Transitions and Desistance from Crime." *Criminology* 36, no. 2:183–216.

Weaver, Velsa M. 2007. "Frontlash: Race and the Development of Punitive Crime Policy." *Studies in American Political Development* 21, no. 2:230–65.

Weaver, Velsa M., and Amy E. Lerman. 2010. "Political Consequences of the Carceral State." *American Political Science Review* 104, no. 4:817–33.

Weeks, R., and C. S. Widom. 1998. "Self-Reports of Early Childhood Victimization
among Incarcerated Adult Male Felons." *Journal of Interpersonal Violence* 13,
no. 3:346–61.

Wehrman, Michael M. 2010. "Race, Concentrated Disadvantage, and Recidivism:
A Test of Interaction Effects." *Journal of Criminal Justice* 38, no. 4:538–44.

Weiman, David F., Michael A. Stoll, and Shawn Bushway. 2007. "The Regime of
Mass-Incarceration: A Labor-Market Perspective." In *Barriers to Reentry? The
Labor Market for Released Prisoners in Post-industrial America*, ed. Shawn
Bushway, Michael A. Stoll, and David F. Weiman, 29–79. New York: Russell
Sage.

Weisberg, Robert, and Joan Petersilia. 2010. "The Dangers of Pyrrhic Victories
against Mass Incarceration." *Daedalus* 139, no. 3:124–33.

West, A. D., and Richard P. Seiter. 2004. "Social Worker or Cop? Measuring the
Supervision Styles of Probation and Parole Officers in Kentucky and Missouri."
Journal of Crime and Justice 27, no. 2:27–57.

West, Heather C., William J. Sabol, and Sarah J. Greenman. 2010. "Prisoners in
2009." Bureau of Justice Statistics Bulletin, NCJ 231675. Washington, DC: US
Department of Justice, Bureau of Justice Statistics.

Western, Bruce. 2002. "The Impact of Incarceration on Wage Mobility and Inequality." *American Sociological Review* 67, no. 4:526–46.

———. 2006. *Punishment and Inequality in America*. New York: Russell Sage.

———. 2007. "The Penal System and the Labor Market." In *Barriers to Reentry?
The Labor Market for Released Prisoners in Post-industrial America*, ed. Shawn
Bushway, Michael A. Stoll, and David F. Weiman, 335–60. New York: Russell
Sage.

Western, Bruce, Jeffrey R. Kling, and David F. Weiman. 2001. "The Labor Market
Consequences of Incarceration." *Crime and Delinquency* 47, no. 3:410–27.

Wexler, Harry K., Gregory P. Falkin, and Douglas S. Lipton. 1990. "Outcome Evaluation of a Prison Therapeutic Community for Substance Abuse Treatment."
Criminal Justice and Behavior 17, no. 1:71–92.

Wildeman, Christopher, and Christopher Muller. 2012. "Mass Imprisonment and
Inequality in Health and Family Life." *Annual Review of Law and Social Science*
8:11–30.

Wildeman, Christopher, Jason Schnittker, and Kristin Turney. 2012. "Despair by
Association? The Mental Health of Mothers with Children by Recently Incarcerated Fathers." *American Sociological Review* 77, no. 2:216–43.

Wildeman, Christopher, and Kristin Turney. 2014. "Positive, Negative, or Null? The
Effects of Maternal Incarceration on Children's Behavioral Problems." *Demography* 51, no. 3:1041–68.

Wilson, James A., Yury Cheryachukin, Robert C. Davis, Jean Dauphinee, Robert
Hope, and Kajal Gehi. 2005. *Smoothing the Path from Prison to Home: An*

Evaluation of the Project Greenlight Transitional Services Demonstration Program. New York: Vera Institute of Justice.

Wilson, William Julius. 1987. *The Truly Disadvantaged: The Inner City, the Underclass, and Public Policy.* Chicago: University of Chicago Press.

Wozniak, Abigail. 2015. "Discrimination and the Effects of Drug Testing on Black Employment." *Review of Economics and Statistics* 97, no. 3:548–66.

Wyse, Jessica J. B. 2013. "Rehabilitating Criminal Selves: Gendered Strategies in Community Corrections." *Gender and Society* 27, no. 2:231–55.

Wyse, Jessica J. B., David J. Harding, and Jeffrey D. Morenoff. 2014. "Romantic Relationships and Criminal Desistance: Pathways and Processes." *Sociological Forum* 29, no. 2:365–85.

Index

abuse: physical, 24, 26, 30, 210, 217–18; sex-
    ual, 24, 38, 39, 43, 90, 217–18
addiction, 3, 19–23, 25, 27, 30–31, 43, 44–46,
    63, 107–8, 216–17, 247; and housing, 88–
    92; postincarceration treatment of, 240;
    recovery, 66–67; relapse, 102–4, 211–12;
    treatment for in prison, 238–39. *See also*
    relapse; sobriety
Affordable Care Act (ACA), 240

ban-the-box legislation, 233
behavioral health problems. *See* addiction;
    mental health, and incarceration

capital: economic, 10; human, 146, 191, 218;
    social, 10–11. *See also* education
carceral state. *See* incarceration
caregiving, as role, 96–97, 119, 121
childhood: crime during, 34; experience of
    incarcerated individuals, 23; experience
    of study participants, 19–20, 25–27, 29–
    30, 34, 38, 43, 122. *See also* abuse
churches, 165–66
class, social, 222
Clear, Todd R., 6
coercion. *See* social control, informal
cognitive transformation, 223–24, 226–27
cohesion. *See* neighborhoods: connected-
    ness of
collateral punishment, 170–73; reducing,
    231–35
community, 165–66; addiction-recovery, 140–
    41. *See also* neighborhoods
community supervision, 7; as alternative to
    prison, 229–31; and housing, 88; as ob-
    stacle to housing security, 91–94

credentialing, 234–35
crime: childhood, 34; impulsive, 43
criminal records, expungement of, 234

death, risk of, 61
demeanor, in prison, 127
desistance, barriers to, 8
disculturation, 49, 64–65
driver's licenses, 170–73. *See also* transpor-
    tation
drug abuse. *See* addiction

economic resources of formerly incarcer-
    ated people, 10
education: and discipline, 5; as financial
    strategy, 104–5; prior to incarceration,
    24; in prison, 236
electronic monitoring, 70, 147, 192
emotional support, 128–31. *See also* family
    support
employment, 17, 24, 36, 42, 69, 175–76, 219;
    and addiction, 211–12; barriers to, 86–87,
    190–96; before incarceration, 38; changes
    over time, 189; direct effects of impris-
    onment on, 191–92; and education, 186–
    87; and gender, 186–87; and geographical
    context, 177–78; and health, 191, 209–10;
    by industry, 180–83, 200–203; informal,
    204–5; and local labor market, 199–202;
    maintaining, 180, 189, 208–12; as part
    of reintegration, 213; postincarceration
    programs, 240–41; preprison factors for,
    190–91; and public benefits, 101; and
    race, 179–80, 182–83, 186–87, 195; rates
    of, 166–67, 178–87; and recidivism, 177–
    78, 184–88; search experience, 196–203;

employment (*continued*)
and stigma, 194–96, 233–35; successful,
189, 196–99, 205–9; and successful reintegration, 178; trajectories, 184–87; volatility in, 188–89
expungement of criminal records, 234

family, 17, 78, 220–21, 224–27; conflicts
within, 88–89; as context for reintegration, 50, 79; effects of incarceration on
nonincarcerated members, 59; emotional stress from, 111; as employment
resource, 197, 205–8; enabling addiction, 111; and housing, 88–89; improving experience of prison for, 236–37; as
motivation, 107–10, 123–25; need to support, 110; and public benefits, 101; and
reintegration outcomes, 115; relationships with during incarceration, 56–59;
and social control, 114; as temptation,
32, 107–10, 126–27
family support, 76–77, 109–10, 116–19, 131;
during and after incarceration, 55; and
housing stability, 95–100; material, 95–
100, 110. *See also* fatherhood; marriage;
motherhood
fatherhood, 38; as motivation, 28, 117–19,
123. *See also* family
fear, 53, 62–63, 140–41, 158
fees, for supervision, 70, 73–74

gangs, 26–27
gender, 13–14; and emotional support, 130–
31; and incarceration, 53; and risk, 158
Goffman, Erving, 49–50, 64

health, 13–14, 22, 24–25, 216–17; and
employment, 191, 209–10; health care in
prison, 238–39
homelessness, 41, 44, 83–84, 86–87; postincarceration, 40
housing, 17, 29, 36–37, 78–81, 218; instability,
drivers of, 88–94; institutional, 68, 69, 78,
80, 81–82, 84, 148; obstacles to, 88; preprison vs. postprison, 80–81; as source of
risk, 82; stability in, 82–85, 87–88, 94–100
housing, public, 147
hybrid state institutions, 13

identity, 122–25, 221. *See also* role strain
immigration, parallels to reintegration, 9–10

incarceration: collateral consequences of,
7; cost of, 4; growth of, 3–4; improving
experience of, 235–39; and inequality, 2,
6; isolation during, 39; and likelihood of
reoffending, 228–30; and personal transformation, 35–36; and race, 2, 4–5; reducing rate of, 227–31; scale of, 2–5; and
slavery, 5; and sobriety, 27–28; as social
framework, 5
inequality, 2–3
institutionalization, Goffman's definition,
49–50, 53
intermediate sanctions, 230–31
intimate partners, and reintegration, 45
isolation, 142; during reintegration, 65–67;
strategic, 39–40, 42–44, 52–53, 65–67,
150–52, 154, 157, 162–65; unintentional,
140; within neighborhood, 162–65

jobs. *See* employment

labor market conditions, 199
labor market intermediaries, 196, 198–99
labor markets, 11. *See also* secondary labor
market
letter writing, 56–58
libraries, 139
life-course analysis, 222–27

marriage: and attachment, 114; rates, 115;
and reintegration outcomes, 115. *See
also* family
mental health, and incarceration, 4, 25, 53,
80, 81, 191, 209, 216–17, 237–39
methodology of present study, 14–16
military service, 34–35
mobility, social, 145–48
motherhood: and incarceration, 30–31; as
motivation, 21–23, 32, 77, 124–25; single,
20. *See also* family

neighborhoods, 17, 218–19; chaotic connected, 153–54; chaotic detached, 150–
52, 157–58; connectedness of, 149–54;
constraints of, 146–48; effects of, 143–44;
geography of, 166–67; as networks, 155–
59; perceptions of, 162; safe connected,
152–53, 159; safe detached, 149–50;
safety of, 142–43, 149–54; services and
amenities, 139; as sites of risk, 160–62; as
sites of temptation, 142–43, 161, 163–65;

social services within, 167; supportive,
139–40, 141; types, 143–48; unemployment within, 166–67

parole, 12–13, 147, 220; as barrier to employment, 192–93; as context for reintegration, 50; cost of, 71; experience of, 60–62,
67–74, 192–93; improving, 235; precari-
ousness of, 71–72; requirements of, 169;
scale of, 71; and transportation, 169–73;
violations, 60–61. *See also* community
supervision
policing, 72, 167, 172–73
policy recommendations, 227–42
poverty, 3, 144–48; and incarceration, 23
prison: age dynamics of, 54; conditions
within, 16, 54–55; emotional effects of,
54; entry into, 48–49; experience of, 48–
53, 56–59, 191–92; familial and pseudo-
familial relations within, 54; isolation of,
55; lack of privacy in, 51; and sobriety,
21; status within, 51, 52–53; as turning
point, 222–27; women's, 53–54
prisonization, 53; secondary, 55
probation. *See* community supervision
provider role, 116–21
public benefits, 5, 101–3

race, 13–14, 215–16; and employment, 182–
83, 195; and incarceration, 24; and location, 145–48; and neighborhoods, 167;
and study design, 243
Raphael, Steven, 4
recidivism, 104, 126–27, 188; as framework
for understanding reintegration, 7–8;
overall likelihood, 233; predictive factors
for, 167, 177–78; prevalence and timing
of, 60–61; and social bonds, 7
rehabilitation: decline of, 12–13; programs
for, 225
reintegration: contexts for, 9–10; creating
positive conditions for, 3, 222, 227–42;
emotions during, 63–65; and family support, 28; as framework for considering
incarceration, 12; parallels to immigration, 9–10; as process, 8–10; and recidivism, 7–8; resources for, 9–10; responsibilities during, 62, 64–65; successful, 28, 38,
102, 137, 205–8; support during, 239–42

relapse, 102–4, 211–12
relationships: emotionally supportive, 128–
31; as predictors of success in reintegration, 137–38; in the reintegration process,
136; source of stress, 132–35
release from prison (homecoming), 60–68
risk, 157–59; assessment of, 69–70; perceptions of, 160–61
role strain, 116–21. *See also* identity
romantic relationships: avoidance of, 112–
13; economic inequality in, 112; prevalence of, 113. *See also* family; isolation;
marriage

sanctions, monetary, 73–74
secondary labor market, 180–81, 197, 200–
203, 219; volatility of, 182–83
segregation, residential, 147–48
self-care, balancing with family care, 121
sobriety, 32, 41, 45, 129–31, 142, 163–64; in
prison, 58. *See also* addiction
social control, informal, 121–27, 155–56
social networks, and temptation, 29
SSI (supplemental security income), 99,
101–4, 117
stability, 79–80; housing, 82–85, 87; and
public assistance, 103. *See also* employment
stigma, 194–96, 220, 231–35
Stoll, Michael A., 4
student debt, 105
supplemental security income. *See* SSI (supplemental security income)

temptation, 157. *See also under* family;
neighborhoods
therapy, 37
trajectories and transitions. *See* life-course
analysis
transportation, 163, 170–73; difficulties of,
67–68; and employment, 177; as site of
risk and temptation, 168–69

violence, exposure to, 24, 26
visitation, in prison, 55–56

Wacquant, Loïc, 5, 7, 11
welfare, 22
work. *See* employment

Printed and bound by CPI Group (UK) Ltd, Croydon, CR0 4YY

09/06/2025

14685712-0004